深圳国际仲裁院
北京大学法学院 主办

China International
Arbitration
Review

中国国际仲裁评论

总第五卷

刘晓春　潘剑锋·主　　编
林一飞　何　音·执行主编

法律出版社
LAW PRESS·CHINA
北京

图书在版编目(CIP)数据

中国国际仲裁评论. 总第五卷 / 刘晓春, 潘剑锋主编. -- 北京 : 法律出版社, 2023
ISBN 978 - 7 - 5197 - 7387 - 8

Ⅰ. ①中… Ⅱ. ①刘… ②潘… Ⅲ. ①国际仲裁 - 文集 Ⅳ. ①D994 - 53

中国版本图书馆 CIP 数据核字(2022)第 238705 号

中国国际仲裁评论(总第五卷)
ZHONGGUO GUOJI ZHONGCAI PINGLUN
(ZONG DI - WU JUAN)

刘晓春　潘剑锋 主编

策划编辑 谢清平
责任编辑 谢清平
装帧设计 李　瞻

出版发行 法律出版社
编辑统筹 法律应用出版分社
责任校对 王　丰　李景美
责任印制 刘晓伟
经　　销 新华书店

开本 710 毫米 × 1000 毫米　1/16
印张 21　　**字数** 332 千
版本 2023 年 2 月第 1 版
印次 2023 年 2 月第 1 次印刷
印刷 三河市兴达印务有限公司

地址:北京市丰台区莲花池西里 7 号(100073)
网址:www. lawpress. com. cn
投稿邮箱:info@ lawpress. com. cn
举报盗版邮箱:jbwq@ lawpress. com. cn

销售电话:010 - 83938349
客服电话:010 - 83938350
咨询电话:010 - 63939796

书号:ISBN 978 - 7 - 5197 - 7387 - 8
定价:82. 00 元

凡购买本社图书,如有印装错误,我社负责退换。电话:010 - 83938349

《中国国际仲裁评论》(总第五卷)编委会

目录

【国际投资仲裁】

【国际商事仲裁】

【国际投资仲裁】

国际投资仲裁中仲裁员公正性保障探析

甘　瑛*

摘　要:国际投资中,仲裁员的公正性决定着仲裁过程与裁决的权威性和专业性,深刻地影响公众对国际投资仲裁制度的信心,并由此影响国际投资仲裁的未来发展。作为仲裁员公正性的保障制度设计,应在界定"公正性"内涵的前提指导下,以仲裁庭成立为界,从事前预防的披露措施和事后补救的回避措施两方面着手,预防和杜绝国际投资仲裁中因身份冲突、争议点冲突以及重复任命等各类严重影响到仲裁员公正性的情形。本文以ICSID相关规则与实践为核心,探析仲裁员公正性在这具备相辅相成性质的两方面保障中所显露的关键缺陷和问题:一是以披露为核心的事前预防中的主观标准与实践缺陷及粗放型规则导致的披露不确定性;二是以回避为核心的事后救济中的模糊性证明标准所导致的实践矛盾,并研论二者在标准差异化情况下引起的衔接强化问题。由此提出改进二者标准规则并强化衔接的相关建议,以期从完善相辅相成制度上保障国际投资仲裁中的仲裁员公正性。

关键词:国际投资仲裁　仲裁员公正性　事前预防　事后救济　披露　回避　ICSID

---

* 甘瑛,华东政法大学国际法学院副教授。

一、问题的提出

仲裁员的公正性是投资仲裁制度的基石,仲裁员若不能公正裁决,则投资仲裁制度如立于流沙。

在国际投资仲裁中,一方当事人为东道国政府,是维护国家利益的主体,这使国际投资仲裁在一定程度上具备公法性质和特点。而大多数国际投资仲裁的仲裁员往往身兼数职,多有国际商事仲裁经验,倾向于国际商事仲裁的私法思维,奉行"私权至上"而否定东道国社会利益目标,而国际投资仲裁"商事化"表现,如裁决过程秘密性、仲裁员的临时性、裁决结果相互独立且一裁终局等因素,都导致诸多被诉国对国际投资仲裁产生信任危机。因此,在国际投资仲裁中裁决公平且无倾向性的发展要求,对于掌控着仲裁全过程的仲裁员的公正性提出更高要求。

从制度设计上看,自有裁判以来,法律实践中就逐步摸索出了保障裁判公正性的核心制度:以披露制度为代表的事前预防措施;以及以回避制度为代表的事后救济措施。在国际投资仲裁实践中,由于公正性的内涵与外延界定不明,在规定和运用这类制度时仍不免产生种种问题。例如,在披露制度设计中,以何种标准要求仲裁员披露哪些事实,才能真正实现事前保障公正性的目标?又如,在回避制度设计中,以何种证明标准来确定影响仲裁员公正性的情况?按《关于解决国家和他国国民之间投资争端公约》①(以下简称《华盛顿公约》)规则,即便一位仲裁员的道德高尚且具备公认的专业能力,一旦当事方能够提供明显证据证明仲裁员存在缺乏独立性(以存在利益冲突为最典型)的情形,即可对其申请回避。然而,如何解读"明显"一词,见解各异,导致由非专职仲裁员组成的临时仲裁庭在不同案件中解释各异,导致仲裁员公正性的判断标准处于不断变化中,形成公正性判断的不可预测性。

本文将从国际投资争端解决中心(International Center for Settlement of Investment Disputes,ICSID)的有关规则和实践出发,探讨国际投资仲裁制度中,为保障仲裁员公正性而设计的事前防范之披露和事后救济之回避措施,尤其针对上述矛盾焦点,探讨其中存在的主要缺陷——确定仲裁员公正性的内涵、明

---

① Convention on the Settlement of Investment Disputes between States and Nationals of Other States (March 18th,1965).

确其标准，细化事前预防和事后救济制度，以期在下层制度设计完善的基础上，确保上层目标——仲裁员公正性——得以最佳保障。

二、仲裁员公正性之内涵

何谓“公正”？在国际仲裁中，公正性是指仲裁员不对任何当事方有所偏向，能够公平地审理案件。[①] 即仲裁员能公平地在遵循仲裁程序的情况下，仅依据相关案件事实和法律规定作出裁定，对任何当事方皆无偏袒或偏见的思想状态。[②] 它作为评价标准，具有较强的心理主观性[③]，它以天平两边所称的价值相等为意象，具有不确定性。由此，需对案件仲裁程序设置限制性规定，确保仲裁员与当事方或利害关系方之间不存在影响仲裁员裁判的关系因素，以保障仲裁员公正性。[④] 此即裁判独立性，意指仲裁员具有不受他人影响而独立思考判断的内在稳定性，包括不得接受他人贿赂、不得利用仲裁员身份满足私利、不得让与外界关系影响判断等。缺乏独立性最终影响仲裁员公正性，因此，独立性要求最终是为仲裁员公正性提供保障，服务于公正性的终极目标，换言之，公正性是上位概念，独立性为下位概念，公正性涵盖了独立性。[⑤]

要保障仲裁员公正性，首先需在公正性界定问题上应有所突破，明确仲裁员公正性的要求。

在国际投资大环境中，以 ICSID 为核心的现有国际投资仲裁机制，大多并

---

① A. Redfern, M. Hunter, ed., Law and Practice of International Commercial Arbitration, Sweet & Maxwell, 1991, p. 215.

② UNCITRAL Arbitration Rules, G. A. Res. 31/98, art. 10, U. N. Doc. A/31/17 (Dec. 15, 1976).

③ T. Vardy, John J. Barcelo, Arthur T. Von Mehren, International Commercial Arbitration, Eagan West Group, 2003, p. 131 – 132.

④ 如业务、金钱、种族、亲缘、朋友、雇佣等关系，参见 Christopher Schreuer, et. al. ed., The ICSID Convention: A Commentary, Cambridge University Press, 2009, p. 518 – 519。又如，亲人、朋友、民族等“关系”、经济利益等“利益冲突”，以及其他方面（比如仲裁员与当事人之间存在重大投资项目，又如仲裁员公开发表过观点，对一方当事人持有不友善的态度）。参见杨良宜、莫世杰、杨大明：《仲裁法：从 1996 年英国仲裁法到国际商务仲裁》，法律出版社 2006 年版，第 561 页。

⑤ 当然，具有独立性本身并不等同于仲裁员具有公正性，譬如，若某仲裁员的一贯理念是维护资本利益，即使他与当事人并无任何不当关联，其裁定也可能存在明显偏向。

未直接明确仲裁员公正性的问题,公正性仅体现于《华盛顿公约》[①]等国际条约的原则性描述中,或是实践中针对仲裁员回避异议、撤销仲裁裁决等问题的判定理由当中体现出对仲裁员公正性的要求。

《华盛顿公约》第 14 条要求仲裁员应“可被信赖做出独立的判断”,并为保障仲裁员公正性设计一套规则:仲裁庭的组成中首席仲裁员须不同于当事方国家的国民担任[②];仲裁员应当具备高尚的道德品质、突出的专业能力和独立性三个基本条件[③];若有“明显”证据表明仲裁员不符合这三个基本条件,则当事方可以提出取消仲裁员资格[④]。《ICSID 仲裁规则》第 6 条要求仲裁员应当签署声明“依据准据法,在双方当事人间公正地进行裁判,并始终保持独立性”,应当披露除了所列举的披露事项之外,还须披露“任何其他可能导致其独立判断的可靠性被一方质疑的情况”。尽管上述文件均未明确“仲裁员公正性”内涵,但其措辞强调的“保持独立性”以“公正”裁决,以及由此展开的相关保障制度设计显然表明:仲裁员公正性是国际投资仲裁机制的基本目标。

但是,仲裁员公正性未被明确界定,就需要仲裁庭从条款、条约历史等诸多方面加以解释和推论,导致在实践中的理解差异和具体事项的判断分歧。公正性作为仲裁员制度的根本前提,应从条文上加以明确界定,并完善判断标准。就此,可采用反向定义法,从仲裁员客观关系和主观思想状态两方面加以界定,包含仲裁员不应当与争端方及其代理律师间存在任何形式的亲密依赖关系(包括过去或现在的职业、经济、社交、亲属关系等)而形成直接和间接的利益冲突,或仲裁员不应当对于争议事项具有偏见而偏向于某一当事方而作出不得体和看似不得体的行为。明确了仲裁员公正性内涵,争端方才能够在其指引之下判断仲裁员应当作出的披露,并寻找可能影响仲裁员公正性的证据以提出回避申

---

① 《华盛顿公约》第 14.1 条要求,“指派在小组服务的人应具有高尚的道德品质,并且在法律、商务、工业和金融方面有公认的能力,他们可以被信赖作出独立的判断。对仲裁员小组的人员而言,在法律方面的能力尤其重要”。《ICSID 仲裁规则》第 13(1)条要求,“根据本规则行事的仲裁员应是公正和独立的”。

② 《华盛顿公约》第 13 条规定:“一、每一个缔约方可以向每个小组指派四人,他们可以是但不一定是该缔约方国民;二、主席可以向每个小组指派十人,所指派人员应具有不同的国籍。”

③ 《华盛顿公约》第 14.1 条。

④ 《华盛顿公约》第 57 条规定:“一方可以根据明显缺乏《华盛顿公约》第 14 条规定有关品质的任一事实向原仲裁庭或专门委员会提议撤销其任职的资格。”

请,而且仲裁庭也可在内涵确定的前提下更明确地判断某种具体社会关系是否影响仲裁员公正性。

三、为仲裁员公正性之事前预防:以披露为核心的规则与实践分析

作为国际投资仲裁员公正性之保障,披露是事前预防的核心手段。《ICSID仲裁规则》对仲裁员披露的要求在不断地修订过程中。该规则早期版本仅要求仲裁员于仲裁开始前需要签署声明性质文件,其中需要披露"与争议当事方过去和现在的专业、商业和其他关系(如有)"①,到2006年修改为进一步要求披露"任何其他可能导致其独立判断的可靠性被一方质疑的情况",同时承担仲裁程序期间持续披露义务。② 2019年修订建议增加披露范围:要求披露第三方资助情况以及涉案争议冲突情况。尽管ICSID的规则在不断修改进步,但尚未很好解决两个关键问题:一是合理的披露标准,二是披露的细化事项。对这些问题的差异观点和做法导致实践的混乱。

(一)ICSID的主观标准与实践缺陷

明确的披露标准是披露制度的前提,是确定有关披露是否恰当的重要保证。确定披露标准的关键,在于确定判断披露事项的主体③,国际仲裁实践中就此形成两类披露标准④,一是客观标准,即以"合理第三人"(或"客观第三方")为判断应予披露事项的主体;二是主观标准,即以仲裁员或案件当事方为判断主体。客观标准假设存在通晓案件事实的公平客观的第三方,在合理公正的前提下判断应予披露的相关事实。典型代表为《联合国贸法会仲裁示范法》(以下简称《示范法》)的规定,应当披露可能对仲裁员公正性产生"正当怀疑"的任何情况。⑤ 此即以客观第三人角度在全盘明确事实情况基础上对被怀疑事项是否需披露的正当性进行判断。国际律师协会曾在其《国际仲裁员行为准则》中同

---

① 《ICSID仲裁规则》(2003)第6.2条规定:"... A statement of my past and present professional, business and other relationships (if any) with the parties is attached hereto..."

② 《ICSID仲裁规则》(2006)第6.2条。

③ Yves Derains and Eric A. Schwartz, A Guide to the ICC Rules of Arbitration (2nd ed.), Kluwer Law International 2005, p. 135.

④ Swiss Federal Supreme Court, Case No. 4A/506/2007 (20 March 2008), 26 ASA Bull. 575 (2008).

⑤ 《示范法》第12条第1款。

样采用此标准。①主观标准则从仲裁员或当事方角度来判断有关事项是否影响仲裁员公正性而应予披露。②

《ICSID 仲裁规则》第 6 条的规定显然采用仲裁员主观标准,以此标准,仲裁员仅需根据自己的理解从自身立场角度确定应披露事项。如 Alpha 公司诉乌克兰案③,被申请取消仲裁员资格的 Turbowicz 博士认为,如果自己认为在客观上,表面上或主观上都对该案的审议具有最轻微的偏见,就不会接受指定为该案仲裁员,正是由于自己认为,当事方所以为应披露的共学经历或简短电话联系等情况的性质、范围和强度或性质,并不属于应予披露的关系,是允许仲裁员自我裁量是否披露的权限范围内的,因此才未予披露(详见下文)。

基于这种"仲裁员主观标准"而进行的披露存在局限性——仲裁员的主观标准与仲裁当事方的主观标准存在差异——仲裁员认为无须披露的事项可能成为当事方人认为有必要披露的事项。尽管在通常情况下,仲裁员往往具有相当的社会名望,可以推定其根据维护仲裁员公正性的要求会进行合理披露,但无可避免的是,有些事项仲裁员认为无关紧要无须披露,当事方却不以为然,而披露的目的在于保证仲裁员本身能够让当事人看起来他会进行公正裁判。④

但是,如果采用当事方主观标准,则可能导致当事方滥用披露程序而大量提出不当披露要求。仲裁员的业务关系往往是非常广泛的,如果期待仲裁员向当事方提供完整无删的所有业务或其他信息,很可能引发仲裁员隐私权和当事方知情权之间的冲突。一方面,滥用信息披露会造成仲裁员时间和精力的浪费;另一方面,披露无论是轻微的还是严重的任何关系,可能将引致无根据的或

---

① IBA《国际仲裁员行为准则》(1987 年)第 4 条对披露采用客观标准:"如果存在当事人看来对其公正性和独立性产生怀疑的事实或者情况,仲裁员应当在接受任命前或者其知情后尽快向当事人、仲裁机构或者其他任命当局以及其他仲裁员披露这些事实或者情况。"参见宋连斌、林一飞编译:《国际商事仲裁资料精选》,知识产权出版社 2004 年版,第 233 页。

② Alan Redfern & Martin Hunter: Law and Practice of International Commercial Arbitration, Sweet and Maxwel, 2004, p. 204.

③ Alpha Projecktholding GMBH v. Ukraine (2007), https://icsid. worldbank. org/en/Pages/resources/ICSID – Caseload – Statistics. aspx, last visit on October 2nd, 2022.

④ Anne K. Hoffmann, Duty of Disclosure and Challenge of Arbitrators: The Standard Applicable Under the New IBA Guidelines on Conflicts of Interest and the German Approach, Arbitration International, Vol. 21, No. 3 (2005), p. 427 – 436.

琐碎的回避申请[①],由此不当拖延程序。

然而,如果采用客观标准,也并不容易把握,因为合理第三人作为虚拟人,不同评判者在以"合理第三人"考察是否应披露事实,终究是评判者的一种主观体现,因此,即便是采用客观标准,也可能存在披露范围不确定、不统一的问题。因此,有必要改进披露标准,使之合理化,在仲裁员、当事方,乃至仲裁机构之间形成平衡之势,才是有效解决披露的关键。

(二)ICSID 的粗放规则与披露的不确定性

尽管《ICSID 仲裁规则》一直在不断完善中,但迄今所要求披露的措辞仍是相当概括的,其模糊性导致在实践中仲裁庭往往对于究竟何种事项需要披露产生极大的不确定性。

在 Alpha 公司诉乌克兰案 [②]中,仲裁员 Turbowicz 博士被提议取消该案仲裁员资格,理由是该仲裁员与申请人委托的代理律所中的某律师曾经在哈佛大学共学,且他们之间在案前曾有简短电话联系,而该仲裁员在披露声明中并未披露此点。对此,该仲裁员表示,除了该段共学过程,此后从未有过包括职业、商业、社交、个人关系在内的任何形式的关系。仲裁庭认为,过去关于仲裁员公正性的质疑决定大多"基于被质疑的仲裁员与其中一方之间的某些所谓的专业或业务关系",上述微不足道的事实无法证明该仲裁员的公正性,尽管与一当事方的具有个人、家庭或商业性质关系可能影响仲裁员资格,但并非过去与当事方的任何专业或私人联系都会导致仲裁员资格的丧失。该案中,仲裁庭提到国际律师协会(International Bar Association,IBA)的《国际仲裁利益冲突指南》(IBA Guidelines on Conflicts of Interest in International Arbitration,以下简称《冲突指南》)(2004 年版),认为此文件虽未指出共学信息是否应披露,但肯定不鼓励必须披露此信息,因为如果要求披露琐碎的或表面的事实,将给当事人和仲裁员带来不必要的自由选择的限制性负担,披露应具备合理性。该案所涉电话联系仅涉及仲裁员与指定方初步联系,以仲裁员的空缺和服务资格,也属于《冲突指南》中无须披露的"绿色清单",该电话并没有使人怀疑该仲裁员对案件公正判断的能力。所有这些问题都指向一点:国际投资仲裁规则能否细化披露事

① 《国际律师协会国际仲裁利益冲突指南》"前言"第 1 段。

② 参见前注 Alpha Projecktholding GMBH v. Ukraine (2007)。

项,以便为仲裁员和当事方提供指引。

在 Burlintong 公司诉厄瓜多尔案中[①]涉及某仲裁员被特定律师事务所多次重复任命,厄瓜多尔要求该仲裁员披露在该律所代理任何案件中的所有任命以及这些仲裁程序中支付的赔偿金,并在该仲裁员提供了被要求披露的案件清单后,申请取消其仲裁员资格,其理由是,该仲裁员接受该律所指定的案件数量高得令人无法接受,违反了披露影响其独立判断可靠性情况的义务,且该仲裁员曾多次在主持会议过程中发表损害厄瓜多尔利益的言论,明显缺乏公正性。这些具体事项究竟是否应当披露,都成为争议的问题。

再如,Cemex 公司诉委内瑞拉案[②]中,接受指定的某仲裁员也受到披露争议的困扰,因其作为本案当事方的代理律师事务所的退休合伙人,一直接受该律所提供的办公室和秘书服务并且收取根据退休前收入计算的养老金,其信息也在律所网站上保留。所有这些是否属于仲裁员应披露的范围,都无法在仲裁规则中找到具体依据。

可见,《ICSID 仲裁规则》所设置的仲裁员披露义务是相当模糊的,披露事项的范围不明,这种高度概括的规则形式,叠加上现实社会利益冲突情况的复杂性,以及仲裁员与争端方的文化法律背景差异,极易导致在实践中的理解分歧。仅要求仲裁员自行披露自己认为应当披露的事项,往往可能出现非故意的遗漏。从披露范围的规则看,要穷尽列举引发仲裁员公正性质疑的情况是不可能的;但是仅以模糊规定要求披露又无法满足现实需求。如果能以应披露信息与仲裁员公正性之间存在紧密联系为标准,用适当指导的方式——如借鉴《冲突指南》的做法来细化披露事项——解决人们对于披露的差异性理解,有助于建立更完善的披露制度。

四、为仲裁员公正性之事后救济:以回避为核心的规则与实践分析

回避制度作为仲裁庭成立后发现仲裁员披露瑕疵或其他可能影响其公正性的事后救济,是国际投资仲裁机制高效公正运转的重要保障。《华盛顿公约》

---

① Burlington Resources, Inc. v. Republic of Ecuador (2008), UNCTAD. 2016. Investor – State Dispute Settlement: Review of Developments in 2015, UNCTAD IIA ISSUES NOTE.

② Cemex Caracas Investments B. V. v. Bolivarian Republic of Venezuela, UNCTAD. 2016. Investor – State Dispute Settlement: Review of Developments in 2015, UNCTAD IIA ISSUES NOTE.

第 57 条规定,申请回避的当事方必须证明仲裁员明显缺乏公约第 14.1 条所规定的品质[①]的任何事实而作出独立裁判的可靠性。

从规则文字上看,当事方必须"证明",也就是提供存在某种事实的客观证据。回避申请方的主观信念不足以满足公约的要求,"明显"是证据规则,并非证明标准。[②] 这一客观证据要求也是仲裁庭的实践共识。在 Suez 诉阿根廷案[③]中,东道国阿根廷对投资方选任仲裁员提出回避申请,因该仲裁员在 Vivendi 诉阿根廷案中就担任仲裁员,而 Vivendi 案仲裁在事实认定、举证责任等诸多方面漏洞百出,最终导致阿根廷错误地被判高额赔偿;让这样的仲裁员再次参与涉及阿根廷的类似案件,明显缺乏公正性。审理该回避申请的仲裁员认为,公约的要求抽象模糊,缺乏实际的定量标准或者衡量依据,异议方须提供可以衡量"明显缺乏公正性"的明显证据,不能仅以"观点""态度"等不确定因素来考量仲裁员的内心想法,此案"没有客观证据支持",仲裁员与某当事方对一系列案件事实以及司法判断的不一致也不表明该仲裁员缺乏公正性。Alpha 诉乌克兰案延续此观点,该案有关仲裁员未披露相关事实而遭回避申请,审理回避申请的仲裁员认为,《华盛顿公约》第 57 条要求异议方提供有说服力的客观证据。[④]

然而,公约文字的模糊性导致具体证明标准问题:证据证明要到何种程度,才得以做出回避决定,这是需要实践的具体解释。ICSID 仲裁实践中对于《华盛顿公约》第 57 条的解读存在明显差异,仲裁庭的回避决定对于具体回避理由是否达到了切实影响仲裁员公正性的判断分析,形成不同的认定标准。[⑤] 在较早期的案件中采用的往往是严格证明要求的高标准。例如,在 Amco 诉印度尼

---

① 《华盛顿公约》第 14.1 条要求的品质是:具有高尚的道德操守,并且在法律、商务、工业和金融方面有公认的能力可以被信赖作出独立的判断。《ICSID 仲裁规则》第 6.2 条要求仲裁员"公正地做出判断"所做的列举。

② Loretta Malintoppi and Alvin Yap, "Challenges of Arbitrators in Investment Arbitration: Still Work in Progress?" in Arbitration under International Investment Agreements: A Guide to the Key Issues, ed. Katia Yannaca Small, Oxford University Press, 2018, p. 388.

③ Suez, Sociedad General de Aguas de Barcelona S. A. and Interagua Servicios Integrales de Agua S. A. v. Argentine Repubilc, ICSID Case No. ARB/03/17, Decision on the Proposal for the Disqualification of a Member of the Arbitral Tribunal of 22 October 2007, para. 35.

④ Alpha Projectholding GmbH v. Ukraine, ICSID Case No. ARB/07/16, Decision on Respondent's Proposal to Disqualify Arbitrator Dr. Yoram Turbowicz of 19 March 2010, para. 67.

⑤ Christoph H. Schreuer, The ICSID Convention: A Commentary (2nd ed.), Cambridge University Press, 2009, p. 1197 - 1209.

西亚案①中,印尼认为 Amco 选任的仲裁员曾为 Amco 控股股东提供法律咨询,其所在的加拿大律所与 Amco 代理律师有收益分享协议,两家律所还共用同一办公场和设施,并且该状态从仲裁开始后仍持续了 6 个月,因此该仲裁员与其指定者之间存在客户与代理人的关系。该仲裁员的解释是该咨询费用很低,且该律所是当地唯一加拿大律所,咨询有关加拿大法律咨询也合乎情理;且此后未再对 Amco 提供过法律服务,对其选任自己为仲裁员也并不知情。受理回避异议的仲裁员就此对所涉证据进行综合性的"累积叠加"审查,认为《华盛顿公约》第 57 条中的"明显缺乏"意为不仅要求异议方所提出的事实客观存在,还要求该事实所导致公正性的缺失是显而易见的或高度可能性的,仲裁员与当事人的关联性必须达到"事实上的,几乎确定的,达到高度可能"的实质影响仲裁员公正性的程度。在这一"实际偏见标准"之下,本案所涉事实仅有不太明显的最低关联程度,缺乏关于实际偏见的严格证据。②

此"实际偏见标准"实际上加重异议方的举证责任,申请方不但必须证明客观事实的存在,还必须证明此事实导致实际偏见;甚至还可能导致日后仲裁员即便自认缺乏公正性,却在异议方无法证明无法达到"显而易见"的情况下仍然审理仲裁案。③ 此种严格标准被认为过于严苛,在 Vivendi 诉阿根廷案④中,受理回避异议的仲裁员就认为,Amco 案有关回避决定并不合理,因为这导致回避申请方证明责任相当沉重;仲裁员是否有资格审理案件的判断标准应当取决于任何当事方所合理感知的该资格的缺乏是否会导致裁决不公的真正意义上的危险。但这种"当事方"主观标准也会遭到来自被回避方的质疑,因其可能使得质疑仲裁员程序的运用成为当事方的投机行为。从根本上看,不论异议者提出的是无可争辩的事实,还是根据客观事实所做的推论,审理回避申请时都必须

---

① Amco Asia Corporation, Pan American Development Ltd. and PT Amco Indonesia v. Republic of Indonesia, (1982) ICSID Case No. ARB/81/1.

② ICSID Case No. ARB/81/1, Decision on the Proposal to Disqualified an Arbitrator (24 June, 1982).

③ M. Tupam, Chanllenge and Disqualification of Arbitrators in International Commercial Arbitration, The International and Corporative Law Quarterly, 1989, 38(1), p. 51.

④ Compaía de Aguasdel Aconquija S. A. and Vivendi Universal S. A. v. Argentine Republic, ICSID Case No. ARB/97/3, Decision on the Challenge to the President of the Committee of October 3rd, 2001, Challenge Decision of October 3rd, 2001, para. 25.

确定:以主观标准来判断,还是以理性第三方的客观标准来对证据进行合理评估。

在EDF诉阿根廷案中就采用"客观第三人"标准。该案中,阿根廷以某仲裁员与投资方EDF存在关联关系为由提出回避申请。该仲裁员曾是与EDF关系密切的瑞银集团的董事,而瑞银集团曾为客户推荐投资方的母公司,与投资方共同持有多家公司股份,还持有投资方3%股权的外债。受理申请的仲裁员认为,《华盛顿公约》第57条并未解释用何种标准判断所涉事实达到明显怀疑仲裁员公正性,因此,首先应分析基本事实证据是否确定,然后再依据事实内容来判断其与仲裁员公正性的关联程度,由此决定回避与否。仲裁庭逐一分析每一事实的关联性,认为上述行为或为商业惯例;或关联关系极低,从一个合理且完全知情的客观第三人角度看,该仲裁员审理该案的结果不会对其自身收入或社会评价产生本质影响,也不会对瑞银集团产生任何实质影响。①类似地,Universal诉委内瑞拉案②的回避决定也采纳相同标准,即当事方提供影响仲裁员公正性的证据,须以理性第三人的角度判断该仲裁员是否明显缺失相关品质。Blue Bank诉委内瑞拉案③的回避决定也认为,应基于"客观第三方的合理评估"标准,而不能依据申请方主观推定仲裁员是否明显缺失相关品质。Burlington Resources诉厄瓜多尔案④的回避决定进一步认为,《华盛顿公约》第57条和第14条并不要求证明存在实际偏见,只需足以确定存在依赖性或偏见的表象,以第三方对证据的合理评估为基础的客观标准判断是否"明显"缺失仲裁员应有品质。

综上而言,ICSID的回避标准不明确,从而导致实践各案的较大分歧。有效

---

① EDF International S. A. ,SAUR International S. A. and leon Participaciones Argen – tinas S. A. v. Argentine Republic,ICSID Case No. ARB/03/23,Challenge Decision Regarding Professor Gabrielle Kaufmamn Kohler of June 25th,2008,paras. 71 – 74.

② Universal Compression International Holdings,S. L. U. v. Bolivarian Republic of Venezuela,Decision on the Proposal to Disqualify Professor Brigitte Stern and Professor Guido Santiago Tawil,May 20th,2011,ICSID Case No. ARB/10/9,para. 71.

③ Blue Bank International & Trust (Barbados) Ltd. v. Bolivarian Republic of Venezuela,ICSID Case No. ARB/12/20. Decision on the proposal put forward by the Bolivarian Republic of Venezuela against Mr. salvaro Castellanos,March 2nd,2018,para. 81.

④ Burlington Resources,Inc. v. Republic of Ecuador,Decision on the Proposal for Disqualification of Professor Francisco Orrego Vicuña,December 13th,2013,ICSID Case No. ARB/08/5,para. 67.

的回避制度的根本目的在于维护仲裁员公正性,从而保障争端方权益并增强仲裁合法性。恰当的判断标准才是仲裁员回避裁决的核心,达到争端方利益平衡,从而实现回避制度的价值追求——仲裁员公正性的保障。究竟适用何种标准来判断是否取消仲裁员资格才是恰当呢? 标准过高将加重回避申请方的举证责任,乃至于使回避制度流于形式而无法真正得到有效运用;而标准过低又可能导致回避制度的滥用而使得仲裁员选任处于无法预计的状态,而损害仲裁正义。

如前所述,主观标准有其弊端;但是客观标准并不容易把握,因为"客观第三人"是虚拟人,以"客观第三人"为标准,终究是审理者的主观标准。换言之,"客观第三人"标准可能因为回避申请的审理者本身而导致一定程度的不确定性,由此,确定值得信赖的审理者以确保"客观第三人"的客观程度,就显得很有必要。此外,运用"客观第三方"标准来评估相关事实证据,仍然无法解决《华盛顿公约》规则的"明显证据"要求证明程度的困境:所谓的"明显"一词暗含着较高标准,评判者往往会加诸甚重举证责任, ICSID 实践也表明此情境下的回避申请的低成功率——迄今为止回避申请的成功率仅约为 3%①,这显然是不利于保护当事方利益,也易引发国际社会(尤其是东道国)对国际投资仲裁的信心丧失。

五、仲裁员公正性保障之完善建议

完善仲裁员公正性的保障措施,一方面,要完善包括事前预防的披露措施以及事后救济的回避措施所呈现的上述关键缺陷;另一方面,是要强化披露与回避之间的衔接,尤其是其评判标准的衔接。

(一)事前预防——披露问题的完善

1. 披露标准的改革建议

披露标准的实行,无论是主观标准还是客观标准,都存在一定局限性。比较现实的做法是采用一定标准加上规则明确指导的方式,以尽可能地避免仲裁员与当事方之间因披露而引发的冲突。

① "Decisions on Disqualification", ICSID, https://icsid.worldbank.org/en/Pages/Process/Decisions-on-Disqualification.aspx#, last visit on October 2nd, 2022.

如前所论,仲裁员和当事方对于信息披露是存在潜在冲突的。仲裁机构在其中亦发生一定作用——若其侧重程序公正,则可能倾向于当事方而强化披露要求;若其程序效率,则可能倾向于仲裁员而弱化披露要求。而确定披露标准的目的在于"寻求平衡当事人、代理人、仲裁员和仲裁机构之间的各种利益"。[①]不论是客观标准或主观标准,都可结合"利益平衡标准",也即考虑特定信息在平衡三方利益过程中,居于何种保护次序、保护限度以及保护方式,由此来实现披露规则的均衡化和可接受性。

前述案例中有仲裁庭考察 IBA《冲突指南》来评判有关事实是否应当披露。《冲突指南》的思路是根据有关信息对仲裁员公正性的影响程度对有关情形进行分类(参见后文阐释)。此种思路确是可取的。ICSID 可以结合披露目的、当事方证明难易程度、上述利益平衡等多重目标来设置披露标准,然后参考《冲突指南》的分类思路,来划分信息是否应予披露、如何具体披露。

2. 披露规则的细化改进

(1)以倒推法增设披露情形

关于仲裁员公正性,无论是事前防范的披露还是事后救济的回避,所涉信息或事项的矛盾焦点,都特别集中于仲裁员身份冲突、涉案争议点冲突以及重复任命问题这三方面。因此,可考虑以实践中引发仲裁员回避的结果来倒推仲裁员需披露的情形。

首先,是身份冲突与思维定式的矛盾。国际投资仲裁中的仲裁员多为执业律师、法律顾问、法律学者、法官等专业人才,此类人才数量紧缺,仲裁机构不可能直接禁止兼职担任仲裁员,从而导致身兼两职乃至身兼数职、交叉选任[②]的情况。作为仲裁员与当事人代理人等的角色切换导致仲裁员身份与其他身份之间的冲突,从而影响仲裁员公正性。从人类思维定式角度看,国际投资仲裁领域在很大程度上受到西方国家法律先例拘束力理念的影响,使仲裁中参照、援引先前裁决的做法比比皆是,[③]仲裁员有意或无意地受思维定式影响甚重,使裁决具有倾向性而导致不公正。即使仲裁员自认为有能力划清界限,但如何证

---

① 《利益冲突指引》"前言"第 4 段。

② 如 X 案的代理人 A 指定某仲裁员 B,而 B 作为 Y 案的代理人则指定 A 在 Y 案中担任仲裁员。

③ Thomas W. Wälde, New Aspects of International Investment Law, Martinus Nijhoff Publishers, 2006, p. 66.

明？仲裁员能否进行完全的角色切换，或提出应以“理性第三人”角度判断，[①]然而实践中的判断标准亦颇参差。其次，是仲裁员与涉案争议点的矛盾。即仲裁员对争端事项(法律问题或者事项)具有先入为主的立场和预判而导致实际或表面偏见。在投资仲裁中，涉案双边投资条约的条款往往非常相似，仲裁员在审理案件时，很可能遇到与自己曾经所做裁决中类似的事实和法律问题，从而导致潜在矛盾，引起当事方对仲裁员公正性的质疑。最后，是重复任命的矛盾。国际投资仲裁机制允许当事方选择仲裁员。仲裁员在期待被一当事方重复多次选择的动机下，可能会倾向于支持某当事方的立场，由此被怀疑其公正性。

将上述典型实践情形纳入仲裁员应予披露事项中，可以在一定程度上明确仲裁员披露范围，提升仲裁效率，或可较大程度避免启动回避程序。

在这点上，《ICSID 仲裁规则》2019 年修订就建议：①过去五年内争议当事方及其代理人、(目前已知的)仲裁庭其他成员；以及已披露的任何第三方资助者的专业、商业和其他重大关系。②作为律师、调解员、仲裁员、专设委员会成员、事实调查委员会成员，或专家曾经或目前参与的投资争端案件。③其他可能合理导致其独立性或公正性受质疑的情况。且保证不与任何一方当事人或代理人就该仲裁进行单方联系。[②] 此建议首次明确仲裁员须披露其与第三方资助者的关系，须披露由于履行其他职能所可能带来的涉案争议点冲突(issue conflicts)。但其涵盖范围和细化程度还有待提高。就此，IBA《冲突指南》可提供有益的参考。

(2)参考《冲突指南》设置披露事项

IBA《冲突指南》是不同法系法学家参考各国立法或判例基础上反复讨论的结果，自 2004 年公布以来就在国际仲裁界得到广泛支持。上文 Alpha 公司诉乌克兰案就以该文件为参考分析仲裁员的披露标准和披露事项。作为一个参考指导性文件，它可供仲裁员参考以决定自己是否接受指定或者作出披露，也供当事人用以评估仲裁员公正性，同时为仲裁机构提供仲裁员披露与回避决定

---

① Malcolm Langford, Daniel Behn & Runar Hilleren Lie, The Revolving Door in International Investment Arbitration, 20 Journal of International Economic Law (2017) 301, p. 322.

② Schedule 3 of Proposals for Amendment of the ICSID Rules — Working Paper # 3, https://icsid.worldbank.org/en/Documents/WP_3_VOLUME_1_ENGLISH.pdf, last visited on April 5, 2020.

提供参照。该文件经过 2014 年修订,还完善了有关道德披露情形。该文件在其指引中强调,它同样适用于国际投资仲裁,对于国际投资仲裁中仲裁员披露问题具有重要的参考价值。

《冲突指南》首先要求仲裁员在接受指定时以及在审案过程中始终保持公正性。① 在此基础上确定以“合理第三人”审视披露标准,②从而将所有可能需披露的情形以交通信号灯模式进行分类:第一类是不可弃红色清单(不得选任为仲裁员的事项),此类事项即仲裁员披露与否都被视为无可避免存在利益冲突的情况,无论披露与否,都不得被选任,比如,与当事方之间具有实质性经济利益关系、雇佣关系等。第二类是可弃红色清单(争端双方在仲裁员披露后明确同意接受则仲裁员得以选任的事项),包括仲裁员与争端方有着职业、经济、家庭上的关系。第三类是橙色清单,包含争端方认为可能对仲裁员公正性产生合理怀疑的事项。仲裁员披露此类信息后,若争端方未及时异议,则仲裁员得以选任。第四类是绿色清单(仲裁员无须披露的事项),比如,仲裁员曾就过去的仲裁案件中有关问题的公开观点、与争端方曾经参加同一社交活动等。绿色清单所列举的情况是仲裁员无义务披露的,这在一定程度上平衡了当事方知情权和仲裁员个人信息隐私权之间的冲突,而且这类信息从相应的客观角度看来,一般认为不会发生直接利益冲突。

国际投资仲裁本身具有区别于其他商事仲裁的独特性和复杂性,应在此基础上结合投资仲裁在实践中出现的引起注意的情形加以梳理,以软性法律指引,设置明晰的框架,以 ICSID 长期案件实践积累为助益,对影响仲裁员公正性的相关事实进行分类,从经验上升为理论,形成相应标准,然后参考《冲突指南》的做法,分类设置披露信息指导清单,尽可能细化披露信息事项。笔者认为,至少可将披露事项作如下划分:

第一,涉及仲裁员公正性的重大社会关系信息。这类信息主要是仲裁员与

---

① 《冲突指南》第一部分第 1 条规定,“每位仲裁员在接受指定之时应是公正的,独立性于当事人的,并保持如此直至最终裁决作出或仲裁程序另行终止之时。”

② 《冲突指南》第二部分第 2 条规定:“如果存在的事实或情形,或者仲裁员接受指定后产生的事实或情形,在知悉相关事实和情形的合理的第三人看来,将引致对仲裁员的公正性或独立性的正当怀疑,则适用同样的原则,除非当事人已经依据一般标准(4)中所述的规定接受了仲裁员。”第 3 条规定:“如果合理的知情第三人认为,仲裁员在作出裁决时可能会受到当事人陈述的案件是非之外的因素的影响,则怀疑是正当的。”

当事方或其代理人之间的关系,以及具有很大亲密度的商业、家庭关系等。如果仲裁员为某当事方的法人代表或主要任职人员或长期客户,在业务往来或案件结果中有一定经济影响,甚至是在仲裁员给当事方出具参考意见之后,会出现更多的公正性怀疑。[①] 此类重大社会关系信息如:仲裁员所在律师事务所代表或对当事方或其关联方给出建议;仲裁员所在律师事务所曾经或现在代理仲裁当事另一方或关联方的相对方;仲裁员或其律师事务所与一方或其关联方有业务关系,或在争议结果中有任何性质的个人利益;仲裁员或其律师事务所正在或曾经参与争议,或以可能影响其公正性的方式对争议发表了意见;仲裁员与一当事方或其律师事务所的律师有专业或密切的个人关系;仲裁员在涉及一当事方或其关联方的案件中担任或曾经担任仲裁员;仲裁员或未来的仲裁员过去曾由一方或其关联公司,或由一方或其律师事务所的律师指定为仲裁员,等等。当然,仲裁员和律师的关系在现实中是非常复杂的,如果要求仲裁员全面披露此类关系,很可能因披露信息范围过大而违反其他关系中的保密义务。因此,这类关系的披露应有一定限制,即以存在持续性关系且仲裁员很可能会从所涉仲裁案中获取较大利益为限。这也是前述“利益平衡标准”的体现。

第二,很可能影响仲裁员公正性的主观价值判断信息。此类信息往往涉及仲裁员对具有与自己同类经历的当事方的偏袒倾向,或基于宗教或种族等原因形成的歧视倾向,以及其他严重偏见。此外,从广义上讲,这类信息还可以包括基于仲裁员的审理前行判断的很可能影响仲裁员公正性的主观态度信息。

第三,与仲裁员公正性关联度微不足道的其他主观信息。此类信息可以包括仲裁员公开的学术观点、在先前案件中陈述的法律意见,等等。在国际投资仲裁员中,法律人构成较大比重,学术观点差异是国际投资仲裁领域的常态,而学者的基本操守是尊重不同学术观点,本着尊重仲裁员职业操守的基本态度,可先推定学术观点差异本身并不意味着影响仲裁员公正性,无须披露。就先前法律意见来看,如果仲裁员曾就仲裁中对法律问题的决定,对法律条款的解释,本身并不必然影响仲裁员公正性,因为这并未涉及案件具体实质问题,且并非专门针对当前正在进行的仲裁案件发表意见。有调查报告显示,案件中的法律

① The IBA Conflicts of Interest Subcommittee, The IBA Guidelines on Conflicts of Interest in International Arbitration: The First Five Years 2004 – 2009, Dispute Resolution International, 2020(5), p. 7.

问题和事实问题有明显区别①;事实问题则纷繁复杂,即便有相同法律问题的案件也会因为事实问题的区分而可能导致不同结论。以此,《冲突指南》就将“仲裁员先前就仲裁中出现相同的问题公开发表过的一般观点”列入绿色清单,属于无须披露的信息。

第四,与仲裁员公正性关联程度较低的社会关系信息。这主要是仲裁员与当事人之间虽有联系,但此种联系过于微弱,乃至可忽略不计,无须披露。

(二)事后补救——回避问题的完善

如上所论,ICSID 实践中的回避标准有分歧,即便用“客观第三人标准”也难以圆满。笔者认为,如果要加强对当事人免受不合格仲裁员的保护,提高申请回避的成功率,就应考虑适当降低证明标准——如在客观第三人标准的基础上加上“合理/正当怀疑”标准,也即在回避申请方所提供的事实证据,从客观第三人角度判断会引起合理/正当怀疑,即可做出回避决定。

在其他有关投资仲裁案件中有用此“合理怀疑”标准的例子。在 Telkom 诉加纳案②中,加纳对申请方选任的仲裁员提出回避申请,因该仲裁员在同一申请方进行的 ICSID 的 RFCC 诉摩洛哥案的裁决撤销申请③中担任该申请方代理律师,两案涉及类似法律问题,且两种角色并不相容——“Gaillard 以律师身份反对某一具体概念或方法的,在其担任仲裁员的案件中对同一概念或方法的判断不能做到不偏不倚”。④ 海牙国际常设仲裁院秘书长作为该回避申请的指定机构驳回了申请,认为本案中并不存在对该仲裁员公正性产生“合理怀疑”的情形。加纳随后向海牙地区法院起诉,法院最终令该仲裁员在两个角色之间做出选择,不得同时担任,因为从理性第三人标准看,同时担任两种存在潜在冲突的角色足以引起对仲裁员公正性的合理怀疑。

---

① ICCA, Report of the ASIL – ICCA Joint Task Force on Issue Conflicts in Investor – State Arbitration, ICCA, 2016, para. 172.

② Telekom Malaysia Berhad v. The Republic of Ghana, Decision (District Court of the Hague), 18 October 2004, PCA Case No. 2003 – 03, para. 22.

③ Consortium R. F. C. C. v. Kingdom of Morocco, Decision on Annulment of January 18th, 2006, ICSID Case No. ARB/00/6.

④ Republic of Ghana v. Telekom Malaysia Berhad, Hague District Court, Challenge No. 13/2004, Petition No. HA/RK 2004. 667, October 18th, 2004; Challenge 17/2004, Petition No. HA/RK/2004/778, November 5th, 2004.

基于上述“合理怀疑”标准,对仲裁员与选任方之间关联关系的紧密程度、持续时间和可能造成的经济影响等各方面做出是否存在“合理怀疑”的综合判断,较之“明显缺乏”的判断,更可能提升回避申请的成功率,或可成为 ICSID 规则改革的可能方向。

(三)披露与回避的强化衔接

仲裁员披露与回避作为维护仲裁员公正性的两大措施,是相辅相成的,有效的信息披露也是回避措施正常发挥作用的基础。仲裁员应首先依照一定的披露标准进行持续性披露①,通过清单式指引给仲裁员提醒,还需要设置仲裁员未遵守披露义务的后果,在当事方提出异议时,审理者依照一定的回避标准确定相关事实是否导致仲裁员回避。然而,ICSID 仲裁员披露标准与回避标准在实践中并未有效衔接,在各仲裁庭的判断下也呈现不同要求,且往往要求较高,导致回避申请的实现程度极低,回避标准的不确定性也导致仲裁的可预测性受到极大影响。回避作为披露的后续保障,二者之间必须加强联结,对仲裁员披露与回避制度的标准形成内在一致和有效衔接,才有助于实现仲裁员的公正性。要解决此问题,可以考虑适当降低并统一仲裁员回避的标准,将仲裁员披露标准与回避标准有效协调起来。

从前述 ICSID 实践看,《华盛顿公约》第 57 条“明显缺乏”标准,显然是设置颇高门槛,也导致回避成功率极低,打击了当事方对回避制度乃至整个国际投资仲裁制度的信心。因国际投资仲裁处理的案件不仅涉及私人投资主体,也涉及主权国家(东道国),并且标的巨大,利益关系复杂,甚至可能会影响到一国主权,由此对仲裁员的公正性提出更高要求,严苛的回避标准大大增加回避证明负担,相应地就降低了对被回避方的要求,从而导致公正性的降低。适当降低并形成合理的回避标准对国际投资仲裁的益处是不言而喻的。2020 年 ICSID 公布第四次规则修订稿,其中就考虑降低仲裁员回避标准。

“合理/正当怀疑”标准是主观与客观结合较好的产物:基于客观证据来进行审查,从“客观第三人”角度,考察相关事实是否可引起当事方对仲裁员的“合

① 从投资仲裁案件过程漫长,诸如关系紧密程度、持续时间长短、经济利益状况等各类信息不断变化,往往仲裁员最为清楚,因此设置持续性披露审查,及时更新披露事项,不失为完善披露可预测性的措施。

理/正当怀疑”，只要基于客观证据引发的怀疑从第三人角度看是“合理/正当”的，就可确定仲裁员应当回避。此回避标准类似于《冲突指南》对于披露要求的“正当怀疑”标准，[①]也近似于《联合国国际贸易法委员会仲裁规则》对于回避制度所采用“正当怀疑”标准[②]——存在客观事实引发针对仲裁员公正性的合理/正当的怀疑。此种标准更符合回避制度的理性要求，可以较好地平衡各方利益，满足各方对国际投资仲裁中仲裁员公正性的需求。从法与经济学的角度看，制度标准的设计中总是包含所涉各方的利益平衡问题，不论是仲裁员披露标准还是回避标准的确定，所谓的“合理”或“正当”都隐含了仲裁员和当事方以及仲裁机构等多方的利益平衡，沿此利益平衡思路考察下去，在程序公正与程序效率的衡量之间来确定标准问题，是更现实可行的。前文已探讨过的披露中的利益平衡标准，而回避中的利益平衡亦作如是观。

当然，作为“合理怀疑”的审查主体，其本身能否真正以“客观第三人”来判断，也颇为重要。从本质上看，“客观第三人”仍然是审理者借由“第三人”角度而阐发的一种主观价值判断体现。审理者的客观公平，也成为“客观第三人”标准能否真正得以使各方利益得以平衡实施的保障关键。由此，就 ICSID 的回避申请审理主体而言，最好改变现行的由未被异议的仲裁员来审理回避申请的情形。众所周知，在国际高端法律服务共同市场中，投资仲裁案件仲裁员与执业律师的关联性和角色互换从长期来看是难以避免，若以专门委员会匿名审理方式，或以中立的第三方专业机构的方式进行回避申请的审理，或更可使“客观第三人”标准的运用达到其应有效果。

---

① 《冲突指南》第二部分第 2 条及第 3 条。

② 《联合国国际贸易法委员会仲裁规则》第 12.1 条规定，“如果存在可能对任何仲裁员的公正性或独立性产生有正当理由怀疑的情况，均可要求该仲裁员回避”。

One Man's Meat Is Another Man's Poison: Revisiting the Transposition of the Judicial Review Mechanism from Commercial Arbitration to Investment Arbitration

Wanli Ma *

1. Introduction

Over time, academic discussions of the judicial review mechanism in relation to arbitration have flourished and a host of scientific publications have sprung up. Indeed, the judicial review of commercial arbitral awards, as a recurrent topic of debate, has mustered a substantial amount of scholarly attention. ① However, the mechanism of the judicial review of investment awards arguably has not met with the same level of academic interest not least due to the fact that investment arbitra-

* Wanli Ma,马万里,任职于美国凯易国际律师事务所驻北京代表处。

① There are a large body of publications that have been produced with regard to the judicial review of commercial arbitration awards. Scholars and practitioners have discussed this issue from different perspectives. For example, some seem to be intrigued by the rules in this area of a specific jurisdiction, while others prefer to demonstrate the advantages/disadvantages of the judicial review of commercial arbitration awards. But in general, the scope of review and the standards of review are the most dominant themes of these publications. Jessica L. Gelander, "Judicial Review of International Arbitral Awards: Preserving Independence in International Commercial Arbitrations", Marquette Law Review, Vol. 80, No. 2 (1997), p. 625 – 644. Kenneth R. Davis, "When Ignorance of the Law is No Excuse: Judicial Review of Arbitration Awards", Buffalo Law Review, Vol. 45, No. 1 (1997), p. 49 – 140. Stephen P. Younger, "Agreements to Expand the Scope of Judicial Review of Arbitration Awards", Albany Law Review, Vol. 63, No. 1 (1999), p. 241 – 262. Stephen K. Huber, "State Regulation of Arbitration Proceedings: Judicial Review of Arbitration Awards by State Courts", Cardozo Journal of Conflict Resolution, Vol. 10, No. 2 (2009), p. 509 – 578.

tion is not comparable with its commercial counterpart in terms of the number of cases.① Another important factor is that the International Centre for Settlement of Investment Disputes (ICSID) largely dominates investment law scholarship and the judicial review mechanism is not applicable to arbitration conducted pursuant to the Convention on the Settlement of Investment Disputes between States and Nationals of Other States (the ICSID Convention) and the associated Arbitration Rules.

With that said, the setting – aside of investment awards in the wake of the underlying arbitral proceedings, as a critical form of post – award remedy, is not negligible. In case that the claim of the moving party is backed by the review court, the investment award at issue will in all likelihood be fully or partially vacated. Given that the number of investment arbitrations, including non – ICSID arbitration cases,② continue to increase at a rather rapid pace, the relevance of the judicial review mechanism in investor – state dispute settlement (ISDS) would presumably grow in proportion. Meanwhile, the ongoing charged debates about investment arbitration prompt us to get our arms around the judicial review mechanism for investment awards. After all, the understanding and evaluation of the judicial review mechanism would feed into the overall efforts to put investment arbitration in perspective and to mull over related reform proposals. For instance, with regard to the establishment of an appellate review mechanism, whether such a proposal is reasonable and desirable to a large extent hinges on the tradeoffs of the judicial control of investment awards. If the judicial review mechanism works well, the introduction of appellate review sounds less attractive.

---

① There are nevertheless an increasing number of articles that have shed some light on a range of important issues involved in the setting – aside proceedings of investment awards. Jack J. Coe, "Domestic Court Control of Investment Awards: Necessary Evil or Achilles Heel Within NAFTA and the Proposed FTAA", Journal of International Arbitration, Vol. 19, No. 3 (2002), p. 185 – 207. Noah Rubins, "Judicial Review of Investment Arbitration Awards", in Todd Weiler (ed.), "NAFTA Investment Law and Arbitration: Past Issues, Current Practice, Future Prospects", Brill – Nijhoff (2004), p. 359 – 390. Lars Markert and Helene Bubrowski, "National Setting Aside Proceedings in Investment Arbitration", in Marc Bungenberg et al. (eds.), "International Investment Law", Nomos (2015), p. 1460 – 1481.

② Non – ICSID arbitration in this article refers to those investment arbitrations conducted pursuant to all the other arbitration rules other than the ICSID Convention and the associated Arbitration Rules.

Inorder to fill the gap in the literature on this topic and to contribute to the overarching debates of the reform of investment arbitration, this article delves into the institutional design and the practical operation of the judicial review of investment awards by virtue of text analysis, case law study, and empirical evidence. That, in turn, lays the groundwork for a normative assessment of the judicial review mechanism in the context of investment arbitration which sheds light on the path forward for the reconstruction of the post – award remedy. The rest of this article first looks at the origin of the judicial review of investment awards, uncovering that the current mechanism in place is transposed from commercial arbitration to investment arbitration (Section 2). The next section details the review grounds laid out in the UNCITRAL Model Law on International Commercial Arbitration (the Model Law) which serve as a template for the relevant rules in the arbitration legislation of some jurisdictions and resemble those in many other jurisdictions (Section 3). That detailed analysis is followed by an overview of investment arbitrations the awards/decisions out of which have been subject to judicial review by domestic courts at the seat of arbitration (Section 4). The preceding sections combine to provide a foundation for a normative assessment of the judicial review of investment awards, which highlights the flaws of that mechanism despite the recognition of its contributions absent an arrangement of appellate review within the investment arbitration system (Section 5). This article concludes with some thoughts on the reform of the post – award remedy in relation to investment arbitration, such as the implications of the findings in this article for the proposal to establish a centralized appellate review mechanism (Section 6).

2. Transposing Judicial Review from Commercial Arbitration to Investment Arbitration

Compared to commercial arbitration, investment arbitration is a relatively novel phenomenon in the domainof international dispute resolution. ① There are a number of notable divergences between commercial and investment arbitration. Among those would be that while commercial arbitration is founded on an agreement to arbitrate between private parties, investment arbitration is in many cases initiated on the basis of investment agreements. ② Despite all the aspects that distinguish investment arbitration from commercial arbitration, these two types of arbitration share a multiplicity of procedural similarities between them. ③ Wilske and others argue that, on balance, the similarities between commercial and investment arbitration prevail over their divergences. ④ Indeed, the judicial review mechanism which provides parties to non – ICSID arbitration with an opportunity to challenge arbitral awards attests to the statement that commercial arbitration and investment arbitration are "close relatives". ⑤ In other words, the applicability of judicial review of investment awards by domestic courts *loci arbitri* showcases that the procedures of investment arbitration, especially non – ICSID arbitration, largely modelled on that of commercial arbitration. ⑥

The ICSID Convention and the associated ICSID Arbitration Rules are known for the establishment of a self – contained system for ICSID arbitration by creating

---

① The first known treaty – based investment arbitration case was launched by a British investor against Sri Lanka under the Sri Lanka – UK BIT 1987 over the alleged damage to its investment by a military operation by the country's security forces. *Asian Agricultural Products Ltd. v. Republic of Sri Lanka*, ICSID Case No. ARB/87/3. Jonathan Bonnitcha et al., "The Political Economy of the Investment Treaty Regime", Oxford University Press (2017), p. 1 (arguing that the investment treaty regime and investment arbitration went virtually unnoticed until a few years ago).

② Anthea Roberts, "Divergence between Investment and Commercial Arbitration", Proceedings of the Annual Meeting (ASIL), Vol. 106 (2012), p. 298.

③ Gary G. Born, "A New Generation of International Adjudication", p. 834 (arguing that virtually all investment arbitrations are conducted pursuant to procedures that parallel international commercial arbitration procedures).

④ Stephan Wilske et al., "International Investment Treaty Arbitration and International Commercial Arbitration – Conceptual Difference or Only A 'Status Thing'?", Contemporary Asia Arbitration Journal, Vol. 1, No. 2 (2008), p. 228.

⑤ Ibid.

⑥ Gary G. Born, "A New Generation of International Adjudication", Duke Law Journal, Vol. 61, No. 4 (2012), p. 835.

a specific set of procedural rules covering issues that range from request for arbitration to the recognition and enforcement of arbitral awards. ① The ICSID system is also characterized by a unique annulment procedure where an *ad hoc* annulment committee established by the ICSID Secretariat is charged with the task of reviewing awards arising out of ICSID arbitration proceedings. ② The ICSID annulment procedure is notably not meant to operate as an appeals system. ③ Although the recent practice of the annulment procedure has attracted waves of criticisms, ④ domestic courts *loci arbitri* are prevented from scrutinizing ICSID awards. ⑤ However, the awards rendered outside the ICISD arbitration regime, including those out of arbitration proceedings based on the ICSID Additional Facility (AF) Rules, cannot benefit from the exclusive annulment procedure for ICSID arbitration. At the same time, although IIAs often offer investors a few options of arbitration rules that they can choose from to launch an arbitration, ⑥ no treaties have created a tailor – made annulment procedure for awards rendered out of non – ICSID arbitration proceed-

---

① Sundra Rajoo, "Annulment of Investment Arbitration Awards", in Barton Legum (ed.), "The Investment Treaty Arbitration Review", Second Edition, Law Business Research Ltd. (2017), p. 212. Piero Bernardini, "ICSID versus Non – ICSID Investment Treaty Arbitration", http://www. arbitration – icca. org/media/0/12970223709030/bernardini_icsid – vs – non – icsid – investent. pdf (last visited July 15, 2020), p. 5 (arguing that the ICSID arbitration as a self – contained regulation "covers all aspects of the arbitral proceedings and extends to the challenge of the awards, the latter being regulated only by the Convention, without any interference by national courts or other national authorities, no room for the application of the New York Convention being made regarding enforcement of an ICSID award").

② Dohyun Kim, "The Annulment Committee's Role in Multiplying Inconsistency in ICSID Arbitration: The Need to Move Away from an Annulment – based System", New York University Law Review, Vol. 86, No. 1 (2011), p. 250.

③ Ibid.

④ Kateryna Bondar, "Annulment of ICSID and Non – ICSID Investment Awards: Differences in the Extent of Review", Journal of International Arbitration, Vol. 32, No. 6 (2015), p. 621 – 622.

⑤ Kim, *supra* note 11, at 250.

⑥ For instance, Article 1120 (Submission of a Claim to Arbitration) of NAFTA stipulates that satisfying certain conditions, an investor may submit the claim to arbitration under the ICSID Convention, the Additional Facility Rules of ICSID or the UNCITRAL Arbitration Rules. Article 1120, Chapter Eleven: Investment, NAFTA.

ings. ①

As a consequence, the mechanism of the judicial review of non – ICSID awards is governed by the legal framework of the forum state, as some believe that this is the result of the application of the general principle of international law that "*locus regit processum* (procedure is governed by the *lex fori*)". ② Foy argues that the decision of the seat of arbitration, which is a jurisdictional conception and thus not necessarily where the hearings are conducted, is of great importance in that it will inform the legal system that governs the arbitral proceedings and identify the court that supervises the arbitral process, and, in due course, reviews the arbitral award. ③ In the absence of a specialized annulment procedure for non – ICSID awards at the international level, ④ the pursuit of the *vacatur* of a non – ICSID award is governed by the rules applicable to the annulment of awards out of international commercial arbitration proceedings. ⑤ In other words, the legal norms applicable to the judicial review of commercial arbitration awards equally apply to the setting – aside proceedings in relation to investment awards before domestic courts *loci arbitri*. ⑥ Thus, the overlapping regime that simultaneously regulates the challenges against commercial arbitration and investment arbitration awards provides a strong argument that these two types of arbitration are "two sides of the same coin". ⑦

---

① Juan Fernández – Armesto, "Different Systems for the Annulment of Investment Awards", ICSID Review, Vol. 26, No. 1 (2011), p. 131 – 132.

② Ibid., at 132 – 133.

③ Patrick G. Foy, "An Introduction to Judicial Review of International Arbitration Awards", Singapore International Arbitration Academy (Nov. 26 – Dec. 14, 2012, Singapore), https://cil.nus.edu.sg/wp – content/uploads/2012/11/PatrickFoy – An_Introduction_To_Judicial_Review_Of_International_Arbitration_Awards – for – 5 – DECEMBER.pdf (last visited July 15, 2020), p. 35.

④ Fernández – Armesto, *supra* note 16, at 132.

⑤ J. Christopher Thomas and Harpreet K. Dhillon, "The Foundations of Investment Treaty Arbitration: The ICSID Convention, Investment Treaties and the Review of Arbitration Awards", ICSID Review, Vol. 32, No. 3 (2017), p. 493 (arguing that "States have adopted different substantive and procedural rules for the review of arbitral awards and generally have not distinguished between the review of regular international commercial arbitration awards and those rendered by investment treaty tribunals").

⑥ Fernández – Armesto, *supra* note 16, at 132.

⑦ Anthea Roberts, "Divergence between Investment and Commercial Arbitration", Proceedings of the Annual Meeting (ASIL), Vol. 106 (2012), p. 298.

3. The Common Grounds for the Judicial Review of Investment Awards

3.1 Lack or Invalidity of An Agreement to Arbitrate

The first ground noted in Article 34(2) of the Model Law for setting aside an investment award is "*a party to the arbitration agreement referred to in article* 7 *was under some incapacity; or the said agreement is not valid under the law to which the parties have subjected it or, failing any indication thereon, under the law of this State*". ① An arbitration agreement is a consensual declaration of will from the parties to a specific dispute to voluntarily submit the unsettled issues to the competence of an arbitral authority. The agreement to arbitration, also known as the consent of parties, is the cornerstone of arbitration, ② be it commercial arbitration, investment arbitration or interstate arbitration. Thus, an investment award rendered out of an arbitration tainted with the defects in relation to the agreement to arbitrate is vulnerable to judicial denial.

The judicial review proceeding in relation to *Sedelmayer v. The Russian Federation* is representative of the state party challenging the jurisdiction of investment tribunals. Mr. Sedelmayer, as a German, claimed that his assets within the territory of Russia had been confiscated by Russian authorities between 1994 – 1996. On January 15, 1996, Mr. Sedelmayer requested to launch an investment arbitration against Russia under the auspices of the Arbitration Institute of Stockholm Chamber of Commerce, pursuant to Article 10 of the Germany – the Soviet Union BIT, which was succeeded by Russia. The Tribunal in 1998 decided that Russia should compensate Mr. Sedelmayer in the sum of US $ 2.35 million. ③ Russia moved to challenge the award on the basis of lack of jurisdiction of the Tribunal before the Stock-

① Article 34(2)(a)(i), the Model Law.

② Rubins, *supra* note 2, at 363.

③ *Sedelmayer v. The Russian Federation*, Arbitration Award (July 7, 1998), available at https://www.italaw.com/sites/default/files/case-documents/ita0757.pdf (last visited July 28, 2020), p. 118. Pal Wrange, "Sedelmayer v. Russian Federation", American Journal of International Law, Vol. 106, No. 2 (2012), p. 348.

holm District Court.

Russia argued that the assets of Mr. Sedelmayer were indirect investment, which fell outside the definition of "investment" under the German - Soviet BIT. It also insisted that Mr. Sedelmayer could not be treated as an "investor" under the BIT because he did not have his "permanent place of residence" in Germany. The District Court declined to embrace the arguments of Russia, arguing that according to the so - called "doctrine of assertion", ① the statements made by Mr. Sedelmayer with regard to his "investment" and identity of "investor" were sufficient for the Tribunal to establish jurisdiction. Russia later appealed the judgement of the District Court to the Svea Court of Appeal only to see that judgment was upheld. ②

While complete lack of an arbitration agreement, i. e., lack of jurisdiction on the part of arbitral tribunals, is a proper ground for setting aside investment awards, an investor's allegation that the arbitral tribunal wrongly denied jurisdiction over the dispute that it should have assumed jurisdiction may have a bleak outlook to secure support from the review court in some jurisdictions. For instance, in the judicial review proceeding in relation to *Bayview Irrigation District et al. v. United Mexican States*, though the ultimate goal of the applicants was to set aside the arbitral award which denied the jurisdiction of the investment tribunal, the applicants did not rely on denial of jurisdiction *per se* in pursuit of the *vacatur* of the award. Instead, they argued that the award should be set aside because a handful of statutory grounds

① The "doctrine of assertion" is a procedural law principle that originates from the jurisdiction of Sweden, which means that "the dispute falls within the jurisdiction of the arbitral tribunal if one of the parties asserts that its claim comes within the scope of the agreement which contains the arbitration clause, provided that such assertion is not completely without foundation and provided that there is no dispute as to the validity of the arbitration agreement". Kaj Hober and Nils Eliasson, "Review of Investment Treaty Awards by Municipal Courts", in Katia Yannaca - Small (ed.), "Arbitration Under International Investment Agreements: A Guide to the Key Issues", Oxford University Press (2010), p. 645.

② Ibid., at 643 - 645.

had been activated by the tribunal's denial of jurisdiction. ① According to the UNCITRAL 2012 Digest of Case Law on the Model Law on International Commercial Arbitration (hereinafter the 2012 Digest), the German Federal Court of Justice in a review proceeding held that negative jurisdictional rulings are reviewable awards under Article 34. ② But the Court maintained that none of the exhaustively listed grounds in Article 34 allowed the Court to set aside an arbitral award on the sole basis that the tribunal erred in denying jurisdiction. ③

3.2 Inability to Present the Case

Article 34(2)(a)(ii) of the Model Law provides that an arbitral award may be set aside if "the party making the application was not given proper notice of the appointment of an arbitrator or of the arbitral proceedings or was otherwise unable to present its case." ④ A party's inability to present the case is also referred to as the violation of the right to be heard or of due process or of "natural justice", ⑤ indicating that the party was deprived of the possibility to be effectively engaged in the process of the adjudication of the dispute by the arbitral tribunal. Unless a party to arbitration itself is the one that should take the blame for the inability to present its case, lack of involvement in the process of dispute resolution is not in line with the fundamental tenets of natural justice, thus qualifying as a ground for setting aside an arbitral award.

In *Bayview Irrigation District et al. v. United Mexican States*, an investment arbitration conducted pursuant to the ICSID AF Rules, the 46 claimants argued that their water rights under a treaty signed by the United States and Mexico in 1944 to

---

① *Bayview Irrigation District* #11 *et al. v. Mexico*, Ontario Superior Court of Justice, Reasons for Judgment, Court File No: 07 – CV – 340139 – PD2, available at https://www.italaw.com/sites/default/files/case-documents/ita0078_0.pdf (last visited on July 28, 2020), paras. 64 – 78.

② UNCITRAL, UNCITRAL 2012 Digest of Case Law on the Model Law on International Commercial Arbitration (hereinafter the 2012 Digest), http://www.uncitral.org/pdf/english/clout/MAL-digest-2012-e.pdf (last visited on July 27, 2020), p. 143.

③ Ibid.

④ Article 34(2)(a)(ii), the Model Law.

⑤ UNCITRAL, *supra* note 29, at 145.

allocate the water of the Rio Grande were infringed by Mexico, since Mexico had captured, seized and diverted water which they claimed to own, for the use of Mexican farmers. They submitted the dispute to arbitration in 2005, alleging that the practice of Mexico was in breach of Articles 1102, 1105 and 1110 of Chapter 11 of NAFTA. The Tribunal denied jurisdiction over the dispute as it agreed with Mexico that the claimants' water rights under the treaty could not constitute ownership of personal property rights that amounts to an "investment" under Chapter 11 of NAFTA.① The applicants attempted to set aside the arbitral award which precluded the Tribunal from hearing the merits of the dispute before the Ontario Superior Court of Justice. One of the grounds that the claimants mentioned was that the Tribunal had breached a settled practice – the "doctrine of assertion" by denying its jurisdiction, stripping them of a fair opportunity to present their case. Thus, in the applicants' view, the investment award should be set aside under Article 34(2)(a)(ii).②

The Court first made clear that its role in judicial review is not to "conduct a hearing *de novo* of the merits of the Tribunal's decision on jurisdiction" and "the standard of review is narrower in scope than that governing the review by a domestic court of the decision of a domestic administrative tribunal".③ The Court went on by stating that while the losing party of an arbitration is entitled to pose a challenge to the arbitral award, such a challenge is subject to "the 'powerful presumption' that the tribunal acted within its authority".④ As to the applicants' allegation of lack of an opportunity to present their case, the Court did not agree because it

---

① *Bayview Irrigation District et al. v. United Mexican States*, ICSID Case No. ARB(AF)/05/1, Final Award (June 19, 2007), available at https://www.italaw.com/sites/default/files/case-documents/ita0076_0.pdf (last visited on July 28, 2020). David M. Quealy, "*Bayview Irrigation District et al. v. United Mexican States*: NAFAT, Foreign Investment, and International Trade in Water – A Hard Pill to Swallow", Minnesota Journal of International Law, Vol. 17, No. 1 (2008), p. 99–119.

② *Bayview Irrigation District* #11 *et al. v. Mexico*, Ontario Superior Court of Justice, Reasons for Judgment, Court File No: 07-CV-340139-PD2, available at https://www.italaw.com/sites/default/files/case-documents/ita0078_0.pdf (last visited on July 28, 2020), paras. 43, 46–47, & 49.

③ Ibid., para. 60.

④ Ibid., para. 63.

found that "the applicants were provided a full opportunity to know the case they had to meet and fair opportunity to present their case". ① In addition, there was no indication on the record that the applicants objected or asked for an adjournment, allowing them to submit more evidence to sustain their own case. ②

3.3 Excess of Mandate

Article 34(2)(a)(iii) provides that an arbitral award may be (partially) set aside if "the award deals with adispute not contemplated by or not falling within the terms of the submission to arbitration, or contains decisions on matters beyond the scope of the submission to arbitration". ③ In view of the consensual nature of arbitration, the scope of the submission to arbitration, also referred to as the scope of the mandate of the arbitral tribunal, is primarily decided by the parties. ④ Arbitral tribunals are supposed to fulfill duties within the parameters of the parties' consent and should not exceed the mandate conferred upon them by those parties. Markert and Bubrowski argue that, in order to effectively protect the consent of the parties, an arbitral award out of the arbitral proceeding in which the tribunal overstepped this consent has to be set aside. ⑤ Courts have stated that for the purpose of the determination of the "terms of the submission" to arbitration and "scope of the submission," the arbitration agreement, other relevant contractual provisions, the notice of request for arbitration and the pleadings exchanged between the parties are to be taken into account. ⑥

In the judicial review proceeding with respect to the three arbitral decisions

① *Bayview Irrigation District* #11 *et al. v. Mexico*, Ontario Superior Court of Justice, Reasons for Judgment, Court File No: 07 – CV – 340139 – PD2, available at https://www.italaw.com/sites/default/files/case-documents/ita0078_0.pdf (last visited on July 28, 2020), para. 61.

② Ibid., para. 71.

③ Article 34(2)(a)(iii), the Model Law.

④ UNCITRAL, *supra* note 29, at 151.

⑤ Markert & Bubrowski, *supra* note 2, at 1469.

⑥ UNCITRAL, *supra* note 29, at 151.

rendered by the Tribunal in *S. D. Myers v. Canada*,[①] Canada, the claimant, and Mexico, the intervener, attempted to set aside the decisions on the basis that the Tribunal exceeded its authority before the Federal Court of Canada. Canada argued that the respondent in this judicial review case and the claimant in the arbitral proceeding, i. e., the US company S. D. Myers, Inc. (SDMI), was not an "investor", and the Canadian company, Myers Canada, was not an "investment of the investor", as defined under Chapter 11 of NAFTA, which led to the conclusion that the arbitration claim was beyond the scope of the tribunal's jurisdiction.[②] This argument by Canada was discussed under the rubric of "matters beyond the scope of the submission to arbitration."[③] The Court found that in this case the tribunal's decision had not expressly addressed "jurisdiction" and the Canada's argument that SDMI had no "standing" was discussed as a mixed question of fact and law, not as

① S. D. Myers Inc., (SDMI) was a family – held corporation headquartered in Ohio, the US, owned by Mr. Dana Myers (who held 51 percent of the share capital and was the CEO), and his three brothers. The business of SDMI concerned treating or remediating toxic wastes contaminated with polychlorinated biphenyls (PCBs). SDMI entered Canada's remediation market in the 1990s by establishing a Canadian affiliate, Myers Canada. Myers Canada competed with local companies and solicited orders in Canada, and then exported the Canadian – owned PCBs to the US for destruction at SDMI's US facilities. In November 1995, the minister of the environment took regulatory action, banning the export of PCBs on the basis of a purportedly "significant danger to the environment and to human life and health." Contemporaneously, the minister articulated a policy that the remediation of Canadian PCBs should be performed in "Canada by Canadians." The Canadian government reversed that policy and lifted the export restrictions in February 1997. In an arbitration initiated in 1998 on the basis of the NAFTA's investment chapter, SDMI challenged Canada's sixteen – month export ban as an expropriation, an unlawful performance requirement, a denial of national treatment, and a denial of fair and equitable treatment. In the first partial award, the tribunal held that Canada had breached its obligations to provide national treatment to investors from another NAFTA party and accord to investments of investors of another NAFTA party treatment in accordance with international law, including fair and equitable treatment and full protection and security under Article 1105 of NAFTA. In the second partial award and the final award, SDMI was respectively awarded damages and arbitration costs. Hober & Eliasson, *supra* note 26, at 646. Charles H. Brower II, "S. D. Myers, Inc. v. Canada, and Attorney General of Canada v. S. D. Myers, Inc., [2004] F. C. 38", American Journal of International Law, Vol. 98, No. 2 (2004), p. 339 – 342.

② *The Attorney General of Canada v. S. D. Myers, Inc. v. The United Mexican States*, Reasons for Order, Federal Court of Canada, 13 January 2004, available at https://www.italaw.com/sites/default/files/case – documents/ita0756.pdf (last visited on July 29, 2020), para. 76.

③ Ibid., para. 46.

a question of jurisdiction. ① The Court then moved to argue that:

"Jurisdiction is a term of art and a legal objection must be raised clearly at the outset of the arbitration. Canada failed to do so in this case, and cannot now argue that the Tribunal did not have jurisdiction to render the three decisions which are the subject of these applications for judicial review. To find otherwise would undermine the clear and express procedures incorporated in NAFTA for the resolution of disputes. "②

Thus, the Court agreed with SDMI in this regard and reached the conclusion that Canada had lost its right to the judicial review of the jurisdictional decision of the Tribunal by not expressly raising an effective objection to the Tribunal's jurisdiction during the arbitration. Despite no need for the Court to conduct review of the jurisdictional objections that Canada submitted, the Court proceeded to do so in the alternative that it was wrong in the decision that Canada had lost its right to challenge the Tribunal's jurisdiction. ③ The judge decided to review the award with respect to the legal meaning of the word "investor" and "investment of an investor" in NAFTA by the standard of correctness and with respect to the application of the facts to the definitions by the standard of reasonableness. ④ The Court ultimately confirmed that the Tribunal had interpreted the pertinent definition correctly and reasonably applied the facts to the definitions. ⑤

Mexico, which intervened in the case, along with Canada submitted that the respondent's activities in Canada could be properly characterized as cross – border trade in services and should be governed by Chapter 12 of the NAFTA. With that being said, they argued that the application of Chapter 11 to cross – border trade in

---

① *The Attorney General of Canada v. S. D. Myers, Inc. v. The United Mexican States*, Reasons for Order, Federal Court of Canada, 13 January 2004, available at https://www.italaw.com/sites/default/files/case-documents/ita0756.pdf (last visited on July 29, 2020), paras. 51 – 52.

② Ibid., para. 53.

③ Ibid., para. 57.

④ Ibid., para. 60.

⑤ Ibid., para. 70.

services exceeded the tribunal's mandate. ① The Court was of the view that the chapters of NAFTA overlap, and the NAFTA rights are cumulative, unless there is a direct conflict. Although SDMI's business in Canada fell into the scope of trade in services, the company also had investment in Canada with respect to waste remediation services and thus was entitled to the protection accorded by Chapter 11 of the NAFTA. Considering that the rights and obligations under Chapters 11 and 12 were not mutually exclusive or inconsistent, and the arbitral award was based on SDMI's rights under Chapter 11, the Court decided that the tribunal had not exceeded its mandate. ②

3.4 Irregularity in the Composition of the Tribunal and the Arbitral Procedure

Article 34(2)(a)(iv) of the Model Law states that an arbitral award may be set aside by the review court if the composition of the arbitral tribunal or the arbitral procedure was not in accordance with the agreement of the parties, or, failing such agreement, was not in accordance with the applicable arbitration law. ③ The first prong of this test relates to the adjudicative authority that would take charge of the whole process of arbitral proceedings and render decisions that may have significant impact on the parties to arbitration. Unless parties to arbitration have agreed otherwise, an arbitral tribunal in investment arbitration usually comprises a sole arbitrator or three arbitrators, who are usually, in a direct or indirect way, appointed by parties to arbitration. Thus, those parties hold great sway over the exercise of selecting arbitrators to establish an arbitral tribunal for the purpose of deciding a specific case. ④ Considering that the rules concerning the procedure of appointing

---

① *The Attorney General of Canada v. S. D. Myers, Inc. v. The United Mexican States*, Reasons for Order, Federal Court of Canada, 13 January 2004, available at https://www.italaw.com/sites/default/files/case-documents/ita0756.pdf (last visited on July 29, 2020), para. 76.

② Ibid., para. 71.

③ Article 34(2)(a)(iv), the Model Law.

④ According to Articles 8 and 9 of the UNCITRAL Arbitration Rules, parties to arbitration can decide whether a sole arbitrator or three arbitrators are to be appointed to take charge of a case. In principle, the selection of a sole arbitrator should be agreed upon by all the parties. In the case that three arbitrators are to be appointed, each party shall appoint one arbitrator. The two arbitrators thus appointed shall choose the third arbitrator who will act as the presiding arbitrator of the arbitral tribunal. Articles 8 and 9, the UNCITRAL Arbitration Rules.

arbitrators in most cases are relatively clear and unambiguous, it is not very likely that an applicant would claim in a challenge proceeding that it has been deprived of the opportunity to effectively engage with the process of appointing arbitrators. However, a party may still have doubts as to the independence and impartiality of the constitutive members of the arbitral tribunal despite the existence of its own representation within the tribunal. In such a case, this party may move to apply for the setting – aside of the arbitral award on the ground that the arbitral tribunal was not properly constituted because there was conflict of interest or lack of independence and impartiality with regard to arbitrators. ① There is an argument that the improper composition of the arbitral tribunal as a ground for attacking an arbitral award is probably more relevant in investment arbitration than in commercial arbitration because of the high publicity and increased transparency of investment arbitration cases and the small community of arbitrators involved therein. ② The 2012 Digest indicated that, in several decisions rendered out of judicial review proceedings, the failure to object to the composition of the arbitral tribunal during the arbitral proceeding precluded a party from challenging an arbitral award on the ground that the arbitral tribunal was incorrectly composed at the judicial review stage. ③ In this vein, only a party who has objected to the composition of the arbitral tribunal during the arbitration but failed, or who was reasonably unaware of the defect in this regard until after the arbitral award was rendered, is entitled to base the challenge of the award on the improper composition of the arbitral tribunal.

The second prong of the test is connected with the concept of procedural irregularity. Given the self – evident importance of procedural justice in dispensing just and unbiased dispute resolution services, an arbitral award should be, and would be

① The 2012 Digest shows that there are judicial review cases in which the applicant challenged the arbitral award on the basis of alleged lack of independence of the members of the arbitral tribunal. UNCITRAL, *supra* note 150, at 159.

② Markert & Bubrowski, *supra* note 7, at 1472.

③ UNCITRAL, *supra* note 150, at 159.

in most countries,① set aside by domestic courts *loci arbitri* if the arbitration was carried out in a fundamentally arbitrary or unfair way. There are a variety of procedural defects that could subject an arbitral award to *vacatur* at the place of arbitration, including *ex parte* communications, manifestly unequal treatment of the parties, unauthorized consolidation of proceedings, corruption of one or more arbitrators, denial of basic due process, failure to give sufficient reasons, and non-compliance with the formal requirements for an award, etc. ② In practice, in the light of the significant differences between court litigation and arbitration, courts tend to hold arbitrators to looser procedural formalities than those applicable to judges, ensuring considerable procedural flexibility is accorded to arbitrators to streamline arbitral proceedings at their discretion in so far as the parties have not disagreed. ③ That inclination of domestic courts *loci arbitri*, which implies a high threshold of corroboration, could operate as a stumbling block to the success of a claimant seeking *vacatur* of an arbitral award by virtue of procedural defects. On some occasions, along with the existence of a major procedural defect, the claimant also has to further prove that, but for the defect, the decision of the arbitral tribunal would have been different. ④ Furthermore, a party could also lose the right to rely on procedural defects to challenge an arbitral award in a judicial review proceeding if he failed to put the same problem onto the table during the arbitral proceeding subject to that the problem had already become known to the party during that phase. ⑤

In the context of the judicial review proceeding in relation to *CME v. Czech Republic* mentioned in the previous section, Czech Republic also attacked the arbi-

---

① Rubins, *supra* note 7, at 368.

② UNCITRAL, *supra* note 150, at 157 – 159.

③ Rubins stated that "arbitrators enjoy broad powers to arrange hearings as they see fit, including the examination of witnesses, submission of briefs, and timing of oral hearings". According to him, this is particularly true in the context of international dispute resolution because the "fusion of civil law and common law elements have engendered flexible practices that sometimes have little resemblance to court procedures in either civil or common law countries". Rubins, *supra* note 2, at 368 – 369.

④ Ibid., at 369. Markert & Bubrowski, *supra* note 2, at 1473 – 1474.

⑤ Markert & Bubrowski, *supra* note 2, at 1473.

tral awards on a ground that somewhat lies in between improper composition of the arbitral tribunal and procedural irregularity. The Republic argued that its appointed arbitrator, Jaroslav Handl, had been excluded by the other two arbitrators, namely Wolfgang Kuhn (the Chairman) and Stephen M. Schwebel (appointed by CME), from effective participation into the deliberations that led to the drafting of the award. In fact, on September 23, 2001, Handl gave his notice of resignation as an arbitrator, because according to him, *inter alia*, the two arbitrators, in particular Kuhn, had excluded him and deliberated without him. ① The Svea Court of Appeal was of the view that Handl had indeed received all the essential communications between the arbitrators and there was no evidence to show that the two arbitrators had deliberated without him, and that "Handl did not have an opportunity to participate on equal terms, that they worked against him, and that the two other arbitrators ignored his opinions"; on the contrary, Kuhn appears to have treated Handl correctly for the whole time and "Handl appears to have been afforded an opportunity to submit his comments to the extent which reasonably may be dictated by considerations of courtesy between colleagues". It was considered that Handl's feelings of being excluded probably, in all essential regards, related to the fact that his opinion had not won support of the other two arbitrators. The Court further stated that some deadlines proposed by Handl during the proceedings seemed to be unreasonably long and could not be justified by the attached reasons because they were in fact difficult to understand. In its conclusion, the Court found that "the Republic's allegation that Handl was excluded from the deliberations to be unproven and close to groundless", and thus refused to set aside the arbitral awards on the aforesaid ground. ②

① After Handl's resignation, Ian Brownlie took over his position as an arbitrator during the final damages phase. Although Brownlie also ended up in the minority, he signed the final award while issued a lengthy separate opinion. *The Czech Republic v. CME Czech Republic B. V.*, the Svea Court of Appeal, Case no. T 8735 - 01, Judgment of the Court of Appeal, 15 May 2003, available at https://www.italaw.com/sites/default/files/case - documents/ita0182.pdf (last visited on July 29, 2020), p. 19.

② Ibid., at 89 - 90.

3.5 Non – arbitrability of the Subject Matter

Article 34(2)(b)(i) of the Model Law provides that an arbitral award may be set aside by a review court if the court finds that "the subject – matter of the dispute is not capable of settlement by arbitration under the law of this State". ① In other words, the mere fact that the subject matter of a dispute is non – arbitrable could lead to the setting – aside of the arbitral award. Arbitrability entails "a simple question of what types of issues can and cannot be submitted to arbitration and whether specific classes of disputes are exempt from arbitration proceedings". ② While party autonomy would espouse the right of parties to put any dispute to arbitration as they desire, national laws often impose restrictions on the freedom in this regard by not allowing certain issues to be resolved by arbitration but through other methods, such as court litigation. ③ In fact, as of the time of writing, non – arbitrability as a ground for setting aside an arbitral award appears to have not yet forged a close bond with investment arbitration, as evidenced by the fact that there is hardly any instance in which an applicant seeks *vacatur* of an investment award on the ground of non – arbitrability. ④ This does not seem to be surprising when taking into consideration that not infrequently certain issues that are non – arbitrable in some jurisdictions relate to family, labor and consumer law, which, in turn, generally often lack relevance in investment disputes. In addition, there are also a number of states that declare issues in relation to antitrust, security transactions, intellectual property, and insolvency as non – arbitrable. ⑤ Those issues, however, are closely connected to the operation and expansion of foreign investments, thus bearing a rela-

---

① Article 34(2)(b)(i), the Model Law.

② Loukas A. Mistells, "Arbitrability: International & Comparative Perspectives", Kluwer Law International (2009), p. 3 – 4.

③ According to Mistells, "certain disputes may involve such sensitive public policy issues that it is felt that they should only be dealt with by the judicial authority of state courts" and "an obvious example is criminal law which is generally the domain of the national courts: it is undisputed that the sanctioning of criminal activity is in the power of the judiciary." Ibid., at 4.

④ Gaëtan Verhoosel, "Annulment and Enforcement Review of Treaty Awards: To ICSID or Not to ICSID", ICSID Review, Vol. 23, No. 1 (2008), p. 128 – 129.

⑤ Markert & Bubrowski, *supra* note 2, at 1474.

tively high possibility to gain prominence in investment disputes. With that in mind one should not be too surprised if a challenge proceeding against an investment award mounted on the basis of non – arbitrability emerges in the future.

3.6 Violation of Public Policy

In accordance with Article 34(2)(b)(ii) of the Model Law, an arbitral award faces a risk of being set aside by domestic courts *loci arbitri* where "the award is in conflict with the public policy of this State". ① Despite that public policy defenses are not infrequent in the practice of the judicial review of both commercial awards and investment awards, a generally recognized concept or scope of public policy has not yet come into being. ② In fact, public policy is "a broad term with multiple interpretations under different legislative systems". ③ In those jurisdictions in which national public policy is distinguished from international public policy, an investment award would be subject to narrower scope of review in terms of public policy where the court exclusively applies international public policy to awards rendered out of international arbitration. ④

The jurisprudence of the judicial review in relation to investment arbitration has shown that challenges against investment awards on the ground of a violation of public policy are faced with a gloomy prospect in securing endorsement from domestic courts *loci arbitri*. A second look at *Saar Papier v. Poland (II)* mentioned above would reveal a U – turn in the circumstances of both parties in the sense that Saar Papier's claim of compensation was in its entirety dismissed by the Tribunal in the final award dated on 7 June 2001 despite the same Tribunal having decided in favor of the investor in the interim award. Consequently, unlike the setting – aside application regarding the interim award, it was the investor's turn to apply for the

---

① Article 34(2)(b)(ii), the Model Law.

② In fact, it would be extremely hard for a generally accepted definition of public policy to be reached among states, because states seem to have different, sometimes conflicting, public policy considerations, and those considerations would also change with the advancement of time and the changes of circumstances. Markert & Bubrowski, *supra* note 2, at 1475.

③ Rajoo, *supra* note 10, at 219.

④ UNCITRAL, *supra* note 29, at 160.

vacatur of the final award before the Swiss Federal Court. The investor based its challenge against the final award on four separate grounds, including, *inter alia*, a violation of public policy. The public policy argument featured the alleged breach of fundamental principles of "protection of confidence, prohibition of abuse of rights and discrimination, the protection of the weaker party, and the prohibition of expropriation without compensation". ① The investor notably argued that the Tribunal had interpreted certain provisions of the Germany – Poland BIT in a wrong way by equalizing "the damage caused to it" to "the value of the investment" instead of "lost profits". By doing so, the Tribunal allegedly ignored the international law principle – prohibition of expropriation, thus violating public order. ② In its decision on the public policy argument relied upon by Saar Papier, the Court stated that an arbitral award does not violate public order unless it violates a fundamental principle of law both in its reasoning and in its result. Thus, instances such as flawed appreciation of evidence, an incorrect finding of fact, or even a clear breach of a legal norm would not engender the setting – aside of an award. ③ The Court noted that Saar Papier had never argued that it received no consideration for its investments, and that there was no principle of full compensation under international law. In addressing the investor's claim that the Tribunal had erroneously interpreted the BIT, the Court explicitly ruled that a tribunal's mere erroneous interpretation of law would not in any case qualify as a violation of public policy. ④ The Court therefore rejected the setting – aside of the final award on the basis of the public policy argument.

4. Empirical Study: An Overview of Known Cases Concerning the Judicial Review of Investment Awards

Before proceeding to the assessment of themechanism of the judicial review of

---

① Matthias Scherer et al., "Domestic Review of Investment Treaty Arbitrations: The Swiss Experience", ASA Bulletin, Vol. 27, No. 1 (2009), p. 270.

② Ibid.

③ Ibid., at 271.

④ Ibid.

investment awards, it is of much need to pull off a precise understanding of the dynamics of this mechanism in reality. Any efforts to evaluate the judicial review mechanism in the investment arbitration context or seek changes to that should train attention at the empirics in this regard, or risk firing a shot in the dark. While the scholarly and practical benefits of the empirical research of investment arbitration have been made known,① the judicial review of investment awards as a post – award remedy has not been investigated from the empirical perspective to the same extent as other aspects of investment arbitration, such as the impartiality of arbitrators, the costs and length of arbitral proceedings, and the outcomes of those proceedings.② Given that the practice of investment arbitration and the follow – on setting – aside proceedings has been evolving at a rapid pace, the existing empirical literature on the judicial review of investment awards could not reflect the most recent development of that mechanism. Thus, with a view to laying the groundwork for a fact – based appraisal of the judicial review mechanism, this Section is intended to conduct an empirical study of all the known setting – aside proceedings that ensued from investment arbitration cases. All the data presented herein was primarily derived from the Investment Dispute Settlement Navigator (the Navigator) operated by UNCTAD and complemented by the Investment Arbitration Reporter (the IA Reporter), a specialized news and analysis service tracking investment arbitration, as of June 30, 2020.

This Section aims to shed empirical light on the mechanism of the judicial review of investment awards by exploring the answers to the following questions: (1) how often does parties to non – ICSID arbitration submit investment awards to domestic courts *loci arbitri* for judicial review? (2) which legal jurisdictions have been

---

① Chiara Giorgetti, "Is the Truth in the Eyes of the Beholder? The Perils and Benefits of Empirical Research in International Investment Arbitration", Santa Clara Journal of International Law, Vol. 12, No. 1 (2014), p. 275 (arguing that empirical research can provide benefits for the understanding of investment arbitration and offer guidance to its reform).

② Michael Faure and Wanli Ma, "Investor – State Arbitration: Economic and Empirical Perspectives", Michigan Journal of International Law, Vol. 41, No. 1 (2020), p. 25 – 49 (providing an overview of the empirical studies of a host of topics in relation to investment arbitration ranging from arbitration filing to public interest issues).

often involved in the practice of the judicial review of investment awards in the sense that their domestic courts were the review courts and their arbitration legislation was the applicable law? (3) is there symmetry in the number of applications for the setting – aside of investment awards made by the investor party and the state party? (4) how often is more than one court instance is involved in the setting – aside proceedings with respect to investment awards? (5) what are the outcomes of those challenges against investment awards entertained by domestic courts at the seat of arbitration?

Table 1 Investment Arbitrations that Have Triggered Off the Judicial Review of Awards[1]

No.	Case Reference[2]	Year[3]	Jurisdiction[4]	Claimant[5]	Award/Decision[6]	Outcome[7]	Appealed[8]
1	Saar Papier v. Poland (II)	1996	Switzerland	Poland	Interim Award	Upheld	No
				Saar Papier	Final Award	Upheld	No
2	Sedelmayer v. Russia	1996	Sweden	Russia	Final Award	Upheld	Yes
3	Metalclad v. Mexico	1997	Canada	Mexico	Final Award	Partially Set Aside	No
4	Loewen v. USA	1998	The US	Raymond L. Loewen	Final Award	Upheld	No
5	Myers v. Canada	1998	Canada	Canada	Arbitration Awards	Upheld	No
6	Feldman v. Mexico	1999	Canada	Mexico	Final Award	Upheld	Yes
7	Swembalt v. Latvia	1999	Denmark	Latvia	Final Award	Upheld	No
8	CME v. Czech Republic	2000	Sweden	Czech	Partial Award	Upheld	No
9	Saluka v. Czech Republic	2001	Switzerland	Czech	Partial Award	Upheld	No
10	Canfor v. USA	2002	The US	Tembec	Procedural Order & Costs Award	Upheld	No
11	France Telecom v. Lebanon	2002	Switzerland	Lebanon	Final Award	Upheld	No
12	Nagel v. Czech Republic	2002	Sweden	Nagel	Final Award	Upheld	No

Continuation

No.	Case Reference	Year	Jurisdiction	Claimant	Award/Decision	Outcome	Appealed
13	Occidental v. Ecuador (I)	2002	England and Wales	Ecuador	Final Award	Upheld	Yes
14	Thunderbird v. Mexico	2002	The US	Thunderbird	Final Award	Upheld	No
15	AWG v. Argentina	2003	The US	Argentina	Final Award	Upheld	Yes
16	BG v. Argentina	2003	The US	Argentina	Final Award	Upheld	Yes
17	Eureko v. Poland	2003	Belgium	Poland	Partial Award	Upheld	No
18	National Grid v. Argentina	2003	The US	Argentina	Arbitration Award	Upheld	Yes
19	Petrobart v. Kyrgyz Republic	2003	Sweden	Kyrgyz Republic	Arbitration Award	Upheld	No
20	Tembec v. USA	2004	The US	Tembec	Procedural Order & Costs Award	Upheld	No
21	Terminal Forest v. USA	2004	The US	Tembec	Procedural Order & Costs Award	Upheld	No
22	Bayview v. Mexico	2005	Canada	Bayview and Others	Final Award	Upheld	No
23	Binder v. Czech Republic	2005	Czech	Czech	Award on Jurisdiction	Discontinued	Yes
24	Cargill v. Mexico	2005	Canada	Mexico	Final Award	Upheld	Yes
25	EMV v. Czech Republic	2005	England and Wales	Czech	Award on Jurisdiction	Upheld	No
26	Hulley Enterprises v. Russia	2005	The Netherlands	Russia	Arbitration Awards	Pending	Yes
27	Pren Nreka v. Czech Republic	2005	France	Czech	Final Award	Upheld	No
28	RosInvest v. Russia	2005	Sweden	Russia	Award on Jurisdiction	Entirely Set Aside	No
					Final Award	Partially Set Aside	No
29	Veteran Petroleum v. Russia	2005	The Netherlands	Russia	Arbitration Awards	Pending	Yes
30	Walter Bau v. Thailand	2005	Switzerland	Thailand	Final Award	Upheld	No

Continuation

No.	Case Reference	Year	Jurisdiction	Claimant	Award/Decision	Outcome	Appealed
31	Yukos Universal v. Russia	2005	The Netherlands	Russia	Arbitration Awards	Pending	Yes
32	Chevron and Tex-Pet v. Ecuador (I)	2006	The Netherlands	Ecuador	Arbitration Awards	Upheld	Yes
33	Adria Beteiligungs v. Croatia	2007	The Netherlands	Adria Beteiligungs	Final Award	Upheld	No
34	Kaliningrad v. Lithuania	2007	France	Kaliningrad	Final Award	Upheld	No
35	Mobil Investments v. Canada (I)	2007	Canada	Canada	Final Award	Upheld	No
36	Renta 4 S. V. S. A and others v. Russia	2007	Sweden	Russia	Final Award	Unclear	Unclear
37	Achmea v. Slovakia (I)	2008	Germany	Slovakia	Award on Jurisdiction, Admissibility and Suspension	Upheld	Yes
					Final Award	Entirely Set Aside	Yes
38	Clayton/Bilcon v. Canada	2008	Canada	Canada	Award on Jurisdiction and Liability	Upheld	No
				Unclear	Award onDamages	Unclear	Unclear
39	Tatneft v. Ukraine	2008	France	Ukraine	Partial Award on Jurisdiction & Final Award	Upheld	No
40	Chevron and TexPet v. Ecuador (II)	2009	The Netherlands	Ecuador	Interim Awards & First Partial Award	Upheld	Yes
41	EDF v. Hungary	2009	Switzerland	Hungary	Final Award	Upheld	No
42	Gold Reserve v. Venezuela	2009	France	Venezuela	Final Award	Upheld	No
43	Beijing Shougang and Others v. Mongolia	2010	The US	Beijing Shougang and Others	Final Award	Pending	Yes
44	Energoalians v. Moldova	2010	France	Moldova	Final Award	Pending	Yes

Continuation

No.	Case Reference	Year	Jurisdiction	Claimant	Award/Decision	Outcome	Appealed
45	Stati and Others v. Kazakhstan	2010	Sweden	Kazakhstan	Final Award	Upheld	No
46	Al – Kharafi v. Libya and others	2011	Egypt	Libya	Final Award	Entirely Set Aside	Yes
47	Belokon v. Kyrgyzstan	2011	France	Kyrgyzstan	Final Award	Entirely Set Aside	No
48	Crystallex v. Venezuela	2011	The US	Venezuela	Final Award	Upheld	No
49	Ghenia v. Libya	2011	France	Ghenia	Procedural Decision	Upheld	No
50	Mesa Power v. Canada	2011	The US	Mesa Power	Final Award	Upheld	No
51	Oxus Gold v. Uzbekistan	2011	France	Oxus Gold	Final Award	Upheld	No
52	Ryan and Others v. Poland	2011	France	Ryan and Others	Final Award	Upheld	No
53	Devas v. India	2012	The Netherlands	India	Award on Jurisdiction and Merits	Upheld	No
54	GarcíaArmas and García Gruber v. Venezuela	2012	France	Venezuela	Decision on Jurisdiction	Entirely Set Aside	Yes
					Final Award	Pending	Unclear
55	Progas Energy v. Pakistan	2012	England and Wales	Progas Energy	Final Award	Pending	Unclear
56	SanumInvestments v. Laos	2012	Singapore	Laos	Award on Jurisdiction	Upheld	Yes
57	Swissbourgh and Others v. Lesotho	2012	Singapore	Lesotho	Partial Award on Jurisdiction and the Merits	Entirely Set Aside	Yes
58	Beck v. Kyrgyzstan	2013	Russia	Kyrgyz Republic	Final Award	Entirely Set Aside	Yes
59	Berkowitz v. Costa Rica	2013	The US	Costa Rica	Interim Award	Upheld	No
60	De Sutter and Others v. Madagascar (I)	2013	France	Madagascar	Final Award	Entirely Set Aside	Yes

Continuation

No.	Case Reference	Year	Jurisdiction	Claimant	Award/Decision	Outcome	Appealed
61	Deutsche Telekom v. India	2013	Switzerland	India	Interim Award	Upheld	No
62	Natland and Others v. Czech Republic	2013	Switzerland	Czech Republic	Partial Award	Pending	No
63	OKKV v. Kyrgyzstan	2013	Russia	Kyrgyz Republic	Final Award	Entirely Set Aside	Yes
64	RECOFI v. Vietnam	2013	Switzerland	RECOFI	Final Award	Upheld	No
65	Stans Energy v. Kyrgyzstan (I)	2013	Russia	Kyrgyz Republic	Final Award	Entirely Set Aside	Yes
66	Yukos Capital v. Russia	2013	Switzerland	Russia	Interim Award	Upheld	No
67	Ballantine v. Dominican Republic	2014	The US	Ballantine	Final Award	Pending	Unclear
68	Griffin v. Poland	2014	England and Wales	Griffin	Interim Award	Partially Set Aside	No
69	Horthel and Others v. Poland	2014	Switzerland	Poland	Final Award	Upheld	No
70	Luxtona v. Russia	2014	Canada	Russia	Interim Award	Pending	Unclear
71	PL Holdings v. Poland	2014	Sweden	Poland	Final Award	Pending	Yes
72	Uzan v. Turkey	2014	Sweden	Uzan	Final Award	Upheld	No
73	CEF Energia v. Italy	2015	Sweden	Italy	Final Award	Pending	Unclear
74	Dayyani v. Korea	2015	England and Wales	South Korea	Final Award	Upheld	Unclear
75	Everest and Others v. Russia	2015	The Netherlands	Russia	Final Award	Pending	Unclear
76	Foresight and Others v. Spain	2015	Sweden	Spain	Final Award	Pending	Unclear
77	Greentech and NovEngeria v. Italy	2015	Sweden	Italy	Final Award	Pending	Unclear

Continuation

No.	Case Reference	Year	Jurisdiction	Claimant	Award/Decision	Outcome	Appealed
78	JKX Oil & Gas and Poltava v. Ukraine	2015	England and Wales	Ukraine	Final Award	Upheld	No
79	KCI v. Gabon	2015	France	KCI	Final Award	Upheld	No
80	MAESSA and SEMI v. Ecuador	2015	Unclear	Ecuador	Award on Jurisdiction	Pending	Unclear
81	NovEnergia v. Spain	2015	Sweden	Spain	Final Award	Pending	Unclear
82	Stabil and Others v. Russia	2015	Switzerland	Russia	Award on Jurisdiction	Upheld	No
					Final Award		
83	Stans Energy and Kutisay Mining v. Kyrgyzstan (II)	2015	England and Wales	Kyrgyz Republic	Award on Jurisdictional Objection	Upheld	No
84	Ukrnafta v. Russia	2015	Switzerland	Russia	Award on Jurisdiction	Upheld	No
					Final Award		
85	Cengiz v. Libya	2016	France	Libya	Final Award	Pending	Unclear
86	Nurol v. Libya	2016	France	Libya	Decision on Jurisdiction	Pending	Unclear
87	Nissan v. India	2016	Singapore	India	Decision on Jurisdiction	Pending	Unclear

〔1〕This Table provides an inventory of investment arbitration cases out of which arbitral awards or decisions have been subject to the judicial review by domestic courts at the seat of arbitration as of June 30,2020. The data shown herein is mainly derived from the Navigator. Given that this single database suffers from a number of drawbacks,such as an apparent lack of details and a rather slow process of updating,the making of this Table also benefits from the timely reports regularly updated by the Investment Arbitration Reporter.

〔2〕"Case Reference" is informed by the original investment arbitration proceedings instead of the following setting – aside proceedings before domestic courts at the seat of arbitration for the sake of convenience. These references conform to the abbreviations of the related investment arbitration cases as maintained by the Navigator.

〔3〕"Year" refers to the year of initiation of the original arbitral proceedings rather than that of the following setting – aside proceedings.

〔4〕"Jurisdiction" refers to a state or other area in which domestic courts deal with challenges against arbitral awards/decisions arising out of investment arbitration proceedings in accordance with applicable national laws,notably national arbitration legislation.

〔5〕"Claimant" refers to a party to investment arbitration which initiates a challenge proceeding against an investment arbitral award/decision before the domestic court at the seat of arbitration. In case that the setting – aside proceedings involve more one than court instance, it refers to the claimant of the first – instance proceeding.

[6] Both arbitral awards and procedural orders, partial awards and final awards, awards on jurisdiction and awards on merits could potentially be subject to judicial review by domestic courts at the seat of arbitration.

[7] "Outcome" refers to the decision made by domestic courts at the seat of arbitration with regard to whether an arbitral award/decision should be upheld, partially set aside or entirely set aside. In case of the involvement of system of appeals, "outcome" refers to the decision rendered out of the last – instance or the latest proceeding.

[8] This item intends to indicate whether the setting – aside proceedings involve more than one court instance.

4.1 How Often Do Arbitration Parties Challenge Investment Awards?

According to the table above, the judicial review of investment awards, as a post – award remedy for parties to non – ICSID arbitration, is not an insignificant practice. There are at least 87 non – ICSID arbitration cases so far, according to the Navigator and the IA Reporter, that have been followed by judicial proceedings where arbitral awards or decisions were referred to domestic courts *loci arbitri* for review by arbitration parties. That numerical value might not seem so impressive particularly when it is put against the overall amount of investment arbitration cases, which, as indicated by the Navigator, stands at 1,023 as of June 2020. ① However, more than half of the total investment arbitrations, to be precise, 540 of them, were conducted pursuant to the ICSID Arbitration Rules, ② which leave no room for the judicial review of investment awards. ③ In addition, among the residual 483 non – ICSID arbitrations, 165 of them are still pending according to the Navigator. ④ While 12 of those unsettled arbitration cases have already triggered off setting – aside proceedings before domestic courts *loci arbitri*, whether the rest 153 of them

① UNCTAD, "Investment Dispute Settlement Navigator", https://investmentpolicy.unctad.org/investment – dispute – settlement (last visited on August 2, 2020).

② Ibid.

③ Markus Burgstaller and Charles B. Rosenberg, "Challenging International Arbitral Awards: To ICSID or not to ICSID", Arbitration International, Vol. 27, No. 1 (2011), p. 93 (arguing that the ICSID Convention has a self – contained procedure for the annulment of an investment award and that ICSID awards are not subject to challenges under local law).

④ UNCTAD, *supra* note 88.

will entail the judicial review of investment awards is uncertain at this stage.① Thus, when the frequency of the activation of the judicial review mechanism is to be measured correctly, those 153 arbitration cases should be excluded from the total sample since it is too early to say whether arbitration parties will challenge arbitral outcomes or not. Therefore, of the 330 non-ICSID arbitration cases comprising all the concluded cases and some pending cases with the involvement of challenge proceedings, arbitration parties activated the judicial review mechanism before domestic courts *loci arbitri* in at least 87 instances. In other words, as Figure 1 shows, empirically speaking, more than 26 percent of non-ICSID arbitrations have been followed by the setting-aside proceedings initiated by arbitration parties at the place of arbitration. Although the majority of non-ICSID arbitration cases have not triggered off the judicial review of investment awards, we should factor in that in some instances, such as when a settlement was achieved, arbitration parties would have no need to challenge investment awards at all. Therefore, it is safe to say that in those non-ICSID arbitration cases where arbitral tribunals made substantial decisions which set apart the winning party and the losing party, the losing party arguably not infrequently refer the unfavorable outcome to domestic courts *loci arbitri* in an attempt to take a second bite at the apple.

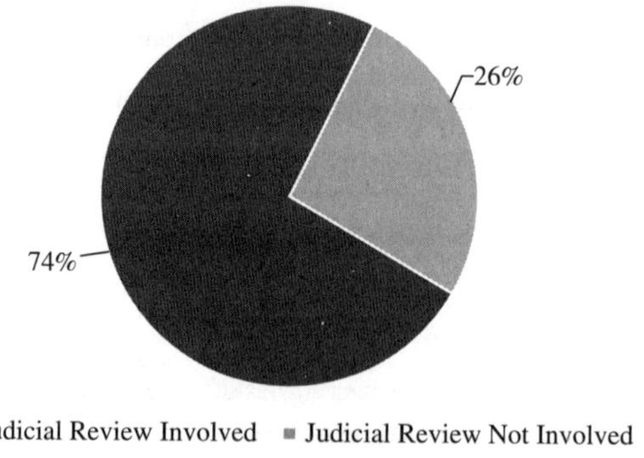

Figure 1　The Ratio of Non-ICSID Arbitrations Followed by Judicial Review

① UNCTAD, *supra* note 88.

4.2 Forum States Involved in the Judicial Review of Investment Awards

Insofar asthe information is available, there are at least 14 jurisdictions in which domestic courts have exerted judicial control over arbitral awards in relation to investment arbitration, including Belgium, Canada, Czech, Denmark, Egypt, England and Wales, France, Germany, Russia, Singapore, Sweden, Switzerland, the Netherlands, and the US. Those jurisdictions are mainly from the continents of North America and Western Europe, corresponding to the dominance of developed countries in the international arbitration industry and to their sheer popularity among disputing parties (in this context foreign investors and host states) and arbitrators as the seat of arbitration. ① Figure 2 suggests that France, the US, Switzerland, Sweden, Canada, the Netherlands, and England and Wales are legal jurisdictions where domestic courts were most frequently involved in the practice of the judicial review of investment awards. One can also safely infer that most of those selected jurisdictions feature modern and effective arbitration laws, an independent and efficient judiciary, and a good track record of enforcing agreement to arbitrate and arbitral awards, thus satisfying the benchmarks of the Chartered Institute of Arbitrators (the CIArb) London Centenary Principles for an effective and efficient seat in international arbitration. ② It can also be drawn from the table above that, in most cases, parties to non – ICSID arbitration or the arbitral tribunals established tend to avoid choosing either the host state or the home state of the foreign investor as the seat of arbitration in order to ensure the neutrality of arbitral proceedings. That to some extent ensures that the domestic courts of the host state or the home state of the foreign investors would not be entrusted with the task of reviewing an arbitral award for or against the interest of their states or nationals. There are ex-

① Gary G. Born, "International Arbitration: Law and Practice (Second Edition)", Kluwer Law International (2015), p. 111 (arguing that, in practice, the seat of arbitration is almost always specified by arbitration parties in their arbitration agreement or by arbitrators or arbitral institutions in the absence of an agreement between the parties for that purpose).

② The CIArb, "Introduction CIArb London Centenary Principles", http://www.ciarb.org/docs/default – source/ciarbdocuments/london/the – principles.pdf? sfvrsn = 4 (last visited on August 2, 2020).

ceptions, though. For instance, in *Myers v. Canada*, the arbitration was seated within the territory of Canada albeit that the respondent was indeed the government of Canada. Thus, the judiciary of Canada was tasked with reviewing the three investment awards rendered by the Tribunal in that case. In addition, most of the judicial review proceedings unfolded before the domestic courts of the US and Canada were related to investment arbitration cases initiated under NAFTA which has been replace by the USMCA Agreement. ①

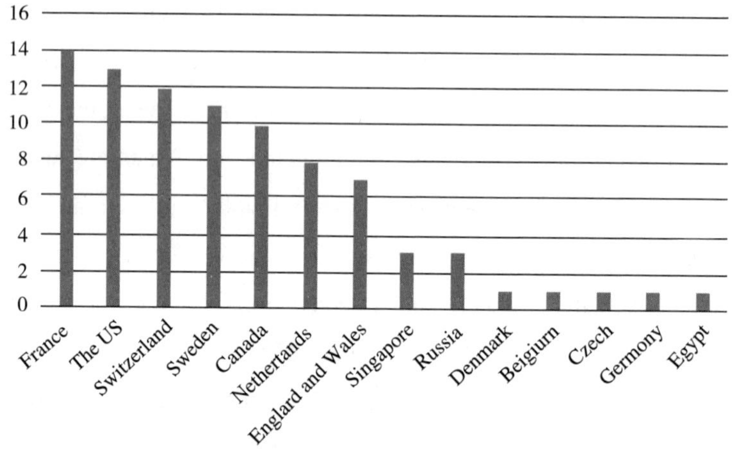

Figure 2　Jurisdictions Where Review Courts Are Located

4.3　Investor versus State: Which Party Made More Setting – Aside Applications?

The jurisprudence of the judicial review of investment awards shows that both the investor party and the state party to non – ICSID arbitration cases are likely to resort to domestic courts *loci arbitri* to challenge arbitral awards/decisions rendered against them. In other words, the judicial review mechanism in relation to investment arbitration can be activated by either the investor party or the state party. If

---

① Those NAFTA cases include *Metalclad v. Mexico*, *Loewen v. USA*, *Myers v. Canada*, *Feldman v. Mexico*, *Canfor v. USA*, *Thunderbird v. Mexico*, *Tembec v. USA*, *Terminal Forest v. USA*, *Bayview v. Mexico*, *Cargill v. Mexico*, *Mobil Investments v. Canada (I)*, *Clayton/Bilcon v. Canada*, and*Mesa Power v. Canada*.

two or more arbitral awards are issued by the tribunal in an investment arbitration and those awards are not homogeneous in the distribution of interests as in *Saar Papier v. Poland (II)*, the foreign investor and the host state could even respectively initiate setting – aside proceedings in relation to the specific award that consigns them to an adverse situation. Although both foreign investors and host states could make applications for the setting – aside of investment awards, empirical evidence has shown that most judicial review proceedings in relation to investment arbitration were initiated by host states. To be precise, as shown in Figure 3, the instances where the judicial review was commenced by the state party (67) are around 3 times as many as those by the investor party (21).

Assuming that the state party and the investor party are equally loath to swallow the bitterness of unfavorable arbitral outcomes, that much more applications for the setting – aside of investment awards were made by host states is a thought – provoking finding. At first sight, one possible explanation could be that states lost more often in investment arbitrations than foreign investors, otherwise they would not have had the need to challenge investment awards before domestic courts *loci arbitri*. This proposition resonates with the cliché in investment law that investment arbitration is inherently biased against host states. ① However, according to the Navigator, among those non-ICSID arbitrations in which the clear – cut victory of a party is discernible, a decision was made in favor of host states in 276 instances and of foreign investors in 237 instances. ② Thus, that host states lost more often in non – ICSID arbitrations does not seem to be a reasonable explanation.

However, the effects of the setting – aside of investment awards may be held to account for the discrepancy in theproportions of challenge proceedings in relation to investment awards initiated by host states and foreign investors. Once the appli-

---

① Charles N. Brower and Sadie Blanchard, "What's in a Meme? The Truth about Investor – State Arbitration: Why It Need Not, and Must Not, Be Repossessed by States", Vol. 52, No. 3 (2014), Columbia Journal of Transnational Law, p. 709 (asserting that there is a school of thought holding that investment treaty protections and investment arbitration structurally favor foreign investors).

② UNCTAD, *supra* note 88.

cation for the setting - aside of an investment award is granted, the award would be deprived of all legal purposes, at least within the forum state. ① However, the underlying dispute would remain unresolved, and there would be no *res judicata* effect with regard to the merits of an annulled award. ② Thus, for the state party which succeeds in setting aside an unfavorable investment award, the consequential benefit is immediate and definite, such as depriving the investment tribunal of its jurisdiction or obviating the need to pay all of or any of the amount of damages accorded to the investor by the tribunal. On the contrary, even if an investor manages to set aside an unfavorable investment award, the claims of the investor via arbitration equally cannot be satisfied because domestic courts *loci arbitri* in all likelihood would not revise the award on their own. ③ The benefit that the investor can acquire is that the dispute might be remitted to the original investment tribunal or the investor would get another opportunity to launch a *de novo* arbitral proceeding against the host state, ④ yet still facing uncertain outcomes.

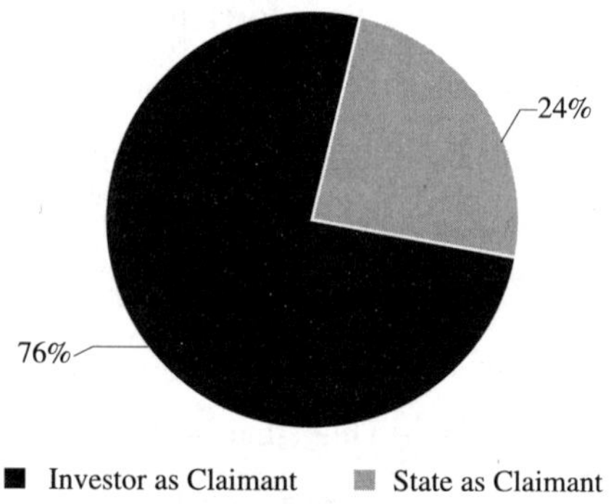

Figure 3　A Breakdown of Judicial Review Cases by Claimant

---

① Fernández - Armesto, *supra* note 16, at 142.

② Ibid.

③ Barbara H. Steindl, "ICSID Annulment vs. Set Aside by State Courts - Compared to ICSID ad hoc Annulment Committees, Is It the State Courts that are Now More Hesitant to Set Aside Awards?", Yearbook on International Arbitration, Vol. 4 (2015), p. 201 (arguing that domestic courts sitting on set - aside will not "substitute their own decision for the successfully challenged award").

④ Piero Bernardini, *supra* note 10, at 34 - 35 (revealing that, under different national arbitration legal orders, the effects of the setting - aside of investment awards could be different).

4.4 How Often Is More than One Court Instance Involved?

Unlike the ICSID annulment procedure where the decision made by an *ad hoc* annulment committee is not subject to any review or appeal, a court judgement made in judicial review proceedings either upholding or setting aside an investment award might be appealed to a higher court in a number of jurisdictions. ① As shown in Figure 4, insofar as the information is available, in a sizable minority of judicial review proceedings in relation to investment arbitration (34% or 26 instances), the judgment made by a lower court was later appealed to a higher court within the forum states. In a majority of those judicial review proceedings (66% or 50 instances), the appeals system common to national judiciaries was not activated by disputing parties. In fact, the reasons that the judgment of a lower court was not appealed to a higher court in some judicial review proceedings could be multi – dimensional, such as the deterrence of increased length and cost and a gloomy prospect of having the trial judgment reversed. In addition, sometimes disputing parties involved in a judicial review proceeding in relation to investment arbitration choose not to appeal the judgment of a court merely for the fact that they are not granted the right to do so in a given jurisdiction. For instance, in Switzerland, any request to set aside investment awards must be filed with the Swiss Federal Supreme Court, thus effectively precluding disputing parties from appealing the judgments made by the Court. ② It is also worth mentioning that, according to a previous study, although judicial review proceedings before domestic courts might involve more than one instance of court, these proceedings do not necessarily take more time than annulment proceedings in the context of ICSID arbitrations. ③

---

① Verhoosel, *supra* note 68, at 145.

② Matthias Scherer, "Arbitration Guide: Switzerland", International Bar Association, IBA Arbitration Committee, Jan. 2018, https://www.ibanet.org/Document/Default.aspx?DocumentUid=8DA26206-5B7E-49A5-A69F-4BEF37D6408A (last visited July 17, 2020), p. 19 – 20.

③ Verhoosel, *supra* note 68, at 145 (identifying in the year of 2008 that "the ICSID annulment review process still took on average nearly five months longer than non – ICSID setting aside proceedings").

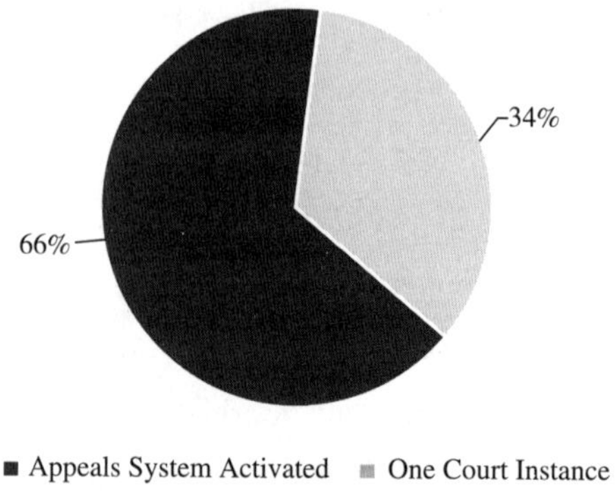

Figure 4　The Proportion of Judicial Review Proceedings Where the Appeals System Was Activated

4.5　The Outcomes of Judicial Review Proceedings

When it comes to the outcomes of the applications for the setting - aside of investment awards, a notable pattern is that only a small portion of judicial review proceedings have seen the investment awards partially or entirely set aside by domestic courts *loci arbitri*. To be more precise, as shown in Figure 5, review courts upheld original investment awards in 81% of judicial review proceedings (56 instances); 15% (10 instances) and 4% (3 instances) of those proceedings have led to the entire and partial setting - aside of investment awards respectively. It can be inferred that, in most of the time, domestic courts *loci arbitri* have refrained themselves from taking an unduly intrusive approach and shown a high level of deference to the decision - making of investment tribunals in judicial review proceedings. Fernández - Armesto put forward three possible explanations to account for the high level of deference: first, arbitrators in charge of investment arbitrations are usually renowned and respected experts selected by disputing parties; second, investment disputes are complicated and do not fall into the jurisdiction of review courts; third, those courts recognize that the disputing parties agreed to submit their disputes for arbitration and stood ready to accept the decisions made by arbitral tribunals.① Therefore, it is safe to say that parties to non - ICSID arbitration, both foreign investors and host states, are faced with formidable challenges in

① Fernández - Armesto, *supra* note 16, at 146.

vacating investment awards before review courts.

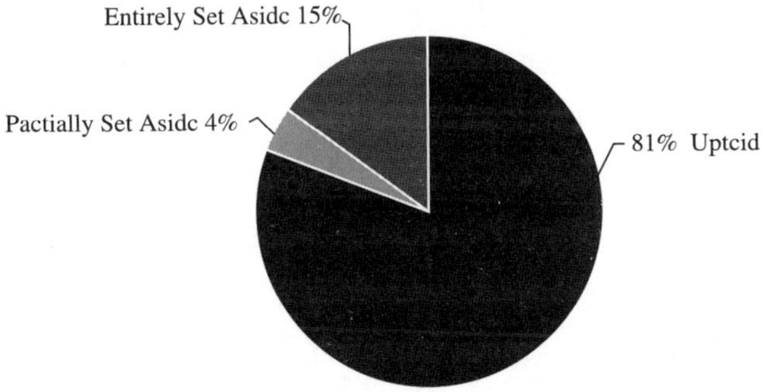

Figure 5 The Outcomes of Judicial Review Proceedings

When the success rates of the investor party and the state party in applying for the *vacatur* of investment awards are viewed separately, an asymmetry is rather conspicuous in the sense that all but one setting – aside applications initiated by foreign investors were rejected by review courts. ① All the other court decisions to entirely or partially set aside investment awards were rendered out of the judicial review proceedings initiated by the state party. The underlying reasons for the notable divergence between the success rates of the two sides are difficult to gauge. One possible explanation could be that, given that arbitral tribunals have less incentive to wrongly deny their jurisdiction over investment disputes than to wrongly claim their jurisdiction, the threshold to have negative jurisdictional rulings reversed through setting – aside applications could be rather high. In any way, it would be imprudent and insufficient to conclude that domestic courts *loci arbitri* are biased against foreign investors in reviewing the awards made by investment tribunals merely on this point.

With respect to the court decisions to entirely or partially set aside investment awards, it is noted that France and Russia have each entirely set aside three investment awards. The fact that France is one of the jurisdictions that set aside the most investment awards is somewhat surprising given that France has for long been

① The only exception took place in the judicial review proceeding in relation to *Griffin v. Poland* where the interim awards was partially set aside by an English court at the request of Griffin.

viewed as one of the most arbitration – friendly places in the world. However, recalling that French courts have handled the most applications for the setting – aside of investment awards so far, three instances of *vacatur* decisions do not seem to be intolerably out of proportion. Russia, as a jurisdiction less known for its friendliness towards arbitration, has gone so far to set aside all the three investment awards submitted to its courts for judicial review. Nevertheless, concluding thereby that Russian courts show little deference to the decisions of investment tribunals and demonstrate burning inclination to vacate investment awards risks untenable generalization. For one thing, since only three applications for the setting – aside of investment awards were filed with Russia courts, the sample size is arguably too small to reach any conclusion. For another thing, the three underlying investment arbitrations for the setting – aside applications were closely related, effectively reducing the oddity of making three entire setting – aside decisions. In the meantime, the US and Switzerland stand out as two jurisdictions that have hitherto issued no (final) judgments to entirely or partially set aside investment awards, though both countries have received a good number of applications for the setting – aside of such awards due to their popularity as places of non – ICSID arbitration.

With the help of the updated data from more recent years, this empirical work improves previous studies by rectifying an obsolete judgment. Indeed, across the existing literature on the judicial review mechanism with respect to investment arbitration, a widespread argument is that ICSID awards are more likely to be annulled by *ad hoc* annulment committees than non – ICSID awards set aside by review courts.① However, with the sample size of both ICSID annulment proceedings and the judicial review proceedings in relation to non – ICSID arbitration increasing over the last several years, it becomes clear that applications for the annulment of IC-

① Verhoosel, *supra* note 68, at 122 (arguing in 2008 that the annulment ration of ICSID awards was much higher than the setting – aside ratio of non – ICSID awards). Veijo Heiskanen and Laura Halonen, "Chapter 16: Post – Award Remedies", in Chiara Giorgetti (ed.), "Litigating International Investment Disputes: A Practitioner's Guide", Brill (2014), p. 511 (arguing that challenges against ICSID awards are more likely to succeed than challenges against non – ICSID awards before domestic courts *loci arbitri*).

SID awards are not necessarily easier to succeed than those for the setting – aside of non – ICSID awards. Figure 6 shows that, in 79% of all the annulment proceedings (48 instances), the *ad hoc* committees upheld the ICSID awards concerned. In addition, in 6% (4 instances) and 15% (9 instances) of those proceedings, the ICSID awards were entirely and partially annulled respectively. Measured against the setting – aside ratio of non – ICSID awards (19%), the annulment ratio of ICSID awards (21%) does not seem to be strikingly different. Therefore, generally speaking, the odds are rather heavily against the losing party of the underlying investment arbitration proceeding in its effort to strike down either ICSID or non – ICSID awards.

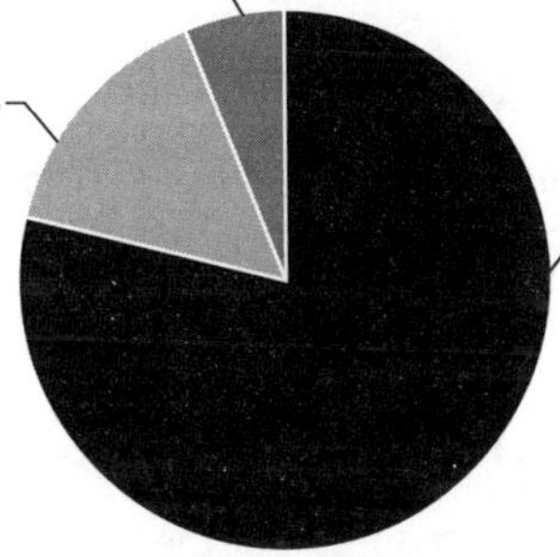

Figure 6 The Outcomes of ICSID Annulment Proceedings

5. Critical Analysis of the Judicial Review Mechanism for Investment Awards

The supervisory role of domestic courts at the seat of arbitration in reviewing arbitral awards has been regarded as the most important role of national judiciaries in respect of non – ICSID arbitration. ① Although the judicial review of investment awards only pertains to non – ICSID arbitration, it is indeed closely relevant for the ongoing discussions about the reform of the investment arbitration system. The

① Gabrielle Kaufmann – Kohler and Michele Potestà, "Investor – State Dispute Settlement and National Courts: Current Framework and Reform Options", Springer Open (2020), p. 65.

question of how to handle the long – lasting call for the establishment of an appellate review mechanism is a burning issue on the agenda for the reform of investment arbitration.① Whether an extra layer of appeal – style review should be put in place in turn requires us to take a step back and carry out an assessment of the current mechanism by which parties to investment arbitration may apply for the *vacatur* of investment awards. Thus, an evaluation of the judicial review mechanism in relation to non – ICSID arbitration would to a large extent contribute to the debate on the path forward for the reform of investment arbitration insofar as post – award remedy is concerned.

Before going into a critical analysis of the judicial review mechanism in relation to investment arbitration, it is necessary to give this mechanism credit wherever it is due. Considering that the right to appellate review is in general not a part of the investment arbitration system, the judicial review mechanism to some extent bridges a gap in the dispute resolution process. The mechanism first of all represents a trade – off between the rivaling goals of fairness and efficiency. By filing an application for the setting – aside of investment awards, arbitration users are afforded an opportunity to seek further redress if for instance gross procedural deviations arose out of arbitral proceedings. In the meantime, the judicial review mechanism is expected to fulfil an important role of safeguarding procedural integrity of the overall dispute resolution process and preventing egregious injustice from going unnoticed and uncorrected. The supervisory role that domestic courts *loci arbitri* assume versus arbitral tribunals may also benefit investment arbitration in a less apparent manner by generating positive impact on the behavior of arbitrators. The underlying assumption is that the existence of the judicial review mechanism imposes pressure on arbitrators, prompting them to avoid suspicious procedural irregularities in the arbitral process and to increase the quality of their decision – making.② If

---

① Albert Jan van den Berg, "Appeal Mechanism for ISDS Awards", ICSID Review, Vol. 0, No. 0 (2019), p. 2 (arguing that the debate on the establishment of an appeal mechanism within the investment arbitration system has going on for some 25 years).

② Coe, *supra* note 2, at 191.

they fail to do so, there is a chance that the decisions made by them will be set aside by review courts at a later stage. Although an occasional annulment decision issued by a review court will not likely materially reduce their likelihood of being re – elected as an arbitrator, a bad record in judicial review proceedings of often having arbitral awards vacated by those courts would only do damage to their reputation and prestige rather than the inverse. Additionally, the judicial review mechanism is likely to step up the public's confidence in investment arbitration since flawed investment awards and deficient procedures stand a chance if being corrected thereby. However, the benefits mentioned above cannot justify the judicial review mechanism as the optimal option for the post – award control of investment arbitration nor offset the concerns that the mechanism causes. The rest of this section is devoted to a critical analysis of the judicial review mechanism, revealing that the negative by – products are so grave that it is time for reform to be introduced for an improved version of post – award remedy for non – ICSID arbitration.

5.1 Domestic Courts *loci arbitri* as an Inconvenient Review Forum

5.1.1 Blending International Politics and Dispute Resolution

The judicial review mechanism where domestic courts loci arbitri are vested with the power to scrutinize investment awards could also unnecessarily bring international politics back into the domain of investor – state dispute resolution. There is a possibility that the forum state (State A) where an investment arbitration is seated is locked in a diplomatic row with the state party (State B) to the underlying arbitration. In that case, subjecting the investment award that significantly impacts the interest of State B to the jurisdiction of the courts of State A will be a politically inconvenient arrangement. If the courts of State A rendered a judgment to State B's detriment, it is likely that State B would claim that the review courts had a pre – determined bias against it driven by political calculation and the judicial review proceedings were partial. Even if the judgment at issue was made strictly as per applicable laws by the courts, the overall dispute resolution process might be cast into shadow by the allegation made by State B. After all, whether justice was actually dispensed would in all likelihood become an issue where the truth lies in the eye of the beholder.

Take the Yukos case as an example, the judicial review proceeding took place before the Dutch courts amidst the rising tensions in the relationship between the Netherlands and Russia. The harrowing and infuriating incident of the downing of Malaysia Airlines MH17 on 17 July 2014 dealt a blow to the Dutch – Russian diplomatic relations. The Hague District Court reversed the awards of more than US $ 50 billion in favor of Russia in 2016 when Russia was a primary suspect of the tragedy but the investigations were underway. However, the Hague Appeal Court overruled the judgment of the District Court and revived the obligation of Russia to pay astronomical damages in February 2020 after the Netherlands and Australia came to the conclusion that Russia should be held responsible for its part in the horrific air crash on 25 May 2018. ① While the Netherlands is known for a good record of the rule of law and there is apparently no evidence to show the judges had a bias against Russia, ② the judgment which is disadvantageous to Russia came at a politically inconvenient time. Meanwhile, with respect to the handling of a number of key issues on which controversies have long existed, the Appeal Court chose to adopt an interpretation that undermined Russia's positions. For instance, the Appeal Court was of the opinion that the underlying disputes between the former Yukos shareholders and Russia were of civil – legal nature, thus rendering the non – arbitrability of public disputes provided by Russian Law irrelevant. However, not everyone would agree that investment disputes are private in nature. Considering that the case is pending before the Dutch Supreme Court, that Russia has not issued a politically charged statement so far does not mean it will not if the judgment by the Supreme Court is not in its favor.

---

① Government of the Netherlands, "MH17: The Netherlands and Australia Hold Russia Responsible", https://www.government.nl/latest/news/2018/05/25/mh17 – the – netherlands – and – australia – hold – russia – responsible (last visited on Aug. 16, 2020).

② In the Rule of Law Index 2020 released by the World Justice Project, the Netherlands admirably ranks 5 out of 128 jurisdictions. World Justice Project, "WJP Rule of Law Index", https://worldjusticeproject.org/rule – of – law – index/country/2020/Netherlands/ (last visited on Aug. 16, 2020).

Conceivably, under certain circumstances, subjecting a state party to investment arbitration to the jurisdiction of the courts of another sovereign state would not only cast a cloud on the procedural integrity of the dispute resolution process but also further complicate the strained relationship between the two countries. Again, it should be stressed that the review courts of the forum state might have handled the judicial review case at hand in a way that is perfectly consistent with the spirit of the rule of law, but that is not the focus in the opposition against unnecessarily blending interstate politics with investor – state dispute resolution via the judicial review mechanism. After all, the political inconvenience in this regard and the ensuing suspicion and confusion could have been avoided in the first place by rejecting ineptly transposing the judicial review mechanism tailored for commercial arbitration to the context of investment arbitration.

5.1.2 Impaired Neutrality

The unwanted politicization of dispute resolution accompanying the judicial review mechanism in relation to investment arbitration apparently could also raise concerns over the fairness of the proceedings before review courts. However, the presumed involvement of international politics in the judicial review of investment awards is not the only element that might chip away at the general public's confidence in the dispute resolution process. In practice, particularly in the context of NAFTA – related investment arbitrations, there are cases where the designated place of arbitration was in the territory of the respondent state. It follows from that the judicial review proceedings in the wake of those investment arbitrations took place before the courts of the respondent states which were the very targets of the investment claims initiated by foreign investors. ① Although that part of judicial review

① The judicial review proceedings in relation to at least the following investment arbitrations are known to have been entertained by the courts of the respondent states: Loewen v. USA, Myers v. Canada, Canfor v. USA, Tembec v. USA, Terminal Forest v. USA, Binder v. Czech Republic, Mobil Investments v. Canada (I), and Clayton / Bilcon v. Canada.

proceedings only accounts for a minority of the ensemble,① foreign investors may speculate that the neutrality of adjudicative authority is compromised at the judicial review stage if the review courts are located in the respondent states. ② It is true that speculation may be made without any merits and judicial bias should not be easily assumed or insinuated. ③ However, one of the advantages of investment arbitration in comparison to court litigation via the domestic courts of host states is that international tribunals are in general believed to be a more neutral forum. If the awards issued by investment tribunals are to be subjected to the control of the courts of host states via the judicial review mechanism, the raison d'être of investment arbitration would be questioned and the advantage of investment arbitration in terms of neutrality would be somewhat neutralized.

The neutrality of the review courts of forum states could be further impaired by the fact that, unlike investment arbitration where the procedural formats are orchestrated to accommodate participants of different legal cultures,④ the specific court procedures at the seat of arbitration could be inherently in favor of one side of the disputing parties. For instance, imagine a situation where both the forum state and the state party to investment arbitration are common law jurisdictions while the foreign investor is from a home state with the civil law system. While the expertise of appointed legal counsels could narrow the gap in a way, the state party is likely to have a pre – existing edge over the foreign investor at the judicial review stage due to a higher level of familiarity with the procedural rules applicable to the setting – aside proceedings.

5.1.3 The Casual and Loose Link between the Forum State and the Underlying Arbitration

While the seat of an international arbitration could be any city around the

---

① Heiskanen and Halonen, *supra* note 107, at 499 (arguing that parties to investment arbitration rarely agree on a place within the respondent state as the seat of arbitration).

② Coe, *supra* note 2, at 193 – 194.

③ Ibid.

④ Ibid.

world in theory, arbitration rules provide guidance on the choice of the seat to ensure a degree of certainty of arbitration proceedings. In the practice of non – ICSID arbitration, the seat of arbitration is determined by the agreement of the disputing parties as the default rule. ① In case that the agreement between them on this issue is not forthcoming, which is often the case, ② the way of designating the seat of arbitration largely depends on whether the arbitration concerned is administered by an arbitration institution or not. If so, the arbitration institution is often vested with the power to designate the seat of arbitration and the place where the institution is located is often preferred. ③ In the case of *ad hoc* arbitrations under the UNCITRAL Arbitration Rules, the seat of arbitration is decided by arbitral tribunals "having regard to the circumstances of the case." ④

In practice, the seat of arbitration is often selected by taking into consideration a host of factors, such as neutrality and convenience, and the forum state often does not have a close connection with the underlying dispute. ⑤ Goode, for instance, challenges the importance of the seat of arbitration on several grounds, in particular: (1) the choice of seat is often a matter of convenience; (2) the choice of seat is often determined not by the parties but by the arbitral institution they have selected; (3) the choice of seat is often governed by the desire for neutrality; and (4) the role of the arbitral tribunal is transitory, and the seat has no necessary connection with the dispute. ⑥ Therefore, the contingent nature of the choice of the seat in

① Fernández – Armesto, *supra* note 16, at 133.

② Ibid.

③ Fernández – Armesto, *supra* note 16, at 133. For instance, Article 18.1 of latest version of the ICC Rules of Arbitration provides that: "The place of the arbitration shall be fixed by the Court, unless agreed upon by the parties." Article 18.1, the ICC Rules of Arbitration.

④ Article 18.1 of the UNCITRAL Arbitration Rules provides that: "If the parties have not previously agreed on the place of arbitration, the place of arbitration shall be determined by the arbitral tribunal having regard to the circumstances of the case. The award shall be deemed to have been made at the place of arbitration." Article 18.1, the UNCITRAL Arbitration Rules.

⑤ Pippa Read, "Delocalization of International Commercial Arbitration: Its Relevance in the New Millennium", American Review of International Arbitration, Vol. 10, No. 2 (1999), p. 185.

⑥ Roy Goode, "The Role of the Lex Loci Arbitri in International Commercial Arbitration", Arbitration International, Vol. 17, No. 1 (2001), p. 19 – 40.

international arbitration is evident, which means, for example, for an arbitration where Paris was selected as the seat, the place of arbitration could also have been Singapore.

Despite the casual and loose link between the forum state and the arbitration, the judicial review mechanism leads to a situation where domestic courts *loci arbitri* somehow are granted the power to decide whether an arbitral award should be set aside in accordance with national arbitration acts. Considering that local judges usually have broad discretion and national arbitration legislation not infrequently demonstrates particularities, the arbitral seat which is not irreplaceable in practice might have significant impact on the underlying arbitration and the distribution of interests between arbitration parties. However, bearing in mind that the forum state and the dispute arbitrated often have no material connections, that significant impact is actually inexplicable and unreasonable to a large extent. At the end of the day, investment arbitration is based on mutual consent to arbitration of the investor and the state rather than the tolerance of the place of arbitration. ① Thus, the judicial review mechanism gives meaning to the casual link between the forum state and the underlying arbitration out of all proportion by putting the courts of that state on the top of the arbitral tribunal.

5.2 Keep It in the Family: The Monopoly of Review Power

Figure 2 reveals that it is the domestic courts of a small groupof jurisdictions comprising in the main countries from Western Europe and North America (the developed North) that are vested with the power to entertain setting – aside applications in relation to investment awards. On the contrary, the judiciaries of countries from the developing South are nearly excluded from the exercise of review power although those countries are also often subject to investment claims initiated by foreign investors before international tribunals. Certainly, in a way this monopoly of review power is understandable since the developed countries most often involved in the judicial review of investment awards are celebrated hubs for international ar-

① Read, *supra* note 124, at 185.

bitration. It is small wonder that in practice arbitral institutions and tribunals would prefer to designate those places known as arbitration – friendly jurisdictions as the seat of arbitration. Therefore, the concentration of review power in the hands of a number of developed countries to some extent reflects the reality of uneven development of the international arbitration market in geographical terms.

However, the fact that the monopoly of review power is most likely developed through a spontaneous process does not mean that no changes should be introduced to reform the judicial review mechanism under discussion. As a matter of fact, the investment arbitration system has been under attack for long by a multiplicity of stakeholders involved in FDI activities, particularly by developing host states. Some of them tend to believe that developing countries are put in a disadvantaged position in the investment arbitration system for the mere fact that developed countries have a higher success rate than their developing counterpart in the face of challenges from foreign investors as evidenced by some empirical studies. ① Others believe so citing that the pool of arbitrators in the system is mostly made up of nationals of western countries, which gives rise to concerns over their neutrality and impartiality in decision – making. ② Not least due to the concerns mentioned above, a growing number of developing countries have become alert to the alleged bias inherent in the investment arbitration system and some of them have taken actions to disengage themselves from the dispute resolution method. ③

The monopoly ofreview power at the judicial review stage is likely to amplify

① Thomas Schultz and Cedric Dupont, "Investment Arbitration: Promoting the Rule of Law or Over – empowering Investors? A Quantitative Empirical Study", European Journal of International Law, Vol. 25, No. 4 (2015), p. 1165 – 1167. Daniel Behn, et al., "Poor States or Poor Governance? Explaining Outcomes in Investment Treaty Arbitration", Northwestern Journal of International Law and Business, Vol. 38, No. 3 (2018), p. 380 – 381.

② Chiara Giorgetti, "Who Decides Who Decides in International Investment Arbitration?", University of Pennsylvania Journal of International Law, Vol. 35, No. 2 (2013), p. 460 (arguing that lack of diversity of arbitrators becomes more of a problem in the context of investment arbitration where a wide variety of viewpoints would benefit the handling of complex and public policy cases).

③ Leon E. Trakman, "Choosing Domestic Courts over Investor – State Arbitration: Australia's Repudiation of the Status Quo", University of New South Wales Law Journal, Vol. 35, No. 3 (2012), p. 979.

the perceived bias and lend ammunition to the critics of investment arbitration. In response, more developing countries will probably stay away from investment arbitration as the dominance of the western world in the judicial review of investment awards might further lock in their perception that the mechanism is intrinsically biased against their interests. So far developing countries seemingly have been largely oblivious to the dominant position of western judiciaries in handling challenges to investment awards and have not unambiguously expressed concerns over that particularity of the judicial review mechanism. But that is the case probably because the scale of judicial review proceedings in relation to investment awards has not become notable enough until more recent years. Thus, with the continued growth of non – ICSID arbitration and the following setting – aside applications, the dominant position of the judiciaries of developed countries in the judicial review mechanism could exacerbate the legitimacy crisis at least from the perspective of less developed countries.

5.3 The Judge Judging the Arbitrators: Not Necessarily Qualified

One of the recurrent concerns raised about the judicial review mechanism is that the judges from the place of arbitration probably do not have the required knowledge and expertise to entertain the applications for the setting – aside of investment awards submitted to them. For instance, Hobér and Eliasson argue that domestic judges are typically not knowledgeable nor experienced in the domain of international law, implying that they sometimes could not effectively address international law issues arising out of judicial review proceedings. ① Some other commentators maintain that, unlike ICSID annulment committee members who are leading experts in arbitration of investment disputes, domestic judges usually do not deal with investment law as part of their usual practice. ② It follows from that the lack of expertise on the part of the judges from review courts would curtail the

---

① Leon E. Trakman, "Choosing Domestic Courts over Investor – State Arbitration: Australia's Repudiation of the Status Quo", University of New South Wales Law Journal, Vol. 35, No. 3 (2012), p. 979.

② Heiskanen & Halonen, *supra* note 284, at 513.

quality of their decision – making with regard to setting – aside applications.[①] For those who question the competence of domestic judges in this regard, it could be argued that the limited number of the judicial review proceedings in relation to investment arbitration in general also impedes the accumulation of experience for those judges. However, this line of generic attacks against the qualification of the judges from review courts does not necessarily hold water, particularly considering that the review courts involved in practice are nearly always located in international arbitration hubs and those judges tasked with the handling of setting – aside applications could also be assigned to this post for their expertise. In addition, in at least some judicial review proceedings, such as those related to *Sanum v. Laos* (*I*) and the Yukos case, the judges from review courts have conducted in – depth analysis of issues of international law in nature by the employment of techniques that are commonly adopted by international courts and tribunals, such as by referring to Articles 31 and 32 of the VCLT.

However, the expertise of the judges from domestic courts *loci arbitri* is not indisputable especially considering that the judicial review mechanism to some extent places those judges in a higher position than arbitrators handling investment disputes. The question that matters thus becomes whether domestic judges are expert at investment law – related issues enough that they could be relied on to provide even higher – quality decision – making than arbitrators. Indeed, the expertise of domestic judges with regard to investment disputes as compared with that of arbitrators may suggest the judicial review of investment awards is not an ingenious design in the first place. It is conventional wisdom that arbitrators in general tend to be specialized in a particular area of law while judges in many cases are expected to be versatile so that they could cope with disputes of different types registered

① Heiskanen & Halonen, *supra* note 284, at 513.

with the courts that they serve. ① This is especially true in the context of investment arbitration given that arbitrators are often faced with complex and high – stake disputes, the resolution of which often requires not only the interpretation of vague and open – ended provisions of IIAs but also the application of relevant rules of customary international law.

Although the expertise of investment arbitrators is also questioned by some commentators, ② there are good reasons to believe that those arbitrators are more specialized in public international law and investment law than domestic judges rather than the inverse. First, the party – appointment system established in investment arbitration for the selection of arbitrators indicates that the disputing parties and their legal counsels would participate in a process of deciding the most appropriate arbitrators, which in turn to some extent ensures the eligibility and qualifications of those selected arbitrators. That is arguably one of the reasons for that at least a notable proportion of investment arbitrators are experts with a background of public international law, especially with respect to international investment law. Second, critics have bluntly asserted that investment arbitration has been dominated by a small cohesive community of arbitrators who have been routinely engaged in the adjudication of investment disputes. ③

For the reasons above, an inference that the arbitrators involved in often massive investment arbitrations are "among themost experienced and qualified in the

① Gellaine T. Newton, "Like Oil and Vinegar, Sitting Judges and Arbitrations Do Not Mix: Delaware's Unique Attempt at Judicial Arbitration", Arbitration Law Review, Vol. 5, No. 1 (2013), p. 149 (arguing that one of the benefits that makes arbitration especially attractive to large businesses is that arbitrators usually have specialized expertise).

② Colin M. Brown, "A Multilateral Mechanism for the Settlement of Investment Disputes. Some Preliminary Sketches", ICSID Review, Vol. 32, No. 3 (2017), p. 673 (arguing that many of them have had involvement only in commercial arbitration, thus lacking necessary experience to assess the regulatory authority of states when public actions are measured against the terms of international treaties).

③ Pia Eberhardt and Cecilia Olivet, "Profiting from Injustice: How Law Firms, Arbitrators and Financiers Are Fuelling an Investment Arbitration Boom", Corporate Europe Observatory and the Transnational Institute (2012), p. 36.

world". ① In the light of the scathing criticisms against the investment arbitration system, those arbitrators also "have proven themselves as a general rule meticulous in their observance of procedural rules, proper techniques of communication with the parties, and thorough evidence collection". ② However, domestic judges cannot be supposed to be on a par with those selected arbitrators in terms of expertise and experience with respect to public international law in general and international investment law in particular. Thus, with due respect to judges who are in general legal professionals with broad knowledge and acute judgment, it is debatable, if not unreasonable, to subject the decisions of arbitrators who are more specialized in investment law to the scrutiny of the judges from the place of arbitration who may lack comparable knowledge and techniques. The deficiency of expertise on the part of domestic judges relative to investment arbitrators can sometimes be worsened by the phenomenon that a single judge from domestic courts may be assigned to review the decisions made often by an investment tribunal that in the main comprises three experienced arbitrators. ③

5.4 Augmented Costs and Procedural Delay

Despite previous studies which revealed that the average length of setting – aside proceedings before review courts is comparable to, or even shorter than, that of ICSID annulment procedures, ④ more recent jurisprudence shows that in some instances judicial review proceedings can be very lengthy and costly. Indeed, while in some countries, such as Switzerland, applications for the setting – aside of investment awards can be handled rather efficiently, judicial review proceedings elsewhere can drag on for several years with considerable costs incurred by disputing parties. ⑤ Considering that investment arbitration proceedings in many cases are not

---

① Rubins, *supra* note 7, at 369.

② Ibid.

③ For instance, a single judge from the High Court of Singapore was assigned to review the jurisdictional ruling rendered by the Tribunal in *Sanum v. Laos (I)* on his own.

④ Heiskanen & Halonen, *supra* note 284, at 517.

⑤ Ibid.

fast and cheap as they have been expected to be,① the judicial review mechanism would in all likelihood make the overall dispute resolution process even less efficient. For instance, the judicial review proceeding in relation to *Achmea v. Slovakia*(I) involved several instances of court in Germany and invited the intervention of the Court of Justice of the European Union (the CJEU). As a result, nearly 6 years had passed since the issuance of the final award by the Tribunal when the German Federal Supreme Court set aside the award in its entirety based on a preliminary ruling by the CJEU in October 2018. In the similar vein, the request to set aside the awards rendered out of the arbitration proceedings of the Yukos case have been heard by the Hague District Court and the Appeal Court respectively and 6 years have passed since the final awards were issued in July 2016. Given that the judgment of the Appeal Court was appealed by Russia to the Dutch Supreme Court, the final binding judgment will not be available until at least a few months later.

There are a host of reasons that could be held accountable for the not infrequent occurrence of lengthy and costly judicial review proceedings. First of all, in most jurisdictions, an application for the setting – aside of investment awards would often be decided by two or three consecutive court instances and the judges of the higher court are under no obligation or custom to accord deference to the decisions made by the judges of the lower court. ② The multiple layers of court control would doubtlessly prolong the review process and augment financial costs of disputing parties. In fact, with a view to reducing the length and costs required for judicial review proceedings, a number of jurisdictions, are contemplating the reform of the judicial review process via limiting the court instances involved in setting – aside

① Lars Markert, "Improving Efficiency in Investment Arbitration", Contemporary Asia Arbitration Journal, Vol. 4, No. 2 (2011), p. 216.

② Heiskanen & Halonen, *supra* note 284, at 517.

applications. ① Second, since the judges from domestic courts *loci arbitri* in general are less specialized than arbitrators, more information arguably has to be transferred from disputing parties to the judges in judicial review proceedings than to arbitrators in arbitration proceedings. Consequently, the costs of dispute resolution would be increased and delays in procedure would be caused. Third, unlike investment arbitration in which the scarcity of enough legal practitioners has not yet been heard of, there may be a dock – related backlog within domestic courts *loci arbitri*, thus rendering the dispute resolution lengthy and inefficient. ② Fourth, according to Fernández – Armesto, in the context of the judicial review of investment awards, "Domestic law normally requires that parties be represented by counsel admitted to the local bar, that the local language be used throughout the procedure, with foreign language documents duly translated, and that its own procedural rules and requirements be applied throughout." ③ It leads him to believe that the judicial review mechanism embodies "a complete break with the practices followed in the past arbitration." ④ Fifth, the submissions from *amici curiae* and the participation of new parties at the judicial review stage are also contributing factors of the occurrence of length and costly proceedings. ⑤ Last, the complicated nuances of domestic procedural rules could exacerbate the situation and one example would be that in some cases the higher court tends to remand the case to the lower court for retrial instead of correcting the errors on its own. For instance, in the context of the judicial review of the jurisdictional award of *García Armas and García Gruber v. Venezuela*, the French Supreme Court overruled the first decision by the Paris Court of Appeal but asked the latter to reopen the case rather than writing down its own opinions on

① Ibid., at 519 (noting that, for instance, in the ongoing arbitration law reform in the Netherlands, a proposal that has been put forward is to "have setting aside proceedings heard directly before the appeals court, with the possibility of the parties agreeing to exclude further appeals to the Supreme Court").

② Coe, *supra* note 2, at 201.

③ Fernández – Armesto, *supra* note 52, at 134.

④ Ibid.

⑤ Coe, *supra* note 2, at 201.

contested issues. ①

5.5 The Real Beneficiaries: Those Made of Money

Given the fact that the judicial review proceedings are often lengthy and costly, to claim victory under the present system, i. e. non – ICSID arbitration plus the judicial review of investment awards, "a disputant must have not only a meritorious claim, but ample financing and considerable resolve". ② This worrying issue in relation to the rising costs actually speaks to the question of fairness of the judicial review of investment awards. Since the judicial review process requires considerable devotion of time and finance by disputing parties, this mechanism may entail the risk of being hijacked by the party that has an upper hand in the dispute, be it the rich investor or the powerful state, to drain the other party. In the light of the multiple court instances involved in the handling of setting – aside applications, the likelihood that the financially superior party exploits the system by extending the battle as long as it can possibly be would only increase. If there is an apparent imbalance between the disputing parties in terms of financial resources, the availability of the judicial review mechanism would likely put the poorer one in a rather disadvantaged position. Considering that setting – aside proceedings to some extent serve the interests of the richer party or at least further elevate the significance of financial resources in dispute resolution, the legitimacy of the judicial review mechanism is thereby undermined.

5.6 The Extension of the Infamous Inconsistency Issue

Investment arbitration is bashed by many because of the infamous issue of inconsistent decisions rendered by investment tribunals in like circumstances as a result of lack of an official precedent system and an appellate review procure. It has been argued that such inconsistencies have caused a loss of confidence in arbitration of investment disputes and calls for an overhaul of the current investment arbitration

---

① IA Reporter, *supra* note 465.

② Coe, *supra* note 2, at 201 – 202.

system.① However, the inconsistency problem is not restricted to arbitral proceeding but extends to the judicial review of investment awards as well. In all likelihood, domestic courts *loci arbitri* across different jurisdictions may issue inconsistent or even contradictory judgments with regard to the same application for the setting - aside of an investment award. The fundamental reason is that the judicial review mechanism applicable to investment arbitration is nothing but a mere transplantation of that applicable to commercial arbitration, leaving the supervisory power over investment awards scattered among and anchored to various national law regimes at the seat of arbitration.

There are, however, more specified reasons to account for the inconsistency issue in judicial review of investment awards. First, there are different grounds for the setting - aside of investment awards across relevant jurisdictions because at the end of the day the power to decide the scope of the judicial review of investment awards is held in the hands of the legislature of each jurisdiction. Therefore, it is conceivable that an investment award that may be set aside in a jurisdiction for a specific ground turns out to be impossible to be set aside in another jurisdiction for the simple reason that the specific ground is not recognized by the arbitration law of the latter jurisdiction. Second, although the Model Law has brought a certain extent of unification to the grounds for judicial review, different courts may still interpret the common text in a conflicting way.② Third, the standard of review adopted may also differ from one court to another, resulting in a varying level of difficulty in sat-

---

① Eun Young Park, "Appellate Review in Investor State Arbitration", in Jean E. Kalicki and Anna Joubin - Bret edited, "Reshaping the Investor - State Dispute Settlement System Journeys for the 21st Century", Koninklijke Brill (2015), p. 444.

② Coe, *supra* note 2, at 194.

isfying the grounds for setting aside investment awards.① Thus, by applying the same review ground to the same circumstance of an application for setting aside an investment award, different courts may have different answers towards the question of whether a reversal decision should be granted. For instance, while both the Canadian court in the review proceeding related to *Bayview v. Mexico* and the Singaporean court in the review proceeding related to *Sanum v. Laos* were tasked with reviewing the jurisdictional decisions by the investment tribunals, but the former court firmly asserted that its roles was not to conduct a de novo review of the merits of the tribunal's jurisdiction, in marked contrast to the position adopted by the latter review court. Fourth, related to the difference in standard of review is the fact that the varying legal cultures dictate that domestic courts across different jurisdictions tend to have different judicial attitudes towards arbitration and arbitral decisions. While some jurisdictions may argue for considerable respect and deference to arbitral decisions, other jurisdictions may have a different stand on this issue. The different judicial review attitudes would in turn influence the outcomes of setting – aside proceedings against investment awards. Last but not least, the trial class system also contributes to the inconsistency problem embedded in judicial review of investment awards since courts of different instances within a certain jurisdiction may also have their opinions against each other as evidenced by the review proceedings in relation to *BG v. Argentina* and *Sanum v. Laos*. This inconsistency problem engenders considerable unpredictability for disputing parties resorting to non – ICSID arbitration, extending a major loophole in investment arbitration to the judicial review

① Thomas and Dhillon also illustrate the potential conflicting handling by domestic courts across distinct jurisdictions in the face of judicial review of investment awards by giving an example that involves the diverging ways adopted by the courts respectively from three states to deal with questions of jurisdiction. They argue that: "State A might employ a de novo standard of review, permitting the parties to adduce evidence that was not before the tribunal and permitting the judge to decide the issue for her/himself. The courts of State B, on the other hand, might apply a correctness standard, but restrict the review to the evidence that was before the tribunal. The courts of State C, employing presumptions of correctness, might be inclined to apply an even more deferential standard of review." Thomas & Dhillon, *supra* note 20, at 493.

phase and encroaching upon the legitimacy of the judicial review mechanism for investment awards.

6. Conclusion

The critical analysis against judicial review of investment awards reveals that this form of post – award remedy, despite serving the purpose of exercising control over investment awards and arbitral proceedings, is far from beyond reproach. All these doubts against the judicial review of investment awards also naturally trigger a question of whether a better alternative can be introduced to take place of the current regime. The deficiencies that have been discussed above seem to suggest that the judicial review mechanism for investment awards is problematic and ready – for – change not least because of the heavy reliance of investment arbitration (including the following post – award remedy) on the procedural formats originally designed for the conduct of commercial arbitration. ①

Taking all the critical analysis mentioned in the above text into account, the proposal that has been put forward for a long time which advises the establishment of a centralized appellate review system could shed light on the potential reform of the judicial review mechanism for investment arbitration. One of the prevailing arguments for the introduction of an appeals system is that it would help to correct the inconsistency problem that has been troubling investment arbitration and restore the legitimacy of this dispute resolution method. However, the appeal system may also be desirable in that it is a better alternative as a form of post – award remedy compared to the judicial review of investment awards.

However, it should not be taken that this article is suggesting the establishment of an appeal system that is often seen in national judicial systems in which the appeal court may review the decision of the lower court in each and every aspect often with no or little deference or respect. In effect, this article intends to arrive at a conclusion that a standing centralized review panel within the arbitration system is

---

① Brown, *supra* note 141, at 673.

more desirable than the current judicial review mechanism for investment arbitration, leaving the prescription of an appropriate scope of review, which is absolutely an important yet complicated issue, out of the picture for now. The proposed arbitral review system is by no means a perfect solution, but it at least avoids some of the mentioned problems by way of detaching domestic courts *loci arbitri* from the process of reviewing investment awards.

ICSID 仲裁管辖权争议中证明责任的适用失范与规则构建*

马明飞　蔡斯扬**

摘　要:ICSID 仲裁逐渐开始区分结果意义上的法定证明责任和程序意义上的举证证明责任。就管辖权争议而言,投资者与东道国须围绕ICSID 公约与涉案投资条约规定的若干管辖权要件进行证明活动。依据一般证明责任分配原则,提出主张的一方应当承担要件事实的法定证明责任。然而,这一原则在仲裁管辖权裁决实践中的适用,表现出了要件事实主张者确认困难、过重的说服义务引起双方地位失衡、证明责任规则代替对仲裁合意的解释三个突出的失范问题,为此更宜采用国际法院对证明责任适用的方法予以克服。在 ICSID 管辖权证明责任适用的规则构建上,应对管辖权具体要件优先适用举证证明责任,强化对仲裁合意条款的全面解释,仅将法定证明责任用为具体要件认定上的兜底条款。

关键词:ICSID 仲裁　管辖权　法定证明责任　举证证明责任

一、问题的提出

随着近年来国际投资仲裁①的案件数量呈指数增长,投资者与东道国在案件管辖权问题上的激烈交锋已成为该领域的关注焦点之一。国际仲裁界就曾

---

* 特此注明:本文主要内容已于 2021 年 7 月在《社会科学家》发表。

** 马明飞,法学博士,大连海事大学法学院教授;蔡斯扬,法学博士,大连医科大学法学系讲师。

① 本文讨论的国际投资仲裁,范围仅限于外国投资者与投资东道国基于投资争端而提起的条约仲裁,不包括一国与他国因投资争端所引发的国家间仲裁。

统计,在全部国际投资仲裁案件中,因管辖权而全部驳回或部分驳回申请人仲裁申请的案件比例高达 60% 。[①] 联合国贸易和发展会议(United Nations Conference on Trade and Development, UNCTAD)在《2018 年投资者—东道国争端解决案件报告》中指出,截至 2018 年年底全球约有 600 起已审结投资仲裁案件,在东道国胜诉的案件中,约一半因管辖权异议而驳回投资者的仲裁请求。[②] 可见,管辖权问题很大程度上决定了仲裁案件的后续进程与最终结果。

在作为当前最重要的投资争端解决机制——“解决投资争议国际中心”(The International Center for Settlement of Investment Disputes, ICSID)仲裁中,绝大多数的投资东道国都会对投资者的仲裁申请提出管辖权异议。[③]实践中,ICSID 仲裁庭确定能否对个案拥有管辖权,除了审查具体争议是否符合涉案双边或多边投资条约对诸如条约时间效力、地域范围与仲裁合意等投资保护的限定条件之外,还须审查该争议是否满足《关于解决国家与他国国民之间投资争议公约》(以下简称 ICSID 公约)第 25 条规定的同意管辖、属物管辖与属人管辖等要件。[④] 如 SGS v. Paraguay 案仲裁庭就指出,其在管辖权阶段应根据涉案双

---

① See Ian A. Laird, Borzu Sabahi, Frédéric G. Sourgens, Nicholas J. Birch, Kabir Duggal & Joanna Coyne, International Investment Law and Arbitration: 2013 in Review, in Yearbook on International Investment Law& Policy 2013 – 2014, edited by Andrea K. Bjorklund, New York: Oxford University Press, 2015, p. 71 – 72.

② See Review of ISDS Decision in 2018: Selected IIA Reform Issues, UNCTAD, p. 3, available at https://unctad.org/en/PublicationsLibrary/diaepcbinf2019d6_en.pdf,最后访问日期:2020 年 6 月 8 日。

③ 国际投资仲裁的管辖权基础是东道国与投资者母国缔结投资条约中的仲裁合意。实践中该投资条约被解释为东道国将投资争议提交仲裁的持续要约,投资者甫一启动仲裁程序即被视作对该要约的承诺。所以,投资者可以随时作为仲裁申请人启动仲裁程序,东道国在国际投资仲裁中一般只能作为被申请人进行应诉。

④ 参见 ICSID 公约第 25 条规定:(1)中心的管辖适用于缔约方(或缔约方向中心指定的该国的任何组成部分或机构)和另一缔约方国民之间直接因投资而产生并经双方书面同意提交给中心的任何法律争端。当双方表示同意后,任何一方不得单方面撤销其同意。(2)“另一缔约方国民”系指:①在双方同意将争端交付调解或仲裁之日以及根据第 28 条第 2 款或第 36 条第 3 款登记请求之日,具有作为争端一方的国家以外的某一缔约方国籍的任何自然人,但不包括在上述任一日期也具有作为争端一方的缔约方国籍的任何人;②在争端双方同意将争端交付调解或仲裁之日,具有作为争端一方的国家以外的某一缔约方国籍的任何法人,以及在上述日期具有作为争端一方缔约方国籍的任何法人,而该法人因受外国控制,双方同意为了本公约的目的,应看作另一缔约方国民。(3)某一缔约方的组成部分或机构表示的同意,须经该缔约方批准,除非该缔约方通知中心不需要予以批准。(4)任何缔约方可以在批准、接受或核准本公约时,或在此后任何时候,把它将考虑或不考虑提交给中心管辖的一类或几类争端通知中心。秘书长应立即将此项通知转送给缔约方。此项通知不构成第 1 款所要求的同意。

边投资条约(Bilateral Investment Treaty,BIT)和 ICSID 公约的有关规定,对适格国籍、受保护的投资、投资位于的领土、条约保护的时间范围与提交 ICSID 仲裁合意等直接决定管辖权的事实进行确定。① 仲裁庭在对案件管辖权进行审查过程中,必然要求仲裁双方对涉及管辖权争议要件事实进行举证与说明。由于 ICSID 公约及《解决投资争议国际中心仲裁规则》(以下简称 ICSID 仲裁规则)均未对证明责任规则作出明文规定,是故仲裁庭在管辖权要件事实的证明责任分配上拥有较为广泛的自由裁量权。②

目前的 ICSID 仲裁实践中,对于以征收与补偿为主要内容的实体问题,广泛运用"谁主张,谁举证"这一世界范围内所公认的证明责任分配的一般原则。然而,由于 ICSID 公约和具体涉案投资条约就管辖权要件规定的多重性与复杂性,以及不同背景的仲裁员往往会选择性援引以往相异案情仲裁裁决中的证明责任分配方法,"谁主张,谁举证"这一原则在案件管辖权认定上的适用业已出现相应的失范与异化。仲裁庭简单而机械地凭借此原则,不但无法满足部分案件中特殊管辖权要件事实的证明需要,而且也容易导致在一些管辖权裁决中出现实质不公的消极后果。基于此,本文从证明责任的概念分野出发,通过考察证明责任一般分配原则适用于部分 ICSID 管辖权争议案件时已出现的若干困局,并在剖析导致管辖权证明实践难题之背后原因的基础上,对如何更为合理地构建 ICSID 管辖权的证明责任适用规则提出建议。

二、ICSID 仲裁实践对证明责任的理解与适用

对证明责任内涵的准确认识,有助于深刻理解 ICSID 仲裁中证明责任的分配原理。ICSID 仲裁实践发展至今,已经逐渐对法定证明责任与举证证明责任两种概念有所区分。

(一)ICSID 仲裁中证明责任的双重内涵

国内法上,证明责任是有自身逻辑内涵的一个整体概念。英美法系的证明

---

① See SGS Société Générale de Surveillance S. A. v. The Republic of Paraguay, ICSID Case No. ARB/07/29, Decision on Jurisdiction(12 February 2010), paras. 53 – 55.

② 参见 ICSID 公约第 43 条第 1 款第 1 项仅规定:"除双方另有协议,仲裁庭可在程序的任何阶段认为有必要时,要求双方提出文件或其他证据。"而 ICSID 仲裁规则第 34 条只是原则性地规定,"仲裁庭对于所提供的证据,应就其是否接受及其证明价值作出判断"。

责任(burden of proof)包括说服责任(burden of persuasion)(或称法定证明责任,legal burden of proof)和提出证据责任(burden of producing evidence)(或称举证证明责任,evidential burden of proof)。[①] 大陆法系的证明责任理论体系则区分客观证明责任与主观证明责任。[②] 尽管在制度起源与具体适用方式上存在差异,然而"法定证明责任"和"客观证明责任"均强调不能说服法官而产生的败诉风险,是结果意义上的证明责任,在案件审理中均始终不发生转移。[③] 而且,"举证证明责任"与"主观证明责任"大体上都是行为意义上的证明责任,可在个案进程中随具体情况发生转移。[④] 这种证明责任双重内涵的区分,在国际投资仲裁理论界被较为一致地认可。学者们指出,证明责任作为一项课以事实主张者的基本负担,其中的法定证明责任或说服责任在国际仲裁整个过程中从未发生转移;而举证证明责任作为程序事项,可以在主张者与抗辩者之间来回转移。[⑤] 更有学者论及,用证明责任术语来代替举证负担(burden of evidence)是不准确的,证明责任由事实主张者承担,直到案件所涉整个主张得到证明。[⑥]

ICSID 仲裁实践中,这种区分经历了一个逐渐形成共识的过程。早在 20 世纪 90 年代初,AAPL v. Sri Lanka 案就指出"如果一方举出的证据在表面上支持该方的主张,则证明责任转移给了另一方"[⑦]。虽然此后若干仲裁案件援引这一表述,但均未能道明转移的是哪一种证明责任内涵,并回避了证明责任两种

① 法定证明责任,是指整个诉讼过程中,当事人提出证据以说服裁判者相信其主张的事实为真的责任;举证证明责任,是指在诉讼各个阶段,当事人就争议事实提出证据,并在质与量两方面达到最低要求,否则其将诉请将被驳回。参见张卫平:《民事证据法》,法律出版社 2017 年版,第 271、272 页。

② 客观证明责任,是指在庭审的最后阶段若要件事实依然真伪不明,由主张该事实的当事人承担不利的裁判后果;主观证明责任是指当事人为了获得对其有利的裁判、避免败诉,通过提供证据的方式对争议事实进行证明的一种必要负担。参见[德]普维庭:《现代证明责任问题》,吴越译,法律出版社 2006 年版,第 35 页。

③ 参见李昌盛:《积极抗辩事由的证明责任:误解与澄清》,载《法学研究》2016 年第 2 期。

④ 参见易延友:《证据法的体系与精神——以英美法为特别参照》,北京大学出版社 2010 年版,第 293 ~ 295 页。

⑤ See Mojtaba Kazazi, *Burden of Proof and Related Issues: A Study on Evidence Before the International Tribunal*, Kluwer Law International, 1996, p. 36. See also Anna Riddell & Brendan Plant, *Evidence before the International Court of Justice*, British Institute of International and Comparative Law 2009, p. 111.

⑥ See Chittharanjan F Amerasinghe, *Evidence in International Litigation*, Martinus Nijhoff Publishers, 2005, p. 253 – 254.

⑦ See Asian Agricultural Products Ltd. v. Republic of Sri Lanka, ICSID Case No. ARB/87/3, Final Award (27 June 1990), para. 56.

内涵的区分。直到 Apotex v. the United States 案仲裁庭明确作出“法定证明责任不转移,举证证明责任随着证据出示的情况而在当事人之间发生转移”的论证后,[①]ICSID 仲裁开始有意对两种证明责任内涵进行区分,这也体现在 Mercer v. Canada 案、Koch Minerals v. Venezuela 案和 Gavazzi v. Romania 案等一系列仲裁实践中。[②] 由此,ICSID 仲裁中的证明责任概念融合了两大法系的制度内涵,逐渐将说服裁判者的义务和提供证据的义务区别开来。

(二)ICSID 仲裁中证明责任分配的一般原则

“提出主张者承担证明责任”(onus probandi incumbit actori)这一起源于罗马法的原则,已被两大法系的国内诉讼作为一项普遍接受的证明责任分配原则而持续恪守。在国际争端解决层面,该原则在实践中得到常设国际法院(Permanent Court of International Justice,PCIJ)、国际法院(International Court of Justice,ICJ)和世界贸易组织(World Trade Organization,WTO)争端解决小组等国际机构广泛认可的同时,[③]也为国际仲裁中经常适用的《联合国国际贸易法委员会仲裁规则》(UNCITRAL Arbitration Rules)所明文规定。[④]

虽然 ICSID 公约与 ICSID 仲裁规则均未明文确认此项规则,但是仲裁庭在处理实体争议的实践中广泛地遵循了该原则。同样在 AAPL v. Sri Lanka 案中,仲裁庭开创性地总结出关于证明责任的两条首要原则:第一,法律的一般原则将证明责任课予权利主张者;第二,不能仅从程序立场出发而机械地让原告

---

① See Apotex Holdings Inc. and Apotex Inc. v. the United States, ICSID Case No. ARB(AF)/12/1, Award (25 August 2014), para. 8.8.

② See Mercer International Inc. v. Government of Canada, ICSID Case No. ARB(AF)/12/3, Award (6 March 2018), paras. 7.11 – 7.14; Koch Minerals Sàrl and Koch Nitrogen International Sàrl v. Bolivarian Republic of Venezuela, ICSID Case No. ARB/11/19, Award(30 October 2017), paras. 7.18 – 7.23; Marco Gavazzi and Stefano Gavazzi v. Romania, ICSID Case No. ARB/12/25, Award of the Tribunal(18 April 2017), para. 224.

③ 例如,WTO 上诉机构适用这一规则时指出:“在民法、普通法以及事实上大多数司法管辖区内普遍接受的证明准则均是:当事方无论是主张还是抗辩,证明责任课以提出某一特定主张或抗辩的一方。” See WTO, United States—Measure Affecting Imports of Woven Wool Shirts and Blouses from India(25 April 1997), WT/DS33/AB/R, para. 14.

④ 参见《国际贸易法委员会仲裁规则》第 27 条第 1 款规定:“每一方当事人应对其仲裁请求或答辩所依据的事实负举证责任。”

承担证明责任,而应从具体争议来检视谁是真正的权利主张者。[①] 嗣后,大多数 ICSID 仲裁庭对上述分析予以呼应,[②]其中以 Rompetrol v. Romania 案与 Bernhard v. Zimbabwe 案仲裁庭对该原则的阐释最为典型。前案指出,如果被申请人提出自己的新主张以反驳或破坏申请人的事实请求,则该新主张的证明责任由被申请人承担;[③]后案论道,若主张与抗辩涉及相同的事实问题,每一方都承担证实自身观点的提出证据责任,管辖权异议提出时并不存在证明责任转移的概念。[④] 而且,部分仲裁庭在承认"提出主张者承担证明责任"的基础上还进一步澄清,证明责任的分配原则不会因为获取与提交证据中存在困难而发生改变,[⑤]也不能因为另一方更容易获得证据而改变。[⑥] 故此,证明责任一般由提出事实主张的申请人或提出新事实抗辩的被申请人自始承担,[⑦]这是仲裁庭为解决某一投资争议所设立的认知起点。此处所指的证明责任应理解为法定证明责任或说服责任,尽管没有统辖 ICSID 仲裁证明责任分配的明文法律,然而上述证明责任分配原则被大多数国际争端实践与国内法所明确使用和规定,构成了一项仲裁员普遍遵循的一般法律原则。

由于举证证明责任是一种程序推进责任,故而实践中的仲裁庭对其须满足何种条件方得以转移的论述不多,且多未区分证明责任的双重内涵。[⑧] 国际仲

---

① See Asian Agricultural Products Ltd. v. Republic of Sri Lanka, ICSID Case No. ARB/87/3, Final Award (27 June 1990), para. 56.

② See Hussein Nuaman Soufraki v. United Arab Emirates, ICSID Case No. ARB/02/7, Award (7 July 2004), para. 58; RosInvestCo UK ltd. v. Russian Federation, SCC Case No. V079/2005, Final Award (12 September 2010), para. 250; Saopem S. p. A. v. People's Republic of Bangladesh, ICSID Case No. ARB/05/07, Decision on Jurisdiction and Recommendation on Provisional Measures (21 March 2007), para. 83.

③ See Rompetrol Group NV v. Romania, ICSID Case No. ARB/06/3, Award (6 May 2013), para. 179.

④ See Bernhard von Pezold and Others v. Republic of Zimbabwe, ICSID Case No. ARB/10/15, Award (28 July 2015), para. 174.

⑤ See Lao Holdings N. V. v. Lao People's Democratic Republic, ICSID Case No. ARB(AF)/12/6, Decision on the Merits (10 June 2015), para. 11.

⑥ See Azurix Corp. v. The Argentine Republic, ICSID Case No. ARB/01/12, Decision on the Application for Annulment of the Argentine Republic (1 September 2009), para. 215.

⑦ 须注意抗辩与否认之间概念的区别。否认是指对于一方当事人主张的事实,另一方当事人向法院或仲裁机构表示是不真实的;抗辩则是一方当事人通过主张与对方当事人不同的事实或法律关系来排除对方的主张。参见李浩:《民事诉讼法适用中的证明责任》,载《中国法学》2018 年第 1 期。

⑧ 实际上,一些 ICSID 仲裁庭在论述证明责任的转移时,均使用了"shift the burden of proof",并未就证明责任中的举证证明责任加以单独阐释。从笔者目前查阅的案例来看,既往仲裁庭对所谓"burden of proof"的转移标准一般为形成"表面证据案件"(prima facie case)。

裁理论界对此进行了弥补:O' Malley 教授认为,国际仲裁中当事人提出的证据至少需要达到表面上的确定性(prima facie certainty),才能将证据负担转移给对方。[①] Amerasinghe 教授指出,一方当事人提出表面证据(prima facie evidence)[②]后,实际上免除自身的提出证据责任,在对方当事人反驳该已经成立的表面证据之前,不再承担该待证事实进一步的举证负担。[③] 质言之,虽然表面证据不一定能满足某一案件的最终说服责任标准,但其包含的最低程度之说服责任意义却可辅助仲裁庭对举证证明责任的履行情况进行检验并决定是否转移。

综上,ICSID 仲裁中的两种证明责任内涵所引致的证明分配结果应当有所不同。在仲裁程序启动之初,对某一案情事实的法定证明责任与举证证明责任均归于同一当事人(提出主张的申请人或提出新事实抗辩的被申请人)。当该当事人提出事实证据并形成了一项表面证据时,则意味着他满足了待证事实的最低程度的说服标准,举证证明责任由此转移给对方,而且在对方对该表面证据反驳之前,他都不会承担进一步的法定证明责任。[④] 对方当事人为阻止对其自身的不利裁判,提出证据反驳该表面证据,举证证明责任再次回到原方当事人而迫使他提出更多针对该待证事实的证据。上述过程中,法定证明责任始终居于一方当事人,举证证明责任的来回转移,引导双方对特定事实论证的说服力不断发生变化,从而有助于仲裁庭认识证据的全貌和判断一方当事人是否完成了法定证明责任。

---

① See Nathan D O' Malley, *Rules of Evidence in International Arbitration: An Annotated Guide* (Informa Law 2012), p. 212 – 213.

② 表面证据是指除非提出相反证据,否则据此证据已能确立某项事实或支撑某项判决。表面成立的案件是表面证据在证明案件成立时的一种证明标准,也即说服责任的标准,其在说服责任中表现为:如果对方当事人不提供相反证据,对方当事人就将承担败诉的风险。表面证据的作用可以是转移提出证据责任,也可以作为一种减轻当事人证明责任的推定。参见徐康:《英国表面证据规则初探》,载《司法改革评论》2013 年第 2 期。

③ Amerasinghe 教授还进一步列举了四种申请人提交表面证据的后续可能结果:(1)相对人没有回应,法庭最终认定申请人提交的证据满足适用的证明标准,并支持其主张;(2)相对人没有回应,但法庭认定申请人提交的证据无法满足适用的证明标准,不认可其主张;(3)相对人以提出证据或进行解释的方式提出抗辩,但仲裁庭最终发现该抗辩无法动摇申请人证据对证明标准的满足,因此支持申请人主张;(4)相对人以提出证据或进行解释的方式提出抗辩,仲裁庭最终发现申请人证据无法满足适用的证明标准,因此不认可申请人的主张。See Chittharanjan F Amerasinghe, *Evidence in International Litigation*, Martinus Nijhoff Publishers, 2005, p. 251.

④ See Mojtaba Kazazi, *Burden of Proof and Related Issues: A Study on Evidence Before the International Tribunal*, Kluwer Law International, 1996, p. 273.

(三)ICSID 多重管辖权要件事实上的证明责任适用

不同于国际商事仲裁的管辖权争议集中在平等商事主体间订立的仲裁条款之约束范围,借鉴商事仲裁方法的 ICSID 仲裁,因涉及的仲裁条款包含在国际公法性质的条约之中,东道国往往针对条约若干具体条款提出管辖权异议,其管辖权上的争议相对广泛得多。① 为保持仲裁效率并兼顾公正,ICSID 仲裁常对仲裁程序进行管辖权审理阶段与实体问题审理阶段的"二元划分"(Bifurcation),②以便通过对管辖权争议要件进行审查而驳回没有适格管辖权的仲裁申请,由此避免对后续实体问题再进行徒劳审理,③这也就塑造了 ICSID 仲裁管辖权争议审理阶段的相对独立性,管辖权结果之于仲裁双方的重要性亦得以凸显。而证明责任在 ICSID 管辖权确立上的适用,实践中则表现出如下特点:

一方面,根据前述被 ICSID 实践所广泛运用的"提出主张者承担证明责任"原则,作为仲裁提起人的投资者需要对管辖权的整体成立承担法定证明责任,并肩负就 ICSID 公约第 25 条规定的"双方书面同意将争端提交给中心解决"之同意管辖要件、"涉案争端系直接因投资而产生"之属物管辖要件、"仲裁双方必须是缔约方与另一缔约方国民"之属人管辖要件上的事实逐项说服仲裁庭的义务。正如 National Gas v. Egypt 案仲裁庭所指出,尽管被申请人可能提出若干具体的管辖权异议,对各项管辖权要件事实的证明责任仍应由申请人承担。④

---

① 参见[德]Karl – Heinz Böckstiegel、傅攀峰:《商事仲裁与投资仲裁:当今两者差异几何?》,载《仲裁研究》2014 年第 2 期。

② 这种程序划分的案件管理方式为 ICSID 公约第 41 条第 2 项所明确规定:"仲裁庭有权决定是否将管辖权异议作为先决问题处理,或与该争端的实体问题一并处理"。即使其他仲裁机构也不同程度地支持此种程序处理方法。例如,被其他仲裁机构广泛适用的《联合国国际贸易法委员会仲裁规则》(UNCITRAL 规则)(2010 年版)第 23 条第 1 款也规定:仲裁庭"对管辖权作为初步问题还是一并与实体问题作出裁决"有自由裁量权;《国际商会仲裁院仲裁规则》第 2 条指出,裁决分为"临时、部分以及最终的裁决",并于该规则附录 4 补充道:"如果诸如二元切分的案件管理技术能更为高效地处理案件,仲裁庭可以使用"。

③ 在 ICSID 仲裁语境下,实体问题(Merits)是指投资者基于东道国违反涉案国际投资条约中投资保护条款而享有的条约请求权。为支撑针对东道国违反种种具体条约义务的诉请,投资者需列举若干基础事实,这就可能与关涉管辖权要件的事实发生重叠。实践中,仲裁庭一般以管辖权与实体问题中事实的重叠程度为基础决定是否进行程序的二元切分。由于讨论的主题及篇幅有限,对实体问题与管辖权问题的重叠程度如何具体判别,本文暂不作详细论述。

④ See National Gas S. A. E. v. Arab Republic of Egypt, ICSID Case No. ARB/11/7 , Award (16 April 2014), para. 118.

可见,作为申请人的投资者所承担的管辖权证明责任显然较重。

另一方面,ICSID 公约及仲裁规则中证明责任具体条文缺位,加之绝大多数涉案投资协定未对证明责任予以明确约定,使得投资仲裁庭对具体案件管辖权的证明责任适用拥有较大的自由裁量权。同时,目前的 ICSID 仲裁也尚未形成有拘束力的判例法体系供仲裁庭遵循。故此,如果仲裁庭在管辖权裁判实践中回避与混淆证明责任两种内涵,或是在要件事实上对证明责任分配不清甚至运用错误,就容易产生裁决结果有失公允。

三、ICSID 管辖权争议中证明责任适用失范的突出表现

当前在 ICSID 管辖权问题上证明责任的适用失范,主要体现在部分仲裁庭过分依靠法定证明责任这一单一内涵来判断要件事实的存在与否,而且对当事人说服义务的承担与卸除的解释不甚统一,裁决结果也难免容易引起争议。

(一)确定管辖权要件事实的真正"主张者"并非易事

仲裁界学者们曾对在国际仲裁中运用"提出主张者承担证明责任"的一般分配原理提出了担忧。Amerasinghe 教授就提出过五点适用上的问题,一是在国际法程序中有效区分事实主张者与抗辩者可能存在困难;二是在国际争端中同时提交诉请是被允许的;三是仲裁庭审理案件所依据的相关基础文本材料对证明责任分配保持缄默;四是国际仲裁中的证据规则是"非技术性的";五是争议双方有义务与国际仲裁庭合作,以此构建出案件的真相。① 其他较有影响力的学者也对证明责任的适用表达了相似看法。② 而 ICSID 仲裁管辖权审理实践中,于特定案件中确定"主张者"的确也出现过困难与争议。例如,Rompetrol v. Romania 案仲裁庭在东道国罗马尼亚提出投资并非受申请人控制且投资资金源于罗马尼亚公民的管辖权异议后,将此适格投资的法定证明责任课以罗马尼亚。③ 又如 Lao holding v. Lao 案中,老挝政府就案件管辖权提出的唯一异议是

---

① See Chittharanjan F. Amerasinghe, *Evidence in International Litigation*, Martinus Nijhoff Publishers, 2005, p. 90.

② See Mojtaba Kazazi, Burden of Proof and Related Issues: A study on Evidence Before the International Tribunal, Kluwer Law International, 1996, p. 234; See also V S Mani, *International Adjudication: Procedural Aspects*, Martinus Nijhoff Publishers, 1980, p. 203.

③ See The Rompetrol Group N. V. v. Romania, ICSID Case No. ARB/06/3, Decision on Respondent's Preliminary Objections on Jurisdiction and Admissibility (18 April 2008), para. 50.

在争端发生时申请人还不是投资者,仲裁庭将“争端何时发生”的法定证明责任分配给了老挝政府。[①] 然而,按照证明责任分配的原则,适格投资、条约时间保护范围等要件事实的法定证明责任一般应由提出仲裁申请的投资者承担,提出管辖权异议的东道国只需承担举证证明责任。

而以投资者适格国籍为例,按照证明责任一般分配原则,投资者应当承担该要件事实的法定证明责任,即说服责任。但是在面临投资者具有双重国籍的案件时,问题就变得较为棘手。[②] 在 Ambiente v. Argentina 案中,依涉案意大利与阿根廷 BIT 的相关条款规定,投资者的适格国籍要件包括具有意大利国籍(积极事实)、不具有阿根廷国籍(消极事实)和未在阿根廷居住两年以上(消极事实)三个要素。[③] 该案仲裁庭的多数仲裁员将具有意大利国籍的法定证明责任课以投资者,同时把证明该投资者不具有阿根廷国籍且未在该国居住两年以上的法定证明责任分配给东道国阿根廷。该案少数仲裁员在其反对意见中则指出,应由投资者承担适格国籍的积极要件与消极要件的总体法定证明责任,否则将有违国际法上对证明责任的一般公认原则。[④] 此案若按多数意见处理,东道国对该国籍消极要素只存在反驳的举证证明责任,课以其该要素的法定证明责任则导致一个要件事实中出现了两个说服责任,显然有悖于证明责任分配原理;而依少数仲裁员意见处理,则存在申请人(事实主张者)承担对不存在的消极事实进行证明这一显然有违常理的做法。该案仲裁庭对证明责任的分配也由此在理论界被不断探讨与争论。

(二)投资者被赋予过重法定证明责任所导致的不平等

尽管实践中 ICSID 仲裁因只能由投资者发起而看似在程序上对其有利,但作为被申请人的东道国在管辖权的证明责任规则上拥有较大优势。因为投资

---

① See Lao Holdings N. V. v. Lao People's Democratic Republic, ICSID Case No. ARB(AF)/12/6, Decision on Jurisdiction, paras. 64 – 67.

② 依 ICSID 公约第 25 条第 2 款第 1 项的规定,对于争端中作为投资者的一方当事人,必须同时满足两项国籍要求:必须具备另一缔约方的国籍(也称积极要求),且其不得同时具备投资东道国的国籍(也称消极要求)。

③ 该仲裁涉案 BIT 规定,具有阿根廷国籍的投资者不受该 BIT 保护以外,开始进行投资之前已在阿根廷居住满两年以上者,也不受在该 BIT 的保护。See Ambiente Ufficio S. p. A et al. v. Argentine Republic, ICSID Case No. ARB/08/9, Decision on Jurisdiction and Admissibility (8 Feburary 2013), para. 312.

④ See Ambiente v. Argentine, Dissenting Opinion of Santiago Torres Bernárdez (2 may 2013), para. 141.

者对国籍、适格投资、仲裁合意与可归责性等管辖权事实需提供证据予以证明，而东道国往往就这些事实提出多项管辖权异议，且东道国所独享的警察权力也使其可能坐拥投资者永远无法获取的信息。是故，赋予投资者以过于苛刻的证明责任，会使仲裁双方的程序地位严重失衡。

Caratube v. Kazakhstan 案是畸高的法定证明责任导致投资者败诉的典型实例。该案缘于 CIOC 公司因哈萨克斯坦政府征收其石油与天然气开采特许权项目而申请 ICSID 仲裁，其中管辖权确立的焦点在于美国公民 Hourani 是否有效控制了位于东道国的合资企业 CIOC。[①] 仲裁庭虽然依间接证据认可了 Hourani持有涉案企业 92% 的股权，但认为这并不能够充分说明对涉案企业的实际控制。[②] 在哈萨克斯坦政府提出可能存在他人实际控制企业的异议后，仲裁庭命令申请人证明投资资金的来源、对投资项目的实际贡献和参加股东会与董事会频率等事项，以此说服仲裁庭 Hourani 对企业实际控制。[③] 问题在于，自 CIOC 公司的业务被征收时起，其办事处已遭到哈萨克斯坦警方多次搜查，相关重要文件被没收且部分工作人员已被拘留与审讯，[④]这种严格的法定证明责任和畸高的说服义务使申请人难以诉诸充分举证而最终败诉，何况这些附加给申请人的额外证明事项并非与通常意义上的企业控制权直接相关。而且，纵观该案审理过程，摆脱举证义务却掌握相关记录证据的哈萨克斯坦政府，也未有效地证明其所主张的投资者举证不真实、CIOC 是由 Hourani 以外的其他人所实际控制的事实。

无独有偶，Libananco v. Turkey 案仲裁庭亦课予投资者绝对化的说服责

① 依 ICSID 公约第 25 条第 2 款第 2 项的规定，法人的国籍问题存在“国籍标准”与“控制标准”两种适合标准，即外国法人可以是东道国以外的某一缔约方国籍的任何法人（国籍标准）；而受外国控制的且具有东道国国籍的法人，经双方特别约定，也可以视为另一缔约方国民（控制标准）。只有能够证明 CIOC 公司（全称 Caratube International Oil Companyllp）被美国公民 Hourani 实际控制，才能符合涉外 BIT 与 ICSID 公约对属人管辖要件事实的规定。

② See Caratube International Oil Company LLP v. The Republic of Kazakhstan, ICSID Case No. ARB/08/12, Award (5 June 2012), paras. 407, 457.

③ See Ibid, paras. 425 – 427.

④ See Ibid, paras. 2, 15, 171, 194.

任,从而导致投资者最终败诉。① 该案管辖权争议的焦点是,Libananco 公司是否在土耳其军警查封 CEAS 公司和 Kepez 公司的日期之前拥有此两个公司的控制权,以此证明其是否为适格的外国投资者。Libananco 公司在该案中出示了包括无记名股份交易记录在内的表明其控制权的关键要素事实,并指出在涉案关键日期之后不可能再进行股权交易,因为土耳其方面已经没收了存放股份的相关设施。② 然而,土耳其方面坚持不懈地主张投资者的股权是由其欺诈行为所得,并依靠投资者的证人证言与书证之间的不一致之处,③成功地让仲裁庭对投资者合法持有股权产生了怀疑。仲裁庭认为,申请人对于已发生事件的描述存在一定的矛盾与抵触,而证明所有权存在的负担必须被"确定性地解除",故而最终驳回了投资者的管辖权申请。④ 然而,该案中东道国所主张的投资者对两公司的股权系欺诈所得,自始至终没有得到有效证明。⑤

从上述两案分析可知,在投资争议提交 ICSID 后,东道国实际上有大量机会通过主张投资者存在欺诈行为或证据缺乏真实性等事由,在可能掌握对其有利证据的同时,促使仲裁庭将投资者对某一要件事实的说服责任提高至"明确和令人信服的标准"。在面对投资者主张与东道国反驳的要件事实存在两种不同解释时,仲裁庭很可能超越现有双方提交证据的记录,以说服责任来替代对证据进行全面调查和相应的权衡比较,最终作出对投资者较为不利的判断。

(三)以说服责任的适用替代对同意仲裁条款的合理解释

近十几年来,ICSID 仲裁案件数量不断增加过程中的一个凸显的现象是,越来越多的投资者认为涉案 BIT 中的最惠国待遇条款(Most – Favored – Nation-

---

① 该案是一家名为 Libananco 的塞浦路斯控股公司针对土耳其政府提出索赔,理由是土耳其军队和警察部队于 2003 年 6 月 12 日,查封扣押了 Libananco 控股的位于土耳其境内的两家垂直一体化电力公用事业公司(CEAS 公司和 Kepez 公司)并撤销了其特许经营权,从而违反了《能源宪章条约》(Energy Charter Treaty,ECT)。See Libananco Holdings Co. Limited v. Republic of Turkey,ICSID Case No. ARB/06/8 ,Award(2 September 2011).

② See Ibid. ,paras. 145 – 146,155.

③ 这种不一致之处源于案件中投资者公司人员作为证人,对其飞往塞浦路斯准备股权交易事宜的时间与航班的描述。该证人称当日只有一家从约旦至塞浦路斯的直航航班,而仲裁庭掌握的证据表明,这架航班在当天于黎巴嫩做过一次中途停留。See Ibid. ,paras. 414 – 415.

④ See Ibid. ,para. 536.

⑤ 土耳其出示其动用技侦手段得到的涉案股权先前受益人 Uzan 家族的电子邮件与传真,以表明 Libananco 与该家族的股权交易是在查封扣押行为之后进行的。然而这些书面证据的真实性也遭到了作为 Libananco 的证人的 Hakan Uzan 的强烈质疑。See Ibid. ,para. 441.

treatment,MFN)(以下简称 MFN 条款)[①]可适用于争端解决等程序事项,从而援引东道国与第三方国家 BIT 中对争议解决更为放宽的条件,作为其主张东道国对本争议提交仲裁的同意基础。然而,不同 BIT 中对 MFN 条款在措辞、范围等方面都不甚统一,仲裁庭对 MFN 条款能否及于东道国对提交仲裁的同意的解释莫衷一是。以 Maffezini v. Spain 案[②]和 Siemens v. Argentina 案[③]为代表,仲裁庭强调争端解决条款是在涉案 BIT 项下赋予投资者的权利中重要组成部分,与他们所受待遇紧密联系,因而符合"同类原则",进而认定 MFN 条款代表了东道国对仲裁的同意。[④] 而以 Plama v. Bulgaria 案为典型,明确否认投资者基于 MFN 条款的管辖权请求。该案仲裁庭指出,MFN 条款适用于争端解决程序是一种例外,若要通过 MFN 条款引入第三方条约中的争端解决机制,该条款也必须是明确而不模糊的,能够使缔约方毫不怀疑地认为同意仲裁的意思包含在其中。[⑤]

以上两种针锋相对的观点被后续不同的仲裁庭援引,尤其在 Impregilo v. Argentina 案中激烈碰撞。该案仲裁庭的多数仲裁员援引 Maffezini 案中的论证

---

① MFN 条款是指根据条约,缔约方一方有义务使缔约方另一方国民享受该国给予第三国国民的同等权利。无论何时缔约方给予第三国更优惠的条件,则缔约他方有权享有这种新的更优惠的条件。参见余劲松主编:《国际投资法》,法律出版社 2014 年版,第 246 页。

② 该案中,依 1991 年阿根廷与西班牙 BIT,阿根廷投资者须先向西班牙国内法院寻求救济,并且在 18 个月后也未获裁决的情况下方可提起 ICSID 仲裁。而该投资者依照智利与西班牙 BIT 中"仅需 6 个月磋商期后即可提起 ICSID 仲裁"而援引 MFN 条款,绕开 18 个月的等待期而直接将投资争议向 ICSID 提交仲裁。See Emilio Agustín Maffezini v. The Kingdom of Spain, ICSID Case No. ARB/97/7, Decision of the Tribunal on Objections to Jurisdiction (25 January 2000).

③ 该案中,德国投资者援引阿根廷与智利 BIT 中不要求优先采用当地救济的条件,从而避开德国与阿根廷 BIT 中规定的"争端发生 18 个月内先向阿根廷法院寻求救济"条款,径直向 ICSID 提交仲裁。See Siemens A. G. v. The Argentine Republic, ICSID Case No. ARB/02/8, Decision on Jurisdiction (3 August 2004).

④ 在解释最惠国待遇条款时,两项解释工具经常被使用:一是《维也纳条约法公约》第 31 条确定的"善意解释规则";二是"同类原则"(ejusdem generis principle),即只有在第三方条约与基础条约规定的事项属于同一类别,并且该事项本身须与最惠国待遇相关时,方可援用最惠国待遇条款。参见赵骏:《论双边投资条约中最惠国待遇条款扩张适用于程序性事项》,载《浙江社会科学》2010 年第 7 期。

⑤ 该案中塞浦路斯投资者认为保加利亚与芬兰 BIT 中对提交 ICSID 仲裁的关于征收的争议并未限定范围,而优惠于塞浦路斯与保加利亚 BIT"仅限于征收补偿额的争端提交 ICSID 仲裁"的规定,故援引 MFN 条款申请 ICSID 仲裁。See Plama Consortium Limited v. Republic of Bulgaria, ICSID Case No. ARB/03/24, Decision on Jurisdiction (8 February 2005), paras. 198, 199, 223.

观点和分析方法,认为投资者可以依据 MFN 条款直接对阿根廷提起仲裁。① 而仲裁员 Stern 援引 Plama 案观点并在其反对意见中指出,在没有明确且清晰的仲裁合意表示的情况下,必须对该 MFN 条款进行解释,然而任何对 MFN 条款的"解释"都必须得出该条款无法应用于 BIT 中关于同意的规定。② 纵观上述几个案件的分析论证,可以察觉出仲裁庭就两种不同观点,均试图发展出一种支配同意条款证明的法定证明责任规则,即"除非证明另有明确的消极规定,MFN 条款一般可以适用于争端解决的程序性事项"(肯定规则)或"除非证明另有明确的积极适用规定,MFN 条款一般不可适用于争端解决程序性事项"(否定规则)。依证明责任分配的一般原则,投资者应承担说服仲裁庭 MFN 条款适用与否的责任。通过课以投资者这种要么较轻或要么很重的说服责任,仲裁庭往往回避对争议双方提交的有关 MFN 条款背景材料的审查与解释。

这种通过异化出的证明责任规则来处理对仲裁合意条款文本解释的方法,在 Brandes v. Venezuela 案中的运用尤甚。该案仲裁庭引用 Plama 案的观点,认为"东道国对提交仲裁的同意应当以毫无疑问的方式表达,而且这是'不证自明'的"③。然而,在投资者已向仲裁庭提交了与《委内瑞拉国内投资法》第 22 条(MFN 条款)起草阶段有关的、包括专家意见在内的书面证明材料后,仲裁庭却拒绝对该条款能否囊括对争端解决程序的同意进行深入解释,并认为"该条款本身表述是混乱且不精确的,不可能从语法上解释其包含国家同意仲裁管辖与否","每一项事关该条款的证明材料均未达到该国同意仲裁的证明标准"。④ 从该案证据提供上看,投资者比东道国提供了更为合理的同意仲裁解释;而从裁决书中的论证考察,仲裁庭认为投资者之所以无法满足对仲裁合意的说服责任,总体上缘于其承认了委内瑞拉不断提出的且宽泛的该国历史上长期反对仲

① 该案意大利投资者援引第三方投资条约中的 MFN 条款,绕开了意大利与阿根廷 BIT 中"投资争议须提交阿根廷国内法院,并在未获判决 18 个月后方可提交仲裁"的规定,直接向 ICSID 提起投资仲裁。See Impregilo S. p. A. v. Argentine Republic, ICSID Case No. ARB/07/17, Award (27 June 2011).

② See Impregilo S. p. A. v. Argentine Republic, ICSID Case No. ARB/07/17, Concurring and Dissenting Opinion of Professor Brigitte Stern(20 June 2011), paras. 14 – 17.

③ 该案中,美国投资公司 Brandes 在委内瑞拉政府将其业务国有化后,以委内瑞拉国内投资法的 MFN 条款中比美国与委内瑞拉 BIT 中争端解决条款更为优惠的条件,向 ICSID 仲裁庭主张存在管辖权。Brandes Investment Partners, LP v. Venezuela, ICSID Case No. ARB/08/3, Award (Aug. 2, 2011), paras. 72, 113.

④ See Ibid., paras. 83 – 83, 103, 115.

裁的态度。[①]

可见,通过经典判例中的观点而试图发展出正式的法定证明规则之做法,并未起到平衡投资者与东道国在 ICSID 仲裁管辖权利益上的效果。若适用肯定规则,那么投资者能够轻易地满足说服责任,为投资者通过 MFN 条款扩张管辖权范围大开方便之门。若依据否定规则,投资者显然被课以了极为沉重的说服责任和绝对明确的证明标准,直接后果是阻塞了投资者唯一公平地解决投资纠纷的有效途径。仲裁庭以相对武断的说服责任规则偏好来替代对当事方证据材料的平衡检验与合理解释,容易造成管辖权裁决结果的实质不公。

总而言之,管辖权证明责任适用中业已出现的事实主张者确定困难甚至错误、过重的法定证明责任招致的争议双方间实质不平等、说服责任取代本应对同意仲裁条款作出的合理解释等问题,也是 ICSID 仲裁证据制度自身特点所引致的必然副产品。一方面,ICSID 制度在证明责任的适用上为仲裁庭留有极大的裁量空间且不同背景的仲裁员在证明责任运用的方法与范围上难免有所出入。另一方面,被赋予较大自由裁量权的仲裁庭,面对具体个案时也常选择性地引用先前裁决,而这些先例中对法定证明责任的适用方式,可能因案情与证据获取情况等方面的不同而并非适合于当前案件。

四、ICSID 管辖权争议中证明责任适用的方法完善与规则构建

对于上述管辖权争议中证明责任适用的突出问题,ICSID 制度自身的裁决撤销机制所能提供的矫正效果极为有限。尽管 ICSID 公约第 52 条规定了对可能的错误裁决可启动撤销程序予以救济,[②]然而该条款中"严重地背离基本程序规则""仲裁庭显然超越其权力"等撤销事由只是蕴含了要求仲裁庭在作出裁决过程中不能过于偏离国际诉讼与仲裁在证明规则上普遍采用的做法,受到裁决不利的一方很难通过主张证明责任分配上的偏颇,使作为 ICSID 的裁决监督机构的特别委员会认定该裁决达到了"严重"或"显然"的错误程度。实际上,IC-

---

① Brandes Investment Partners, LP v. Venezuela, ICSID Case No. ARB/08/3, Award (Aug. 2, 2011), paras. 75 – 78, 106.

② 参见 ICSID 公约第 52 条第 1 款规定:"任何一方可以根据下列一个或几个理由,向秘书长提出书面申请,要求撤销裁决:(一)仲裁庭的组成不适当;(二)仲裁庭显然超越其权力;(三)仲裁庭的成员有受贿行为;(四)有严重的背离基本程序规则的情况;(五)裁决未陈述其所依据的理由。"

SID 裁决撤销机制的预设功能是关注程序性问题,最终的裁决结果是否具有实质上的抽象正确性不在其评价范围之内。① 有的特别委员会就曾指出,其不认为仲裁庭应被要求在解决争议过程中强制适用任何特定的证明责任或证明标准。② 前文 Caratube 案的投资者以证明责任过重为由提出撤销裁决请求后,该案特别委员会亦维持了原仲裁庭在证明责任上的认定。③ Impregilo 案特别委员会亦表示,撤销裁决作为一种特殊的补救机制,应当保持对裁决终局性的尊重。④ 故此,在现有 ICSID 仲裁框架内对管辖权争议中证明责任的适用失范加以克服,只宜从原仲裁庭的裁判规则与方法上寻求突破。

ICSID 仲裁作为"私人—主权国家"型争议主体所决定的国际公法性质的争端解决机制,其突出的特点是不存在一个具有一般管辖权的审理机构,也不存在预见性较强的一整套法律规范。不似私人性质的商事仲裁管辖权问题可以被国内法中强制性的支持仲裁政策所克服,⑤也不像国内法院在面对国家成为被告时所援引的主权豁免制度,ICSID 仲裁管辖权是一种有限的管辖权,它必须在确保提供给投资者以唯一获得起诉国家的救济机会、贯彻国家有限同意参与仲裁的意图之间作出权衡。ICSID 仲裁适用的是措辞极为简约、许多概念与规则未明确界定的投资条约为主的国际法,其相较于适用准据法为各国国内法的国际商事仲裁而言,在操作上具有模糊性,在裁决上缺乏可预见性。⑥ 基于以上特质,ICSID 仲裁管辖权裁决规则参考同样依国际公法解决纠纷,也仅具备有

---

① See R Doak Bishop & Silvia Marchili, *Annulment Under the ICSID Convention*, Oxford University Press 2012, p. 4, 94, 130. See also David D Caron, Reputation and Reality in the ICSID Annulment Process: Understanding the Distinction Between Annulment and Appeal, ICSID Review 21, 1992(7), p. 24.

② See Continental Casualty Company v. The Argentine Republic, ICSID Case No. ARB/03/9, Decision on the Application for Partial Annulment and the Application for Partial Annulment (16 September 2011), para. 135.

③ See Caratube International Oil Company LLP v. The Republic of Kazakhstan, ICSID Case No. ARB/08/12, Decision on the Annulment (21 February 2014), paras. 261 – 274.

④ See Impregilo S. p. A. v. Argentine Republic, ICSID Case No. ARB/07/17, Decision on Annulment (24 January 2014), para. 118.

⑤ 当今主要发达国家,对案件的可仲裁性和仲裁条款的适用范围上的争议,总体上越发倾向以支持仲裁的立场加以解决。See Edward M. Morgan, Contract Theory and the Sources of Rights: An Approach to the Arbitrability Question, 60 S. CAL. L. Rev (1987), p. 1059, 1061.

⑥ 参见袁杜娟:《投资条约仲裁对"国际商事仲裁"之借鉴与改革》,载《上海财经大学学报》2012 年第 1 期。

限管辖权的 ICJ 与国际仲裁庭对证明责任的适用方式,不失为一条突破现有证明责任适用失范局面的有效进路。

(一)通过善意推定以强化举证证明责任在管辖权要件上的优先适用

强加给投资者严格的说服责任所导致的程序地位不平等问题,根本上还是源于仲裁庭回避或无法进行清楚的事实发现,而最后不得不援用法定证明责任规则。此种困境可以通过运用“善意推定”这一国际公法上的裁判方法加以破解。依善意推定,一国的所有行为都应被认作更有可能是正常的、与国际法相一致的,与此相反的主张须由其提出人加以证明。[①] 善意推定规则的法律渊源是国际条约、[②]国际习惯以及 ICJ 的判例,其在 ICJ 与法庭若干案件中获得承认与适用。[③] 而 ICSID 仲裁庭作为国际法上的争端解决机构,根据 ICSID 公约第 42 条第 1 款的规定,其有权力适用可能适用的国际法规则。善意推定运用于 ICSID 仲裁中,是预设投资者在投资有关的交易中的行为是诚实与合理的,一旦东道国提出了与此推定相左的反驳主张,则其需要承担相应的举证证明责任。[④] 由此,善意推定可以推动仲裁各方就案情进行积极的攻防举证,从而成为一种有效的事实发现工具。

在 ICSID 仲裁管辖权的证明中适用善意推定规则,在不违反证明责任分配一般原理的同时,又可避免课以投资者畸高的说服责任所产生的实质不公,因为推定制度本身不转移法定证明责任,而仅转移举证证明责任。在英美法系,

---

① 参见郑斌:《国际法院与法庭适用的一般法律原则》,韩秀丽、蔡从燕译,法律出版社 2012 年版,第 313 ~ 315 页。

② 1969 年《维也纳条约法公约》第 26 条就提及该善意推定,即“每一生效条约对当事方均有约束力,必须善意履行”。该公约第 27 条还补充道:“条约缔约方不得援引其国内法的规定作为其不履行条约的理由”。

③ See Cf. P. C. A: North Atlantic Coast Fisheries Case (1910), 1 H. C. R., p. 141, 157. See also PCIJ: German Interests Case (Merits) (1926) A. 7, p. 30; See also ICJ: Corfu Channel Case (Merits) (1949) D. O. by Ecer, ICJ Reports 1949, p. 4, at 119.

④ See Frédéric G Sourgens, Reason & Reasonableness, the Necessary Diversity of the Common Law (2014) 67 Maine L. Rev. 73.

经过长期学术争论与司法斗争,[①]最终由美国《联邦证据规则》第301条确认了"即使存在推定,也不能转移说服责任和整个案件的法定证明责任"的结论性立法,[②]此后虽偶有个案突破该规定,但这一权威立法仍得到广泛的恪守;在大陆法系,德国学者认为法官的任务是从实体法规范中区分与界定隐含其中的证明责任规范而无权创造,推定的效果也不是证明责任的转移或免除。[③] 而日本较为流行的"修正的证据提出说",也只是更加强调具有一定证明力的反驳才可以转移提出证据责任。[④] 可见,两大法系经典主流观点均认为,推定不能转移含有说服责任内涵的法定证明责任。推定之所以能够转移举证证明责任,是由于在当事人提出证据对基础事实加以证明后,仲裁庭运用善意推定规则得出了对投资者有利的推定要件事实,投资者暂时无须进一步对要件事实予以举证,而东道国为反驳此善意推定事实,必须对其提供有一定说服力的证据。可以说,善意推定对阻却东道国提出无充分证据且对仲裁员心证形成不利影响的反驳意见,具有相当重要的作用。

具体到ICSID管辖权适格投资要件上,前文Caratube案仲裁庭更为合理的证明责任运用方法是对投资者Hourani拥有CIOC公司92%股权的事实进行善意推定,得出该投资者拥有公司控制权的推定事实,使得投资者的法定证明责任暂时得以解除,举证证明责任交由作为被申请人的东道国承担,以促使其向仲裁庭出示更为全面的证据。该案东道国对其提出所谓"掌握公司实际控制权另有其人"的反驳,须提供具有一定证明力的证据加以支持。仲裁庭在权衡推定事实与反驳事实两者间证据说服力后,得出的倾向性结论才能被视为经过了

---

① 英美学术界对推定能否转移整体上的证明责任存在大致四种学说:(1)塞耶学说,即推定只转移提证责任而不转移说服责任;(2)摩根学说,主张"强推定"与"超级推定"能够转移证明责任;(3)波伦学说,主张基于经验法则的推定转移提证责任,按公共政策的推定转移证明责任;(4)艾伦学说,建议法官抛弃推定,在个案中便宜分配证明责任。参见张乐乐:《民事推定规范研究》,南京大学2015年博士学位论文,第162~165页。

② 该条规定:"在所有民事诉讼中,除国会制定法或本证据规则另有规定外,一项推定赋予其针对的当事人举证反驳或满足该推定的责任,但未向该当事人转移未履行说服责任即需承担风险意义上的证明责任,该证明责任仍由在审判过程中原先承担的当事人承担。"参见《美国联邦刑事诉讼规则和证据规则》,卞建林译,中国政法大学出版社1996年版,第104页。

③ 参见[德]普维庭:《现代证明责任问题》,吴越译,法律出版社2006年版,第32、73页;[德]莱奥·罗森贝克:《证明责任论——以德国民法典和民事诉讼法典为基础撰写》,庄敬华译,中国法制出版社2002年版,第224~227页。

④ 参见叶峰、叶自强:《推定对举证责任分担的影响》,载《法学研究》2002年第3期。

审慎事实检验,也更具有实体结果的正当性。同理,Libannaco 案的东道国,亦应承担对投资者无记名股权系欺诈所得和股权取得系发生在该国军警强制措施之后的这两项反驳意见的举证证明责任。仲裁庭凭借善意推定,使东道国出示更多的证据,以此缓解投资者在适格投资要件上承担过重的总体证明责任,维持争议双方在举证方面的大体平等。

而对于由事实主张者确认困难所引起的要件事实上的法定证明责任争议,同样可以通过强化双方的举证证明责任来加以解决。具言之,仲裁庭应尽可能地向仲裁双方强调其各自的举证证明责任,运用推定事实以暂时解除某要件事实主张者的法定证明责任,促使对方当事人将各自掌握的全部证据向仲裁庭展示,从而进行动态上的证据分量权衡,以查清管辖权的某一要件事实。[①] 国际投资仲裁实践中,也已存在这种搁置法定证明责任分配的案例。较早的 Grand River v. United States 案中,虽然争议双方对管辖权要件事实的证明责任之负担问题僵持不下,但是鉴于双方在仲裁程序中业已展示出充足的证据,仲裁庭未分配证明责任而作出了最终事实认定,且该案也并未因证明责任问题被提出撤销裁决请求。[②] Muhammet Cap v. Turkmenistan 案的仲裁庭也指出,其不认为管辖权的法定证明责任应课以仲裁的任意一方,而应通过比较双方提出证据分量大小和论证过程,权衡管辖权的确立与否。[③] 这种动态强化双方举证证明责任的"中间立场",在特定情况下有助于纾解特殊管辖权要件事实上证明责任分配的两难境况。

(二)以举证证明责任来促进对仲裁合意条款的深入解释

前文 Impregilo 案和 Brandes 案仲裁庭对 MFN 条款能否扩展至提交仲裁合意的裁决出发点,是试图创设出一种国际投资仲裁上正式的法定证明责任,而不是对条款本身是否包含合意表示的解释。仲裁庭这种针对一方当事人而预设的主观标准,使同意仲裁要件的裁断结果很难具有较强的说服力。

---

① See Frederic G. Sourgens, By Equal Contest of Arms: Jurisdictional Proof in Investor – State Arbitrations, 38 N. C. J. Int' L L. & Com. Reg. 875(2013), p. 952 – 953.

② See Grand River Enterprises Six Nations, Ltd. et al. v. United States, NAFTA/UNCITRAL Arbitration, Decision on Jurisdiction(20 July 2006), para. 37.

③ See Muhammet Cap & Sehil Insaat Endustri ve Ticaret Ltd. Sti. v. Turkmenistan, ICSID Case No. ARB/12/6, Decision on Jurisdiction under Article VII(2) (13 February 2015), paras. 119 – 120.

解决这一问题需要进行规则适用上的转变:仲裁庭不任意适用法定证明责任,而是通过运用举证证明责任,将重点置于理解决定管辖权成立与否的国际法上。ICJ 在判例中所采用的方法,为此提供了答案。PCIJ[①] 在审理 Factory at Chorzów 一案时最先指出了 ICJ 确定自身管辖权的一般法律解释规则:"考虑是否具有管辖权时,法庭始终的目的是确定当事方是否存在向其赋予管辖权的意图。如果这种意图能够以一种具有说服力的方式表现出来,那么就不需要考虑可能存在的质疑管辖权无效这一问题。"[②]而且该案法庭基于争议双方通过具体举证所提供的解释材料,运用一种盖然性标准来对待管辖权问题:"为建立管辖权,法庭必须考虑一系列因素,包括仲裁条约的历史发展、这些条约的术语学问题、字面上的语法和逻辑意思、可归因于缔约双方对管辖权同意的功能意图。"[③]有学者对该案解读道,Factory at Chorzów 案所采方法的关键要素是承认事关同意管辖的法律具有不确定性。对于这种不确定性的克服,是通过对比与解释双方当事人关于管辖权的主张和反对主张,最终宣布两者中更可能的一方(而不是"正确的"一方)为管辖权交锋中的胜利者。[④]

以此方法回溯考察 ICSID 仲裁合意问题,实际上在任何特定案件中,对涉及管辖权问题的法律解释都可以支持主张截然相反结果的论点。单独来看,这两种观点均非明显错误的或不可信的。相反,每一种观点都会更多地利用对同意仲裁的解读,以赢得这场投资者步入唯一法律救济渠道和东道国让渡有限的主权间的竞争。又由于不同案件中的涉案投资条约在措辞、上下文背景与立法政策等方面均有所不同,仲裁庭对争议双方就 ICSID 仲裁合意条款提供解释的对比结果就无法具备一致性。这也就说明了在 MFN 条款是否及于同意仲裁问题上,创设固定课予一方当事人的说服责任、过于追求裁决结果一致性做法缘何失败。

在 ICSID 仲裁中运用对同意仲裁条款的盖然性解释方法,要将重点置于争

---

① PCIJ 是根据 1920 年《常设国际法院规约》成立的解决国际争端的常设司法机构,位于海牙,1922 年开始运作。PCIJ 审理由于条约的解释、有关国际法的问题、违反国际义务等事项产生的争端。第二次世界大战期间停止活动,战后为 ICJ 所取代。

② Factory at Chorz6w (Ger. v. Pol.),1927 P. C. I. J. (Ser. A) No. 9 (July 26),p. 89.

③ Ibid.,p. 64.

④ See Martti Koskenniemi,FROM APOLOGY TO UTOPIA (2d ed. 2005),p. 467 – 473.

议双方对条款文本各自解释立场的对比上。根据《维也纳条约法公约》第 31 条规定,“条约应根据条约文本通常所具有的含义,结合条约的目标和宗旨被善意地予以解释”。在管辖权争议的双方当事人依赖语义和语法而对同意仲裁条款进行解释后,仲裁庭可以要求双方对其观点进一步举证,根据他们各自提供的书面材料与证人证言,就涉案协定中同意仲裁相关部分进行上下文比对,以发现一方的解释与条约的其他规定之间可能产生矛盾,从而权衡出说服力较强的一种解释。同时,ICSID 仲裁庭可以参阅过去的仲裁裁决的相关争议点来测试本案双方提出的论证,通过类比过去的案例的方式来区分或确认现在本案的权衡解释观点。[①] 通常情况下,任何一方当事人都不能提出完全优于另一方当事人的解释。这种通过敦促双方提供更多背景证据而进行综合解释的模式,使管辖权分析中的盖然性标准变得具体而丰满,也使最终裁决更具有合理性。

(三)法定证明责任仅应在具体管辖权要件上进行兜底适用

证明责任制度本身的产生,源自裁判者对待证事实的认识手段不足与认识能力局限,[②]其中的法定证明责任更是旨在对事实真伪不明或是无法说服裁判者后的不利后果的承担。[③] 然而,不似国内法上对相应的实体权利义务关系作出证明责任分配的明文规定,ICSID 公约本身的证明责任适用规则尚付阙如。

在目前的 ICSID 仲裁管辖权认定实践中,存在争议双方之间对整体管辖权分配证明责任和不明确课以一方整体证明责任的两种方式。在前一种方式中,仲裁庭机械地调用国内法理中的法定证明责任概念,以取代对涉案投资条约中相关条款进行深入解释、充分对比与权衡争议双方就要件事实所提出的证据,除了可能造成争议双方程序地位严重失衡以外,也很可能致使其作出管辖权裁决建立在事实认定不明、法律含义不清的基础上。这就意味着仲裁庭未能有效行使 ICSID 公约第 42 条赋予的裁决职能,以法律含义模糊为由作出不甚清楚

① See Frédéric G. Sourgens, Keep the Faith, Investment Protection Following the Denunciation of International Investment Agreements, 11 Santa Clara J. Int'l L.

② 参见[德]莱奥·罗森贝克:《证明责任论——以德国民法典和民事诉讼法典为基础撰写》,庄敬华译,中国法制出版社 2002 年版,第 1、2 页。

③ 大陆法系只能在事实真伪不明时求诸证明责任分配理论,英美法系在陪审团、对抗式庭审和法官高权威性等因素作用下,以是否满足说服责任为标准仅区分事实存在与不存在,并运用推定这一重要的事实发现工具,根据具体案情来辅助证明责任的分配。参见曹志勋:《“真伪不明”在我国民事证明制度中确实存在么?》,载《法学家》2013 年第 2 期。

的裁决。①

不对任何一方事先课以法定证明责任的方式，更为符合运用国际公法解决纠纷、仅具备有限管辖权的ICSID仲裁。这种方式借鉴了ICJ依据国际法对国家间领土争端的做法。ICJ在"渔场案管辖权裁决"（Fisheries Jurisdiction）中认为，"尽管提出主张者应对相关事实承担证明责任，但这与国际法院的管辖权无关，该管辖权是一个根据相关事实来解决的法律问题"②。ICJ不预先对整体管辖权分配法定证明责任的观点，被诸多ICSID仲裁庭援引，③其中具有代表性的CSOB v. Slovak案仲裁庭直接指出："对于仲裁双方是否有效地表达了其接受ICSID管辖，不能由国内法相关内容与原则来确定，而应由ICSID公约第25条这一国际法规来掌管。"④由此，具体案件中也就不存在对ICSID整体管辖权这一法律问题的证明责任，而只涉及对决定管辖权的相关事实的证明。

同时须明确，在仲裁庭运用举证证明责任对适格国籍、合法投资等管辖权要件事实进行充分调查与证据权衡后，抑或对仲裁合意的要件事实依靠更为翔实的证据予以充分解释后，认定作为仲裁申请人的投资者仍未就该事实进行更具盖然性的证明，方宜凭借法定证明责任对其作出不利的管辖权裁定。将优先适用举证证明责任与兜底适用法定证明责任相结合，管辖权要件事实的认定才能更为公正与合理。

---

① ICSID公约第42条第2款规定："仲裁庭不得借口法律无明文规定或含义不清而暂不作出裁定。"

② 在西班牙诉加拿大的渔场国际仲裁案中，ICJ认为："尽管法庭认为仲裁庭不受当事人争论的束缚而由自身决定行使管辖权是毋庸置疑的，但其不能容忍被要求课予申请人以管辖权的证明责任……尽管一方当事人对其主张的事实需要担负举证责任，但这与国际法庭的管辖权确立不具有相关性，后者是一个根据各个相关事实而待解决的法律问题……对于管辖权的事项，法庭将根据所有事实和考虑所有争论后而做出决定。"Fisheries Jurisdiction（Spain v. Canada），1998 I. C. J. at paras. 450 – 451.

③ See ADF Group Inc. v. United States, ICSID Case No. ARB（AF）/00/1, Award（9 January 2003）, para. 145; Impregilo S. p. A. v. Pakistan, ICSID Case No. ARB/03/3, Decision on Jurisdiction（22 April 2005）, para. 241; See Saipem S. p. A. v. People's Republic of Bangladesh, ICSID Case No. ARB/05/07, Decision on Jurisdiction（21 March 2007）, para. 14; Inmaris Perestroika Sailing Maritime Services GmbH and Ors v. Ukraine, ICSID Case No. ARB/08/8, Decision on Jurisdiction（8 March 2010）, paras. 57 – 59.

④ See Ceskoslovenska Obchodni Banka, A. S.（CSOB）v. The Slovak Republic, ICSID Case No. ARB/97/4, Decision of the Tribunal on Objections to Jurisdiction（24 May, 1999）, para. 35.

五、结论

由于公约条款的缺位和对证明责任内涵的认识不足，部分 ICSID 仲裁庭在面对管辖权问题时裁量失当，以设置法定证明责任取代本应在各管辖权要件事实上的全面与审慎的判断，由此造成争议双方程序地位失调、裁决结果不公且缺乏说服力的困境。仲裁庭应在管辖权要件事实的判定上优先适用举证证明责任，这一过程既要对当事人各自主张的法律理论价值深入理解，也需对据以左右法律理论的事实证据加以均衡分析。只有通过对各方当事人提出的证据进行比较而得出的裁决结果，才更为合理与公平。诚然，ICSID 公约赋予仲裁庭在证据事项上广泛的裁量空间和 ICSID 仲裁判例法体系的尚未成熟，举证证明责任优先适用、法定证明责任兜底适用这一更为合理的裁判规则尚不可能为所有仲裁庭采纳。不过，只要更多的仲裁庭能够对法定证明责任的误用与滥用予以克制，更加重视管辖权证明的动态举证过程，就能有效避免本文所列举的证明责任适用中产生的突出失范问题。

中国在国际投资仲裁中适用第三方资助的法理基础与实践审视

汤 霞*

摘 要:第三方资助是一把“双刃剑”,既为处于经济困境或意图分担投资仲裁风险的申请人提供了接近正义的机会,也因缺乏规制可能损害被申请人的利益。国际社会目前日渐重视对第三方资助的利用及对其负面影响的规制。在“一带一路”建设的推进过程中,投资仲裁需求的推动、国际仲裁市场的竞争压力以及降低仲裁成本的考量使得中国在投资仲裁中适用第三方资助极为必要,而域外经验的借鉴、国内软法的推进、法无禁止即可为原则的赋权以及完善的承认执行机制等为我国在投资仲裁中适用第三方资助提供了可行性。我国应在条件成熟时赋予第三方资助合法地位,提升我国建立亚太国际仲裁中心的竞争力。

关键词:国际投资仲裁 第三方资助 接近正义 披露

投资者与国家间的争议解决(Investor - State Dispute Settlement, ISDS)因费用高昂、耗时较长而给当事方带来较大的经济负担。虽然我国目前所涉投资仲裁案件不多,但随着习近平主席在2013年提出共建“丝绸之路经济带”和“21世纪海上丝绸之路”的倡议,以及2015年国家发展和改革委员会、外交部、商务部联合发布《推动共建丝绸之路经济带和21世纪海上丝绸之路的愿景与行

* 汤霞,法学博士,华南师范大学法学院特聘副研究员。

动》,鼓励本国企业到"一带一路"沿线国家投资并欢迎沿线各国企业到中国投资之后,沿线各国的投资明显增加。从联合国贸易和发展会议(United Nations Conference on Trade and Development,UNCTAD)国际投资争端数据库的统计数据来看,"一带一路"沿线国作为被申请人的案件占全球投资案件的54.4%,①表明沿线国面临的投资争议较多。由于"一带一路"沿线国的法制基础较为薄弱,我国在推进"一带一路"建设的过程中与沿线国的投资争议可能增多。投资仲裁领域日益普遍的第三方资助可为有需要的投资者提供资金支持,以促进投资争议的及时有效解决。从现有研究来看,国内外学者们多是对第三方资助投资仲裁的具体法律问题如披露、费用担保以及费用分配等问题进行研究,②还未有学者结合第三方资助发展的最新实践探讨其在中国关涉投资仲裁程序的适用问题。本文的写作目的在于分析中国在国际投资仲裁中适用第三方资助的必要性和可行性,为第三方资助在我国的合法化提供学术支撑。本文主要分为四部分,首先从学理角度考察中国在国际投资仲裁中适用第三方资助的法理基础,其次分析中国在国际投资仲裁中适用第三方资助的必要性和可行性,最后结合最新实践探讨第三方资助在我国的发展前景。

一、中国在国际投资仲裁中适用第三方资助的法理基础

ISDS中投资者和国家间主体的不对等性以及高昂的投资仲裁费用等给投资者带来了较大的经济负担。申请人投资者受制于经济困境可能无法提起投资仲裁请求维护自身权益,资助者为申请人提供资金使其获得了接近正义的机

---

① UNCTAD Date Center, at http://unctadstat. unctad. org/wds/ReportFolders/reportFolders. aspx?sCS_ChosenLang = en(Last visited on 10 August,2020).

② 国内学者主要有:张亮、杨子希:《第三方资助国际仲裁的费用担保问题研究》,载《国际经济法学刊》2020年第2期;范冰仪:《论国际投资仲裁中第三方资助披露问题》,载《国际商务研究》2020年第2期;汤霞:《第三方资助国际投资仲裁费用担保的必要性标准研究》,载《国际经济法学刊》2019年第3期;肖芳:《国际投资仲裁第三方资助的规制困境与出路——以国际投资仲裁"正当性危机"及其改革为背景》,载《政法论坛》2017年第6期。国外学者主要有:Inna Uchkunova, "Allocation of Costs in ICSID Arbitration", *Kluwer Arbitration Blog*, December 3,2014; Jenny Power, "Investment Arbitration – Determination of Costs in ICSID Arbitration", *Australian Yearbook on International Arbitration*,2010; Jonas von Goeler, "Security for Costs and Third – Party Funding", *Kluwer Law International*,2016; Maxi Scherer, "Third – Party Funding in International Arbitration Towards Mandatory Disclosure of Funding Agreements?", *Kluwer Law International*,2013.

会。同时,鉴于资助者的营利本性,其可能资助骚扰性的主张损害被申请人利益。随着第三方资助在国际投资仲裁领域的适用日渐普遍,国际社会也意识到对第三方资助进行规制以维持投资者和东道国利益平衡的重要性。这两方面的考虑反映了第三方资助投资仲裁蕴含的法理。

(一)接近正义

"接近正义"运动最初出现在20世纪六七十年代的西方国家,其目的是改善传统诉讼的繁杂、拖沓和高昂的费用,为人们提供更为高效便捷的救济途径。[①] 西方国家围绕更好地保护个体接近正义的权利进行了三次司法改革,推动了"司法社会化"的趋势,越来越多的人倾向于选择司法的替代方式如仲裁来解决纠纷。但由于低收入群体的基数庞大,接近正义这一运动对于贫困群体的巨大司法需求而言仍是杯水车薪。因此,让一部分社会资金参与进来,通过投资诉讼或仲裁主张的方式来获得相应收益,不仅有助于贫困的申请人获得接近正义的机会,也增加了多元化争议解决机制如仲裁的利用频率。[②]

随着经济全球化的进一步扩张,投资者的跨国投资活动也日益频繁,加剧了纠纷的复杂性和耗时性,仲裁所需费用也日益高昂。在诉讼领域具有成熟实践的第三方资助顺势而为,为有资金需求的争议方提供资金支持,并根据案件结果获得收益,在国际投资仲裁领域具有庞大的市场需求。第三方资助增加了申请人保护其权利的机会,处于资金困境或意图通过外部资金分担仲裁风险的申请人都可从第三方资助中受益。资助者通过尽职调查对案件的选择犹如一个"过滤器",只投资"有胜诉前景"的主张,这一过程过滤掉了骚扰性或无价值的主张,对社会和被申请人来说都是有益的。因为它使得有价值的主张有接近正义的机会,挫败骚扰性的主张以避免被申请人承担不必要的损失。我国投资者在对外投资的过程中若与东道国发生投资争议,也可寻求第三方资助来分担风险保持资金流动。

(二)投资者和东道国的利益平衡原则

国际投资仲裁的高风险高回报吸引了第三方资助者的参与。资助者为了

---

① 参见张鸿绪:《"接近正义"视阈下我国大调解格局的制度构想》,载《西南石油大学学报(社会科学版)》2014年第1期。

② 参见高陈:《接近正义——美国纽约州法院司法改革项目研究》,中国政法大学出版社2015年版,第74~87页。

获得利益的最大化,通常会对案件的管理、申请人律师的选择以及仲裁员的任命等施加一定影响。资助者参与投资仲裁程序可能导致投资者和东道国利益的不平衡:首先,双方承担风险的不平衡。在 ISDS 之下,来自西方发达国家的投资者提出的投资主张很少被驳回,[①]在大多数情况下仲裁裁决中的数额由国家来负担。[②] 国际投资仲裁中申请人对仲裁员的直接决定权、国际投资仲裁裁决一裁终局的效力以及完善的承认执行机制等特性,使得资助者在资助案件胜诉时可以获得可观的利润,而风险只是其投入的成本。[③] 资助者通常和投资者约定败诉时不承担不利费用,即使东道国胜诉也可能面临仲裁费用无法获得补偿的风险。因此,第三方资助被一些仲裁员视为"赌徒的天堂"(Gambers' Paradise)也不足为奇。[④] 其次,双方获得资助机会的不平衡。由于国家通常作为被诉方且很难提起反请求,资助者为了获得最大收益通常资助申请人一方。资助者为投资者提供资金支持一定程度上导致了投资仲裁案件的增加,一些对抗国家的骚扰性主张也在资助者的资助下被提起,国家不得不投入大量的人力和财力应对。最后,裁决赔偿资金来源的不平衡。在 ISDS 之下,第三方资助者的利润来自败诉国和其公民,东道国的纳税人是败诉裁决的最终承担者,国家公共财政流向非 ISDS 体制内的受益者——私人资助者,甚至可能影响一国的国家政策或社会公共利益。而若申请人败诉,则其赔偿来源仅是其股东,影响较小。

为了维护东道国的利益,近年来一些区域贸易协定如《跨大西洋贸易和投资伙伴协议》(Transatlantic Trade and Investment Partnership,TTIP)以及《综合性经济贸易协议》(Comprehensive Economic and Trade Agreement,CETA)等都包含了要求披露第三方资助的条款,国际知名仲裁机构的仲裁规则也对第三方资

① See Richel Denae Thrasher, "The Regulation of Third Party Funding: Gathering Data for Future Analysis and Reform", *Boston College Law Review*, 2018, p. 5.

② Ibid.

③ See Frank J. Garcia & Kirrin Hough, "The Case Against Third – Party Funding in Investment Arbitration", *Columbia FDI Perspectives on Topical Foreign Direct Investment Issues*, No. 253, June 3, 2019.

④ See Gavan Griffith draws this analogy in RSM Production Corporation v. St. Lucia, ICSID Case No. ARB/12/10.

助进行了规制,[①]要求受资助者披露资助者的存在和资助协议的相关条款,当受资助者存在不当行为时仲裁庭可通过费用担保和费用分配来加重申请人的费用责任,避免申请人利用第三方资助滥诉。新加坡和中国香港还通过立法的方式明确受资助者和资助者的披露义务。[②] 上述规定对规范受资助者的行为,保障东道国的利益起到了积极作用。因此,当外国投资者利用第三方资助资金对我国提起投资仲裁时,我国须从保护本国利益出发,要求受资助者进行披露。

二、中国在国际投资仲裁中适用第三方资助的必要性

我国目前已是兼具资本输出和输入双重身份的投资大国,中国投资者主动提起和中国作为东道国被动应诉的案件也将与日俱增,但我国目前还未正视第三方资助的作用。我国国内立法中未赋予第三方资助相应的合法地位,也不存在限制第三方资助对投资仲裁程序带来不利影响的规制措施。在第三方资助日益产业化和被广泛应用于投资仲裁的背景下,其在我国有一定的市场需求,尤其是我国"一带一路"建设的推进,沿线国家投资争议的增加使得这种需求更为迫切。

(一)投资仲裁需求的推动

根据 2019 年世界投资报告的统计数据,中国的吸引外资量和对外投资量均位居世界第二。[③] 我国近年来对"一带一路"沿线国家累计投资达 986.2 亿美元,国内投资者在沿线国设立境外企业超 1 万家。[④] 我国对外投资的主体既包括国有企业也包括相当一部分民营企业,且投资领域日益多元化。但我国企业在对外投资的同时也面临不小的风险和挑战。一方面,近年来一些国家保护主义盛行,以国家安全为由严格审查中国对外投资企业,影响了我国的对外投资。另一方面,中国企业与国外跨国公司相比在竞争力和抗风险能力上还有待增强。尤其是"一带一路"沿线国家政治不稳定、法律制度不完善,投资风险较大。

---

① 如新加坡国际仲裁中心、香港国际仲裁中心、ICSID、中国国际经济贸易仲裁委员会、北京仲裁委员会等仲裁机构颁布的仲裁规则都出现了对第三方资助的规制条款。

② 香港律政司 2018 年 12 月 3 日公布《2018 年〈2017 年仲裁及调解法例(第三方资助)(修订)条例〉(生效日期)公告》,新加坡发布 2017 年《民法(修正)法案》和《民法(第三方资助)规则》。

③ See World Investment Report 2019, p. 2 – 4.

④ 参见商务部:《中企对"一带一路"沿线国家直接投资超过 900 亿美元》,载中新网,https://www.chinanews.com/gn/2019/04-18/8813147.shtml。

中国投资者与"一带一路"东道国间产生了大量的投资争议,许多在建项目因战争或政府更迭被迫中止,中国投资者损失惨重。

我国投资者向国际投资争端解决中心(The International Center for Settlement of Investment Disputes ICSID)或其他国际仲裁机构相继提起了平安诉比利时案、北京城建诉也门政府案等投资仲裁案件。上述案件中我国投资者尚未借助第三方资助分担仲裁风险,漫长的仲裁程序和高昂的仲裁费用使得我国企业面临巨大的经济压力。随着"一带一路"投资争议的日益增多,一方面,我国投资者遇到的投资争议将逐渐增加;另一方面,我国吸引外资的力度逐渐加大,作为被诉东道国的可能性也将增加。对此,我国要未雨绸缪,积极利用第三方资助,减轻投资者的经济压力,同时也须防范我国作为被诉东道国时面临的仲裁风险。

(二)国际仲裁市场的竞争压力

目前,接近正义的价值目标已被人们广泛接受。美国最高法院首席大法官在2013年指出,诉诸法庭是一项权利,国家不应妨碍个人行使这项权利。① 很多司法辖区如英格兰、威尔士、澳大利亚、加拿大和美国等都已取消了禁止助讼和包揽诉讼这一普通法原则,允许第三方资助。例如,在英格兰和威尔士,若将资助协议等同于助讼或包揽诉讼,必须存在不适当的因素,如资助者获得不成比例的利润或资助者过度控制案件等。澳大利亚法院积极认可第三方资助,其指出即便资助者既给当事方的诉讼提供资金也控制诉讼,仍不违反公共政策。②

取消禁止助讼和包揽诉讼的做法也延伸至仲裁领域,为第三方资助在该领域的迅速增长提供了合法性基础。新加坡通过立法在国际仲裁中允许第三方资助,意在推动其作为世界主要国际仲裁地的优势,增强与中国香港争夺亚洲国际仲裁中心的竞争力。中国香港也积极更新立法,允许第三方资助适用于仲裁地位于香港的仲裁,为寻求此类投资的资助者和缺乏资金提起仲裁的当事方提供机会。亚洲日益增加的投资流动以及双边和多边投资条约的盛行,表明纠纷解决也将更多地向这一地区转移。我国内地若想成为亚太国际仲裁中心,也

① Lord Neuberger, From Barretry, *Maintenance and Champerty to Litigation Funding*, Gray's Inn Speech, 2013, p. 5.

② James Rogers, *International Arbitration Report*, Norton Rose Fulbright, 2016, p. 9.

须适时对第三方资助问题进行回应,为投资者提供仲裁友好型国家的比较优势,进一步提升自身竞争力。

(三)降低仲裁成本的考量

根据 Jeffery 的研究数据,ICSID 仲裁案件从登记到裁决,ICSID 程序的平均持续时间为 3.75 年,即 1370 天;联合国国际贸易法委员会(United Nations Commission on International Trade Law,UNCITRAL)程序下从仲裁通知到裁决作出的平均持续时间为 3.96 年,即 1446 天;斯德哥尔摩商会仲裁院(Arbitration Institute of Stockholm Chamber of Commerce,SCC)裁决的投资案例平均时长为自登记之日起至最终裁决之日止 21 个月。① 伴随着漫长投资仲裁程序的是高昂的仲裁费用。2014 年 Matthew 的研究指出,投资仲裁中申请人的平均费用约为 440 万美元,被申请人的平均费用为 450 万美元。② 2017 年 Matthew 的研究数据显示投资仲裁当事人的平均费用较 2014 年相比有所增加,申请人平均费用为 740 万美元,较 2014 年增幅达 68%,被申请人的平均费用为 520 万美元,也比 2014 年增加了 16%。③ 高昂的仲裁费用对申请人和被申请人来说都是不小的负担。以尤科斯诉俄罗斯案为例,申请人的律师费用就高达近 6000 万美元,④对主权国家来说尚且不堪重负,对中小企业而言更是无力承担。国际投资仲裁的高额费用和漫长的仲裁程序使其饱受诟病。第三方资助者的参与在一定程度上降低了投资者面临的仲裁风险,资助者为投资者提供的资金支持也可

① See Jeffery P. Commission, "How Long is too Long to Wait for an Award?", *Global Arbitration Review*, 2016, 18; Jeffery P. Commission, "How Much does an ICSID Arbitration Cost? A Snapshot of the Last Five Years", http://arbitrationblog.kluwerarbitration.com/2016/02/29/how-much-does-an-icsid-arbitration-cost-a-snapshot-of-the-last-five-years/ (Last visited on 28 July, 2020); Vannin Capital, *The Duration and Costs of ICSID and UNCITRAL Investment Treaty Arbitration*, Funding in Focus Report Three, 2016, p. 7; The Study is based on An Analysis of 138 ICSID Arbitration between 2011 and 2015, https://www.vannin.com/downloads/funding-in-focus-three.pdf (Last visited on 4 August, 2020).

② See Matthew Hodgson, "Counting the Costs of Investment Treaty Arbitration", Global Arbitration Review, 24 March, 2014, http://www.allenovery.com/SiteCollectionDocuments/Counting_the_costs_of_investment_treaty.pdf (Last visited on 6 August, 2020).

③ See Matthew Hodgson & Alastair Campbell, "Damages and Costs in Investment Treaty Arbitration Revised", *Global Arbitration Review*, 14 December 2017, http://www.allenovery.com/SiteCollectionDocuments/14-12-17_Damages_and_costs_in_investment_treaty_arbitration_revisited_.pdf (Last visited on 10 August, 2020).

④ See Yukos Universal Limited (Isle of man) v. The Russian Federation, UNCITRAL, PCA Case No. AA 227, Final Award, 18 July 2014.

缓解后者的资金困境,投资者可通过让渡一部分胜诉收益的方式来降低其仲裁成本。因此,我国投资者可积极利用第三方资助来缓解因高昂的仲裁费用产生的资金周转问题。

三、中国在国际投资仲裁中适用第三方资助的可行性

我国立法目前尚未明确第三方资助的地位,我国投资者也没有利用资助者的资助提起投资仲裁。鉴于我国近年来已跃居世界第二大外商直接投资目的国和资本净输出国,①吸引外资和对外投资的过程中不可避免地会出现投资争议。如何合理利用第三方资助分担仲裁风险已成为我国需要考虑的问题,而我国也存在积极利用第三方资助的实践基础和规范支撑。

(一)中国香港特区和新加坡关于第三方资助的经验借鉴

伦敦玛丽女王大学关于国际仲裁的一项调查显示,中国香港特区和新加坡已位列世界上最受欢迎仲裁地的第三位和第四位。当事方对中国香港国际仲裁中心(Hong Kong International Arbitration Centre,HKIAC)和新加坡国际仲裁中心(Singapore International Arbitration Center,SIAC)的选择远超过去五年的数量。② 其他国际仲裁地如伦敦、纽约、斯德哥尔摩等都在国际仲裁领域允许第三方资助,③中国香港特区和新加坡受传统的禁止助讼和包揽诉讼的普通法原则的限制,第三方资助市场已落后于其他国际仲裁地。

在中国香港特区,相当一部分人明确表达了对禁止助讼和包揽诉讼这一传统普通法原则妨碍当事方间协商一致同意的不满。香港不允许第三方资助的做法已落后于其他受欢迎的国际仲裁中心。④ 2015 年 10 月,香港法律改革委员会(The Law Reform Commission of Hong Kong,LRC)下设的第三方资助仲裁委

---

① See World Investment Report 2020, p. 12 – 15.

② See 2015 International Arbitration Survey: Improvements and Innovations in International Arbitration, Queen Mary University of London, 2015, p. 12.

③ See Lisa Bench Nieuwveld & Victoria Shannon Sahini, *Third – Party Funding in International Arbitration*, 2nd ed., Kluwer Law International, 2017, p. 219 – 236.

④ See Leslie Perrin, *Third Party Litigation Funding Law Review*, Law Business Research Ltd., 2017, p. 85 – 86.

员会发布一份磋商文件,建议香港允许第三方资助。① 2017 年 6 月 14 日,香港特区立法会颁布《2017 年仲裁及调解法例(第三方资助)(修订)条例草案》,允许在仲裁和调解领域适用第三方资助。② HKIAC 2018 年颁布的《机构仲裁规则》授权仲裁庭可以要求一方当事人为仲裁费用提供担保、仲裁庭在分配仲裁费用时考虑第三方资助协议的存在,以及受资助者对第三方资助协议和资助者的披露义务。③ 2018 年 12 月 7 日香港特区律政司发布《第三方资助仲裁实务守则》,第 2 条第 10 款至第 14 款规定了资助者有责任提醒受资助者披露与其有关的信息、资助协议中须规定资助者的费用担保义务和承担不利费用的义务以及资助者可以终止资助协议的情形,限制资助者的随时终止权。④ 上述规定较为详尽地规范了第三方资助仲裁产生的问题,对仲裁实践具有指导作用。

新加坡上诉法院在 2007 年的判例中认为第三方资助有违新加坡公共政策。⑤ 鉴于第三方资助在国际仲裁领域适用日益普遍的事实,新加坡司法部于 2011 年向公众征求第三方资助在国际仲裁领域合法化的意见,⑥新加坡议会终在 2017 年 1 月通过《民法修正案》,⑦废除了助讼和包揽诉讼的侵权责任,在国际和国内仲裁及调解程序中可以适用第三方资助。⑧ 2017 年 1 月 1 日生效的 SIAC《投资仲裁规则》进一步明确了受资助者对第三方资助协议和资助者的披

---

① See LRC,"LRC Release Consultation Paper on Third Party Funding for Arbitration", p. 1 – 3, https://www. hkreform. gov. hk/en/index/index. htm(Last visited on 15 August,2020).

② 参见《香港修例容许仲裁第三方资助》,载史蒂文生黄律师事务所官网,http://www. sw – hk. com/zh/litigation – 20170616 – 1/。

③ 2018HKIAC Administered Arbitration Rules, Art. 24,34.4,44.

④ LRC, *Code of Practice for Third Party Funding of Arbitration*, https://www. doj. gov. hk/eng/public/pdf/2018/pr20181207e4. pdf(Last visited on 16 August,2020).

⑤ Otech Pakistan Pvt. Ltd. v. Clough Engineering Ltd. and Another [2006] SGCA 46.

⑥ *Review of the International Arbitration Act Proposals for Public Consultation*, https://www. mlaw. gov. sg/content/dam/minlaw/corp/assets/documents/linkclickf651. pdf(Last visited on 4 September,2020).

⑦ 新加坡《民法修正案》适用的第三方资助范围仅限于国际仲裁程序、国际仲裁引起的或与之相关的诉讼程序、国际仲裁所引起的或与之相关的调解程序,明确了第三方资助者须具备的经营范围以及缴纳资本要求,即主营业务为第三方资助,实缴资本不低于五百万美元或其他等额资金。

⑧ Ministry of Law,"Speech by Minister (Law and Home Affairs) K Shanmugam at the Opening Ceremony of Law Society at Maxwell Chamber Suits", https://www. mlaw. gov. sg/news/speeches/speech – by – minister – k – shanmugam – at – opening – ceremony – of – lawsoc – at – maxwell – chambers – suites (Last visited on 5 September,2020).

露要求，以及仲裁庭认为适当时可要求受资助者提供费用担保的权力。①

中国香港特区和新加坡认为国际仲裁是一个完全独立和相对自治的体系，当事方可选择仲裁来避免传统法院诉讼的限制。为了进一步吸引资助者参与国际仲裁市场，中国香港特区和新加坡在国际仲裁领域赋予第三方资助合法地位。中国内地可借鉴中国香港特区和新加坡的做法，先在国际仲裁领域适用第三方资助，提升国际仲裁的竞争力。在立法模式方面，借鉴新加坡通过修改国内民法赋予第三方资助合法地位，限定第三方资助的适用范围仅为仲裁领域，再辅之以后续补充立法的方式，根据适用效果推广到国内诉讼或仲裁领域的模式。这一灵活方式考虑了第三方资助发展的特点和存在的问题，并及时予以调整，有助于规范第三方资助市场的良性运转。在监管问题上借鉴香港通过软法规制的方式，明确受资助者的披露义务和违反该义务的法律后果，避免第三方资助给仲裁员的独立性和公正性以及仲裁程序造成不利影响。②

（二）国内软法的先行推进

第三方资助者作为仲裁程序之外的主体参与投资仲裁，为当事方提供便利的同时也给其蒙上了资助骚扰性主张、危害当事方保密信息、引发利益冲突等阴影。针对第三方资助带来的负外部性，国际仲裁界目前对第三方资助已渐有规制。这些软法性质的国际仲裁规则弥补了硬法的缺失，为投资仲裁庭处理第三方资助问题提供了依据。鉴于中国香港已先行一步，拥有巨大仲裁市场需求的中国内地也采取积极行动，如中国国际经济贸易仲裁委员会（China International Economic and Trade Arbitration Commission，CIETAC）《国际投资争端仲裁规则（试行）》第27条、CIETAC香港仲裁中心《第三方资助仲裁指引》第2条第7、8款，以及北京仲裁委员会（Beijing Arbitration Commission，BAC）《国际投资仲裁规则》第39条都明确规定了仲裁当事方披露第三方资助的义务和满足条件时提供仲裁费用担保的要求。这些软法虽不具有硬法的强制力，但仲裁机构在当事人选择采用上述仲裁规则时即可预见到第三方资助产生的问题并采取相应的威慑措施，一定程度上预示着我国对第三方资助的积极态度。

---

① International Arbitration Rules of the Singapore International Arbitration Centre，1st Edition，1 January 2017，Arts. 24，33.

② 参见唐琼琼：《第三方资助纠纷解决规制模式的国际经验及思考》，载《上海财经大学学报》2018年第6期。

（三）“法无禁止即可为”原则的赋权

“法无禁止即可为”原则最初来源于古希腊、古罗马对法律与自由的思考，即自由和法治是良好政体不可或缺的两个方面。① 在自由国家，个人只要不违背法律的精神，不侵犯他人利益，就应允准他按照自己的方式去追求利益。② 这一原则在法国1789年《人权宣言》和1791年宪法以及美国1789年宪法修正案中都具有明确规定。③ 该原则通过法律解释和法律论证相结合的方式，意在给公民赋权，即只要法律不禁止的事情都可以做。其适用的主体为包括自然人、法人、非法人在内的公民；④适用的内容为权利，即公民依自己意愿为或不为某种行为的能力或资格。我国的法律体系中不存在类似于禁止助讼和包揽诉讼的普通法原则，立法中也未禁止第三方资助。第三方资助对处于资金困境或意图分担风险的私主体而言是其实现接近正义权利的物质保障，并未违反道德上的义务。因此，我国投资者在适用第三方资助时存在正当性基础。

（四）完善的执行制度和广阔的资金需求

第三方资助者通常在案件获得胜诉且得到有效执行时，才能获得约定比例的回报。因此，良好的执行制度对资助者来说极为必要。国际投资仲裁领域主要存在两种执行机制，即《关于解决国家与他国国民之间投资争议的公约》（以下简称《ICSID公约》）执行机制和《承认及执行外国仲裁裁决公约》（以下简称《纽约公约》）执行机制。前者是投资争议当事方较为信赖的争议解决机制，《ICSID公约》第54条第1款要求各缔约方执行ICSID裁决如同执行其本国法院终审判决，执行裁决中涉及的金钱义务。我国于1993年加入该公约，若我国作为被诉东道国败诉了，ICSID裁决在我国的执行不会存在太大障碍。在我国投资者作为申请人的投资仲裁案件中，投资者大多经历了旷日持久的仲裁程序。若这些ICSID裁决进入执行程序，在《ICSID公约》较为完善的执行机制之下，投资仲裁裁决大多能得到承认执行，我国投资者的胜诉权益也可以得到保

① 参见[美]唐纳德·坦嫩鲍姆、[美]戴维·舒尔茨：《观念的发明者》，叶颖译，北京大学出版社2008年版，第29页。

② 参见[英]亚当·斯密：《国富论》，郭大力、王亚南译，上海三联书店2009年版，第121页。

③ 1789年法国《人权宣言》和1791年宪法都规定了凡未经法律禁止的行为即不得受到妨碍，以及1789年美国《宪法修正案》第9条规定，本宪法对某些权利的列举不得被解释为否定或轻视人民保有的其他权利。

④ 参见马爱平：《“法不禁止皆自由”的宪政监督》，载《政法学刊》2017年第2期。

障。非 ICSID 裁决的执行需要根据《纽约公约》这一机制来进行。我国于 1987 年加入《纽约公约》,此后也很好地履行了公约的规定。《纽约公约》第 5 条规定了执行地国法院可以拒绝执行的理由。我国在加入《纽约公约》时作了互惠保留和商事保留①,虽然商事保留会阻碍投资仲裁裁决在我国的执行,但我国《民事诉讼法》第 283 条规定了互惠原则,即在《纽约公约》无法适用之时,我国法院处理投资仲裁裁决的执行问题可以适用互惠原则。② 只要裁决不违反我国的公共政策或我国放弃了执行豁免,一般会执行国际投资仲裁裁决。

从我国参与国际投资仲裁的案件来看,就我国作为被申请人而言,目前只有我国被诉的第一案——伊桂兰案进入执行程序,双方和解结案。③ 韩国安城住房案中仲裁庭驳回了申请人的仲裁请求,案件不涉及执行问题。④ 从我国作为申请人的投资仲裁案件来看,除了北京城建诉也门案⑤和中国平安诉比利时案⑥不涉及执行问题外,其他案件多会进入执行阶段,但都经历撤销程序,耗费了大量时间和财力。鉴于国际投资仲裁耗时较长且费用高昂,申请人可能既要承受因东道国的征收等不法行为带来的经济困境,又要负担昂贵的仲裁费用,对其自身长远发展也极为不利。若投资者利用第三方资助来分担仲裁过程中面临的风险,则既可保证自身投资活动平稳进行,也可为被申请人胜诉要求投资者提供费用担保时提供"定心丸"。随着"一带一路"建设的推进,投资者在对外投资过程中发生的投资争议和我国作为被诉东道国面临的仲裁风险也日益增加。我国不妨在条件成熟时赋予第三方资助合法地位,既便利我国投资者利用第三方资助提起投资仲裁,也通过对第三方资助进行相应规制来降低我国作为被诉东道国时面临的仲裁风险。

---

① 商事保留主要是指我国依照《纽约公约》仅执行"根据中国法律属于契约型和非契约性商事关系"的裁决。

② 参见肖芳:《国际投资仲裁裁决在中国的承认与执行》,载《法学家》2011 年第 6 期。

③ See Ekran Berhad v. People's Republic of China, ICSID Case No. ARB/11/15.

④ See Ansung Housing Co., Ltd. v. People's Republic of China, ICSID Case No. ARB/14/25.

⑤ See Beijing Urban Construction Group Co. Ltd. v. Republic of Yemen, ICSID Case No. ARB/14/30.

⑥ See Ping An Life Insurance Company of China, Limited and Ping An Insurance (Group) Company of China, Limited v. Kingdom of Belgium, ICSID Case No. ARB/12/29.

四、我国对第三方资助国际投资仲裁的回应

如上所述,我国在 ISDS 中利用第三方资助有其必要性和可行性。虽然我国立法目前对第三方资助未作规定,但我国仲裁界和国家对外实践对第三方资助进行了回应,通过在仲裁规则中明确第三方资助的披露要求、提高仲裁程序的透明度以及提升我国仲裁制度的国际化水平等措施来应对。我国应争取在符合现实的情况下与国际通行做法接轨,不仅为我国投资者在国际仲裁中积极利用第三方资助提供制度保障,也通过对第三方资助进行规制来维护我国的社会利益。

(一)明确披露第三方资助的要求

我国原有的仲裁规则多规定了仲裁员的信息披露义务,即仲裁员认为存在可能影响其独立性和公正性的怀疑时应立即披露。由于第三方资助者参与仲裁程序的隐秘性,仲裁员和第三方资助者之间存在的利益关系可能难以为外界所知,或者仲裁员无法知晓第三方资助者的存在进而无法判断是否存在利益冲突。上述情形可能使得仲裁程序遭受正当性质疑。CIETAC 2017 年 9 月 12 日颁布的《国际投资争端仲裁规则(试行)》第 27 条对第三方资助的披露和费用分配问题进行了规定。该规则不仅明确了何为第三方资助,规定了受资助的申请人在签订资助协议后的披露对象和披露内容,还赋予仲裁庭要求受资助者披露和分配费用时可以将第三方资助作为考量因素的权力。[①] 该规定将申请人的披露行为作为决定其费用承担的做法不仅迫使受资助者自动履行披露义务,也保障了仲裁程序的顺畅进行,减少了影响仲裁结果的因素。CIETAC 香港仲裁中心《第三方资助仲裁指引》也对第三方资助者的资金状况、责任承担、披露等进行了明确,为第三方资助者在我国的资助活动提供了指导。[②] BAC 2019 年 7 月 4 日通过的《国际投资仲裁规则》第 39 条规定了第三方资助的含义,受资助者向对方当事人、仲裁庭和仲裁机构披露的内容和时间要求,明确了仲裁庭在决定仲裁费用承担时可以将第三方资助作为考虑因素,若资助者在资助协议中未

---

① 参见《中国国际经济贸易仲裁委员会国际投资争端仲裁规则(试行)》第 27 条。

② See China International Economic and Trade Arbitration Commission Hong Kong Arbitration Center, Guidelines for Third Party Funding for Arbitration.

承担受资助者的不利费用责任或受资助者未及时履行披露义务，仲裁庭可在必要时要求受资助者提供费用担保。① 另外，ICSID 投资仲裁机制改革以及 UNCITRAL 改革中都涉及第三方资助问题，我国也积极参与国际规则制定并发出中国声音。

（二）增强仲裁程序的透明度

投资仲裁程序的公正、透明有助于投资者和第三方资助者全面评估投资仲裁程序，为投资者选择经济且合理的争议解决方式、有针对性地对争议焦点进行举证，从而尽快解决争议。同时，投资仲裁程序和仲裁规则的透明度也影响着投资者对仲裁机构的选择。② 透明度的提高有助于增强仲裁机构的竞争力和影响力，我国在中国—加拿大双边投资协定（Bilateral Investment Treaty，BIT）③以及中日韩投资协定④中对透明度的态度发生了转变，都在协定中规定了透明度条款，联合国《投资人与国家间基于条约仲裁透明度公约》也着意于强化投资者—国家间仲裁程序的透明度。2019 年 BAC《国际投资仲裁规则》第 50 条对仲裁程序的透明度也进行了规定，即在当事方书面同意的情况下优先适用 UNCITRAL《投资人与国家间基于条约仲裁透明度规则》；若当事方未就适用该透明度规则达成一致，则除相关机密信息或其他受保护信息外，其他仲裁文件须公开。⑤ 这一规定有效地保障了投资仲裁程序的透明度。2019 年 7 月 18 日，我国政府对投资人与国家间争端解决机制可能的改革所提的意见中也指出，第三方资助者的参与可能导致其与仲裁员的利益冲突，需要加强关于第三方资助规定的透明度纪律，披露第三方资助的存在以避免利益冲突。若未披露，则须承担相应的法律后果。⑥ 这也是我国官方首次对第三方资助及其引发的仲裁程序透明度问题表态，为第三方资助在我国的适用提供了政策指导。

---

① 参见《北京仲裁委员会/北京国际仲裁中心国际投资仲裁规则》第 39 条。

② 参见朱明新：《联合国国际贸易法委员会“投资仲裁透明度规则”评析》，载《武大国际法评论》2017 年第 1 期。

③ See Agreement between the Government of Canada and the Government of the People's Republic of China for the Promotion and Reciprocal Protection of Investments, Arts. 28 – 29.

④ See China – Japan – South Korea Investment Agreement, Arts. 10 and 16.

⑤ 参见《北京仲裁委员会/北京国际仲裁中心国际投资仲裁规则》第 50 条。

⑥ 《投资人与国家间争端解决制度可能的改革》，中国政府提交的意见书，A/CN. 9/WG. III/WP. 177，19 July，2019。

(三)提升我国仲裁制度的国际竞争力

经济全球化的进程加快了资本的全球流动,亚太地区因其庞大的市场、低廉的劳动力和丰富的资源等对跨国资本产生了巨大的虹吸效应。近年来,中国实力的增强提升了其在国际舞台的地位和话语权,并提升了中国参与国际规则制定的积极性。同时,国内规则的制定也应紧跟国际形势。承认第三方资助的合法地位将在一定程度上增强我国成为亚洲国际仲裁中心的吸引力。为了推动国内争议解决机制改革,国务院在 2015 年专门发布《进一步深化中国(上海)自由贸易试验区改革开放方案》,着力推动上海自由贸易试验区与国际争议解决机制进行深度接轨,将优化自由贸易试验区仲裁规则与引进国际知名争议解决机构并举,加强我国与国际争议解决机构的交流和合作,提升我国建设国际仲裁中心的竞争实力。[①] 国务院于 2019 年 7 月 27 日印发的《中国(上海)自由贸易试验区临港新片区总体方案》中更是明确允许境外知名仲裁及争议解决机构经有关部门登记备案后可以在临港新片区设立业务机构并开展业务。[②] 2020 年 10 月,世界知识产权组织仲裁与调解上海中心落地并进行实质化运作,主营业务为涉外知识产权争议案件的仲裁与调解业务。[③] 随着我国仲裁业务对外开放的步伐加快,在中国开设分支机构的国际仲裁机构也将更多。国际知名仲裁机构的入驻一方面给我国本土仲裁机构带来了挑战,另一方面也倒逼国内仲裁机制改革。

为了适应“一带一路”建设的需求,武汉仲裁委员会于 2016 年设立“一带一路”(中国)仲裁院,处理“一带一路”沿线的投资争议。[④] 我国国内仲裁机构也扩大了其受案范围,将投资仲裁争议纳入其管辖范围。2019 年 2 月 21 日开始生效的《深圳国际仲裁院 2019 仲裁规则》第 2 条第 2 款规定,仲裁庭可以受理投资者与东道国之间的投资争议。[⑤] 我国仲裁机构进行的一系列创新不仅为我

---

① 参见《进一步深化中国(上海)自由贸易试验区改革开放方案》。

② 参见《中国(上海)自由贸易试验区临港新片区总体方案》。

③ 参见《全国首家国际组织仲裁机构落地上海并实质化运作》,载中国长安网 2020 年 10 月 24 日,https://baijiahao.baidu.com/s?id=1681449045835399399。

④ 参见《武汉仲裁委员会发起组建“一带一路”(中国)仲裁院成立》,载 http://www.whac.org.cn/index.php/news/details/type/26/id/3399.html,最后访问日期:2020 年 10 月 2 日。

⑤ 参见《深圳国际仲裁院 2019 仲裁规则》,载 http://www.sccietac.org/web/doc/view_rules/913.html,最后访问日期:2020 年 10 月 2 日。

国投资者的投资争议提供了解决的场所，有助于推广我国优秀的争议解决方式，提升我国仲裁机构的国际竞争力，也为第三方资助者资助"一带一路"投资争议提供了契机。虽然上述仲裁院处理投资争议案件的经验有限，但至少表明了我国参与全球经济治理的意愿和行动。①

五、结语

随着"一带一路"建设的稳步推进，我国投资者对外投资和我国作为东道国吸引外资的过程中面临的投资争议可能增加。第三方资助投资仲裁在我国有存在的必要性和可行性，我国仲裁机构也在其投资仲裁规则中对第三方资助进行了规制，以降低资助者对仲裁程序的影响。在中国香港特区、新加坡等相继赋予第三方资助合法地位以争夺亚洲国际仲裁中心之时，借鉴中国香港特区和新加坡的立法实践，条件成熟时赋予第三方资助合法地位，有助于提升仲裁制度的国际化水平。

① 参见马亚伟、漆彤：《论"一带一路"投资争议解决机制的构建》，载《国际商务研究》2018 年第 5 期。

投资争端解决中的调解机制:功能、案例与趋势

苏伟康*

摘　要:调解机制在全世界范围内引发了共鸣,非约束性裁决偏好理论可能成为调解繁荣的重要依据。投资争端调解机制正在朝着制度化、规范化的方向发展。考察既有的案例可以发现,调解机制可以满足投资争端解决的基本需求。调解机制在维护合作关系、控制纠纷进展和降低解纷成本上具有不可比拟的优势。然而,保密性的桎梏、岔路口条款的影响以及约束力的缺失等可能会成为制约调解机制适用的理由。《新加坡公约》的开放签署和巴西 CFIA 模式是投资争端调解的最新进展,体现了投资争端调解机制的发展前景和制度活力,并为投资争端调解的发展提供了可能的方向。

关键词:投资争端解决　调解机制　新加坡公约

调解(mediation)会取代仲裁吗? 这一设问或许有些危言耸听,但如果结合近几十年国际纠纷解决格局的变迁就会发现,这确实是一个值得思索的问题。无论是在商事纠纷或是投资争端中,调解机制已经吸引了越来越多的注意力。《联合国宪章》第 33 条明确鼓励成员国使用调解与和解(conciliation)的方式解决纠纷。在这一框架之下,调解的价值日益凸显。2017 年 9 月,东帝汶民主共和国与澳大利亚联邦通过和解程序就海上边界划定问题达成了共识,①这标志

* 苏伟康,上海交通大学凯原法学院博士研究生。

① *Conciliation between the Democratic Republic of Timor – Leste and the Commonwealth of Australia*, 1st September 2017, https://pcacases.com/web/sendAttach/2230.

着《联合国海洋法公约》附件五中的调解程序被正式激活。在国际投资争端领域，2016 年 7 月，国际能源宪章会议通过了“投资调解指南”（Guide on Investment Mediation），[①]鼓励投资者与东道国通过调解程序解决纠纷。该指南涵盖了调解的规则与结构，探讨了调解规则与和解规则之间的区别。2017 年 6 月国际投资争端解决中心（International Centre for the Settlement of Investment Disputes，ICSID）为专门针对投资者与国家之间争端的调解员举办了培训。[②] 在欧盟与越南签订的投资协议中，将调解程序列为主要争端解决方式，规定于附件中。[③]

国际法学界对于投资争端中的调解机制的研究已有较多成果。遗憾的是，在中国此项研究尚处于起步阶段。本文将围绕投资争端中的调解机制适用问题展开讨论。但需要言明的是，本文无意于全景式地展现投资争端调解机制的全貌，而是希望通过本文的探索发现和归纳调解机制的固有特征以及其在投资争端中的特殊价值，并对中国投资争端调解机制的发展提供具体思路。首先，展示作为一般纠纷解决机制的调解，阐明其趋势与功能。其次，归纳和总结既有的规则与案例。再次，在前述研究的基础上总结提炼调解机制的适用优势与问题。最后，论述调解机制的最新进展，以期把握调解机制发展的基本方向。

一、调解的趋势与功能

调解一般被界定为中立第三人以当事人的需求和利益为依据，在双方或多方当事人之间促进沟通交流的过程。[④] 在国际争端解决的体系中，调解程序扮演着与众不同而又不可或缺的角色。调解既可以作为一种独立的替代性纠纷解决机制，也可以是仲裁程序的前奏。[⑤] 在国际法的实践中，和解也被视为调解

---

① Energy Charter, *Decision of the Energy Charter Conference*, 19th July 2016, https://energycharter.org/fileadmin/DocumentsMedia/CCDECS/2016/CCDEC201612. pdf.

② https://icsid. worldbank. org/en/Pages/resources/ICSID% 2NewsLetter/207 - Issue3/Considering - theFuture - of - Investor - State - Mediation. aspx, retrieved on 30th May 2020.

③ 参见 https://trade. ec. europa. eu/doclib/docs/2018/september/tradoc_157378. pdf，最后访问日期：2020 年 7 月 12 日。

④ 参见王福华：《现代调解制度若干问题研究》，载《当代法学》2009 年第 6 期。

⑤ Reif, L. C., "Conciliation as a Mechanism for the Resolution of International Economic and Business Disputes," *Fordham International Law Journal*, Vol. 14, Iss. 3, 1990, p. 578 - 638.

程序的表现形式之一。例如,常设仲裁法院(Permanent Court of Arbitration,PCA)中的和解规则可以与调解进行互换。[①] 尽管国际法学界尚未对和解的概念达成共识,但一般认为,和解与调解一样,都是通过中立的第三方——可能是个人,也有可能是一个小组或当事人指定的机构——解决纠纷的方法。两者在解决方案上略有不同:调解员"努力使争议各方进行对话,以便他们自己可以达成折中解决方案"。相较而言,和解人"在与争议各方讨论案情之后,将起草并提出纠纷解决的条款,代表着和解人对于纠纷公正解决的理解"[②]。大体上看,调解与和解之间没有明确的界限,因为调解员与和解人的共同目标都是帮助争议各方以某种方式达成和解协议(settlement agreement)。因此本文不对 mediation 与 conciliation 进行区分,统称为调解/和解程序。[③]

与仲裁庭的裁决不同,调解所达成的和解协议不具有约束力,但是可以为争议各方进一步的谈判奠定基础。调解员也可能有义务根据某些调解程序发布书面报告,ICSID 即是如此,[④]而 PCA 无此要求。

(一)调解的流行与非约束性裁决偏好

几个世纪以来,调解一直是东方国家解决国内争端的一种普遍形式,[⑤]无论在大陆法地区还是普通法地区,调解都成为社会普遍接受的纠纷处理方式。从文化角度来看,在不喜欢对抗的亚洲文化中,调解确实具有特别的吸引力。[⑥] 日

---

① 参见《常设仲裁法院选择性和解规则》"引言":在现代国际惯例中,"调解"一词有时用于表示与本规则中所述的"和解"程序非常相似的过程,https://docs. pca - cpa. org/2016/01/Permanent - Court - of - Arbitration - Optional - Conciliation - Rules. pdf。

② A. Redfern& M. Hunter, *The Law and Practice of International Commercial Arbitration*, Cambridge University Press, 2008, p. 46.

③ 负责《新加坡公约》的联合国贸易法委员会第二工作组同样认为,mediation 与 conciliation 是可以互换的。See UNGA, International commercial mediation: draft model law on international commercial mediation and international settlement agreements resulting from mediation, 2nd March 2018, A/CN. 9/943, p. 9;也有学者认为应当对 mediation 与 conciliation 进行区分。See Sussman, E., "The Advantages of Mediation and the Special Challenges to its Utilization in Investor State Disputes," *Revista Brasileira de Arbitragem*, Vol. 7, Iss. 27, 2010, p. 54 - 67.

④ 参见《ICSID 调解规则(2006 年版)》,载 https://icsid. worldbank. org/en/Pages/icsiddocs/ICSID - Convention - Conciliation - Rules,最后访问日期:2020 年 6 月 12 日。

⑤ Reif, L. C., "Conciliation as a Mechanism for the Resolution of International Economic and Business Disputes", *Fordham International Law Journal*, Vol. 14, 1990, p. 578 - 638.

⑥ Harpole, S. A, "The Combination of Conciliation with Arbitration in the People's Republic of China," *Journal of International Arbitration*, Vol. 24, Iss. 6, 2007, p. 623 - 634.

本早在20世纪80年代后期便创设了“辩论兼和解”程序,并通过1996年新民事诉讼法中的辩论准备程序使之制度化,在法院附设的调停程序之后又为当事人提供了一次和解的机会。[①] 韩国将调解制度广泛地运用于诉讼前后。[②] 香港国际仲裁中心的仲裁规则允许在仲裁过程中使用调解,同时允许仲裁员作为调解员采取行动,[③]《香港仲裁条例》同时适用于国内纠纷和国际纠纷的解决。与之类似,在新加坡,仲裁员同样可以在仲裁程序中担任调解员。[④]

在中国,得益于儒家文化浸润[⑤]与“枫桥经验”的提倡,调解程序在纠纷解决体系中占据重要地位。中国的调解程序主要是在基层人民调解委员会、仲裁机构和法院进行。台湾地区的乡市镇调解也扮演着消解社会基层矛盾的角色。[⑥] 在国际商事争端的处理中,很多规则允许争端者在使用约束性裁决机制之前先进行调解或和解。比如美中贸易全国委员会(National Council for US - China Trade)和中国国际经济贸易仲裁委员会(China International Economic and Trade Arbitration Commion,CIETAC)。[⑦] 内地与香港特别行政区之间的《内地与香港关于建立更紧密经贸关系的安排》也将调解列为解决投资争端的方式之一。[⑧]

有理论认为,仲裁之所以普遍盛行“是建立在西方偏好于通过约束性、对抗性的方法解决冲突的传统之上”[⑨]。如果这一理论成立,则在东方国家越来越多地参与国际经济的格局之下,争端解决将会朝着“基于共识”的模式转变。换言之,东方文化中的自觉与妥协将会影响到纠纷解决机制的选择。在东方国家在国际商贸体系中的地位日益增长的当下,当事人关于纠纷解决方式的选择可能

---

① 参见史长青:《裁判、和解与法律文化传统——ADR对司法职能的冲击》,载《法律科学》2014年第2期。

② 参见郑圭相:《韩国司法型调解制度小考》,载《东南司法评论》2012年第0期。

③ 参见《香港仲裁条例》第32、33条。

④ 参见《新加坡国际仲裁法》(International Arbitration Act)第16、17条。

⑤ 参见陈弘毅:《调解、诉讼与公正——对现代自由社会和儒家传统的反思》,载《现代法学》2001年第3期;胡旭晟、夏新华:《中国调解传统研究—— 一种文化的透视》,载《河南省政法管理干部学院学报》2000年第4期。

⑥ 参见范愉:《人民调解与我国台湾地区乡镇市调解的比较研究》,载《清华法学》2001年第1期。

⑦ 参见《中国国际经济贸易仲裁委员会仲裁规则》(2015年版)第47条。

⑧ 参见《内地与香港关于建立更紧密经贸关系的安排》第19、20条。

⑨ Reif,L. C.,“Conciliation as a Mechanism for the Resolution of International Economic and Business Disputes”.

会从对抗性的仲裁程序向协商性的调解机制转变。

如果将目光扩展至全球范围就会发现,调解并不完全是“东方”国家的专属。在西方,调解同样获得了广泛的支持和应用,越来越多的国际商事仲裁法将辅助性调解条款作为解决争端的初步或替代方法。例如,美国加利福尼亚州将调解条款作为仲裁前的可供选择的前置步骤。① 州立法甚至明确指出加利福尼亚州的政策是鼓励进行国际合作的商业主体签署通过调解解决其争端的商业协议。在澳大利亚,仲裁员可以担任国内仲裁程序的调解员。② 德国利用积极的“管理性判断”(managerial judging)为调解提供便利,即在仲裁程序中,仲裁员可以对案件的是非曲直表达初步意见,并提出可能和解的建议。这并不构成偏见或预先判断。③ 在法国,调解被确定为法官和仲裁员的职能之一。④

非约束性裁决偏好是指相对于具有强制约束力的诉讼程序和仲裁程序(通过司法保障),在一些情况下,当事人可能会更钟情于不具有约束力的纠纷解决方式。非约束性裁决更具灵活性,其争议解决程序可以与其他争议解决方式相衔接,当事人可以选择获得一个具有约束力的裁决,也可以在裁决作出后采取其他方式寻求进一步的救济。非约束性裁决的理想结果是,当事人对争议结果满意并自愿执行,或者仅仅损失不多的时间和金钱解决纠纷,同时保有采取其他手段解决争议的权利。⑤ 总之,非约束性裁决的价值在于它为当事人提供了一种不同于其他纠纷解决方式的可供选择的纠纷解决机制,其成本低廉且能促进公正的实现。

调解规则可在东西方任意国家的国内争端解决机制中找到。随着东西方文化的交流与时间的推移,调解程序在世界各地都引发了文化共鸣。更重要的一点是,如果上述非约束性裁决偏好理论得到证实,那么调解程序可能还存在更加广阔的适用空间。

---

① 《加利福尼亚民事诉讼法典》第1297条。

② 《澳大利亚商业仲裁法》第27条。

③ Sim, C. "Conciliation of Investor - State Disputes, Arb - Con - Arb, and the Singapore Convention," *Singapore Academy of Law Journal*, Vol. 31, 2019, p. 670 - 712.

④ 《法国民事诉讼法典》第1460条。

⑤ 参见高薇:《非约束性网上仲裁解决电子商务争端的法律分析》,载《中州学刊》2012年第2期。

(二)调解与国际关系中的实用主义

与经济学上的成本效益分析相比,政治因素往往会成为政府在投资争端解决中的重要关切。随着全球合作的不断深入,国家之间的相互依存的发展关系得到承认,国际投资中的主体都认识到根据不断变化的情况对长期合同进行反复调整的必要性,国际关系中的实用主义日益发展,也产生了对非约束性解决机制采取更开放的态度的可能性。

首先,实用主义要求纠纷解决的同时能够保持合作关系的存续。世界银行总法律顾问阿隆·布罗奇斯(Aron Broches)指出:"当您在商业合作关系中走到尽头时,您最好还是通过仲裁程序作出明确的决定。另一方面,如果双方希望继续他们的伙伴关系,调解程序可能是更优的选择。"①

调解与协商在最为重视维持友好关系的贸易纠纷中(一般是长期国际合同的纠纷)发挥良好的效果,②它有助于维持和谐的商业关系,进而达成纠纷解决中的"双赢"局面。而诉讼或是仲裁的裁决形式可能会破坏这种联系。③ 油气开采、采矿和基础设施建设项目中的争议就是非常典型的范例,这种项目往往涉及大量的沉没成本,而且有必要在项目仍在继续进行的时候解决纠纷。例如在 Hess Equatorial Guinea 和 Tullow Equatorial Guinea 诉赤道几内亚案中,④投资者与东道国之间的关系尽管受到了调解机制暂停的威胁,但两公司仍然继续进行了进一步的投资。这是争端解决与长期合作关系兼容的典范。因此,如果投资争端的争议主体希望保留其现有合同和商业合作时,应首选调解解决纠纷。尤其是在长期合约或合资关系中,调解的优势将更加明显。

其次,实用主义的另一要求是对东道国主权的维护。国际投资争端往往是政治对抗的衍生或延续。一般而言,外交和政治纷争通常以调解和谈判的方式解决,因为终局性的手段无疑会让政府产生忧虑,非裁决性的方式可以在温和、

---

① Seymour J. Rubin, Ewell E. Murphy, Jr., Detlev F. Vagts, K. Scott Gudgeon, Gerhard Wegen, Aron Broches & Samuel K. B. Asante, Avoidance and Settlement of International Investment Disputes, *American Society of International Law Proceedings* 78, 1984, 38 – 54.

② [日]多喜寛『國際仲裁と國際取引法』,转引自[日]梶田幸雄、王丹:《对中日两国间商事纠纷解决的提案》,载《东方法学》2016 年第 1 期。

③ Constain, S., "Mediation in Investor – State Dispute Settlement: Government Policy and the Changing Landscape," *ICSID Review – Foreign Investment Law Journal*, Vol. 29, Iss. 1, Winter 2014, p. 25 – 40.

④ ICSID Case No. CONC(AF)/12/1.

宽松的环境下解决纷争。在一些由于政治事件而导致的投资争端中,政府方的顾虑同样会对寻求解决方案造成障碍,尤其是某些国家会将针对其的争端解决程序(如 ICSID 的仲裁程序)视为“不友好行为”。在这种情况下,调解程序及其协商一致的调解协议具有了较高的可接受性。因为相对而言,它们是争端解决机制中“较软”的形式,对东道国主权的威胁较小,也有助于政府形象的维护。

最后,实用主义对于纠纷解决的灵活性有较高的需求。调解程序所具备的灵活性可以适应参与者及其利益的多样性,其具备的半外交性质可以提供政治性的而非严格的法律解决方案。例如,在 Kardassopoulos 和 Fuchs 诉格鲁吉亚共和国案中,①申请人寻求美国前国务卿基辛格的协助解决纠纷,来自中立第三方的外交干预无疑增加了纠纷解决的机会。调解程序所具备的半外交性可能对于带有政治背景的纠纷(如当外国投资者是国有企业时)特别有效。

二、调解机制的规则与案例

实践中不乏利用调解机制解决投资争端的规则设计和实际案例。对规则的检视将有助于提炼调解程序的普遍原则,对案例的回看可以发现调解机制的具体运作模式。

(一)投资争端解决的调解规则

《关于解决国家和他国国民之间投资争端公约》(以下简称《华盛顿公约》)在 1965 年诞生伊始就设立了调解机制用以解决纠纷,起草者们在公约中纳入了关于调解的规定以及具体规则。在很多双边投资协议中也规定了调解的适用。例如“索赔人和被诉人应首先通过协商和谈判解决争端,其中可能包括使用不具有约束力的程序,例如斡旋、调解或和解”②。但一般来说,调解往往是作为仲裁的补充或替代的角色出现,其具体适用规则也较为模糊,一般表述为:如果当事任何一方提出为解决争端进行协商的六个月内未能解决,则根据该国民或公司的要求,可提交参考《华盛顿公约》而组成的调解委员会或仲裁委员会。缔约任何一方和缔约另一方国民或公司关于其他事项的争端,可根据当事双方

① ICSID Case No. ARB/07/15.

② 2014 年《埃及—毛里求斯双边投资协定》第 10 条。

的同意,提交如上所述的调解委员会或仲裁委员会。[①]

然而,在最近的国际投资协议中,调解机制正在朝着制度化方向转变,投资协议开始制定具体的规则而不只是作出宽泛的指引。例如,《澳大利亚与印度尼西亚全面经济伙伴关系协定》(2019 年)规定:"调解(1)如果在争端方收到书面协商请求之日起的 180 天内仍无法解决争端,则争端方可启动调解程序。该程序对有争议的投资者而言是强制性的,以期达成友好和解。调解程序应由争议方向争议投资者提出的书面请求启动。(2)本条所述的调解程序只能由争端方在收到争端方提出的书面协商请求之日起 180 天内提出的书面请求才能启动。(3)与调解程序有关的费用应由争端各方平均分担。"[②]《欧盟—加拿大综合经济贸易协议》(2016 年)、《欧盟—新加坡投资保护协议》(2018 年)都出现了类似的条款。

尽管如此,与仲裁程序相比,调解机制的规范化和制度化都还有很大差距。明确的标准将有助于当事人解决争端。替代性纠纷解决机制(Alternative Dispute Resolution,ADR)的多元化构成和法律文化的差异性都要求明确的调解规则,以厘清其适用条件,确定调解程序中的具体流程。诚然,过于精确的程序安排可能会减损调解程序的灵活性,进而加剧其成本和时间损失。但不可否认的是,原则性的规则明确是调解机制活跃生长的必备条件。

1.《联合国国际贸易法委员会调解规则》(UNCITRAL Conciliation Rules)[③]

1980 年 12 月 4 日,联合国国际贸易法委员会通过了调解规则。该规则仅有 20 个条款,比大多数 ADR 机构的调解规则都为简略。

规则开宗明义,明确了主体自治的核心地位:根据第 1 条第 2 款,当事方可以合意变更或限制适用本规则,只要该协议不与当事方所遵循的强制性法律规定相抵触。该规则第 2 条第 1 款规定,任何一方当事人如欲发起调解程序,必须书面邀请另一方参加,并说明争端的性质。第 2 条第 3 款规定,如果另一方当事人拒绝邀请,则不会进行调解程序。第 4 条规定,如果当事方未另行达成

---

① 参见 1988 年《中华人民共和国和日本国关于鼓励和相互保护投资协定》第 11 条。

② 2019 年《澳大利亚与印度尼西亚全面经济伙伴关系协定》(Australia – Indonesia Comprehensive Economic Partnership Agreement)第 14 条。

③ United Nations, UNCITRAL Conciliation Rules, 1980, https://www.jus.uio.no/lm/un.conciliation.rules.1980/doc.html.

协议,则调解由单独的调解员主持,通常由当事方共同决定。当事人可以寻求第三方机构或个人担任调解员。第 13 条规定,当和解协议的基本要素已经具备时,调解员可以制定和解协议的条款。如果双方达成协议,他们将签署书面和解协议。

2.《华盛顿公约》与《国际投资争端解决中心调解规则》(ICSID Conciliation Rules)①(以下简称《ICSID 调解规则》)

由 ICSID 主持的调解程序受《华盛顿公约》第 28 ~ 35 条和《ICSID 调解规则》的约束。同时,《国际投资争端解决中心附加便利规则》(ICSID Additional Facility Rules)②为 ICSID 管辖范围以外的争议提供调解指引。调解员或调解委员会的组成原则与仲裁程序相同。

根据《华盛顿公约》第 28 条规定,希望提起调解程序的当事方应向秘书长书面提出请求,其中应包括有关争端的事项、双方的身份以及他们同意依照调解的程序规则进行调解等内容。第 29 ~ 31 条规定了调解委员会的组成。第 32 条规定调解委员会应是其本身权限的决定人。第 33 条则确保了调解程序的灵活性,并允许在当事各方同意时修改调解规则。第 34 条是公约关于调解程序的核心条款,其规定委员会有责任澄清双方发生争端的问题,并努力使双方就共同可接受的条件达成协议。为此目的,委员会可以在程序进行的任何阶段,随时向双方建议解决的条件。当事方不得随意拒绝,并对建议给予最认真的考虑。如果双方达成协议,委员会应起草一份报告,指出争端中的焦点,并载明双方已达成协议。该报告必须包含有关双方当事人、争议的性质和调解程序过程的详细信息。尽管委员会必须在报告中指出各方是否达成和解协议,但除非双方共同要求披露和解协议的具体内容,否则报告不包括和解协议的详细信息。

除了《ICSID 调解规则》外,ICSID 于 2018 年开始制定一套新的调解规则,新的调解规则是投资争端解决程序更新和现代化的进程的重要组成部分,同时是专门为投资争端设计的第一批机构调解规则。调解规则旨在补充 ICSID 现有的仲裁、调解和调查(fact - finding)程序,各方当事人可以单独适用或是配合

① Rules of Procedure for Conciliation Proceedings (Conciliation Rules), ICSID, http://icsidfiles.worldbank.org/icsid/icsid/staticfiles/basicdoc/parte.htm, retrieved on 25th June 2020.

② Ibid.

其他程序适用。

3.《国际律师协会投资争端调解规则》(International Bar Association Rules for Investor – State Mediation)

国际律师协会国家调解小组委员会(以下简称小组委员会)于2008年开始着手起草关于国际投资争端的调解规则。小组委员会起草相关调解规则时不仅重视投资争端中调解程序运作的实际情况,而且着重考虑到以下要素:大多数投资条约中没有具体提及调解;缺乏针对投资人与国家间争端的调解规则;《ICSID调解规则》与仲裁程序过于相似;普遍缺乏对调解在国际投资界中的潜在作用的认识;缺乏合格的调解员;缺乏明确的国际框架(与《承认及执行外国仲裁裁决公约》类似的)等。2011年年初,小组委员会启动了规则起草项目。① 该规则于2012年获得批准,旨在调解涉及国家或国家实体的投资争端(第1条第1款)。第7条第2款和第8条第2款明确划定了调解员的职能,其中规定:"调解员无权强制各方当事人以任何方式部分或全部解决争端……调解员应协助当事方在各方自愿解决的基础上达成协议以解决争端。各方当事人可以对程序进程和调解结果作出自由的选择。"最终,调解过程在当事方之间达成的和解协议、当事人一方决定中止调解程序和调解员确定不可能继续调解的情况下终止(第11条)。

4.《国际商会调解规则》(ICC Mediation Rules)②

国际商会(International Chamber of Commerce, ICC)于2014年发布的《国际商会调解规则》取代了之前的《国际商会友好争议解决规则》(ICC Amicable Dispute Resolution Rules),而更为久远的是1988年施行的《国际商会选择性调解规则》(ICC Rules of Optional Conciliation)。

尽管ICC的调解机制主要在国际商事争端中使用,但根据其第1条第2款,该规则适用于所有"争议"(dispute)。因此在理论上《国际商会调解规则》完全可以覆盖投资争端。第1条第3款划定了极为广泛的适用范围:"适用于

---

① See Joubin – Bret, A. & Legum, B., "A Set of Rules Dedicated to Investor – State Mediation: The IBA Investor – State Mediation Rules," *ICSID Review – Foreign Investment Law Journal*, Vol. 29, Iss. 1, Winter 2014, p. 17 – 24.

② See *ICC Mediation Rules*, ICC, https://iccwbo.org/dispute – resolution – services/mediation/mediation – rules/, retrieved on 14th July 2020.

纠纷解决程序。"这意味着当事人可以在任意程序中使用该规则,包括仲裁、调解、协商和斡旋等。当事人可共同提名一名调解员,如果当事人未共同提名一名调解员,第 5 条规定由中心任命调解员。根据规则第 8 条,在当事方已签署和解协议或当事方之一放弃调解时,调解程序应当终止。

(二)投资调解机制的典型案例

由于调解机制的保密性,获取调解案件信息披露十分困难,目前仅能够在 ICSID 系统查询投资调解的案例。根据 ICSID 调解规则解决纠纷的有 12 起案件,其中 9 起案件已经结案,而 3 起案件仍在审理中。ICSID 中的调解案件从登记到结案(发布报告或达成和解)的平均时间为 541 天,其中最短的是 173 天,最长的是 1047 天。(见表 1)具体情况如下:

表 1 ICSID 调解程序案件(截至 2020 年 7 月 10 日)

案号	申请人	被申请人	状态	用时[1]
CONC/82/1	SEDITEX Engineering Beratungsgesellschaft für die Textilindustrie m. b. H.	马达加斯加民主共和国	结案(Settled)	258 天
CONC/83/1	Tesoro Petroleum Corporation	特立尼达和多巴哥	结案(Concluded)	824 天
CONC/94/1	SEDITEX Engineering Beratungsgesellschaft für dieTextilindustrie m. b. H.	马达加斯加民主共和国	结案(Concluded)	767 天
CONC/03/1	TG World Petroleum Limited	尼日尔共和国	结案(Settled)	487 天
CONC/05/1	Togo Electricité	多哥共和国	结案(Concluded)	321 天
CONC/07/1	Shareholders of SESAM	中非共和国	结案(Concluded)	366 天
CONC/11/1	RSM Production Corporation	喀麦隆共和国	结案(Concluded)	631 天
CONC(AF)/12/1	Hess Equatorial Guinea, Inc. and Tullow Equatorial Guinea Limited	赤道几内亚共和国	未决(Pending)	

续表

案号	申请人	被申请人	状态	用时
CONC(AF)/12/2	CMS Energy Corporation and others	赤道几内亚共和国	结案(Concluded)	1047 天
CONC/16/1	Xenofon Karagiannis	阿尔巴尼亚共和国	未决(Pending)	
CONC/18/1	Société d'Energie et d'Eau du Gabon	加蓬共和国	结案(Concluded)	173 天
CONC/19/1	La Camerounaise des Eaux(CDE)	喀麦隆共和国	未决(Pending)	

资料来源:世界银行官网。

〔1〕指从在 ICSID 登记到发布报告或达成和解所用的时间。

1. ICSID 调解第一案:Tesoro Petroleum Case

1968 年特索罗石油公司与特立尼达和多巴哥政府建立了合资企业,用于在东道国购买和开发油田。1981 年,投资者与东道国之间的关系开始紧张,主要原因是东道国征收的新石油税、封锁勘探领域以及拒绝返还股息。随后,特索罗石油公司决定出售其商业活动,并开始与东道国进行谈判。

调解程序的启动源于当事各方合同义务:特索罗于 1984 年 1 月 6 日根据 ICSID 规则发起了调解程序。在双方进行了两次程序协商并交换了文书后,1985 年 2 月,调解员提出了解决建议。1985 年 10 月,特索罗石油公司发布新闻,宣称其与特立尼达和多巴哥政府根据调解员的建议已经达成和解。1985 年 11 月,当事双方将调解书告知调解员,调解员结案并提交了调解报告。调解程序的总费用为 11,000 美元。①

2. The Vattenfal *v.* Polskie Sieci Elektroenergetyczne Case

此案始于 2002 年瑞典国有电力公司(以下简称瑞典电力公司)和波兰国家综合电力公司(以下简称波兰电力公司)之间的合作。具体争议源于一项长期合约,根据该合约,瑞典电力公司将为瑞典和波兰之间的能源运输提供资金并

① Nurick, L. & Schnably, S. J., "The First ICSID Conciliation: Tesoro Petroleum Corporation v. Trinidad and Tobago," *ICSID Review – Foreign Investment Law Journal*, Vol. 1, Iss. 2, Fall 1986, p. 340 – 353.

提供互联器,而波兰电力公司将在未来 20 年内通过该互联器从瑞典电力处购买电力。在能源环境发生变化及电力价格大幅下跌之后,波兰电力公司认为继续履行合约明显不公平,开始了与瑞典电力公司的谈判。

随着谈判失败,瑞典电力公司威胁启动仲裁程序。后双方合意决定通过调解程序以寻求满意的解决方案。双方任命了托马斯 · 瓦尔德(Thomas Wälde)作为调解员,理由在于:他在争议解决上依靠技术专家的协助,并着重消除妨碍双方进行谈判的客观障碍以及主观因素因素(心理和情感方面),而不仅是根据法律评估各方立场。在最初的 75 天内,调解员与双方组织了单方面的磋商和联席会议。然后,调解员对政府、欧盟和两国监管机构等第三方进行了会谈。100 天后,双方达成协议,并为剩余合作期间建立了新的合约,使双方之间的合作关系得以继续。① 值得一提的是,此后瑞典电力公司与德国在 ICSID 仲裁中的纠纷同样以谈判的形式解决。②

3. ICC 投资争端调解第一案

在本案中,西欧某国和某东南亚国家签署了促进和保护投资的双边协定。尽管该协议规定将仲裁作为解决争端的程序,但投资者仍建议通过调解程序解决其与东道国政府之间的争端。投资者根据 2014 年《国际商会调解规则》第 3 条和 2012 年《国际律师协会投资争端调解规则》提交了调解请求。基于《国际商会调解规则》的灵活性,ICC 接受了这一请求,并同意适用《国际律师协会投资争端调解规则》。

本案的调解程序持续了大约两年半,原因在于:第一,在向相对国发出调解请求通知与该国同意参加调解程序之间相隔了两个月;第二,在调解程序进行中该国举行大选,政权和人事的更迭推迟了程序进程。尽管调解程序未能解决争端,但通过调解当事人之间的谈判取得了重大进展:当事人重新建立了沟通

---

① Wälde, T. W., "Efficient Management of Transnational Disputes: Case Study of a Successful Interconnector Dispute Resolution," TDM 1, 2007, http://www.transnational-dispute-management.com/article.asp?key=970, 14th July 2020.

② Vattenfall AB, Vattenfall Europe AG, Vattenfall Europe Generation AG v. Federal Republic of Germany ICSID Case No. ARB/09/6.

渠道,并为未来的和解与合作打开了大门。①

三、调解适用的潜力与困境

上述讨论清晰地展现了这一事实:调解程序具备解决投资争端的能力,在某些场景中,调解甚至优于仲裁。调解解决投资争端的潜力清楚地体现在以下数据中:ICSID 仲裁案件中有 40% 的案件是在最终裁决之前解决的。迄今为止,在 444 宗已解决的投资者与东道国之间的争端中,有 26% ~28% 的案件是在裁决之前解决的。② 然而,考察调解机制与投资争端解决的适配度,仍需具体分析投资争端解决的现实需求与调解机制的功能特性。

(一)调解机制的适用优势

伦敦玛丽女王大学于 2019 年 12 月进行了一项关于投资者对拟议的投资者—国家争端解决(Investor - State Dispute Settlement,ISDS)改革的调查,其中一些问题与投资者与国家之间的调解有关。在调查询问受访者是否欢迎在仲裁程序开始之前引入强制调解的态度时,受访者有五种选择:强烈支持、支持、无视、反对、强烈反对。总体上,受访者认为该要求的引入是有利的(64%),其中 34% 的受访者选择"支持",30% 的受访者"强烈支持"该建议。

在理论上论证调解对于解决投资争端的优势是简单的。早在 1984 年,世界银行起草《华盛顿公约》的总法律顾问阿隆 · 布罗奇斯就观察到,尽管仲裁程序仍是纠纷解决的首选项,但是"全世界存在着很强的调解倾向"③。如果可以实现强有力的监管且政府具有开放宽容的态度,则调解将会是解决投资纠纷的

① See Leoveanu, A. & Erac, A., "ICC Mediation. Paving the Way Forward," in Titi, C. & Fach Gómez, K. (eds.), *Mediation in International Commercial and Investment Disputes*, Oxford University Press, 2019, p. 81 - 100.

② See *Background Information on the International Centre for Settlement of Investment Disputes (ICSID)*, ICSID, https://icsid. worldbank. org/en/Documents/ICSID% 2Fact% 2Sheet% 20 - % 20ENGLISH. pdf., retrieved on 15th July 2020.

③ Seymour J. Rubin, Ewell E. Murphy, Jr., Detlev F. Vagts, K. Scott Gudgeon, Gerhard Wegen, Aron Broches & Samuel K. B. Asante, Avoidance and Settlement of International Investment Disputes, *American Society of International Law Proceedings* 78, 1984, p. 38 - 54.

首选方法。[①]

首先,调解机制允许当事方即使在发生争执的情况下也能保持良好的业务或外交关系。[②]

其次,调解机制可以显著地降低时间和经济成本。[③] ICSID 中的仲裁程序因其程序冗长、花费巨大而饱受诟病。投资仲裁程序平均需 3.5 年,每一当事方的平均费用为 80 万美元。这些成本无论是对跨国公司还是发展中国家,都是极大的负担。[④] 在 Metalclad 诉墨西哥合众国案中,Metalclad 公司最终获得了 1700 万美元的赔偿,该公司的首席执行官却感叹"此案中没有真正的赢家"[⑤],因为投资者和东道国政府都为争端解决付出了巨大代价。相比较之下,投资调解相对于投资仲裁而言具有显著的经济优势,因为当事方可以进一步协商,并就解决争端所要支付的金额达成最佳的经济议价。[⑥] 根据现有的调解案件的披露情况来看,调解机制的成本远低于仲裁程序的耗费。

再次,调解机制的灵活性更加有利于争端的解决。仲裁庭必须在国际法、投资协定、合同以及国内法设定的框架中权衡各方提出的请求与抗辩,从而确定违约赔偿责任和赔偿额。但在调解程序中,投资者和国家将有更大的空间实施创造性的解决方案,[⑦]调解程序所具备的灵活性可以更好地应对投资争端固有的技术复杂性。阿隆·布罗奇斯在报告中以牙买加案件为例指出,尽管牙买加单方面更改了协议中规定的特许权使用费,并且由于长期协议的情况发生了

---

① See Shannon, M., "Preventing War and Providing the Peace? International Organizations and the Management of Territorial Disputes," *Conflict Management and Peace Science*, Vol. 26, Iss. 2, 2009, p. 144 – 163.

② 第一部分已经涉及,此处不再赘述。

③ See Salacuse, J. W., "Is There a Better Way? Alternative Methods of Treaty – Based, Investor – State Dispute Resolution," *Fordham International Law Journal*, Vol. 31, Iss. 1, 2007, p. 138 – 157.

④ 参见王寰:《投资者——国家争端解决中的调解:现状、价值及制度构建》,载《江西社会科学》2019 年第 11 期。

⑤ ICSID Case No. ARB(AF)/97/1.

⑥ See Coe Jr, J. C., "Toward a Complementary Use of Conciliation in Investor State Disputes A Preliminary Sketch," *U. C. Davis Journal of International Law & Policy*, Vol. 12, 2005, p. 7 – 46.

⑦ See Constain, S., "Mediation in Investor – State Dispute Settlement: Government Policy and the Changing Landscape".

变化,但是争议各方仍然通过调解程序设法达成和解。①

最后,调解程序维持了当事人对于案件的高度控制。调解程序融合了中立第三方参与的同时,保留了争议主体对程序的最终控制权。在投资关系中,无论是政府还是投资者都希望能够掌握对争端的控制权,世界贸易组织的"成员驱动"(member - driven)机制就是国家保留控制权的典型范例。

(二)调解程序的适用困境

今天,ICSID 仍是解决投资争端的主要方式。1965 年之前,起草人曾预测,当《华盛顿公约》生效时,调解将证明"比仲裁程序更为重要"。② 在上述讨论中,也确实论证了调解对于纠纷解决的熨帖。但事实相反,在公约签署 50 年后,调解机制并未如预期一般发挥重要的作用。截至 2016 年,只有 12 例 ICSID 调解案件。尽管调解的保密性意味着还存在其他尚未披露的案件。但这也无法掩盖调解程序在投资争端解决机制中的弱势地位。

为什么调解在投资争端中很少使用?这一问题并不难回答。例如,相较于仲裁规则,调解规则往往具有更高的复杂性和技术性;寻找熟悉国际投资法领域的专家担任调解员并不容易;如果当事方无法通过调解达成协议,争端仍将诉诸仲裁,这意味着调解程序将浪费时间和经济资源;等等。然而,影响当事人选择调解最关键的三个原因是:第一,调解程序的保密性与投资争端解决领域旨在提高透明度和一致性的现行政策相抵触。③ 第二,投资协议中广泛存在的岔路口条款对调解程序适用空间的压缩。第三,目前为止尚未完全建立起允许各方当事人在世界范围内通过调解执行和解协议的机制。

1. 保密性的桎梏

保密性是调解机制最为显著的特性,也是其特殊价值的重要体现。④ 一次

---

① See Seymour J. Rubin, Ewell E. Murphy, Jr., Detlev F. Vagts, K. Scott Gudgeon, Gerhard Wegen, Aron Broches & Samuel K. B. Asante, Avoidance and Settlement of International Investment Disputes, *American Society of International Law Proceedings* 78, 1984, p. 38 – 54.

② See ICSID, *History of the ICSID Convention* (*Volume II* – 1), Washington, DC: ICSID, 1968, p. 242.

③ See Reisman, W. M, "International Investment Arbitration and ADR: Married but Best Living Apart," *ICSID Review – Foreign Investment Law Journal*, Vol. 24, Iss. 1, Spring 2009, p. 185 – 192;又见漆彤、范晓宇:《论投资者与东道国争端调解机制的透明度规则问题》,载《国际经济法学刊》2020 年第 3 期。

④ 参见《联合国贸易法委员会调解规则》第 10 条第 4 款;《华盛顿公约》第 33 条第 3 款;《国际商会调解规则》第 9 条第 1 款和第 10 条第 4 款;《国际律师协会投资争端调解规则》第 10 条第 1 款。

保密的调解可以避免产生不利的先例,进而避免为其他投资者的索赔打开闸门。[①] 这一功能可能会受到东道国政府的青睐。在 2001 年的阿根廷比索危机[②]和 2012 年西班牙政府对能源部门的管制[③]所引发的纠纷案中,一个案件背后潜藏着同一类型的多件纠纷。在 ICSID 仲裁中,仲裁程序是公开且具有约束力的,在这种情况下,政府别无选择,只能花费大量的成本对每一个案件进行仲裁,而且担忧因为输掉一个案件,而影响所有相关案件。调解的保密性则可以有效地避免先例裁判的影响。然而,保密性的存在不可避免地与投资争端的透明度规则之间产生矛盾。一方面,投资争端往往涉及公共利益,公众对于和解协议享有知情权。同时,如果纠纷涉及公民的基本权利,就其本质而言不能成为调解的对象。另一方面,一些国家的内部立法禁止政府及其官员进行调解和解决争端,调解机制保密性可能会面临国内法的挑战。

2. 岔路口条款的影响

如果缔约方在国际投资协定中明确约定岔路口条款或类似规定,当事方一旦作出选择就不能再次启动其他程序寻求救济。[④] 岔路口条款主要是为了避免纠纷久拖不决,陷入无尽的程序泥沼中。一般来说,岔路口条款最大限度地维护了东道国作为争端一方的利益,被广大发展中国家推崇,[⑤]其设置背景是,实质性的时间限制在投资协议中普遍存在,这就极大限制了投资者在短时间内对发生的纠纷提起仲裁的权利,无疑会影响投资者对调解程序的选择。例如,大多数中国双边投资协定规定了 3 个月的冷却期,要求投资者务必在该期间内进

---

① Coe Jr, J. C., "Toward a Complementary Use of Conciliation in Investor State Disputes A Preliminary Sketch".

② Sempra Energy International v. The Argentine Republic ICSID Case No. ARB/02/16, Award (28th September 2007); Enron Corp v. The Argentine Republic ICSID Case No. ARB/01/3, Award (22nd May 2007); LG&E Energy Corp et al. v. The Argentine Republic ICSID Case No. ARB/02/1, Award (25th July 2007).

③ Watkins Holdings S. i r. l. v. Kingdom of Spain ICSID Case No. ARB/15/44; NextEra Energy Global Holdings BV & NextEra Energy Spain Holdings BV v. Kingdom of Spain ICSID Case No. ARB/14/11.

④ 参见刘梦非:《论国际投资争端解决平行程序的规避——以程序安排为中心的思考》,载《甘肃政法学院学报》2020 年第 2 期。

⑤ 参见徐崇利:《国际投资条约中的"岔路口条款":选择"当地救济"与"国际仲裁"权利之限度》,载《国际经济法学刊》2007 年第 3 期。

行国内行政复议程序。[①] 在此种时间压力之下,某些调解规则进行调解的前提是“岔路口条款”或者禁止诉诸仲裁。《常设仲裁法院选择性调解规则》(PCA Optional Conciliation Rules)第 16 条规定:当事人承诺在调解程序中不针对与和解程序有关的争议提起任何仲裁或司法程序,除非当事方可以在其认为此类程序为维护其权利所必需的。

尚无法确定《华盛顿公约》第 26 条是否应解释为适用 ICSID 的调解程序。第 26 条指出,同意仲裁视为“排除任何其他救济措施”。在阿莫可诉印度尼西亚案中(Amco v. Indonesia),仲裁庭建议对第 26 条的理解应为“救济措施仅意味着司法救济”。换言之,选择仲裁并不当然意味着拒绝调解。然而,这仅是一家之言,岔路口条款的存在依然是调解程序适用的重要阻碍。

3. 执行力的缺乏

当事方倾向于具有约束力的裁决是调解不被重视的主要原因,[②]“仲裁条款的预防作用(约束力的威慑)是减少案件数量的主要因素”[③]。在投资争端解决的进程中,投资者可能已经与东道国政府进行了长期的谈判和斗争,也正因如此,疲倦的投资者不太可能再去选择无约束力的争端解决方式。为避免和解成为一种浪费的程序,有观点曾建议,争议各方可事先同意接受和解人的建议具有约束力。但是,基于《华盛顿公约》和《承认及执行外国仲裁裁决公约》(以下简称《纽约公约》)的规定,争议方提前约定的具有约束力和解建议可能无法在广阔的国际范围内获得执行力。所以,争议当事人并没有太强的动机选择调解。

四、调解机制的新趋势与启发

(一)《新加坡公约》的影响

应该如何构建调解程序,以经济高效、及时的方式帮助解决投资纠纷?布

---

① 参见沈伟:《投资者—东道国争端解决条款的自由化嬗变和中国的路径——以中国双边投资协定为研究对象》,载《经贸法律评论》2020 年第 3 期。

② See Onwuamaegbu, U. O., “The Role of ADR in Investor State Dispute Settlement: The ICSID Experience,” TDM 1 (2007), http://www.transnational-dispute-management.com/article.asp? key = 964, 14th July 2020.

③ Seymour J. Rubin, Ewell E. Murphy, Jr., Detlev F. Vagts, K. Scott Gudgeon, Gerhard Wegen, Aron Broches & Samuel K. B. Asante, Avoidance and Settlement of International Investment Disputes, *American Society of International Law Proceedings* 78, 1984, p. 38 - 54.

罗奇斯在1982年指出:“(国际法学界)越来越希望探索和解的可能性,可能是试图结合两种程序(调解与仲裁)的优点。著名的德国仲裁法专家 Otto - arndt Glossuer 博士提出了调解后达成的承认和执行协议的公约构想,但我认为这对企业来说太棘手了。我们还有其他更紧迫的担忧。”①

因此,融合调解和仲裁的尝试暂时被搁置了。然而,赋予调解协议以执行力的努力一直未曾停止。在纽约和维也纳进行了三年多的谈判之后,2018年2月9日,联合国国际贸易法委员会第二工作组结束了就执行争端解决协议的公约和示范法的谈判,在2018年秋季会议上最后敲定了文书细节。2019年8月7日,联合国大会宣布《联合国关于调解所产生的国际和解协议公约》(以下简称《新加坡公约》)开放签署。公约规定在第三个国家批准后的6个月后,即2020年9月12日正式生效。

《新加坡公约》被设计为通过《纽约公约》的模式进行调解,规定缔约方承诺赋予由和解产生的和解协议以执行力,《新加坡公约》要求成员国以与《纽约公约》对待仲裁裁决的方式类似的方式执行调解所产生的和解协议。如果《新加坡公约》在全球范围内被迅速批准,那么它可以消除调解的主要缺点之一——执行力的缺失,标志着对调解机制现代化的重大承诺,在解决跨境和国际争议的优先应用。②

众所周知,《纽约公约》通过为裁决的执行提供广泛的司法支持,使国际仲裁成为解决国际商事纠纷的主流方式,并为投资者—国家仲裁机制奠定了基础。《新加坡公约》旨在为国际商事争端解决添加一种新的可能性,尽管其最初动机是完善国际商事争端机制,但《新加坡公约》也可以应用于解决投资争端。ICSID 早在2018年 ICSID 调解规则改革中就提到了使用《新加坡公约》的可能性,并试图将和解协议纳入拟议的《新加坡公约》中关于执行调解协议的范围之内。《新加坡公约》中对于“调解”的定义是:“一种过程,无论所使用的表达方式或执行过程的基础如何,当事方都试图在缺乏向争端各方施加解决方案的权力的情况下,通过第三人或多人(调解人)的协助以友好方式解决争端。”可以肯

① Seymour J. Rubin, Ewell E. Murphy, Jr., Detlev F. Vagts, K. Scott Gudgeon, Gerhard Wegen, Aron Broches & Samuel K. B. Asante, Avoidance & Settlement of International Investment Disputes, *American Society of International Law Proceedings* 78, 1984, p. 38 – 54.

② 参见漆彤:《论“一带一路”国际投资争议的预防机制》,载《法学评论》2018年第3期。

定的是,《新加坡公约》能够适用于国际投资争端中投资者与东道国政府达成的和解协议。尽管如此,但《新加坡公约》第8条允许成员方进行保留,排除了与该政府或政府机构之间达成的和解协议。考虑到政府比商业团体更有可能执行与外国投资者达成的和解协议,同时也关注到欧盟和东盟等国际组织将更多地参与国际经济法和投资争端,《新加坡公约》也将由"由主权国家组成的"区域经济一体化组织开放签字。

(二)巴西CFIA示范法

巴西在2015年至2018年缔结的新一代《合作与促进投资协定》(Cooperation and Facilitation Investment Agreement,CFIA)(以下简称CFIA示范法)代表了调解发展的另一趋势。2015年巴西发布了CFIA示范法,期望能够替代传统的双边投资条约,在国家主权监管、投资者保护、可持续发展与促进投资便利化之间寻求一个平衡模式。[①] CFIA项下的争端解决机制为国际投资争端提供了替代方案。CFIA为了尽可能避免诉诸诉讼,各缔约方已经建立了两个机构安排来解决投资交易产生的问题或分歧:联合委员会(Joint Committee)[②]和国家联络点(Focal Point)[③]。协议详细说明了这两个机构的作用以及当发生争端时双方必须遵循的程序。具体而言,当联合委员会收到投资者的书面请求后,应在60日内(有正当理由并经双方同意可延长60日)评估案件的相关信息并提交报告,报告应包括协商措施的说明以及缔约双方协商的最后结果。同时,为了便于缔约双方寻求更合理的解决办法,联合委员会应尽可能地邀请受影响的投资者代表以及政府或非政府实体代表参加协商会议。如果未达成协议并且当事方决定不遵循联合委员会的报告,将会启动国家—国家仲裁机制,而非传统的投资者—东道国仲裁。

(三)新趋势对投资调解发展的启示

《新加坡公约》与巴西CFIA示范法在强化调解形式多样性的同时,也为投资争端调解的发展提供了有益的参考。

---

① 参见魏丹、唐妍彦:《从国际投资规则的旁观者到引领者——巴西CFIA模式研究》,载《武大国际法评论》2019年第5期。

② 联合委员会将在国家间层面进行对话,由双方政府代表组成。

③ 国家联络点是投资者与东道国的对话机构,由各个缔约方各自提名本国政府机构为联络点,并持续为外国投资者提供支持援助。

首先,投资调解应当为当事人提供约束力裁决的选项。尽管存在非约束性裁决偏好的可能,但《新加坡公约》的实践表明,为调解协议注入约束力是有必要的。在投资调解中,可以在征询投资者与东道国同意的情况下,通过双方合意的方式使得调解协议具有约束力。这样既可以强化调解机制的实效性,同时也可以卸下有"岔路口条款"情形下争议当事人选择调解的忧虑。这样的方式包括但不限于:将纷争递交仲裁机构,产生具有约束力的裁决(考虑到投资者与东道国已经达成一致,这一过程并不会占用太多时间);就双方认同的争端解决结果订立新的协议;协议中承担义务的一方提供抵押物等。

其次,扩展投资调解调解人的范围或多元性。投资仲裁对于仲裁员具有较高的要求,这固然有利于纠纷解决的专业性、中立性和严肃性,但也在一定程度上限制了当事方的选择余地。投资调解在此方面可以扩展自身优势,吸纳各界人士加入调解,尤其是可以考虑将投资者母国人员加入调解程序,如投资者母国驻东道国外交人员和商会负责人等,最大限度地发挥调解机制的灵活性,保证调解协议的公正性,提升纠纷一次性解决的可能。

最后,可以考虑有选择地公开调解结果。诚如前述,保密性对调解来说是一把双刃剑,它既吸引了一部分当事人,也将很多潜在对象拒之门外。在此,或许可以借鉴金融仲裁程序的做法,在删除部分敏感信息后公布调解结果,①以缓和调解机制保密性所产生的道德危机和国内法制约。

五、结语

通过对调解机制的功能分析、案例归纳和问题揭露,本文揭示了这样一个事实:在过去的几十年中,投资仲裁并未成为国际投资争端各方的首选方法。与之相对的是,调解程序成为了广受关注的方法。在《新加坡公约》开放签署的背景下,这一趋势必将更加流行。当然,在 ISDS 体系下,调解程序完全取代仲裁是不现实的:解决方式的选择将取决于冲突的性质、争端的政治化程度和利益攸关方的态度和意图。然而,国际法应当欢迎和鼓励所有 ADR 的发展。调解机制当然不适用于所有类型的投资者与国家之间的争端,但如果有当事人愿

① 参见苏伟康:《论国际金融仲裁发展及我国仲裁机构的应对》,载《研究生法学》2018 年第 4 期。

意启动更快、更灵活的程序,国际法律体系应当为当事方提供新的选择。在中国"一带一路"倡议不断落地的当下,调解机制的发展与完善将是学界与实务界共同应对的课题。

论国际投资仲裁中的第三方资助披露制度改革

贾　宏*

摘　要：国际投资仲裁领域的第三方资助虽然定义尚未形成共识，但在国际投资仲裁领域发展迅猛，呈现出资助目的多样化、隐秘性高、资助当事方单一等特征。本文置利益冲突及披露议题于讨论核心，认为第三方出资导致的仲裁员利益冲突问题与涉及第三方出资信息披露和透明度缺失密切相关。然而，目前国际投资仲裁第三方资助的相关规制存在披露主体混乱、披露范围界定不清、披露时间模糊以及无法对第三方资助者进行有效规制的现实困境。作为国际投资仲裁的主要竞技场，国际投资争端解决中心及联合国国际贸易法委员会分别启动国际投资仲裁适用规则的改革，其中第三方资助是热点议题之一。当前改革总体上具有合理性，通过在仲裁规则中广泛纳入和修订第三方资助披露制度、制定第三方资助者行为准则以及利用《透明度规则》中的存储处可避免仲裁员利益冲突影响国际投资仲裁的合法性。

关键词：第三方资助　国际投资仲裁　利益冲突　披露制度　ICSID 规则修订

---

* 贾宏，外交学院国际经济法专业硕士研究生。

一、国际投资仲裁中的第三方资助

(一)国际投资仲裁中第三方资助的概念界定

第三方资助最早发源于德国及澳大利亚,并于21世纪进入美国、英国等市场,随着在西方国家的市场建立及规模扩大,第三方资助近年来出现在部分亚洲国家及地区(如新加坡、中国内地与香港)。简言之,第三方资助是指当事人以外的第三人承担一方当事人在诉讼或仲裁程序中的费用并以该方当事人胜诉判决或裁决收益为回报的一种纠纷融资模式,①与第三方资助具有相同效用的有风险代理、责任保险、诉讼贷款等其他融资手段。② 与之矛盾的是传统英美法中禁止非当事人资助诉讼并分享胜诉成果的"助讼和帮讼分利原则",③但该原则已逐渐被司法实践抛弃。④ 第三方资助在2008年金融危机以后势头猛涨,一方面市场主体因经济低迷而没有充足现金流起诉或申请仲裁,另一方面投资者也在寻找受市场波动较小的新兴投资对象。⑤ 目前,涉及第三方资助的仲裁案件增速迅猛,⑥涉足国内诉讼、仲裁乃至国际商事和国际投资仲裁领域。出于对第三方资助具有的促进当事人寻求司法救济(access to justice)等积极因素与导致滥诉风险、利益冲突、违背社会公共利益等消极因素⑦的考量,目前部分国内立法机构、国际组织及学术研究机构已发布关于第三方资助的相关法律法规、条约规则、工作报告等。

---

① 参见郭华春:《第三方资助国际投资仲裁之滥诉风险与防治》,载《国际经济法学刊》2014年第2期。

② See Maya Steinitz, "Whose Claim Is It Anyway? Third – party Litigation Funding", 8 *Transnational Dispute Management*, 1278 (2011).

③ See Jones Von Goeler, *Third Party Funding in International Arbitration and its Impacts on Procedures*, Wolters Kluwer Press, 2016, p. 40.

④ See Siegfried Adalbert Unruh v. Hans Joerg Seeberg and Another, [2017] HKCFA10; Lord Mustill in Giles v. Thompson, [1993] UKHL2.

⑤ See *Third – Party Funding in International Arbitration*, *The ICCA Report No.* 4, ICCA – Queen Mary Task Force, 2018, p. 18.

⑥ See James Delaney, Mistakes to Avoid When Approaching Third – Party Funder, Global Arbitration Review, at https://globalarbitrationreview.com/article/1033321/mistakes – to – avoid – when – approaching – third – party – funders (last visited on November 26, 2020).

⑦ 参见唐琼琼:《第三方资助纠纷解决规制模式的国际经验及思考》,载《上海财经大学学报》2018年第6期。

目前国内或地区法层面仅有新加坡及中国香港对第三方资助作出规制,2017 年《新加坡民法修正案》[①]中界定第三方资助协议与第三方资助者;[②]《香港特别行政区 2017 年仲裁及调解法例(第三方资助)(修订)条例》第 10A 部分第 98 条采取罗列构成要素的方式对第三方资助、第三方资助者、资助合同作出定义。[③] 尽管表达形式不同,新加坡与香港特别行政区法中的第三方资助本质为与案件无关的实体向当事人一方提供资金以资助争端解决程序的进行并据此从案件结果中获得收益。不同之处在于第三方资助者身份的界定,新加坡立法修订对第三方资助者身份作严格要求,包括主要营业地在新加坡或其他地区、已缴纳股本不低于 500 万新加坡元或等值外国货币或等值管控资产等;《香港特别行政区第三方资助仲裁实务守则》从资本充足、利益冲突、保密性问题等方面对第三方资助者提出了软性要求。可见,香港对第三方资助实体目前尚无具有强制约束力的要求,新加坡立法则通过注册资本、营业地等限制提高第三方资助者的准入门槛,以此使得适用新加坡实体规则的资助协议下的第三方资助者具备一定专业程度及资金实力。

与国内法中第三方资助主要集中于商业资助且有诸多限定的狭窄定义相比,部分双边投资协定(Bilateral Investment Treaty,BIT)或自由贸易协定(Free Trade Agreement,FTA)中定义囊括范围更广。目前规制第三方资助的 BIT 或

① 《新加坡民法修正案》于 2017 年 1 月 10 日通过议会决议。See A. Henderson and D. Waldek, Singarpore Arbitration Update: Third Party Funding and New Siac Rules 2016, at https://hsfnotes.com/arbitration/2016/07/01/singapore – arbitration – update – third – party – funding – and – new – siac – rules – 2016/(last visited on November 24, 2020).

② 参见《新加坡民法修正案》第二部分规定:"第三方资助协议指争议解决程序的当事人或潜在当事人一方与提供诉讼程序进行的部分或全部费用以获取当事人或潜在当事人一方可能获得的收益的第三方资助者订立的合同或协定。"

③ 参见《香港特别行政区 2017 年仲裁及调解法例(第三方资助)(修订)条例》(2019 年 2 月 1 日起生效)第 98G 条规定:"仲裁中的第三方资助是:(1)以资助合同形式订立的;(2)对象为受资助方;(3)由第三方资助者提供;(4)第三方资助者只有在取得资助合同定义下的支持受资助方裁决结果时才能获得经济利益。"第 98J 条规定:"第三方资助者是:(a)为资助仲裁与被资助方订立资助协议的当事人一方;(b)除资助协议外,与仲裁没有法律上承认的利益。"第 98H 条规定:"资助协议是为第三方资助仲裁而订立的:(a)书面形式;(b)被资助方与第三方资助者之间订立的;(c)在仲裁程序开始或之后订立的。"

FTA 仅限于欧盟、加拿大等，[①]第三方资助定义表述基本一致，资助目的不仅局限于商业目的，资助形式还包括捐赠或赠款，也没有对第三方资助者进行资格限制或类型区分。

仲裁机构和国际组织方面，新加坡国际仲裁中心（Singapore International Arbitration Center，SIAC）、中国国际经济贸易仲裁委员会（以下简称贸仲委）、北京仲裁委员会/北京国际仲裁中心（以下简称北仲）颁布的指引或仲裁规则都有涉及第三方资助。新加坡仲裁机构公布的《第三方资助者指南》[②]、SIAC《涉及外部资助时仲裁员行为准则的实践提示》中[③]的第三方资助或外部资助定义都仅局限于商业性质。《中国国际经济贸易仲裁委员会国际投资争端仲裁规则（试行）》（以下简称《贸仲委投资争端规则》）第 27 条[④]及《北京仲裁委员会/北京国际仲裁中心国际投资仲裁规则》（以下简称《北仲投资规则》）第 39 条第 1 款[⑤]采取的表述方式基本一致，囊括所有协议承担仲裁费用或提供资金支持仲

① 参见《加拿大—欧洲联盟全面经济和贸易协定》（自 2017 年 9 月 20 日暂行）第 8.1 条规定："第三方出资系不属于争端方但与争端一方签订协议的自然人或法人提供任何资金，以捐赠或赠款形式或为根据争端结果换取报酬而支付部分或全部程序费用。"《欧洲联盟—越南投资保护协定》（2019 年 6 月 30 日签署）第 3.28 条规定："i. '第三方出资'系不属于争端方但与争端一方签订协议的自然人或法人提供任何资金，为根据争端结果换取报酬而支付部分或全部程序费用，或不属于争端方的自然人或法人以捐赠或赠款形式提供任何资金。"《欧洲联盟—新加坡投资保护协定》（2018 年 10 月 19 日签署）第 3.1 条规定："2. 在本节中，除非另有规定：（f）'第三方出资'系不属于争端方但与争端一方签订协议的自然人或法人提供任何资金，用于支付部分或全部程序费用，以换取该争议方可能有权获得的程序收益或潜在收益的份额或其他利益，或以捐赠或赠款形式提供任何资金。"《加拿大—智利自由贸易协定》（自 1997 年 7 月 1 日生效）第 G－23 条之二规定 "3. 在本条中，第三方出资系不属于争端方但与争端一方签订协议的人提供任何资金，以捐赠或赠款形式或为根据争端结果换取报酬而支付部分或全部程序费用"。

② 参见新加坡仲裁机构《第三方资助者指南》（2017 年 5 月 18 日）第 1.1 条规定："第三方资助是指为了从胜诉裁决中获得经济利益，第三方提供融资支持争端一方当事人参与仲裁程序或调解程序。" athttps://siarb. org. sg/images/SIArb – TPF – Guidelines – 2017_final18 – May – 2017. pdf, last visited on: 20/12/2020.

③ See Singapore International Arbitration Practice Note of 31 March 2017 Article 3(c)："外部资助是与仲裁程序的裁决结果有直接经济利益的个人或实体", available at http://www. siac. org. sg/images/stories/articles/rules/Third% 20Party% 20Funding% 20Practice% 20Note% 2031% 20March% 202017. pdf, last visited on ：5/12/2020。

④ 《中国国际经济贸易仲裁委员会国际投资争端仲裁规则（试行）》（2017 年 10 月 1 日起施行）第 27 条第 1 款规定："第三方资助是当事人以外的自然人或实体协议承担参与争议的一方当事人在仲裁程序中的全部或部分费用的情形。"

⑤ 《北京仲裁委员会/北京国际仲裁中心国际投资仲裁规则》（2019 年 10 月 1 日起施行）第 39 条第 1 款规定："第三方资助是指并非争端当事人的个人或实体（以下简称'第三方资助人'）向仲裁程序的一方当事人或当事人的关联方或代理人提供资金或其他相当于资金的支持以进行仲裁活动。"

裁活动的第三方,不论资助目的或资助形式。《国际律师协会国际仲裁利益冲突指南》(International Bar Association Guidelines on Conflicts of Interest in International Arbitration)(以下简称 IBA 冲突指南)在 2014 年最早提及第三方资助,但并未直接定义而是采取间接方式,即从仲裁员应当披露的内容方面引出第三方资助。国际商事仲裁理事会与玛丽女王学院在国际仲裁第三方出资问题专门工作报告中对定义采广泛方式,既囊括不同资助形式,也包括不同资助目的。①

尽管目前立法、司法实践以及理论界已对第三方资助基本构成要素有较为统一的认识,包括以下几方面:一是资助方为非争端当事人;二是受资助方包括争端当事人一方;三是资助形式包括向受资助方提供资金支持;四是资助目的包括受资助方获有利裁决,从中获取部分或全部经济利益。但尚不存在对第三方资助的公认概念,对第三方资助的囊括范围尚未形成共识,这集中体现在以下两方面:一是资助目的是否包括无偿行为,在仲裁领域尤其是国际投资仲裁,第三方资助者并非仅考虑获取经济利益。通过无偿资助投资方或母国获得有利裁决有助于实现其特定政治、文化、社会政策等目的。二是资助形式是否包括风险代理、责任保险(以被保险人在争端解决程序中被要求承担不利后果时所负责任为保险标的)、②诉讼贷款、基于股权性质的融资等。

目前学理讨论第三方资助多集中于国际商事仲裁,本文研究背景即国际投资仲裁与国际商事仲裁存在差异。相比于国际商事仲裁中当事人双方私主体身份,国际投资仲裁当事人一方为国家,具有公法人身份主权性特征,这要求国际投资仲裁程序和结果更具透明度、正当性、合法性以及体现特定社会价值和公共政策利益。③ 因而面对国际投资仲裁中的第三方资助时,概念和利益冲突

---

① See Report of the ICCA – Queen Mary Task Force, Third – Party Funding in International Arbitration, The ICCA Report No. 4 (2018), p. 50. 第三方资助为非争端当事方的自然人或法人向当事人或当事人的附属或代表当事人一方的律所:(1)为一个或一系列案件程序进行所需的部分或全部费用提供资金或实质性帮助;(2)这些资金或实质性帮助是以部分或全部根据争议结果计算的报酬或补偿为交换或以保险金作为回报的形式提供的。

② J. Clanchy, "*Navigating the Waters of Third Party Funding in Arbitration*", 3 *The International Journal of Arbitration, Mediation and Dispute Management*, 222 – 232 (2016).

③ Gary B. Born, "Chapter 18: Investor – State and State – to – State Arbitration", *International Arbitration: Law and Practice*, 2nd edn., Kluwer Law International, p. 417 – 449.

影响的界定范围应当更广泛，以囊括形式不同但本质上为非争端当事方为当事人一方提供实质性帮助这一构造的多种资助形式，因此本文将国际投资仲裁中的第三方资助定义为："非争端当事方以获取被资助方有利裁决结果为目的，向当事人一方或其关联主体参与国际投资仲裁案件直接或间接提供任何形式的实质性帮助。"

（二）国际投资仲裁中的第三方资助特点

1. 资助目的多样化

与国际商事仲裁不同，国际投资仲裁中的第三方资助目的更为多元，资助者不仅为获取有利裁决结果的分成，还考虑制造有利的裁决先例、支持某一特定公共政策等。在 Quasar de Valores v. Russia① 案中，Mentalap 资助投资者的目的是为针对俄罗斯提起的另一起仲裁案件创造有利先例。在 *Philip Morris v. Uruguay* 案中，Philip Morris 称乌拉圭政府采取的烟草管控政策违反 1988 年乌拉圭—瑞士 BIT 而将乌拉圭诉至解决投资争端国际中心（International Center for Settlement of Investment Disputes，ICSID），在案件审理过程中，彭博基金会及其旗下的"让孩子远离烟草"运动等无政府组织为乌拉圭政府提供资金支持。在这一案件中，提供资助的无政府组织目的为支持国家为烟草管控作出的努力。②

2. 资助隐秘程度高

国际投资仲裁领域虽存在一定透明度要求，但资助协议中普遍采用的保密条款仍使得第三方资助处于不透明地带。除非另一方当事人申请披露第三方资助或因资助协议本身发生争议等情形外，几乎无法从其他渠道得知此类情况。即便仲裁庭命令披露，内容也仅包括资助者身份，第三方资助协议条款等其他具体内容更是罕为外界所知。

3. 资助当事方单一

理论上，投资者和东道国既可以成为申请方也可以成为被申请方，同时资

---

① See Quasar de Valors and others v. The Russian Federation, SCC Case No. 24/2007.

② 参见乌拉圭政府的律师代表所在律所 Foley Hoag LLP 的相关报道，"Government of Uruguay Taps Foley Hoag for Representation in International Arbitration Brought by Philip Morris to Overturn Country's Tobacco Regulations", p. 8, available at http://www.foleyhoag.com/news-and-events/news/2010/october/uruguay-taps-foley-hoag-for-representation, last visited on: 08/11/2020。

助者既可以选择资助投资者也可以选择资助母国。然而实践中通常为投资方启动仲裁程序,东道国被动应诉。[①] 同时第三方资助者也往往选择向申请方提供出资,一方面投资仲裁的高昂费用使得投资者无法或不愿支付仲裁费用,另一方面高额的损害赔偿金等请求以及“有利于投资者”的裁决倾向使得国际投资仲裁潜在收益极大,[②]因此无论从投资者角度还是资助者角度,资助投资者能在较大程度上实现双赢局面。另外,国家作为公主体,通常处于被动地位,很少提出反诉,且东道国即便是获得有利裁决也不能得到来自投资者的赔偿,[③]因此大多数投资者无法从东道国有利裁决中获得经济利益,也就丧失资助东道国积极性。然而,也存在非出于营利目的的第三方资助者资助东道国的个例。

二、国际投资仲裁中第三方资助下的利益冲突与披露制度

(一)利益冲突的成因及表现方式

仲裁程序公正的核心之一是仲裁员保持独立。独立性指仲裁员与当事人之间没有影响裁决的连带关系,[④]具体体现为经济联系、感情关系以及社会身份关联。[⑤] 利益冲突本质上源自人们对仲裁员独立性、公正性的期待与现实生活中错综复杂的血缘、经济、文化社会关系之间的落差。国际投资仲裁领域关于仲裁员利益冲突议题的讨论早已有之,包括 IBA 冲突指南、《解决国家与他国国民间投资争端公约》(Convention on the Settlement of Investment Disputes between States and Nationals of Other States,以下简称 ICSID 公约)、[⑥]《联合国国际贸易法委员会仲裁规则》(United Nations Commission on International Trade

---

① Gary B. Born,“Chapter 18: Investor - State and State - to - State Arbitration”, in *International Arbitration: Law and Practice*, 2nd edn., Kluwer Law International 2015, p. 417 - 449.

② 参见蔡从燕:《国际投资仲裁的商事化与“去商事化”》,载《现代法学》2011 年第 1 期。

③ Stephen W. Schill, *Arbitration Risk and Effective Compliance: Cost - Shifting in Investment Treaty Arbitration*, The Journal of World Investment and Arbitration, Vol. 7, p. 653.

④ 参见[英]艾伦 · 雷德芬、[英]马丁 · 亨特:《国际商事仲裁法律与实践》,林一飞、宋连斌译,北京大学出版社 2005 年版,第 215 页。

⑤ William W. Park, *Rectitude in International Arbitration*, Kluwer Law International, Vol. 27, 2017, p. 476.

⑥ 参见 ICSID 公约第 14 条第 1 款规定:“指派在仲裁员小组服务的人员应具有高尚的道德品质,并且在法律、商务、工业和金融方面有公认的能力。他们可以被信赖作出独立的判断。”

Law Arbitration Rules,以下简称 UNCITRAL 仲裁规则)①等。

但上述利益冲突的规制主要集中在仲裁员与双方当事人及其代理人之间,第三方资助介入给仲裁员保持独立性、公正性带来新的挑战。第三方资助目的集中体现为获得有利裁决结果并以提取有利裁决结果的一定比例或全部报酬为对价,为保证收益率,第三方资助者利用尽职调查从案件实体、预计损害赔偿额、预计费用支出、被申请方财产状况等方面衡量是否资助某一案件。② 在确定资助后,第三方资助者则通过对案件施以不同程度的直接或间接控制以确保或提高案件胜诉的可能,其中选任仲裁员为重要步骤之一,在此过程中,仲裁员与第三方资助者存在千丝万缕的联系而导致仲裁员潜在利益冲突的可能性大大增加。③

首先,仲裁员与第三方资助者可能存在经济联系,包括仲裁员或仲裁员的重要家庭成员担任第三方资助实体的董事会成员、监事会成员、经理或实际控制人或持有第三方实体或其附属机构股份等雇佣或持股关系,也包括仲裁员经常性地向第三方资助者提供法律意见并获取重要经济来源、仲裁员或所在律所与第三方资助者或其附属机构有重要的商业合作关系等业务往来关系。

其次,仲裁员与第三方资助者可能存在身份关系。身份关系既包括血缘亲属关系也包括工作关系,如仲裁员与第三方资助者及其附属机构的经理、董事、监事会成员及实际控制人有重要的家庭成员关系,仲裁员或仲裁员所在律所的其他律师担任第三方资助者资助的另一案件的代理人等。

(二)国际投资仲裁中的第三方资助披露制度

第三方资助语境下的披露制度属于制度借鉴的产物,它根源于国际商事和

① UNCITRAL 仲裁规则第 11 条规定,可能被指定为仲裁员的人,应在与此指定有关的洽谈中披露可能对其公正性和独立性产生有正当理由怀疑的任何情况。仲裁员应自其被指定之时起,并在整个仲裁程序期间,毫无延迟地向各方当事人以及其他仲裁员披露任何此种情况,除非此种情况已由其告知各方当事人。第 12 条规定,(1)如果存在可能对任何仲裁员的公正性或独立性产生有正当理由怀疑的情况,均可要求该仲裁员回避;(2)一方当事人只能根据其指定仲裁员之后才得知的理由,对其所指定的仲裁员要求回避;(3)仲裁员不作为,或者仲裁员因法律上或事实上的原因无法履行其职责的,应适用第 13 条中规定的程序申请仲裁员回避。

② See Report of the ICCA – Queen Mary Task Force, Third – Party Funding in International Arbitration, The ICCA Report No. 4 (2018), p. 25.

③ 参见周清华、程斌:《第三方资助下仲裁员潜在利益冲突披露的体系建构》,载《中国海商法研究》2018 年第 4 期。

投资仲裁中为保证仲裁员公正性和独立性所作的制度安排。“披露”,顾名思义为使处于不公开状态的信息在一定范围内公开。IBA 冲突指南中认为利益冲突与披露制度密切相关,披露制度为当事人提供判断影响仲裁员公正独立裁决因素的契机,在一定程度上保证仲裁裁决和仲裁程序的正当性,所谓“阳光是最好的防腐剂”。在此制度设计目的下,披露制度呈现出程序先行、程序强制等特点。首先,仲裁员披露制度不同于申请仲裁员回避,仲裁员应当于被任命时及程序进行的任何阶段不断披露,程序上早于当事人申请回避制度,确保尽早发现利益冲突情形,避免程序倒流影响仲裁效率;其次,仲裁员的披露义务为强制性,一般体现为接受任命时向当事人及仲裁机构提交的独立性公正性声明。

然而,第三方资助语境下的披露制度实践却呈现出不同的发展样态。因仲裁具有保密性特征及第三方资助协议规定保密条款等,国际投资仲裁中第三方资助案件的比例尚无可靠数据,但相关数据显示 2013 年所有提交至 ICSID 的仲裁案件中 60% 以上涉及第三方资助,①与庞大受资助投资仲裁案数目形成鲜明对比的是涉及披露制度案件的数量之少。

即便在为数不多的投资仲裁案件中,仲裁庭针对如何命令披露第三方资助这一问题也呈现两极分化的态度。首先,部分仲裁庭认为仅需披露第三方资助者身份,在 *South American Silver v. Bolivia*② 案中,被申请方以保护仲裁程序公正性及公平对待双方当事人为由,要求仲裁庭命令披露申请方的第三方资助者及资助协议内容,但仲裁庭仅同意披露第三方资助者,以无关性为由拒绝命令披露资助协议条款。在 *EuroGas Inc. v. Slovak Republic*③ 案中,申请人已自愿披露其接受了一名来自注册地为卢森堡的资助者的资金支持,但并未披露资助者身份,仲裁庭仅止步于命令披露第三方资助者身份以判断仲裁员利益冲突。在 *Guaracachi v. Bolivia*④ 案中仲裁庭同样拒绝命令披露仲裁协议。其次,部分仲裁庭认为既需披露第三方资助者身份,亦需披露资助协议条款。在 *Muham-*

---

① See Report of the ICCA - Queen Mary Task Force, Third - Party Funding in International Arbitration, The ICCA Report No. 4 (2018), p. 75.

② See South American Silver Limited v. Plurinational State of Bolivia, PCA Case No. 2013 - 15, Procedural Order No. 10 (11 January 2016).

③ See EuroGas Inc and Belmont Resources Inc. v. Slovak Republic, ICSID Case No. ARB/14/14.

④ See Guaracachi America, Inc. and Rurelec PLC v. The Plurinational State of Bolivia, UNCITRAL, PCA Case No. 2011 - 17, Procedural Order No. 13 (21 Feburary 2013).

met Çap v. Turkmenistan[①] 案中，仲裁庭不仅要求披露第三方资助者身份，更以其有内在权力去发布命令以保证当事人权益及程序正当性为由要求披露资助协议的部分条款。最后，部分案件中却从未涉及第三方资助的披露，在 *S &T Oil &Machinery v. Romania*[②] 案中，第三方资助机构 Juridica 资助申请人提出仲裁请求，后因 S&T Oil 起诉 Juridica 第三方资助协议才得以披露。

第三方资助披露制度具有其特殊性。第一，区别于仲裁员披露制度的系统性、事先性、强制性，第三方资助披露实践目前多表现为仲裁员命令模式，即由仲裁员决定是否以及如何披露第三方资助相关信息；第二，披露要求往往发生在另一方当事人通过其他渠道得知存在第三方资助时，申请仲裁庭予以披露，而非由受资助方事先予以披露；第三，被资助方针对披露第三方资助的抗辩往往集中于与案件无关、受资助协议保密条款约束等理由，极少主动予以披露。

三、第三方资助披露制度的缺陷

（一）现有规制缺乏系统性

现有规则缺乏系统性有两方面原因：一是主要国际投资仲裁机构尚无第三方资助利益冲突相关规制；二是现有规制尚未成型。一方面，目前仅有 IBA、SIAC、贸仲委、北仲等组织对国际投资仲裁中第三方资助利益冲突进行规制，而作为国际投资争端解决的主要机构——ICSID、联合国国际贸易法委员会（United Nations Commission on International Trade Law，UNCITRAL）等[③]却暂无成文规定。[④] 同时仅有欧盟或加拿大等的 BITs 或 FTAs 中对第三方资助进行规制，关于第三方资助利益冲突的现有规制尚未得到足够关注或重视，核心监管领域仍呈空白状态。另一方面，现有规制的内容混乱，对于披露主体、披露内容、披

① See Muhammet Çap & Sehil In aat Endustri ve Ticaret Ltd Sti v. Turkmenistan，ICSID Case No. ARB/12/6，Procedural Order No. 3（12 June 2015）.

② See S&T Oil Equipment and Machinery Ltd. v. Romania，ICSID Case No. ARB/07/13.

③ See United Nations Conference on Trade and Development，*Special Update on Investor - State Dispute Settlement：Facts and Figures*，IIA ISSUES NOTE，Nov. 2017，at 5（reporting that between 1987 and mid - 2017，61% of international investment arbitrations were settled through ICSID and 31 % were settled through UNCITRAL）.

④ See Valentina Frignati，*Ethical Implications of Third - Party Funding in International Arbitration*，International Arbitration Law，Vol. 32，p. 505 - 506.

露时间等存在分歧。

1. 披露主体混乱

目前已对第三方资助利益冲突进行规制的仲裁规则存在披露主体混乱问题。IBA 冲突指南既规定仲裁员的披露义务，[①]也规定当事人的通知义务，[②]但并未阐明仲裁员的披露义务与当事人通知义务之间的关系。《贸仲委投资争端规则》及《北仲投资规则》中采取将披露义务施加给被资助方的形式，同时赋予仲裁庭命令当事人披露的权力。目前相关规制中披露主体主要存在仲裁员及当事人均应披露、仅需当事人披露、仅需仲裁员披露三种情形，如何协调仲裁员与当事人两方主体披露的关系，如何处理仲裁员或当事人不知晓相关利益冲突而导致信息未被披露，[③]如何达成统一披露主体的共识，这些问题尚无定论。

2. 披露内容界定不清

目前现有规制的最大分歧之一为披露内容。部分仲裁规则虽直接规制第三方资助主体信息的披露，但披露范围尚未形成共识。《贸仲委投资争端规则》中的披露内容仅包括第三方资助安排的基本事实；SIAC 投资仲裁规则中披露范围还包括资助者与裁决结果之间的利益关系或第三方资助者有无承诺承担裁决的不利费用；《北仲投资规则》在 SIAC 投资仲裁规则的基础上增加了第三方资助人及其实际控制人（如有）与仲裁员之间的关系（如有）。相比于上一种方式，直接披露第三方资助者相关信息的方式虽更为清晰，但仍然存在披露程度的问题，其中核心争议点为是否应当披露资助协议条款及进一步信息。

3. 披露时间模糊

关于第三方资助的披露时间尚未形成共识，目前已有的学术研究和仲裁规则提供的披露时间点包括提交仲裁申请阶段、选择仲裁员阶段、若为在仲裁庭

① IBA 冲突指南 General Standard 3（a）："如果存在以当事人眼光看来能够引起对仲裁员公正性和独立性合理怀疑的事实和情况，那么仲裁员应当在接受指定前，向当事人、仲裁机构或其他指定仲裁员的主体（如果有这样的主体且仲裁规则要求向其披露）和其他仲裁员（如果仲裁庭有其他仲裁员）披露这些情况和事实；仲裁员在接受指定后才知道这些事实和情况的，应在知晓后立即披露。"

② IBA 冲突指南 General Standard 7（a）："当事人一方应当将仲裁员与当事人，或集团下的另一公司，或对仲裁中的当事人一方有控制性影响的个人，或对仲裁裁决享有直接经济利益，或根据作出的仲裁裁决对另一方当事人负有赔偿义务的法人或自然人之间直接或间接的关系通知仲裁员、仲裁庭、另一方当事人、仲裁机构以及任命机构（如有）。"

③ See Report of the ICCA – Queen Mary Task Force, Third – Party Funding in International Arbitration, The ICCA Report No. 4 (2018), p. 112.

组成后签订资助协议则于签订资助协议后,也有部分仲裁规则以“尽早”等字眼表达,披露时间尚未形成共识。

(二)披露制度无法规制第三方资助者

国际投资仲裁庭的管辖权来自国家与国家或国家与投资者之间的合意,该合意也是仲裁庭其他固有程序性或实体性权力的来源。鉴于第三方资助者仅分享有利裁决利益甚至非为获得报酬,当事人一方本质上并未转移诉权,第三方资助者非案件当事人,仲裁庭的权力边界无法到达第三方资助者。

部分国家的国内仲裁员协会或资助者协会颁布了第三方资助者指引,如英国、新加坡等。作为行业自助协会,英国的英格兰威尔士诉讼资助者协会在其2018年发布的《第三方资助者行为准则》①中仅提及第三方资助者与被资助方之间的行为要求,并未提及针对法院的披露义务,且该协会仅针对资助诉讼程序的行为,并未涉及国际投资仲裁。新加坡仲裁员协会于2017年5月颁布的《第三方资助者指南》②区分签订资助协议前及签订资助协议后两个时间段,明确资助人应确保不会因资助而引起任何利益冲突,包括但不限于与被资助方及其代理人、另一方当事人及其代理人、法院或仲裁庭的利益冲突。同时,资助者应当配合被资助方及其代理人进行有关资助信息的披露事宜。但结合2017年《新加坡民法修正案》,该指引范围仅适用于主营业地在新加坡的第三方资助实体。

综上,目前部分国内第三方资助行为准则或仅局限于诉讼资助领域,或对资助者有营业地或注册资本限制,而目前主要国际投资仲裁规则的规制对象仅有仲裁机构、仲裁庭、仲裁员、当事人。除资助协议外,尚无对国际投资仲裁领域第三方资助者资助行为进行规制的条约或仲裁规则,第三方资助者仍处于监管的空白地带,真正掌握利益冲突事实的第三方资助者“逍遥于”披露制度之外。

---

① See Code of Conduct for Litigation Funder, The Association of Litigation Funders of England& Wales, available athttps://associationoflitigationfunders. com/wp – content/uploads/2018/03/Code – Of – Conduct – for – Litigation – Funders – at – Jan – 2018 – FINAL. pdf, last visited on: 13/04/2020.

② See Practice Note of 31 March 2017, available at http://www. siac. org. sg/images /stories/articles/rules/Third% 20Party% 20Funding% 20Practice% 20Note% 2031% 20March% 202017. pdf, last visited on: 13/04/2020.

四、披露制度的改革进展与完善路径

(一)披露制度的改革进展

1. 国际投资争端解决中心的改革进展

作为 ICSID 公约的具体补充,ICSID 仲裁规则于 1967 年施行后历经三次修订。2016 年 10 月 ICSID 启动最新修订并分别于 2018 年 8 月、2019 年 3 月、2019 年 8 月、2020 年 2 月发布第 1、2、3、4 号修订提议工作文件,其中第三方资助为关注热点之一。

2018 年 8 月颁布的 1 号工作文件①中,第三方资助的披露位于第三章"仲裁庭的组成"第 21 条,第 1 款规定第三方资助的定义;第 2 款规定披露内容为第三方资助的存在及名称,提交书面通知的时间为提交仲裁申请时,或在提交仲裁申请后订立第三方资助协议后,立即向秘书处提交;第 3 款规定任何一方当事人都有持续的义务披露发生于披露后的第 2 款所指信息,这些信息包括资助协议的终止。

2019 年 3 月颁布的 2 号工作文件②中,第三方资助被提前至第二章"仲裁庭的组成"第 14 条,与 1 号工作文件相比,2 号工作文件对第三方资助规制主要做结构上调整。鉴于规制第三方资助的主要目的为判断有无利益冲突,2 号工作文件没有以单独定义的方式界定第三方资助,相反,采取直接在披露义务中界定的方式。除此之外,信息披露的接受者发生变化,由 1 号工作文件中的秘书处变更为秘书长。

2019 年 8 月颁布的 3 号工作文件③相比于 2 号工作文件的显著区别为规定秘书长应当将关于第三方资助的通知及变化通知到另一方当事人、拟提议任命的仲裁员或已被提名的仲裁员以完成仲裁员声明。

2020 年 2 月颁布的 4 号工作文件④与第 3 号文件基本相似,增添内容包括:第一,披露内容既包括第三方资助者名称,也包括地址;第二,当事方获取资助既包括直接方式也包括间接方式;第三,第 5 款规定,如果仲裁庭认为有需要,

① See Proposals for Amendment of ICISD Rules Working Paper #1, Volume 3, p. 129.

② See Proposals for Amendment of ICISD Rules Working Paper #2, Volume 1, p. 118.

③ See Proposals for Amendment of ICISD Rules Working Paper #3, Volume 1, p. 37.

④ See Proposals for Amendment of ICISD Rules Working Paper #4, Volume 1, p. 37.

可以根据第36(3)条在程序的任意阶段命令当事人披露关于资助协议和非当事人一方的进一步信息。

2. UNCITRAL 的改革进展

UNCITRAL 第三工作组主要致力于确定并审议投资人与国家间国际投资争端解决方面的关切,并在此基础上审议改革是否可取,[①]其中第三方资助为重大关切之一。工作组、成员国、部分观察员国及国际组织分别于第三十六届及第三十七届会议中对第三方资助可能的改革及解决办法进行讨论。从第三方资助定义范围、法律框架出发,讨论涉及利益冲突和披露、第三方控制和影响、保密和法定保密特权、费用和费用担保、对无根据索赔的影响等多个方面。

工作组将利益冲突和披露这一议题置于讨论的第一顺位,认为仲裁员与第三方出资人之间的利益冲突问题与涉及第三方出资人的信息披露和透明度缺失密切相关,而这一问题被认为与仲裁员与当事方之间的利益冲突问题同等重要。[②] 同时,因其可能对仲裁裁决的可执行性以及更广泛而言对仲裁程序的完整性和国际仲裁的合法性产生影响,[③]所以更值得关注。在披露内容方面,工作组表示要确保最终出资人的身份得到披露,考虑出资人会经常性转售投资资本,此项要求是一项持续性要求;关于披露要求,工作组认为系统性和强制性要求披露第三方出资人相关信息,或者确认仲裁庭有权在任何时候责令披露第三方出资相关信息皆可;未披露相关信息的后果包括暂停程序以责令遵守披露规定、制定费用转移规则、要求违反披露义务的一方承担费用等。除此之外,考虑第三方资助利益披露的监管规定应确保一定的透明度,[④]工作组考虑遵守 UNCITRAL 制定的透明度标准,包括通过根据《投资人与国家间基于条约仲裁透明度规则》(以下简称《透明度规则》)设立的透明度登记处[⑤]提供有关投资争

① 参见《大会正式记录,第七十二届会议,补编第17号》(A/72/17),第263页。

② 参见《投资人与国家间争端解决(投资争端解决)制度的可能改革—第三方出资—秘书处的说明》,A/CN. 9/WG. III/WP. 157,第17段,载 http://undocs. org/en/A/CN. 9/WG. III/WP. 157,最后访问日期:2020年11月15日。

③ 同上注。

④ 参见《第三工作组(投资人与国家间争端解决制度改革)第三十七届会议工作报告》,A/CN. 9/970,第20段,载 https://undocs. org/en/A/CN. 9/970,最后访问日期:2020年11月15日。

⑤ 联合国秘书长通过贸易法委员会秘书处履行透明度登记处职能,参见《透明度规则》第2、3、8条,载 http://www. uncitral. org/transparency - registry/en/introduction. html, last visited on: 19/11/2020。

端解决制度中第三方出资的必要信息。同时,工作组考虑建立第三方出资人的操守准则以规范投资争端解决制度中第三方出资人从业行为。[①]

除部分认为应禁止国际投资仲裁中第三方资助的国家[②]外,其他成员方普遍认为第三方资助需要有更多透明度,[③]中国支持未尽披露义务时明确相关方承担的法律后果的规制。[④] 泰方则提议以现有的 UNICITRAL 仲裁规则和 ICSID 仲裁规则为基础建立新的贸易法委员会投资争端解决规则,其中应要求充分披露任何第三方出资人和出资协议的细节。[⑤] 土耳其提议索赔人与出资人之间的合同应开放给律师和仲裁员审查。[⑥]

(二)披露制度的完善路径

1. 在仲裁规则中广泛纳入和修订第三方披露制度

从上文 ICSID 和 UNCITRAL 的改革进展中不难发现,目前主要的改革措施为广泛制定或修订第三方资助披露制度。披露使得藏在暗处的第三方资助者浮现并得以借此审视第三方资助者与仲裁员在错综复杂的经济社会文化背景下的经济身份关系,从而确保仲裁程序的完整性以及国际投资仲裁的合法

---

① Vers un nouveau moyen de régler les différends entre États et investisseurs Mai 2015, available at https://www.diplomatie.gouv.fr/IMG/pdf/20150530_isds_papier_fr_vf_cle432fca.pdf.

② 参见南非政府提交的意见书,A/CN.9/WG.III/WP.176,http://undocs.org/en/A/CN.9/WG.III/WP.176,最后访问日期:2020 年 11 月 15 日。

③ 参见摩洛哥政府提交的意见书,A/CN.9/WG.III/WP.161,http://undocs.org/en/A/CN.9/WG.III/WP.161,最后访问日期:2020 年 11 月 15 日;泰国政府提交的意见书,A/CN.9/WG.III/WP.162,http://undocs.org/en/A/CN.9/WG.III/WP.162,最后访问日期:2020 年 11 月 15 日;智利、以色列和日本政府提交的意见书,A/CN.9/WG.III/WP.163,http://undocs.org/en/A/CN.9/WG.III/WP.163,最后访问日期:2020 年 11 月 15 日;哥斯达黎加政府提交的意见书,A/CN.9/WG.III/WP.164,http://undocs.org/en/A/CN.9/WG.III/WP.164,最后访问日期:2020 年 11 月 15 日;土耳其政府提交的意见书,A/CN.9/WG.III/WP.174,http://undocs.org/en/A/CN.9/WG.III/WP.17,4,最后访问日期:2020 年 11 月 15 日;中国政府提交的意见书,A/CN.9/WG.III/WP.177,http://undocs.org/en/A/CN.9/WG.III/WP.177,最后访问日期:2020 年 11 月 15 日。

④ 参见中国政府提交的意见书,A/CN.9/WG.III/WP.177,http://undocs.org/en/A/CN.9/WG.III/WP.177,最后访问日期:2020 年 11 月 15 日。

⑤ 参见泰国政府提交的意见书,A/CN.9/WG.III/WP.162,http://undocs.org/en/A/CN.9/WG.III/WP.1,62,最后访问日期:2020 年 11 月 15 日。

⑥ 土耳其政府提交的意见书,A/CN.9/WG.III/WP.174,http://undocs.org/en/A/CN.9/WG.III/WP.174,最后访问日期:2020 年 11 月 15 日。

性、正当性。[①]

(1)披露主体

首先应当明确的是,披露主体应为被资助一方当事人。一方面,第三方资助者非案件当事方,无法参与仲裁程序;另一方面,仲裁员在第三方资助者未被披露之前很难判断其是否与某非当事方有利益冲突以及若有则该等利益冲突是否会影响其公正性和独立性,除非仲裁员事先知晓该第三方资助者。因此,被资助者是披露第三方的最合适人选,这一点也体现在 ICSID 仲裁规则修订和 UCITRAL 关于披露制度的意见中。

(2)披露内容

ICSID 四次工作报告中披露内容的范围逐渐从窄到宽,1 号文件中范围为"第三方资助的存在、第三方资助者的名称及相关信息的变化(如有)"。考虑到披露第三方资助者名称的同时也即表明第三方资助者的存在,2、3 号文件中范围仅包括第三方资助者的名称及相关信息变化(如有)。4 号文件中披露内容不仅增加了第三方资助者地址,还包括特别情况下关于资助协议和非当事人一方的进一步信息。

笔者赞成披露范围包括第三方资助者名称、地址或其他可识别性信息,同时,被资助的当事人一方有持续披露义务,应披露该等信息的任何变化。此外,笔者认为无须系统性披露第三方资助协议,但不排除仲裁庭根据案件情况要求当事人披露资助安排、资助内容等,如资助方以特殊目的实体形式提供资助。[②]

(3)披露时间

ICSID 四次工作报告在披露时间上的规制是统一的,即如订立第三方资助协议是在提交仲裁申请前,则披露时间应为提交仲裁申请时;如订立第三方资助协议是在提交仲裁申请后,则披露时间为一订立资助协议后。同时,应附以"尽早"等概括性表述囊括可能出现的例外情形。

(4)披露性质

受资助方的披露义务应当是系统性和强制性的,即无论第三方资助者与仲

---

① 参见肖璐:《从披露义务的角度看我国内地第三方资助仲裁制度的构建》,载《长江论坛》2018 年第 2 期。

② Proposals for Amendment of ICISD Rules Working Paper #3, Volume 1, p. 295.

裁员的关系是否足以导致利益冲突,受资助方均应全面披露,再交由仲裁庭判断;同时,受资助方有义务披露第三方资助,该义务具有强制性。另外,仲裁庭的固有权力体现在应被授权在仲裁程序进行中命令被资助方披露第三方出资相关信息。①

(5)不披露的后果

ICSID 工作报告 3 号和 4 号工作文件解释部分表示,第 51、52 条关于费用和费用担保规定仲裁庭在决定时考虑第三方资助,上述两条款为受资助方因接受第三方资助而导致的程序上的后果。但笔者认为对不予披露的行为还应从程序本身予以限制,如发现受资助方当事人不主动披露或经仲裁庭命令后不予披露的,应当暂停审理程序,期间产生的相关费用应当由受资助方承担。

2. 制定第三方出资者操守准则

除专门的第三方资助机构,传统投资行业领域也在不同程度上涉足第三方资助领域, ②投资仲裁领域的第三方资助正在逐步产业化。③ 鉴于此,笔者认为应当由联合国贸易和发展委员会等国际经贸投资组织或相关国际投资仲裁机构制定关于第三方资助者行为准则等软法。就披露要求而言,一方面,第三方资助者应主动配合当事人履行披露义务,不得以披露为由认定被资助方违约;另一方面,第三方资助者应承诺维护仲裁程序公平公正,确保不因资助的存在而导致仲裁员产生利益冲突进而影响裁决结果;同时,该准则应鼓励第三方资助者主动向常设仲裁机构或临时仲裁庭披露资助信息。

3. 利用《透明度规则》中的透明度登记处进行披露

2014 年 4 月 1 日正式生效的《透明度规则》突破国际仲裁一贯秉承的不公开审理原则与秘密原则,极大地提升了 UNCITRAL 仲裁规则中的透明度。鉴于国际投资仲裁中的第三方资助披露还涉及国家公权力主体及公共利益等,东道国也表示出第三方资助导致无意义索赔大量出现进而利益受损的担忧。笔

---

① 参见徐树、陈雪雯:《国际投资仲裁中第三方资助的披露规则研究》,载《国际法学刊》2020 年第 3 期。

② 参见肖芳:《国际投资仲裁第三方资助的规制困境与出路——以国际投资仲裁"正当性危机"及其改革为背景》,载《政法论坛》2017 年第 6 期。

③ Eric De Brabandere & Julia Lepeltak, *Third - Party Funding in International Investment Arbitration*, ICSID Review - Foreign Investment Law Journal, Vol. 27, p. 384; Alison Ross, *The Dynamics of Third - Party Funding*, Global Arbitration Review Vol. 7.

者建议将第三方资助的信息披露纳入《透明度规则》,通过向公众披露第三方资助以进一步完善国际投资仲裁的透明度及正当性。另外,可将第三方资助信息列于第3条"文件的公布"清单中,并由仲裁庭以发送至存储处的方式向公众公布。

五、改革第三方资助披露制度的中国因应

第三方资助披露制度的改革是投资者—国家争端解决(Investor - State Dispute Settlement,ISDS)机制面临"合法性危机"变革的缩影。同缺乏纠错机制、条约解释及裁决结果一致性缺失、仲裁员缺乏独立性与公正性等问题一道,第三方资助的负面影响可能波及国际投资领域全球链条上的任何潜在参与方,尤其是外资开放程度较高、有良好国家信誉和以财政收入作担保的新兴发展中国家。[①] 随着中国参与国际投资活动程度的日益加深,我国已经从投资规则的"局外人"逐渐成为投资规则的"制定者"。目前,世界上130多个国家和地区与我国签署BIT,中国是全球第二大对外投资国、第三大吸引外资投入国。中国在UNCITRAL第三工作组第三十八届会议上表示:"中国支持对第三方资助规定透明度纪律,相关方应持续披露有关资助情况,避免因第三方资助者介入而产生直接或间接的利益冲突。如未履行披露义务,应明确相关方承担的法律后果。"[②]从上述中国政府在国际组织的表态来看,中国承认第三方资助对国际投资仲裁带来的挑战,同时认为国际合作加以监管规制而非全面禁止才是解决问题的根本。

从国际立法角度来看,中国应积极参与UNCITRAL及ICSID中心正在进行的第三方资助改革工作,从第三方资助定义、披露内容、披露模式、不披露后果等方面提供具体的可行性方案。从BIT或FTA角度来看,中国应积极倡导在争端解决章节对第三方资助进行规制,构建符合中国投资现状的第三方资助及披露制度模式,以最大程度保护中国作为东道国的国家利益。从投资仲裁角度来看,一方面,中国政府作为投资者母国应鼓励中国企业积极依据投资协定

---

① 参见徐树、陈雪雯:《国际投资仲裁中第三方资助的披露规则研究》,载《国际法学刊》2020年第3期。

② 中国政府提交的意见书,A/CN. 9/WG. III/WP. 177, http://undocs. org/en/A/CN. 9/WG. III/WP. 177,第5页,最后访问日期:2020年4月15日。

或投资协议中的争端解决条款提起国际投资仲裁,合理利用和借助第三方资助以克服国际投资仲裁费用高昂、专业程度高等现实障碍,合法主张权利;另一方面,作为东道国,中国政府应合理预见越来越多投资者利用第三方资助进行国际投资仲裁的现实趋势,如中国参与的国际投资仲裁案件申请方投资人接受第三方资助,中国应尽早在程序阶段申请要求仲裁庭披露相关资助信息,同时可采取申请费用担保等临时措施避免投资者无力支付的情形,合理利用 BIT 或 FTA 及仲裁规则中的相关制度维护自身合法权益。

从中国仲裁机构角度出发,目前我国大陆地区可适用于国际投资仲裁的仲裁规则包括《贸仲委投资争端规则》、《深圳国际仲裁院仲裁规则》①以及《北仲投资规则》,其中《贸仲委投资争端规则》②及《北仲投资规则》③对第三方资助进行规制。尽管目前中国仲裁机构尚未受理国际投资仲裁案件,但在投资仲裁规则中对第三方资助进行规制能吸引投资者选择适用进而扩大中国仲裁机构及仲裁规则的影响力,随着中国企业海外投资步伐的扩大,中国企业可能因东道国违反投资协定而提出投资仲裁请求,辅以中国仲裁机构仲裁费用较

① 参见《深圳国际仲裁院仲裁规则》。

② 参见《中国国际经济贸易仲裁委员会国际投资争端仲裁规则(试行)》第 27 条第 1 款规定:“在本规则中,‘第三方资助’是指当事人以外的自然人或实体协议承担参与争议的一方当事人在仲裁程序中的全部或部分费用的情形。”第 2 款规定:“获得第三方资助的当事人应在签署资助协议后,毫不迟延地将第三方资助安排的事实、性质、第三方的名称与住址,书面告知对方当事人、仲裁庭及管理案件的投资争端解决中心或香港仲裁中心。仲裁庭也有权命令获得第三方资助的当事人披露相关情况。”第 3 款规定:“在就仲裁费用和其他相关费用作出裁决时,仲裁庭可以考虑是否存在第三方资助的情形,以及当事人是否遵守第(二)款的规定。”

③ 参见《北京仲裁委员会/北京国际仲裁中心国际投资仲裁规则》第 39 条第 1 款规定:“第三方资助是指并非争端当事人的个人或实体(以下简称‘第三方资助人’)向仲裁程序的一方当事人或当事人的关联方或代理人提供资金或其他相当于资金的支持以进行仲裁活动。”第 2 款规定:“一方当事人存在第三方资助安排的,应向另一方当事人、仲裁庭和本会提交书面通知,充分披露:第三方资助的存在;第三方资助人及其实际控制人(如有)的身份;在仲裁员已被选定或指定的情况下,第三方资助人及其实际控制人(如有)与仲裁员之间的关系(如有);第三方资助人是否曾承诺承担对该方当事人不利的费用责任。”第 3 款规定:“第(二)款的通知应在申请人或被申请人各自提交仲裁通知或对仲裁通知的答复的同时或之后 7 日内提交;第三方资助安排在提交仲裁通知或对仲裁通知的答复之后达成的,应在达成安排后 7 日内提交。”第 4 款规定:“第(二)款述及的信息在初始披露后发生变化的,包括资助安排终止的,当事人应在变化发生后 7 日内向另一方当事人、仲裁庭和本会披露。”第 5 款规定:“仲裁庭在决定仲裁费用和其他费用的承担时,可以考虑存在第三方资助这一因素,以及接受资助的一方当事人是否遵守了第(二)、(三)、(四)款的要求。如第三方资助人未承诺承担对该方当事人不利的费用责任,仲裁庭在必要时可以要求接受资助的当事人提交适当的费用担保。”

低等优势，中国仲裁机构的国际投资仲裁规则存在被适用的可能。目前贸仲委与北仲颁布的仲裁规则在第三方资助领域的相关规制已领先于 ICSID 仲裁规则、UNCITRAL 仲裁规则等，中国仲裁机构应持续关注第三方资助的境内外发展动态，进一步开发中国仲裁机构的国际投资仲裁市场。

从国内立法层面出发，与澳大利亚、英国、新加坡等第三方资助市场较为发达的地区相比，中国第三方资助市场起步晚且尚未获得充分发展，①因而，英国的行业自治模式以及新加坡的立法模式无法照搬至中国。第一，中国的第三方资助行业远未达到规模化以进行自我规范、自我约束的发达程度；第二，中国第三方资助的行业定位和发展模式尚不清晰，存在与风险代理、诉讼融资、诉讼保险等其他类似模式的交叉；第三，国内第三方资助行业目前业务领域多集中于国内诉讼，触角尚未伸及国际商事仲裁或投资仲裁。因此笔者认为，目前对《仲裁法》或相关部门规章进行“第三方资助”内容的修订为时尚早，立法时机尚不成熟。但考虑到第三方资助市场存在较大发展潜力，结合资本引入法律市场后可能导致的负外部性，建议先行由司法部联合相关部门以指导意见等规范性文件的形式助力第三方资助行业的良性运转，规定内容包括但不限于第三方资助模式的界定、第三方资助的潜在风险、对被资助方的披露要求、资助方的行业自律等灵活宽松的方针政策，不宜限定具体的资助者准入门槛或强制的资助合同备案等，容易阻碍第三方资助行业的进一步发展。同时，考虑到律师在被资助方与资助方之间起沟通枢纽作用，建议地方及全国律师协会强化对律师披露义务的要求，将第三方资助纳入律师的利益冲突披露范围。

六、结论

面对第三方资助在国际投资仲裁领域的现实困境及现有规制的不足，有必要通过广泛纳入和修订第三方披露制度、制定第三方出资者操守准则以及利用《透明度规则》中的透明度登记处公布第三方资助的方式对国际投资仲裁中的第三方资助进行合理规制。我国仲裁机构在投资仲裁规则中纳入第三方资助有助于吸引投资者、提升机构自身影响力；我国投资者应积极参与国际投资仲

---

① 参见张蓓蓓、胡宪：《中国第三方资助市场概述》，张婷婷译，载鼎颂法务创新集团2018年2月11日，https://www.sohu.com/a/222247588_708255。

裁并善于利用第三方资助等更好地参与仲裁、主张权利;我国政府作为东道国,应利用双边投资协定或纳入第三方资助相关规制的仲裁规则维护仲裁程序公正独立,进而保护主权国家正当权益。改革国际投资仲裁中的第三方资助披露制度是国际与国内、立法与司法协调共进的过程,其核心在于平衡第三方资助具有的提供争端解决救济与导致滥诉、利益冲突乃至投资权利义务失衡之间的关系。尤其是在国际投资仲裁领域,面临东道国对于 ISDS 机制的合法性的质疑,如何针对性地回应第三方资助实践、提供切实的改革方案、维护中国在全球资本流动下的合法权益,中国应不断地进行有益探索与实践,积极贡献中国智慧与中国声音。

【国际商事仲裁】

开拓境外仲裁，着力规则创新

——《华南（香港）国际仲裁院仲裁规则》解读

郑聿辰　秦悦民*

华南（香港）国际仲裁院［South China International Arbitration Center (HK)，SCIAHK］是深圳国际仲裁院（Shenzhen Court of International Arbitration，SCIA）在境外设立的一家独立仲裁机构。该机构于2019年在中国香港设立，是受香港法约束的香港仲裁机构。经最高人民法院和香港特别行政区政府律政司共同确认，SCIAHK于2019年9月26日被纳入《关于内地与香港特别行政区法院就仲裁程序相互协助保全的安排》下的香港仲裁机构名单，①标志着SCIAHK作为香港仲裁机构的地位在内地得到了认可。

SCIAHK背靠中国香港、面向全球，向全球当事人提供仲裁服务，因此，制定一部在国际上被广为接受的仲裁规则对其发展至关重要。经过将近两年的努力，SCIAHK于2022年5月1日正式发布和实施了《华南（香港）国际仲裁院仲裁规则》（以下简称《华南规则》）。

《华南规则》由正文（4个章节）和5个附件组成，共52条条文。正文的4个章节分别为："绪则""仲裁庭的组成""仲裁程序""裁决"。附件分别为："紧急仲裁员程序""选择性复裁程序""仲裁院的受理费和管理费""仲裁员的

---

* 郑聿辰，通力律师事务所律师、合伙人，深圳国际仲裁院仲裁员；秦悦民，通力律师事务所律师、合伙人，深圳国际仲裁院仲裁员。

① 香港特别行政区政府律政司，https://www.doj.gov.hk/sc/community_engagement/press/20190926_pr1.html。

收费和开支”“规则说明”。《华南规则》在借鉴《联合国国际贸易法委员会仲裁规则》(以下简称 UNCITRAL 规则)部分条款的同时,也汲取了国际机构仲裁(institutional arbitration)的先进经验,设计了与机构仲裁相适应的制度。

《华南规则》在诸多方面都颇具特色。本文将着重介绍《华南规则》有关受理范围、适应机构仲裁的设计、快速程序、请求和答辩的即决驳回、选择性复裁程序以及紧急仲裁员程序等方面的规定。

一、受理范围

《华南规则》第 1 条是关于受理范围的规定。一般认为,受理范围事关仲裁的属事管辖权(jurisdiction *ratione materiae*)。① 同时,受理范围又与仲裁协议的范围(scope)相呼应,构成判断仲裁协议所约定事项是否可以提交仲裁的标准。

值得关注的是,虽然《华南规则》是商事仲裁规则,但 SCIAHK 同时也明确《华南规则》可以适用于外国投资者和东道国政府之间的投资仲裁。②《华南规则》第 1 条第 4 款规定,对于依照为投资或投资人提供保护的条约或合同提起的投资人与国家间的仲裁,条约或合同赋予仲裁院管辖权的,适用《华南规则》和《贸易法委员会投资人与国家间基于条约仲裁透明度规则》(以下简称《透明度规则》),但以《透明度规则》第 1 条的规定为限。③ 该条规定中,有一点值得注意,即该条除规定了“依照为投资或投资人提供保护的条约提起的投资人与国家间的仲裁”外,还规定了“依照为投资或投资人提供保护的合同提起的投资人与国家间的

① 属事管辖权与属人管辖权(jurisdiction *ratione personae*),以及属时管辖权(jurisdiction *ratione temporis*)一并构成仲裁管辖客观标准的核心内容。但当前一般认为,属时管辖权属于可受理性问题,与管辖权问题区别对待。See Joel Dahlquist, *The Use of Commercial Arbitration Rules in Investment Treaty Disputes Domestic Courts, Commercial Arbitration Institutions and Tribunal Jurisdiction*, Leiden, The Netherlands: Koninklijke Brill NV [2021], chapter 1, p. 7.

② See Joel Dahlquist, *The Use of Commercial Arbitration Rules in Investment Treaty Disputes Domestic Courts, Commercial Arbitration Institutions and Tribunal Jurisdiction*, Leiden, The Netherlands: Koninklijke Brill NV [2021], chapter 1, p. 15. “In theory, the commercial arbitration rules could be used in a way that addresses concerns raised by states about the procedural nature of investment arbitration.”

③ 《华南规则》第 1.4 条规定:“For investor – State arbitration initiated pursuant to a treaty providing for the protection of investments or investors or an investor – State contract to the similar effect by which the SCIAHK is conferred with jurisdiction, these Rules shall apply in conjunction with the UNCITRAL Rules on Transparency in Treaty – based Investor – State Arbitration (the ‘Rules on Transparency’), subject to Article 1 of the Rules on Transparency.”

仲裁”,从而将后者也纳入了《华南规则》的适用范围,为 SCIAHK 受理依据外国投资者和东道国政府签订的投资合同(investment contract)产生的争议案件提供了规则依据。

外国投资者以东道国政府为被申请人提起的仲裁,一般分为两类情况:一是认为东道国政府违反了其与外国投资者签订的投资合同而引发的争议;二是东道国政府行使国家权力或实施管理的行为或发生政治事件,致使投资者遭受损失而引发的争议。[①] 换言之,后者并非因为东道国政府违反了其与外国投资者签订的合同,而是其政府行为(包含行政机关、立法机关和司法机关的行为)给外国投资者造成了损失。后者一般都在双边或多边投资保护协定中作出了规定,因此被认为是基于投资条约的争议,而非如前者是基于合同的争议。

基于投资条约提起的投资仲裁与基于投资合同提起的投资仲裁具有不同的特征,两者不能混为一谈。[②] 这一问题涉及争议的性质,即区分公法性质的争议和私法性质的争议(the public - private distinction)。[③] 前者是指政府在行使主权(sovereign)的过程中发生的争议,而后者是指政府商业(commercial)行为引发的争议。尽管一方为政府,但因政府纯粹的商业行为引发的争议并不属于“投资仲裁”。换言之,投资仲裁并非因外国投资者的“投资”而产生的仲裁,而是因东道国政府的政府行为违反了条约和国际法的规定,给外国投资者带来了损失而产生的仲裁。但政府纯粹的商业行为与政府违反条约和国际法的行为,这两者之间并不是非黑即白的关系,其间存在“灰色区域”,这也导致了投资合同争议可能会属于投资仲裁范围的情形。关于这一问题,我们将在下文中进一步阐述。

在投资者是否参与订立仲裁协议的问题上,基于投资合同的投资仲裁和基于条约的投资仲裁亦有所区别。在基于投资合同的投资仲裁中,争议双方同时

---

① 参见杜新力、曹俊编:《国际投资法》,中国政法大学出版社 1995 年版,第 293 页。

② See A M Steingruber, *Consent in International Arbitration*, Oxford 2012, p. 12 with further references; G Wang, *Consent in Investor - State Arbitration: A Critical Analysis*, (2014) 13 Chinese Journal of International Law, p. 2.

③ See Gus Van Harten, *Investment Treaty Arbitration and Public Law*, Stanford Journal of International Law, Vol. 92, No. 1, p. 46. “The argument begins with the premiss that it is both possible and useful to distinguish between the public (or sovereign) and private (or commercial) nature of disputes that are resolved by adjudication. Of course, there is always grey when differentiating black from white, and so it is with the public - private distinction. But the presence of grey does not mean that black and white do not exist.”

也是投资合同的当事双方。它们之间的仲裁协议通常是在争议发生前订立的,而且经过争议双方的协商。而在基于投资条约提起的投资仲裁中,一方面,争议双方是东道国政府和投资者。另一方面,投资条约的缔约双方却是东道国和投资者母国,投资者并非投资条约的一方当事人。由于争议双方并非缔约双方,仲裁协议并非由争议双方在争议发生前协商订立。[①] 质言之,在基于投资条约提起的投资仲裁中,争议双方之间的仲裁协议源于国家在投资条约中的“要约”和投资者请求仲裁时的“承诺”,而非争议双方的合意。在学理上,此类仲裁协议称为不对称的仲裁协议(theoretically asymmetrical arbitration agreement)。[②] 另外,投资合同与投资条约都是当事人合意提交投资仲裁的一种形式,[③]基于投资合同和投资条约提起的两种投资仲裁均会受到投资仲裁管辖权客观标准(objective jurisdictional requirements)的限制。[④] 但在“哪些投资争议可以约定

---

① See Christoph & Schreuer, *Calvo's Grandchildren: The Return of Local Remedies in Investment Arbitration*, in The Law and Practice of International Courts and Tribunals 4: 1 - 17, Brill 2005, p. 10 (citing the ICSID tribunal in *SGS v. Philippines*).

② See Joel Dahlquist, *The Use of Commercial Arbitration Rules in Investment Treaty Disputes Domestic Courts, Commercial Arbitration Institutions and Tribunal Jurisdiction*, Leiden, The Netherlands: Koninklijke Brill NV [2021], chapter 1, p. 8. “Although the notion that this asymmetry is able to create an arbitration agreement has been questioned, it seems to be widely accepted in practice and will not be discussed further this study.”

③ See Christoph & Schreuer et al. *The ICSID Convention: A Commentary on the Convention on the Settlement of Investment Disputes between States and Nationals of Other States*, Cambridge University Press, 2009, p. 190 - 191. “Consent must be obtained from both or all parties. Traditionally this would take place by way of a direct agreement between the host State and the investor (see paras 382 - 389 infra). Consent may also result from a unilateral offer by the host State, expressed in its legislation or in a treaty, which is subsequently accepted by the investor.”

④ See Christoph & Schreuer et al. *The ICSID Convention: A Commentary on the Convention on the Settlement of Investment Disputes between States and Nationals of Other States*, Cambridge University Press, 2009, p. 82. “Art. 25 contains requirements relating to the nature of the dispute (*ratione materiae*) and to the parties (*ratione personae*). In addition, the parties must have given their consent.” Iv, “The jurisdiction of the Centre shall extend to any legal dispute arising directly out of an investment, between a Contracting State (or any constituent subdivision or agency of a Contracting State designated to the Centre by that State) and a national of another Contracting State, which the parties to the dispute consent in writing to submit to the Centre.” p. 73, “consent in writing to submit to the Centre” includes “Consent through Direct Agreement between the Parties”, “Consent through Bilateral Investment Treaties”, “Consent through Multilateral Treaties”. A M Steingruber, *Consent in International Arbitration*, Oxford 2012, p. 84. “Indeed, in arbitration proceedings conducted under ICSID one cannot ignore the fact that ICSID jurisdiction is limited by the nature of the operation at hand, because objective jurisdictional requirements*ratione personae*, *ratione materiae*, and*ratione temporis* have to be fulfilled.”

通过国际仲裁的方式加以解决”的管辖权问题上，和基于合同的投资仲裁相比，在基于条约的投资仲裁中，当事人意思自治在一定程度上受到限制。[①] 因为在投资条约中，条约条款由两个国家拟订，投资者不能修改具体条款。相形之下，在投资合同中，仲裁条款可以由合同双方拟订，具体如何拟订取决于投资者与被投资国的议价能力（bargaining power）。资本实力雄厚的投资者（如拟在自然资源等关键领域开展长期投资的投资者）与东道国政府谈判时，往往有能力在合同中加入较为宽泛的仲裁条款。[②]

如上所述，投资仲裁可以分为“基于条约的投资仲裁”和“基于投资合同的投资仲裁”。因东道国政府违反投资条约提出的仲裁请求（treaty claim）和因东道国政府违反投资合同而提出的仲裁请求（contract claim）之间的区别也已成为国际投资仲裁中争论最激烈的话题之一。[③] 在国际投资仲裁实践中，可以根据违反条约的事实提出 treaty claim，即投资仲裁的诉因（cause of action）是东道国政府违反了投资保护协定；如果违反投资合同的同时也违反了投资条约，亦可以对该既违反投资合同又违反投资条约的事实提出 treaty claim。[④] 但是，违反投资合同并不当然构成违反投资条约。[⑤] 这是因为，在认定是否违反投资条约前，还需要分析：（1）合同权利是否被纳入了条约的主要条款，进而违反投资

① See A M Steingruber, *Consent in International Arbitration*, Oxford 2012, p. 12 with further references; G Wang, *Consent in Investor – State Arbitration*: *A Critical Analysis*, (2014) 13 Chinese Journal of International Law, p. 2.

② See Michael Waibel, *Investment Arbitration*: *Jurisdiction and Admissibility*, in Marc Bungenberg et al. , International Investment Law: A Handbook, C. H. Beck · Hart · Nomos, 2015, p. 1224 – 1225.

③ See Guido Santiago Tawil, *The Distinction between Contract Claims and Treaty Claims*: *An Overview*, International Arbitration 2006: Back to Basics?, ICCA Congress Series, Volume 13 (Kluwer Law International 2007) p. 492.

④ See Crawford, *Treaty and Contract in Investment Arbitration*, 361.

⑤ See Monique Sasson, *Substantive Law in Investment Treaty Arbitration*: *The Unsettled Relationship between International Law and Municipal Law* (*2nd Edition*), Chapter 6: Treaty Versus Contract Claims, and Umbrella Clauses: When a Contract Breach May Become a Treaty Breach, International Arbitration Law Library, Volume 21 (Kluwer Law International 2017) p. 239.

合同即构成违反投资条约;[①](2)合同请求与条约请求是否重合或部分重合,因此,违反投资合同当然也违反了投资条约;[②](3)是否存在保护伞条款,从而根据该规定东道国违反投资合同的行为升级为违反投资条约的行为,进而使 contract claim 转化为 treaty claim [③]。

在 Vivendi Universal v. Argentine Republic 一案中,Compa ía de Aguas del Aconquija S. A. 特设撤裁委员会(ad hoc committee)指出,东道国虽未违反条约,但东道国政府可能存在违反合同的情况。[④] 由此可见,虽然东道国政府没有违反投资条约,也因此未产生公法意义上的国家责任,但其行为可能违反了投资合同,并因此产生了私法意义上的商业赔偿责任。实践中还存在另一种情形,即东道国政府可能违反了条约义务,因此产生了条约和国际法意义上的责任,但其行为并未违反其与投资者之间的投资合同。[⑤]

倘若《华南规则》仅提及投资条约而不提及投资合同,则仅能将投资仲裁中

---

① See Impregilo S. p. A. v. Islamic Republic of Pakistan, ICSID Case No. ARB/03/3, Decision on Jurisdiction, 22 April 2005. 该案中,仲裁庭提出"对合同权利的征收,可能会构成条约项下的征收或具有类似效果的措施"。Occidental Petroleum Corporation and Occidental Exploration and Production Company v. The Republic of Ecuador, ICSID Case No. ARB/06/11, Decision on Jurisdiction, 9 September 2008; LG&E Energy Corp., LG&E Capital Corp. and LG&E International Inc. v. Argentine Republic, ICSID Case No. ARB/02/1, Decision on Objections to Jurisdiction, 30 April 2004; International Thunderbird Gaming Corporation v. The United Mexican States, UNCITRAL, Award, 26 January 2006. 另外,在西方石油公司诉厄瓜多尔仲裁案、LG&E 诉阿根廷仲裁案,以及雷鸟公司诉墨西哥仲裁案中,仲裁庭一致认为,在投资合同签订后,东道国单方面改变合同订立时允诺的法律环境与合同履行条件的行为会令投资者正当的期待受挫,因此,这样的行为违反了投资条约下的公平与公正待遇条款(FET)。

② See Impregilo SpA. v. Argentine Republic, ICSID Case No. ARB/07/17, Award, 21 June 2011. 在 Impregilo 诉阿根廷仲裁案中,仲裁庭对申请人仲裁请求涉及的东道国的不法行为,以及这些行为是否构成征收、不公平待遇,或歧视性措施进行了审查。仲裁庭认为,如果这些不法行为涉及条约下的义务,则其不仅违反了合同,而且同时违反了投资合同和条约。

③ See ALEXANDROV, *Breaches of Contract and Breaches of Treaty*. The Jurisdiction of Treaty - based Arbitration Tribunals to Decide Breach of Contract Claims in SGS v. Pakistan and SGS v. Philippines, op. cit., fn. 8, at p. 566 ("... an umbrella clause in a treaty intends to achieve more than what is already the norm under customary international law").

④ See Aguas del Aconquija - Vivendi v. Argentine Republic, ICSID Case No. ARB/97/3 Decision on Annulment, para 95.

⑤ See Monique Sasson, *Substantive Law in Investment Treaty Arbitration: The Unsettled Relationship between International Law and Municipal Law* (*2nd Edition*), Kluwer Law International 2017, Chapter 6: Treaty Versus Contract Claims, and Umbrella Clauses: When a Contract Breach May Become a Treaty Breach, p. 239.

的 treaty claim 纳入 SCIAHK 的受理范围,不能保证将可能同时产生 treaty claim 的 contract claim 也纳入 SCIAHK 的受理范围。这会导致在 SCIAHK 是否有权受理 contract claim 的问题上出现很大的不确定性。此外,国际投资仲裁实践中,一些双边投资条约或投资合同的争议解决条款并未特别选择国际投资争议解决中心(The International Center for Settlement of Investment Disputes,ICSID)或者海牙常设仲裁法院(Permanent Court of Arbitration,PCA)这类机构,而是约定"将争议提交当事人同意的其他仲裁机构"或"将争议提交某一仲裁机构"。[①] 倘若《华南规则》不提及投资合同,在投资合同一方当事人选择将争议提交 SCIAHK 的情况下,SCIAHK 是否有权受理,会产生不必要的争议。有鉴于此,《华南规则》同时提及了投资条约和投资合同,明确将基于投资条约提起的仲裁和基于投资合同提起的仲裁一并纳入受理范围。这有助于减少有关 SCIAHK 管辖权的争议。

国际投资仲裁是解决投资者与东道国政府之间投资争议的主要方式之一。除如 ICSID 这种为解决国际投资争议而设立的机构外,[②]国际商会国际仲裁院(The ICC International Court of Arbitration,ICC)、伦敦国际仲裁院(London Court of International Arbitration,LCIA)、斯德哥尔摩商会仲裁院(Arbitration Institution of Stockholm Chamber of Commerce,SCC)、新加坡国际仲裁中心(Singapore International Arbitration Center,SIAC)及香港国际仲裁中心(Hong Kong International Arbitration Centre,HKIAC)等国际商事仲裁机构亦可受理国际投资仲裁案件。近年来,我国多家仲裁机构也在积极开拓国际投资仲裁业务,并着手制定相应的投资仲裁规则。SCIA 于 2016 年发布的《深圳国际仲裁院仲裁规则》将一国政府与他国投资者之间的投资争议仲裁案件纳入 SCIA 的受理范围。[③] 中国国际经济贸易仲裁委员会(China International Economic and Trade Arbitration Commion,CIETAC)于 2017 年发布的《中国国际经济贸易仲裁委员

---

① 如中国—瑞士 BIT 第 11 条第 2 款约定:"A dispute between the Contracting Parties, if not settled... may be submitted to an arbitral tribunal at the request of either Contracting Party."

② 截至 2022 年 1 月,基于合同的投资仲裁案件占 ICSID 案件总量的 15%,见 The ICSID Caseload – Statistics (Issue 2022 – 1),第 11 页。

③ 参见《深圳国际仲裁院仲裁规则》第 2 条第 2 项规定:"仲裁院受理一国政府与他国投资者之间的投资争议仲裁案件。"

会国际投资争端仲裁规则》规定 CIETAC 可以受理投资争议，包括基于合同条约、法律法规或其他文件提起的国际投资争议。① 北京仲裁委员会/北京国际仲裁中心（Beijing Arbitration Commission，BAC）于 2019 年发布的《北京仲裁委员会/北京国际仲裁中心国际投资仲裁规则》明确 BAC 可以受理基于条约、合同的投资争议。② 继 CIETAC 和 BAC 之后，SCIAHK 也将国际投资争议中的 treaty claim 和 contract claim 同时纳入受理范围，为包括港澳台投资者在内的中国投资者就近选择投资争议解决机构提供了便利，也进一步拓宽了境内外企业投资争议解决的选择。

二、适应机构仲裁的规则设计

国际仲裁通常分为机构仲裁和临时仲裁（ad hoc arbitration）。

所谓机构仲裁，是指由一个常设的仲裁机构依据其制定的仲裁规则管理仲裁程序，由仲裁机构负责仲裁庭组成，决定仲裁庭费用等事宜的仲裁制度。③ 国际上较为知名的仲裁机构包括 ICC、LCIA、美国仲裁协会（American Arbitration Association，AAA）、SCC、SIAC、HKIAC、CIETAC、SCIA 以及 BAC 等。

截至目前，除 SCIAHK 外，经最高人民法院和香港特别行政区政府律政司

---

① 参见《中国国际经济贸易仲裁委员会国际投资争端仲裁规则（试行）》第 2 条规定："当事人之间解决国际投资争端的仲裁协议可以规定在合同、条约、法律法规或其他文件中。一方当事人通过合同、条约、法律法规或其他文件作出了提交仲裁委员会仲裁或按照本规则仲裁的意思表示，另一方当事人通过提起仲裁或以其他方式予以接受的，视为达成仲裁协议。"

② 参见《北京仲裁委员会/北京国际仲裁中心国际投资仲裁规则》第 2 条第 6 款规定，本规则所称的将争端提交仲裁的约定可以规定在合同、条约、法律法规或其他文件中。

③ See Gary B. Born, *International Commercial Arbitration* (2nd *Edition*), Wolters Kluwer, Chapter 1 Overview of International Commercial Arbitration. "These (and other) arbitral institutions have promulgated sets of procedural rules that apply where parties have agreed to arbitration pursuant to such rules. Among other things, institutional rules set out the basic procedural framework and timetable for the arbitral proceedings. Institutional rules also typically authorize the arbitral institution to select arbitrators in particular disputes and resolve challenges to arbitrators (that is, to serve as 'appointing authority'), to designate the place of arbitration, to fix or influence the fees payable to the arbitrators and (sometimes) to review the arbitrators' awards to reduce the risk of unenforceability on formal grounds. "Nigel Blackaby and Constantine Partasides QC with Alan Redfern and Martin Hunter, *Redfern and Hunter on International Arbitration* (6th *Edition*), Oxford University Press, para 1.146; Klaus Peter Berger, *Institutional Arbitration: Harmony, Disharmony and the "Party Autonomy Paradox"*, Arbitraje: Revista de Arbitraje Comercial y de Inversiones, Kluwer Law International; IproLex 2018, Volume 11, Issue 2, p. 335 – 364.

确认的《关于内地与香港特别行政区法院就仲裁程序相互协助保全的安排》第2条项下的香港仲裁机构及常设办事处还包括HKIAC、CIETAC香港仲裁中心、ICC亚洲事务办公室、香港海事仲裁协会，以及一邦国际网上仲调中心。[①]

所谓临时仲裁，是指当事人没有选择仲裁机构管理仲裁程序，而是选择将争议提交临时组建的仲裁庭进行审理的仲裁制度。[②] 与我国机构本位制度[③]不同，绝大多数国家的仲裁法对于在没有仲裁机构介入和管理仲裁程序的情况下，如何协助当事人顺利推进仲裁程序均有明确规定。UNCITRAL规则即是为临时仲裁而量身定做的仲裁规则。

考虑到SCIAHK属于机构仲裁，其在设计《华南规则》时也采纳了很多适应机构仲裁的规定。

（一）仲裁程序的起算时间以仲裁机构收到仲裁通知之日为准

确定仲裁程序的起算时间十分重要，涉及仲裁时效、请求的可受理性及仲裁程序的启动等多个实体和程序问题。第一，不同的法域对仲裁时效期间的规定和理解有所不同：在一些法域，仲裁时效被视为程序问题，适用仲裁地法律；在另一些法域，仲裁时效被视为实体问题，与其他实体问题适用相同的法律。[④] 如何界定仲裁程序的起算时间关系到当事人是否在仲裁时效期间内提起仲裁，

① 香港特别行政区政府律政司，https://www.doj.gov.hk/tc/mainland_and_macao/pdf/list_of_institutions_c.pdf。

② See Nigel Blackaby, Constantine Partasides QC with Alan Redfern & Martin Hunter, *Redfern and Hunter on International Arbitration* (6th *Edition*), Oxford University Press, para 1.141. "Alternatively, and more usually, the parties may agree that the arbitration will be conducted without involving an arbitral institution, but according to an established set of rules, such as those of UNCITRAL..." Gary B. Born, *International Commercial Arbitration* (2nd *Edition*), Wolters Kluwer, Chapter 1 Overview of International Commercial Arbitration; John Choong, Mark Mangan and Nicholas Lingard, *A Guide to the SIAC Arbitration Rules* (2nd *Edition*), Oxford University Press, p. 308 – 317.

③ 参见《仲裁法》第16条规定，当事人必须在仲裁协议中约定"选定的仲裁委员会"等事项。

④ See Nigel Blackaby, Constantine Partasides QC with Alan Redfern & Martin Hunter, *Redfern and Hunter on International Arbitration* (6th *Edition*), Oxford University Press, para 4.07. "One system of law, for example, may provide that claims under a contract are to be brought within three years, whilst another system of law may allow six years. More importantly, one system of law may classify time limits as matters of procedure, to be governed by the law of the place of arbitration, while another system may classify time limits as matters of substance governed by the same law as that which governs all of the other substantive matters in issue."

即当事人提起仲裁时，仲裁时效期间是否已经届满。[①] 第二，仲裁程序的起算时间可能与仲裁庭计算损害赔偿或利息的起算点有关。[②] 第三，仲裁程序的起算时间也与可受理性（admissibility）问题有关。[③] 因此，仲裁规则通常会明确规定仲裁程序的起算时间。

机构仲裁一般以仲裁机构收到仲裁通知之日作为仲裁程序的起算时间。例如，ICC 规则第 4.2 条、[④]HKIAC 规则第 4.2 条、[⑤]CIETAC 规则第 11 条、[⑥]SIAC规则第 3.3 条[⑦]均规定，仲裁程序于仲裁机构收到仲裁通知之日启动。

临时仲裁中，通常以被申请人收到仲裁通知之日作为仲裁程序的起算时间。例如，根据 UNCITRAL 规则第 3.2 条[⑧]的规定，仲裁程序于被申请人收到仲裁通知之日启动。

不难发现，机构仲裁程序和临时程序的起算时间并不相同。其根本原因在于，临时仲裁中，仲裁机构不会介入仲裁程序。因此，临时仲裁以被申请人收到仲裁通知的时间作为仲裁程序启动的时点更为合理。而对于机构仲裁，通行做法是以仲裁机构收到仲裁通知的时间作为仲裁程序启动的时间。

《华南规则》第 3 条第 3 款考虑了机构仲裁和临时仲裁的区别，遵循了机构仲裁规则的通行做法，将仲裁机构（而非被申请人）收到仲裁通知之日作为仲裁

---

① See Report of the Secretary – General on the Revised Draft Set of Arbitration Rules, UNCITRAL, 9th Session, Addendum 1 (Commentary), UN Doc A/CN. 9/112/Add. 1 (1975), reprinted in (1976) VII UNCITRAL Ybk 166, 168 (Commentary on Draft Article 4(2)). "The time of commencement of the arbitral proceedings may have relevance to the question of whether provisions on prescriptions of rights or limitations of actions under national law are operative in relation to the dispute." David Caron & Lee Caplan, *The UNCITRAL Arbitration Rules: A Commentary* (2nd *Edition*), Oxford University Press, Chapter 10, Commentary on Article 3(2).

② See Clyde Croft, Christopher Kee & Jeff Waincymer, *A Guide to the UNCITRAL Arbitration Rules*, Cambridge University Press, para 3.14. "This can be relevant for limitation periods concerning bringing of actions and might also be used by a tribunal as a trigger point for damages and interest calculations, although this is not necessarily so and may be dependent on applicable substantive law."

③ 国际仲裁实践中的主流观点认为，可受理性问题有别于管辖权问题（jurisdiction）。仲裁管辖权关乎仲裁庭的权限，即某项请求是否可以通过仲裁处理及是否可由仲裁庭审理；而可受理性问题关注的是提起仲裁的时机是否适宜。

④ ICC 规则第 4(2)条。

⑤ HKIAC 规则第 11 条。

⑥ CIETAC 规则第 11 条。

⑦ SIAC 规则第 3.3 条。

⑧ UNCITRAL 规则第 3.2 条。

程序的起算时间。

(二)仲裁地的表述为 Seat of Arbitration,而非 Place of Arbitration

与开庭地不同,仲裁地是一个法律概念。仲裁程序适用仲裁地的仲裁法。因此,当事人选择仲裁地的同时,也确定了适用于仲裁程序的仲裁法和裁决的"国籍"。① 一般而言,仲裁地的仲裁法会对仲裁协议的效力、可仲裁事项、临时措施、当事人申请撤销或者申请执行仲裁裁决的权利等事项作出规定。② 因此,仲裁地的选择对仲裁程序影响甚大。

国际仲裁实践中,存在两种对"仲裁地"的表述。HKIAC 规则第 14.1 条、SIAC 规则第 21.1 条、SCC 规则第 25 条、LCIA 规则第 16 条均采用了"seat of arbitration"的表述。而 UNCITRAL 规则第 18.1 条、CIETAC 规则第 7.1 条、ICC 规则第 18.1 条以及《国际争议解决程序(包括调解和仲裁规则)》(以下简称 ICDR 规则)第 19.1 条采用了"place of arbitration"的表述。

不少学者指出,在不同的情境下,"place of arbitration"可能有两种不同的含义。第一种含义是法律意义上的仲裁地(juridical seat of arbitration),与"seat of arbitration"的内涵一致;第二种含义是开庭地(location of hearings)。③

事实上,在 2010 年《联合国国际贸易法委员会仲裁规则》[以下简称 UNCI-

① See Alice Meissner, *Chapter III: The Award and the Courts, Enforcement of a CIETAC Arbitral Award with Vienna as Place of Oral Hearing*, in Christian Klausegger Peter Klein, et al. (eds), Austrian Yearbook on International Arbitration 2020, Austrian Yearbook on International Arbitration, Volume 2020 (Manz' sche Verlags – und Universitätsbuchhandlung 2020) p. 341 – 353. "Commonly in international arbitration practice, the place of arbitration determines the territory of the applicable procedural law, *lex arbitri*." Gary B. Born, *International Commercial Arbitration* (2nd *Edition*), Wolters Kluwer, Chapter 1 Overview of International Commercial Arbitration.

② See David Caron & Lee Caplan, *The UNCITRAL Arbitration Rules: A Commentary* (2nd *Edition*), Oxford University Press, Chapter 2, Commentary on Article 18. "The law of the place of arbitration may regulate matters, such as the validity of an agreement to arbitrate, the non – arbitrability of certain subject matter, interim measures, the form and validity of the arbitral award, and the parties' respective rights to challenge and enforce the award."

③ See Simon Greenberg, Christopher Kee & J. Romesh Weeramantry, *International Commercial Arbitration: An Asia – Pacific Perspective*, Cambridge University Press, paras 2.5 – 2.11; Clyde Croft, Christopher Kee & Jeff Waincymer, *A Guide to the UNCITRAL Arbitration Rules*, Cambridge University Press, para 3.18. "*The expression 'place of arbitr*ation' is unfortunately used in two contexts in international arbitration. It is sometimes used synonymously with the expression 'seat of arbitration', and in that sense refers to the juridical seat of the arbitration. It is also sometimes used to refer to the location of the hearings. In the context of this rule the meaning is the former."

TRAL 规则(2010)]的制定过程中,UNCITRAL 第二工作组也多次提议采用"seat of arbitration""legal seat of arbitration""juridical seat of arbitration"等表述,以替代 1976 年 UNCITRAL 规则第 16 条规定的"place of arbitration"。[①] 不过,UNCITRAL 规则(2010)第 18.1 条最终还是保留了"place of arbitration"的表述。该部规则在第 18.2 条提及举行会议的地点时采用了"location"的表述,以此区分仲裁地和开庭地。[②]

混用"seat of arbitration"和"place of arbitration"的现象并不罕见,[③]但就两者均指法律意义上的仲裁地这一点而言,已不存在争议。不过,考虑到"seat of arbitration"的表述更为准确,《华南规则》第 18 条采用了"seat of arbitration"的表述。[④]

---

① See UNCITRAL Working Group Ⅱ, 45th Session (11 – 15 September 2006, Vienna), UN Doc A/CN. 9/614, paras 87 – 89; UNCITRAL Working Group Ⅱ, 46th Session (5 – 9 February 2007, New York), UN Doc A/CN. 9/619, paras 138 – 142. "A proposal was made to replace the words 'place of arbitration' in Article 16, paragraphs (1) and (4) with words such as the 'seat', 'legal seat' or 'juridical seat' of arbitration." Clyde Croft, Christopher Kee & Jeff Waincymer, *A Guide to the UNCITRAL Arbitration Rules*, Cambridge University Press, para 18.2.

② See Settlement of Commercial Disputes: Revision of the UNCITRAL Arbitration Rules, Note by the Secretariat, UNCITRAL, UN Doc A/CN. 9/WG. Ⅱ/WP, para 38 (2008). "A draft containing the phrase 'place of arbitration' aims to distinguish between the place of arbitration (meaning the legal seat) and the location where meetings could be held, in terms similar to those adopted under Article 20 of the UNCITRAL Model Law on International Commercial Arbitration"; David Caron, Lee Caplan, *The UNCITRAL Arbitration Rules: A Commentary (2nd Edition)*, Oxford University Press, Chapter 2, Commentary on Article 18.

③ See Michael Hwang and Fong Lee Cheng, *Relevant Considerations in Choosing the Place of Arbitration*, Asian International Arbitration Journal, Singapore International Arbitration Centre (in cooperation with Kluwer Law International); Kluwer Law International 2008, Volume 4, Issue 2, p. 195 – 220. "The words 'seat of arbitration' and 'place of arbitration' are commonly used interchangeably, but the word 'seat is preferable."; Alice Meissner, Chapter Ⅲ: The Award and the Courts, Enforcement of a CIETAC Arbitral Award with Vienna as Place of Oral Hearing, in Christian Klausegger, Peter Klein, et al. (eds), Austrian Yearbook on International Arbitration 2020, Austrian Yearbook on International Arbitration, Volume 2020 (Manz'sche Verlags – und Universitätsbuchhandlung 2020) p. 341 – 353.

④ See Alexander Belohlavek, *Importance of the Seat of Arbitration in International Arbitration: Delocalization and Denationalization of Arbitration as an Outdated Myth*, Academia. "both expressions are treated as synonyms designating the legal localization of a particular dispute in a particular place, with the corresponding connections to the applicable law. 'Seat of arbitration' is probably more precise."

(三)当事人未约定仲裁语言的,应当使用中文或英文进行组庭前的沟通

国际仲裁中,当事人、仲裁员或者其他仲裁当事人可能来自不同的国家,使用不同的语言,且当事人提交的证据,以及当事人在磋商和履行合同阶段使用的语言也有所不同。因此,确定仲裁语言对于仲裁程序的顺利推进至关重要。[①]

许多仲裁规则规定,在当事人未约定仲裁语言的情况下,应当由仲裁庭确定仲裁程序中使用的语言。[②] 确定仲裁语言是当事人交换文件的前置程序,也是仲裁庭必须优先决定的事项。[③] UNCITRAL 规则第 19.1 条[④]和 HKIAC 规则第 15.2 条[⑤]都规定了仲裁庭确定仲裁语言的时间,即必须在组庭后迅速(promptly)决定。

值得注意的是,对于仲裁庭组庭前,当事人应以何种语言通讯的问题,大部分机构仲裁规则没有明确的规定。《华南规则》在这一问题上体现了先进性。《华南规则》第 19 条第 1 款规定,在仲裁庭确定仲裁语言前,当事人应使用中文或英文通讯。这一规定有效地解决了组庭前的仲裁语言问题,避免出现组庭前当事人因语言不同而沟通不畅的局面。

---

① See Sherlin Tung, *The Importance of Language in International Arbitration and How the Impact Parties* Due Process Rights, 10 CONTEMP. Asia ARB. J. 113 (2017). "Also, '[t]he very nature of international arbitration entails parties, arbitrators and any other participant in arbitral proceedings generally being of different nationalities and speaking different languages and often rely on evidence made in different languages,' from the negotiation and finalization of the relevant agreements and the performance of such agreements." Pierre A. Karrer, Arbitration and Language Look for the Purpose, 11 CROATIAN ARB. Y. B. 7 (2004).

② 例如,HKIAC 规则第 15.2 条、SIAC 规则第 22 条、SCC 规则第 26(1)条、ICC 规则第 20 条、ICDR 规则第 20 条、UNCITRAL 规则第 19.1 条。

③ See David Caron, Lee Caplan, *The UNCITRAL Arbitration Rules: A Commentary* (2nd *Edition*), Oxford University Press, Chapter 11, Commentary on Article 19. "The requirement of 'promptness' emphasizes that the decision as to language is a precondition for the commencement of any exchange of pleadings and thus should normally be among the very first acts of an arbitral tribunal."

④ UNCITRAL 规则第 19.1 条。

⑤ HKIAC 规则第 15.2 条。

三、快速程序

近年来,仲裁法和仲裁规则越来越关注仲裁效率、费用和仲裁迟延的问题。① 高效仲裁成为国际上各主流仲裁机构制度改革的重点之一。②《华南规则》第23A 条引入了快速程序(expedited procedure)制度,在双方同意或争议金额不超过 SCIAHK 在其官网上公布的金额(目前为 1000 万港元)的情况下,一方可向 SCIAHK 申请按照快速程序进行仲裁。③ 快速程序的引入贴合国际仲裁实践最新发展趋势,④在提高仲裁效率、降低仲裁成本等方面发挥积极作用。

(一)快速程序的亮点

SCIAHK 的快速程序制度在组庭方式、审理期限、审理方式、裁决书内容等方面均体现了高效、灵活、简便的特点,⑤并且在提高效率的同时也注重保障公正,赋予当事人程序上的选择自由。

---

① See Clyde Croft,Christopher Kee & Jeff Waincymer,*A Guide to the UNCITRAL Arbitration Rules*, Cambridge University Press,para 17.1: In more recent times,arbitral laws and rules have become increasingly concerned with efficiency,expense and delay.

② See Gary B. Born,*International Commercial Arbitration* (3rd *Edition*), Kluwer Law International (2021),2292: leading arbitral institutions have recognized the need to minimize delays and costs in the arbitral process. See also Beom – Cheol Park,E – Wha Joo & Sang – Ryul Shim,*A Comparative Study on the Expedited Procedures of International Arbitration Rules in Four Asian Countries: CIETAC,HKIAC,SIAC and KCAB* (2013) 23 J. Arb. Stud. 177,200: Recently,many international arbitration institutions have responded to the business requirements of their users and have revised their rules to enhance the time and cost efficiency.

③ 参见《华南规则》第 23A 条第 1 款。

④ 例如,UNCITRAL 历时 3 年经 9 次会议,于 2021 年 7 月 21 日第五十四届 UNCITRAL 会议上通过了《贸易法委员会快速仲裁规则》(UNCITRAL Expedited Arbitration Rules),填补了 1976 年《联合国国际贸易法委员会仲裁规则》以及 UNCITRAL 规则(2010)在快速程序这一领域的空白。See also Leng Sun Chan & Weiyi Tan,*Making Arbitration Effective: Expedited Procedures,Emergency Arbitrators and Interim Relief* (2013) 6 Contemp Asia Arb J 349,349: In recent years,arbitral institutions around the world have sought to address the need for swifter resolution of disputes through the introduction of expedited procedures. See also Gary B. Born,*International Commercial Arbitration* (3rd *Edition*),Kluwer Law International 2021, 2478: In recent years,a number of arbitral institutions have adopted rules providing for fast – track or expedited arbitration.

⑤ See Gary B. Born,*International Commercial Arbitration* (3rd *Edition*),Kluwer Law International 2021,2480: the express affirmation of the tribunal's authority to expedite proceedings,the imposition of fixed (short) deadlines and provisions for summary awards and "documents – only" arbitration make it materially more likely that proceedings will actually be conducted in an expedited manner.

(1)简洁的组庭方式

依据《华南规则》第23A条第2款a、b项，快速程序以独任仲裁员为原则，以当事人另有约定为例外。① 即便仲裁协议约定三名仲裁员，SCIAHK也应建议各方当事人将案件提交独任仲裁员处理，并在各方当事人同意的情况下适用独任制审理。② 独任制审理不仅节约了组庭时间和仲裁费用，后续审理过程中在协调仲裁员时间方面面临的挑战也会更少。③

(2)缩短的审理期限

根据《华南规则》第23A条第2款e项，裁决应在仲裁庭组成之日起6个月内作出，SCIAHK仅在特殊情况下可以延长此期限。④ 这与UNCITRAL《快速仲裁规则》(Expedited Arbitration Rules)第16条有关快速程序的审限原则上为6个月的规定一致。

同时，根据《华南规则》第23A条第2款c项，SCIAHK可以缩短《华南规则》规定的或其设定的任何期限。⑤ 这赋予了SCIAHK根据案件实际情况进行调整的自由裁量权，降低裁决在执行阶段被质疑的风险，同时SCIAHK能够采取果断行动而不必担心裁决可能因违反正当程序而被撤销。⑥

---

① 《华南规则》第23A条第2款a项。

② 《华南规则》第23A条第2款b项。

③ See Gary B. Born, *International Arbitration and Forum Selection Agreements Drafting and Enforcing*, (Kluwer Law International BV 2021), Chapter 3, A(5)(b): With respect to expense, three arbitrators cost roughly three times as much as a single arbitrator; there are some ministerial tasks which need to be performed only once even with three arbitrators, but many efforts are tripled in a three – person tribunal. With respect to speed, there are inevitably greater difficulties in scheduling hearings with three arbitrators, where multiple busy calendars must be coordinated (sometimes to accommodate hearings of several weeks or more), See also Leng Sun Chan & Weiyi Tan, *Making Arbitration Effective: Expedited Procedures, Emergency Arbitrators and Interim Relief* (2013) 6 Contemp Asia Arb J 349, 358: Practically, having a sole arbitrator may facilitate a speedier process as the Tribunal is likely to be constituted faster and parties may face fewer challenges in the scheduling of timelines.

④ 《华南规则》第23A条第2款e项。See Gary B. Born, *International Commercial Arbitration* (3rd *Edition*), Kluwer Law International 2021, 2480: if unforeseen circumstances or complexities arise which make it impossible to allow the parties an opportunity to be heard in an expedited proceeding, then both arbitral institutions and tribunals have the authority (and the obligation) to "un – expedite" the proceedings.

⑤ 《华南规则》第23A条第2款c项。

⑥ Explanatory Note to the UNCITRAL Expedited Arbitration Rules (2021), para 68.

(3)灵活的审理方式

根据《华南规则》第23A条第2款d项的规定,仲裁庭应以书面审理为原则,但仲裁庭有权决定是否进行开庭审理(oral hearings)或进行几次开庭审理。[①] 国际商事仲裁的当事人与当事人或当事人与代理人往往位于不同的国家或地区,因此,审理方式直接关系仲裁程序的效率和成本。[②] 在双方当事人同意适用快速程序或者案件标的较小的情况下,书面审理能够避免不必要的延误和开支(如语言障碍所带来的高昂翻译费用等)。[③] UNCITRAL《快速仲裁规则》即采用了快速程序原则上不开庭审理的做法。[④]

国际仲裁实践中,仲裁庭在决定是否开庭审理或进行几次开庭审理时,通常会考虑如下因素:①争议的性质;②争点的复杂性;③争议的金额;④证据和观点的性质,以及证据和观点是由哪一方提供和提出的;⑤节省时间和成本;⑥是不是解决仲裁中所有或部分争点的有效方式。[⑤]

(4)简明的裁决理由

根据《华南规则》第23A条第2款f项的规定,仲裁庭可以简要形式(in summary form)说明裁决依据的理由。[⑥] 这减轻了仲裁庭在快速程序中的说理负担。

由于绝大多数仲裁规则都规定仲裁员应当在裁决中说明裁决理由,若仲裁员以简单的结论代替裁判说理,或者说理不充分,在某些司法管辖区和特定情况下,裁决会有被拒绝执行的风险。例如,在 *Z v. Y* [2018] *HKCFI* 2342 案中,

---

① 《华南规则》第23A条第2款d项。

② 参见杨玲:《国际商事仲裁的审理方式》,载《南通大学学报(社会科学版)》2013年第3期。

③ See The Chartered Institute of Arbitrators, Documents – Only Arbitration Procedures (2015), Commentary on Article 1: Documents – only procedures are particularly effective at speeding up the process and reducing costs. 参见杨玲:《国际商事仲裁的审理方式》,载《南通大学学报(社会科学版)》2013年第3期。

④ UNCITRAL《快速仲裁规则》第11条。

⑤ The Chartered Institute of Arbitrators, Documents – Only Arbitration Procedures (2015), Commentary on Article 1: the factors to take into account when determining whether some or all of the issues are suitable for resolution by a documents – only procedure, to the extent that this information is available, include (1) the nature of the dispute; (2) the complexity of the issues; (3) the amount at stake; (4) the nature of the evidence and arguments to be adduced and by whom; (5) any time and costs savings; and (6) whether it is an effective and efficient way of resolving all, or some, of the issues in dispute in the arbitration. See also 1996 Arbitration Act, Art. 33 (1) (b): The tribunal shall... adopt procedures suitable to the circumstances of the particular case, avoiding unnecessary delay or expense, so as to provide a fair means for the resolution of the matters falling to be determined.

⑥ 《华南规则》第23A条第2款f项。

香港特别行政区高等法院原讼法庭认为,根据内地的法律,作为基础关系的主合同违法或不可执行,从而使被申请人的保证无效或不可执行,是一个重要问题,但仲裁庭没有提供充分理由论述这一问题(not addressed in the award with adequate reasons)。[①] 当裁决可能会被违法因素“污染”(tainted by illegality),且仲裁庭没有对重要问题进行适当的考量和裁断,进而有悖于当事人合法、合理的期待时,执行该裁决就会违反法院的公正和正义理念。[②]

《华南规则》为仲裁庭以简要形式作出裁决提供了规则依据,双方当事人同意适用快速程序即意味着双方同意仲裁庭以简要形式作出裁决。裁决作出后,一方后续很难再以“裁决说理不充分”为由对裁决质疑。[③]

(5)提高仲裁效率的同时保障公正

公正与效率是仲裁的两个基本价值维度,快速程序在实现高效仲裁的同时也必须确保公正。[④] 公正在快速仲裁中主要体现为当事人选择程序的自由,[⑤]

---

① See *Z v. Y* [2018] HKCFI 2342, para 14: “The important issue of whether the underlying HD Contracts and MD Contracts were illegal and unenforceable under PRC law, so as to render the Guarantee void and unenforceable against the Respondent, is not in my view addressed in the Award with adequate reasons...”

② See *Z v. Y* [2018] HKCFI 2342, para 14: “... it would offend our Court’s notions of fairness and justice to enforce the Award when it might be tainted by illegality, and when a significant issue brought before the tribunal for determination has not been seen to be properly considered and determined, contrary to the parties’ legitimate and reasonable expectations.”

③ See Ashurst international arbitration group, ‘Expedited Procedure in international arbitration’ (April 2014), https://www.ashurst.com/en/news-and-insights/legal-updates/expedited-procedure-in-international-arbitration/. 最后访问日期:2022 年 5 月 19 日。

④ See Fabricio Fortese and Lotta Hemmi, *Procedural Fairness and Efficiency in International Arbitration*, (2015) 3 Groningen Journal of International Law 110, 116: Efficiency is often assimilated with only cost and time efficiency, but the other side of the same coin is to gain the efficient proceedings without risking either the correct outcome or the due process. See also Clyde Croft, Shristopher Kee & Jeff Waincymer, *A Guide to the UNCITRAL Arbitration Rules* (Cambridge University Press 2013), para 17.1: ... the second part of Article 17(1) requires a tribunal, in exercising its discretion, ‘to avoid unnecessary delay and expense and to provide a fair and efficient process for resolving the parties’ dispute’. By placing questions of equality and reasonable opportunity alongside concern for efficiency, unnecessary delay and expense, the rules go some way in the direction of an ‘overriding objective’. See also David Caron & Lee Caplan, *The UNCITRAL Arbitration Rules: A Commentary* (*2nd Edition*, Oxford University Press), Chapter 2, Commentary on Article 17(2): Inclusion of the provision in the 2010 Rules aimed to ensure that the arbitral tribunal, where necessary, could modify any time period in the interest of a “fair and efficient process of resolving the parties’ dispute”.

⑤ See Fabricio Fortese & Lotta Hemmi, *Procedural Fairness and Efficiency in International Arbitration*, (2015) 3 Groningen Journal of International Law 110, 112-116.

《华南规则》赋予了当事人一定的决定权。例如,在仲裁协议约定仲裁庭由三位仲裁员组成的情况下,虽然 SCIAHK 建议各方当事人将案件提交独任仲裁员处理,但若当事人不同意,案件仍应提交三位仲裁员处理。又如,经一方当事人要求,且在与各方当事人和任何已确认或指定的仲裁员商议后,SCIAHK 可参酌出现的新情况,决定不再适用快速程序。

(二)快速程序在国际商事仲裁中的意义

2015 年伦敦玛丽女王大学(Queen Mary University of London)发布的国际仲裁调查报告显示,有 68% 的被调查人认为仲裁最大的缺点是成本太高,排在其后的两个缺点分别是缺少对仲裁员效率的监管和速度慢。① 同时,有 92% 的被调查者倾向于适用更加简便、快速的仲裁程序。② 快速程序能够有效降低使用国际商事仲裁的成本与费用,提高仲裁的程序性效率,同时为不同类型的使用者提供多样化选择。多家仲裁机构发布的案件数据表明,越来越多的争议案件通过快速程序得以解决。③《华南规则》引入快速程序制度,无疑将吸引更多商事主体首选 SCIAHK 作为争议解决仲裁机构。

四、请求和答辩的即决驳回

请求和答辩的即决驳回(summary dismissal of claims and defences)是早期处置机制(early dismissal mechanism)的一个重要形式,是指仲裁庭在受理案件

---

① See Queen Mary University of London,2015 Improvements and Innovations in International Arbitration, https://arbitration. qmul. ac. uk/research/2015/. 最后访问日期:2022 年 5 月 8 日。See also Nigel Blackaby & Constantine Partasides QC with Alan Redfern & Martin Hunter, *Redfern and Hunter on International Arbitration* (*6th Edition*), Oxford University Press, para 6. 27: Nevertheless, in recent years, there has been a growing sense of frustration among businessmen involved in international commerce, because of the lengthy delays involved in obtaining the hoped – for promised land of the arbitral tribunal's award.

② See Queen Mary University of London,2015 Improvements and Innovations in International Arbitration, https://arbitration. qmul. ac. uk/research/2015/. 最后访问日期: 2022 年 5 月 8 日。See also Morton & Peter, *Can a World Exist Where Expedited Arbitration Becomes the Default Procedure* (2010) 26 Arb. Int'l 103, 104: There is a growing chorus of discontent from the 'consumers' of the arbitration process (the business community) about the increased time and costs of arbitration.

③ See Haflidi Kristjan Larusson, *Expedited Arbitration – Meeting the Needs of SMEs*, (2017) 63 Scandinavian Stud L 169, 177: Expedited arbitration under the auspices of Arbitration Institute of the Stockholm Chamber of Commerce has grown to the extent that it now counts for almost one – third of all arbitration cases administered by the institution. See also *Statistics – The Arbitration Institute of the Stockholm Chamber of Commerce*, https://sccinstitute. com/statistics. 最后访问日期:2022 年 5 月 8 日。

的早期对当事人的仲裁请求进行评估，在对当事人的具体请求内容和依据进行评估后，如果仲裁庭认为当事人的仲裁请求明显缺乏合理性，则对全部或部分请求和主张予以驳回的一种机制。其目的是尽早结束有明显结果的仲裁以节省时间和成本。①

《华南规则》第 23B 条规定了这项制度。在这一机制下，仲裁庭可以在仲裁程序的早期阶段对当事人的仲裁请求或答辩进行审查，并驳回明显缺乏依据（manifestly without merit）或明显超出仲裁庭管辖权（manifestly outside the jurisdiction）的请求或答辩。②

（一）其他机构仲裁规则中有关即决驳回制度的规定

即决驳回制度正逐步被部分主流商事仲裁机构的规则采纳。

SIAC 是除 ICSID 之外第一个采用即决驳回制度的仲裁机构，③也是首个采用即决驳回制度的主流商事仲裁机构。④ 根据 2016 年 SIAC 规则第 29 条的规定，当事人可基于以下理由向仲裁庭申请早期驳回仲裁申请或答辩：仲裁申请或答辩明显缺乏法律依据，或者仲裁申请或答辩明显超过仲裁庭的管辖范围。⑤

2018 年 HKIAC 规则第 43 条规定，在满足下列条件时，经任何一方当事人申请，并在征求所有其他当事人意见后，仲裁庭应有权通过初期决定程序决定

---

① See John Choong & Mark Mangan, Chapter 11: Early Dismissal of Claims and Defences (SIAC Rule 29), *A Guide to the SIAC Arbitration Rules*, Oxford University Press (2018). "Early dismissal of claims and defences is a mechanism for the early resolution of proceedings in full or in part. The aim is to save time and cost by bringing proceedings or claims that have an obvious outcome to an end as early as possible."

② 参见《华南规则》第 23B 条："(1): A party may apply to the arbitral tribunal for the summary dismissal of one or more claims or defences, including a counterclaim, a claim for the purpose of set - off or any point of law or fact supporting such claims or defences, on the basis that they are manifestly without merit, or manifestly outside the jurisdiction of the arbitral tribunal ('Summary Dismissal')."

③ See Elodie Dulac & Alex Lo, *The SIAC Rules* 2016: *New Features*, Indian Journal of Arbitration Law.

④ Subsequently, SIAC also introduced early dismissal of claims and defences in the new 2017 SIAC Investment Arbitration Rules (see Chapter 19). For an overview of summary dismissal of claims before international courts and tribunals, see M Potestà & M Sobat, *Frivolous Claims in International Adjudication: A Study of ICSID Rule* 41(5) *and of Procedures of Other Courts and Tribunals to Dismiss Claims Summarily*, (2012) 3(1) J Int'l Dispute Settlement 137, 139 - 45, 159 - 67.

⑤ 2016 年 SIAC 规则第 29 条规定："A party may apply to the Tribunal for the early dismissal of a claim or defence on the basis that: a. a claim or defence is manifestly without legal merit; or b. a claim or defence is manifestly outside the jurisdiction of the Tribunal."

一个或多个法律或事实问题：该法律或事实问题明显缺乏依据;或该法律或事实问题明显不在仲裁庭管辖权范围内;或即便该法律或事实问题是由另一方当事人提出且假定是正确的,仲裁庭也无法作出有利于主张该问题一方的裁决(no award could be rendered in favour of that party)。①

2020 年 LCIA 规则第 22 条规定,经一方当事人申请或自主决定,在给予当事人合理机会陈述意见的前提下,仲裁庭可以决定任何请求、抗辩、反请求、交叉请求、对反请求的抗辩或对交叉请求的抗辩明显超出仲裁庭的管辖权、缺乏可受理性(inadmissible),或明显缺乏法律依据,并在适当时作出裁决。②

(二)即决驳回制度在国际商事仲裁中的意义

近年来,国际商事仲裁成本高昂、程序冗余经常被众多仲裁当事人诟病。学者和仲裁实践者一直在寻求如何解决商事仲裁所面临的问题,其中之一即是引入即决驳回制度。③ 即决驳回制度对于降低当事人的仲裁成本、提高仲裁效率具有重要意义。该制度通过在仲裁庭正式审理案件前处置案件,最大限度地将缺乏依据的不合理请求和主张筛除于程序之外,以确保仲裁程序的高效,同时也是对当事人免受滥诉滋扰的重要保护。④

即决驳回制度建立在赋予仲裁庭广泛的自由裁量权的基础上,适用该制度时,当事人进行书面或口头答辩的权利会受到限制,被驳回请求的当事人通常会以仲裁庭超越权限、剥夺当事人陈述权利为由对仲裁裁决提出异议。实践

---

① See HKIAC 规则(2018)第 43 条规定:"The arbitral tribunal shall have the power, at the request of any party and after consulting with all other parties, to decide one or more points of law or fact by way of early determination procedure, on the basis that: ... (c) even if such points of law or fact are submitted by another party and are assumed to be correct, no award could be rendered in favour of that party."

② See LCIA 规则(2020)第 22 条第 1 款 viii 规定:"The Arbitral Tribunal shall have the power, upon the application of any party or [save for sub – paragraph (x) below] upon its own initiative, but in either case only after giving the parties a reasonable opportunity to state their views and upon such terms (as to costs and otherwise) as the Arbitral Tribunal may decide: (viii) to determine that any claim, defence, counterclaim, cross – claim, defence to counterclaim or defence to cross – claim is manifestly outside the jurisdiction of the Arbitral Tribunal, or is inadmissible or manifestly without merit; and where appropriate to issue an order or award to that effect (an 'Early Determination')."

③ See Carlos González – Bueno, *Early Dismissal of Unmeritorious Claims and Defences in International Arbitration*, 40 under 40 International Arbitration (2018).

④ 参见唐塞潇:《国际商事仲裁早期处置机制的价值平衡和制度构建》,载《武大国际法评论》2019 年第 2 期。

中,仲裁庭也曾被认为无权即决驳回被申请人的索赔,除非当事人同意或通过纳入仲裁规则授予仲裁庭此项权力。[①] 然而,在仲裁规则没有规定的情况下,一些仲裁庭作出早期处置(如简易裁决或即决驳回)的做法,可能会受到针对程序正当性的质疑。

例如,在 *Weirton Medical Center Inc. v. Community Health Systems Inc.* 案中,仲裁庭是否有权在不通知当事人的情况下作出简易裁决的问题出现了争议。2016 年,从事医疗健康服务的 Weirton 公司和 Quorum 公司就双方的服务合同达成了仲裁协议,约定因该合同产生的纠纷应提交 AAA 进行仲裁,并适用《美国仲裁协会仲裁规则》(以下简称 AAA 仲裁规则)。2017 年,作为仲裁申请人的 Quorum 公司请求仲裁庭作出简易裁决,并获得了仲裁庭的准许。但被申请人认为,仲裁庭的决定明显超过了其权力范围,因而向美国西弗吉尼亚北区联邦地区法院提出撤销仲裁裁决的申请。该案的关键争议在于,仲裁庭对仲裁的早期处置是否具有法律依据,即在 AAA 仲裁规则对这一问题并没有明确规定的情况下,仲裁庭能否主动通过采取早期处置机制作出简易裁决。[②]

基于此,即决驳回制度过于宽泛的自由裁量权可能会招致当事人和法院对程序正当性的质疑。[③] 因此,《华南规则》引入这一制度的意义在于,为仲裁员适用即决驳回制度提供了仲裁规则上的依据,防止相关质疑者以违反正当程序为由挑战仲裁裁决的效力。[④]

值得一提的是,《华南规则》还明确规定,仲裁庭应在即决驳回申请提交之日起 30 日内,在给予各方当事人针对申请发表意见的机会后,尽快对即决驳回申请作出裁决。SCIAHK 在保障当事人充分发表意见的同时,对即决驳回程序

---

① See David Ryan & Kanaga Dharmananda, *Summary Disposal in Arbitration: Still Fair or Agreed to be Fair, in Maxi Scherer (ed)*, Journal of International Arbitration, "Tribunals were once thought to have no power to summarily dismiss claims unless the parties agreed to confer those powers upon them – directly or through incorporation of arbitration rules."

② See Weirton Medical Center Inc. v. Community Health Systems Inc., N. D. W. Va. June. 27, 2017.

③ See Gary B. Born & Kenneth Beale, *Party Autonomy and Default Rules: Reframing the Debate over Summary Disposition in International Arbitration*, 21 ICC International Court of Arbitration Bulletin 23 (2010).

④ See Philip Chong & Blake Primrose, *Summary Judgment in International Arbitrations Seated in England*, 33 Arbitration International 71 (2017).

明确设置了时间节点。为避免商事仲裁当事人将即决驳回制度作为新的拖延仲裁程序的手段,设置明确的时间限制是必要的。①《华南规则》为仲裁庭作出早期驳回决定设置了30日的时限,显然有助于提高仲裁效率。

一直以来,确保商事仲裁作为替代性纠纷解决机制快速、高效、经济的优势,始终是仲裁机构最重要的目标。《华南规则》引入了"请求和答辩的即决驳回"条款,为仲裁庭的早期处置提供仲裁规则上的依据,对于提高仲裁效率、降低当事人仲裁成本,以及防止滥用程序具有重要意义。同时充分体现了SCIAHK顺应实践发展的趋势和要求,对于推进仲裁机构和仲裁制度的改革发展,必将发挥积极、重要的示范效应和引领作用。在实践中,即决驳回的规定仍然相对较少,但可以预见这一制度将得到更广泛的运用。②

五、选择性复裁

根据《华南规则》第39A条规定,当事人有权约定选择性复裁(Optional Appellate Arbitration)程序。选择性复裁程序的细化规则详细规定于《华南规则》的附件2中,附件2共包括关于"依据""复裁申请""复裁答辩""复裁庭的组成""程序""原裁决的效力""复裁裁决""费用承担""费用担保"9条具体规定。

SCIAHK的这一制度延续了SCIA在内地创设的选择性复裁机制,③是对仲裁内部上诉机制在香港实践的进一步探索。所谓选择性复裁程序,一般是指特定仲裁案件当事人依据约定将仲裁庭作出的裁决提交另行组成的仲裁庭即复裁庭进行复裁,并作出终局裁决的仲裁程序。④

仲裁虽然以其灵活、高效的特点广受欢迎,但与之伴随的代价是缺少纠错

① See Aisatou Diop, *Objection under Rule 41(5) of the ICSID Arbitration Rules*, 25 ICSID Review 313 (2010).

② See Gary B. Born, *Procedures in International Arbitration*, International Commercial Arbitration (3rd Edition).

③ 《深圳国际仲裁院仲裁规则》第68条规定:"(一)在仲裁地法律不禁止的前提下,当事人约定任何一方就仲裁庭依照本规则第八章作出的裁决可以向仲裁院提请复裁的,从其约定。适用本规则快速程序的案件,不适用本条规定的选择性复裁程序。(二)选择性复裁程序按照《深圳国际仲裁院选择性复裁程序指引》的规定进行。"沈四宝、刘晓春、樊奇娟:《一裁终局的重新评估与复裁机制的创新实践》,载《法治日报》2019年11月5日,第10、11版。

④ 刘晓春主编、深圳国际仲裁院编著:《〈深圳国际仲裁院仲裁规则〉理解与适用》,北京大学出版社2020年版,第68页。

机制，特别是争议标的额较大、争议案情较为复杂、对技术和专业知识（如能源、建工、海事等）有较高要求的案件，当事人对实体公正的价值追求可能远远高于对效率的追求。[①] 在内地法院审理的仲裁司法审查案件中，也时常出现当事人不服仲裁实体裁决的处理结果，以此达到“上诉”的最终目的和需求，这却实际与当事人对高效仲裁的期许适得其反。[②]《仲裁法》确立了仲裁“一裁终局”的基本原则，[③]在该原则的指导下，即使当事人在合同中约定如不服仲裁裁决，可向某法院起诉或仲裁机构上诉，基于此类合同约定提出的主张在我国司法实践中通常不会得到支持。[④]

在我国现行仲裁法律制度框架下，选择性复裁制度的设想存在束缚，有违反仲裁法基本原则和规定而不受保护的风险。从境外仲裁立法和实践来看，“一裁终局”似乎越来越多地被认为不是仲裁的“金科玉律”。

纵观现代仲裁制度的发展过程，不同于当前世界仲裁员绝大多数为法律专家，在英国仲裁的早期发展阶段，仲裁员多为行业专家，而非法律专家，这种情况在保险、航运、大宗货物买卖等特定的领域尤为如此。为了防止非法律专家在适用法律的问题上出现明显的偏差，英国一直以来保留了有限的“法律适用错误”上诉制度。[⑤] 因而，1996 年《英国仲裁法》尊重了当事人对仲裁的上诉权利。该法第 58 条规定：“除非当事人另有约定，依据仲裁协议作出的裁决是终局的，对当事人以及通过当事人或以其名义提出请求者都具有约束力。本条规定不影响任何人依据可以利用的仲裁上诉或复审程序或本编之规定对仲裁裁

---

① 参见沈四宝、刘晓春、樊奇娟：《一裁终局的重新评估与复裁机制的创新实践》，载《法治日报》2019 年 11 月 5 日，第 10、11 版。

② 参见刘晓红主编：《仲裁“一裁终局”制度之困境及本位回归》，法律出版社 2016 年版，第 33 页。

③ 《仲裁法》第 9 条规定：“仲裁实行一裁终局的制度。裁决作出后，当事人就同一纠纷再申请仲裁或者向人民法院起诉的，仲裁委员会或者人民法院不予受理。裁决被人民法院依法裁定撤销或者不予执行的，当事人就该纠纷可以根据双方重新达成的仲裁协议申请仲裁，也可以向人民法院起诉。”

④ 参见最高人民法院审理的（2012）民四他字第 39 号案，争议先提交中国国际经济贸易仲裁委员会进行仲裁，“若一方不服该裁决，则再由新加坡国际仲裁法按照该会的有关规定进行仲裁”，该约定违反我国仲裁一裁终局的基本原则。

⑤ English Arbitration Act (1996), Article 69 (Appeal on point of law): “(1) Unless otherwise agreed by the parties, a party to arbitral proceedings may (upon notice to the other parties and to the tribunal) appeal to the court on a question of law arising out of an award made in the proceedings... (3) Leave to appeal shall be given only if the court is satisfied... (c) that, on the basis of the findings of fact in the award (i) the decision of the tribunal on the question is obviously wrong...”

决提出异议的权利。"[①]按照交易协会(Commodity Trade Association)规则在英国进行的诸多商事仲裁,也允许对仲裁裁决提出上诉。[②] 但根据上述条款对仲裁裁决在英国提起的上诉并不是无限制的,当适用的仲裁规则排除了"一裁终局"后的救济时,当事人不再享有上诉的权利。[③] 同时,传统英国法观念认为,外国法(foreign law)是(特殊的)事实问题。[④] 而且,按照1996年《英国仲裁法》第69条,对法律问题提起的上诉限于英国法问题,[⑤]因此,在以英国为仲裁地的国际仲裁中,触发仲裁裁决"法律适用错误"的上诉纠错机制的案件数量有限。[⑥]

此外,在其他法域,根据《香港特别行政区仲裁条例》第73条(裁决的效力)的规定,除非各方另有协议,否则仲裁庭依据仲裁协议作出的裁决,属最终裁决,对仲裁各方具有约束力;但这并不影响当事人按附表2第4条或第5条的规定(基于程序瑕疵质疑裁决或基于法律问题错误对裁决上诉)或按任何可用的

---

① English Arbitration Act (1996), Article 58 (Effect of award): "(1) Unless otherwise agreed by the parties, an award made by the tribunal pursuant to an arbitration agreement is final and binding both on the parties and on any persons claiming through or under them. (2) This does not affect the right of a person to challenge the award by any available arbitral process of appeal or review or in accordance with the provisions of this Part."

② England: VV Veeder, "National Report England" in Lise Bosman (ed), *The International Handbook on Commercial Arbitration*, Chapter VI. 1(a). 如谷物和饲料贸易协会 Grain and Feed Trade Association (GAFTA)、国际油、油籽和油脂协会 Federation of Oils, Seeds and Fats Associations (FOSFA)等。

③ 如 ICC Arbitration Rules (2021), Article 35(6): "Every award shall be binding on the parties. By submitting the dispute to arbitration under the Rules, the parties undertake to carry out any award without delay and shall be deemed to have waived their right to any form of recourse insofar as such waiver can validly be made." LCIA Arbitration Rules (2020), Article 26. 8: "Every award (including reasons for such award) shall be final and binding on the parties. The parties undertake to carry out any award immediately and without any delay (subject only to Article 27); and the parties also waive irrevocably their right to any form of appeal, review or recourse to any state court or other legal authority, insofar as such waiver shall not be prohibited under any applicable law."

④ See Julian D. M. Lew, *Proof of Applicable Law in International Commercial Arbitration*, in Festschrift für Otto Sandrock zum 70. Geburtstag, ed. Klaus Peter Berger & Otto Sandrock (Frankfurt am Main: Verlag Recht und Wirstchaft, 2000), 581, 595.

⑤ Matt Marshall, *Section* 69 *almost* 20 *years on...*, June 24, 2015, Kluwer Arbitration Blog. http://arbitrationblog. kluwerarbitration. com/2015/06/24/section - 69 - almost - 20 - years - on/.

⑥ 在更近的案件中,有观点认为英国法官在认定外国法问题上可以采取更积极主动的方式。See Cassini SAS v. Emerald Pasture Designated Activity Company & Ors [2022] EWCA Civ 102. It held it was entitled to "consider the expert evidence afresh and form its own view of the cogency of the rival contentions in determining whether the trial judge came to the correct conclusion."

上诉或复核的仲裁程序，质疑裁决。[①] 仲裁的上诉在美国也并不陌生，美国的主流仲裁机构诸如 AAA、国际争议解决中心（International Centre for Dispute Resolution，ICDR）、司法仲裁调解服务（Judicial Arbitration and Mediation Services，JAMS）等都有其相应的仲裁程序上诉机制供当事人使用。[②] 美国法院认为，经上诉而作出的仲裁裁决和一裁终局的仲裁裁决在仲裁司法审查上法院都给予同等尊重。[③] 此外，1986 年《荷兰民事诉讼法典》第 1050 条规定："只有当事人已经达成协议，才能对仲裁裁决向另一仲裁庭提出上诉。除非当事人另有约定，就部分裁决向另一仲裁庭的上诉只能同对最终裁决的上诉一并提出。除非当事人另有约定，就临时裁决向另一仲裁庭的上诉也只能同对最终裁决或部分终局裁决的上诉一并提出。"[④]该规定表明，荷兰法律允许当事人协议就仲裁裁决向另一仲裁庭提出上诉，仲裁不实行绝对的"一裁终局"。可见，在上诉问题上，各国仲裁制度存在两种救济路径：一种是默认仲裁上诉权利系法定权利，当事人当然享有，如英国的做法；另一种是允许当事人以协议选择（opt - in）的方式明确约定可以对仲裁裁决提起上诉，如《华南规则》中采取的做法。

结合以上背景，在广泛调研和讨论的基础上，本次《华南规则》的制定中，SCIAHK 充分利用默认仲裁地为香港（《华南规则》第 18 条，另有约定的除外）

---

① See Hong Kong Arbitration Ordinance (Cap. 609), Article 73 (Effect of award): "(1) Unless otherwise agreed by the parties, an award made by an arbitral tribunal pursuant to an arbitration agreement is final and binding both on (a) the parties; and (b) any person claiming through or under any of the parties. (2) Subsection (1) does not affect the right of a person to challenge the award (a) as provided for in section 26 or 81, section 4 or 5 of Schedule 2, or any other provision of this Ordinance; or (b) otherwise by any available arbitral process of appeal or review."

② See Anibal Sabater, *Optional Appellate Arbitration Rules: Are They Good For Your Case?*, http://nysbar.com/blogs/ResolutionRoundtable/Optional%20Appellate%20Arbitration%20Rules%20Are%20They%20Good%20For%20Your%20Case.pdf.

③ See Hamilton v. Navient Solutions, LLC., No. 18 Civ. 5432 (PAC) (S. D. N. Y. February 14, 2019).

④ Dutch Code of Civil Procedure, Article 1050 (Appeal to second arbitral tribunal): "1. An appeal from the arbitral award to a second arbitral tribunal is possible only if the parties have agreed thereto. 2. Unless the parties have agreed otherwise, an appeal to a second arbitral tribunal from a partial final award can be lodged only in conjunction with an appeal from the last final award. 3. Unless the parties have agreed otherwise, an appeal to a second arbitral tribunal from an interim award can be lodged only in conjunction with an appeal from a final or partial final award. 4. Unless the parties have agreed otherwise, an appeal to a second arbitral tribunal shall be lodged within three months after the date of deposit of the award with the Registry of the District Court."

这一规定,在不违反仲裁地法的情况下,赋予当事人通过协议选择的方式,就仲裁裁决的实体问题提请上诉的权利,以适配不同案件和不同利益主体的需求和期望,充分体现了 SCIAHK 以市场需求变化和当事人为中心的理念,积极和持续推动仲裁规则的创新和优化。此外,为了兼顾效率和公平,防止当事人滥用复裁程序,《华南规则》第 39A 条同时规定了复裁程序不能适用的情形,包括争议金额较小或当事人约定适用快速程序进行的案件,以及当事人在仲裁协议中根据《香港仲裁条例》已经约定了有关向原讼法庭上诉的情形(其已享有《香港仲裁条例》赋予的救济途径,无须再适用选择性复裁程序,故不适用复裁程序)。也期待 SCIAHK 在适用《华南规则》项下选择性复裁制度的案件中,在实践中完善复裁仲裁庭的具体权限和审查标准,为增强仲裁结果的可预测性和确定性作出进一步贡献,以更好地服务当事人和相关利益主体。

六、紧急仲裁员程序

《华南规则》第 26 条第 10 款及其附件 1 详细地规定了紧急仲裁员程序(emergency arbitrator procedure)。附件 1 共有 14 个条款,涉及申请紧急仲裁员的方法及时间截点、紧急仲裁员的指定和预付款、紧急仲裁员的回避与替换、仲裁地、紧急决定、费用、提供担保等内容,为紧急仲裁员程序提供了详细的指引。

(一)紧急仲裁员程序概述

紧急仲裁员程序是指在国际商事仲裁中,在提起仲裁的同时甚至提起仲裁之前,或已经提起仲裁但仲裁庭尚未组成前,供当事人寻求临时救济(如证据保全、行为保全、财产保全等)的一种机制。[①] 根据《华南规则》附件 1 第 1 条,申请人可于提交仲裁通知的同时或之后(但在仲裁庭组成前),请求仲裁机构指定

---

① See Gary B. Born, *International Commercial Arbitration*, Chapter 17 "Provisional Relief in International Arbitration", Wolters Kluwer (2nd Edition, 2014). See also 2018 HKIAC Administered Arbitration Rules, Schedule 4 "Emergency Arbitrator Procedures", Article 1, "A party requiring Emergency Relief may submit an application (the 'Application') for the appointment of an emergency arbitrator to HKIAC (a) before, (b) concurrent with, or (c) following the filing of a Notice of Arbitration, but prior to the constitution of the arbitral tribunal." See also Erin Collins, Pre – Tribunal Emergency Relief in International Commercial Arbitration, 10 Loy. U. Chi. Int'l L. Rev. 105 (2013).

一名“紧急仲裁员”以作出临时救济措施。[①] 该机制填补了在仲裁庭组成前,当事人无法直接从仲裁程序中申请临时措施救济的空白,减轻了当事人向一个甚至多个法院申请临时措施的负担。[②]

自 2006 年 ICDR 率先启用紧急仲裁员程序以来,境内外主流仲裁机构相继将该程序纳入仲裁规则。在仲裁规则中采纳紧急仲裁员程序的国际仲裁机构包括但不限于:

(1)ICDR 于 2006 年在其仲裁规则中新增了紧急仲裁员程序;[③]

(2)SCC 于 2010 年在其仲裁规则中新增了紧急仲裁员程序;[④]

(3)SIAC 于 2010 年在其仲裁规则中新增了紧急仲裁员程序;[⑤]

(4)ICC 于 2012 年在其仲裁规则中新增了紧急仲裁员程序;[⑥]

(5)HKIAC 于 2013 年在其仲裁规则中新增了紧急仲裁员程序;[⑦]

(6)LCIA 于 2014 年在其仲裁规则中新增了紧急仲裁员程序;[⑧]

(7)CIETAC 于 2015 年在其仲裁规则中新增了紧急仲裁员程序;[⑨]

(8)BAC 于 2015 年在其仲裁规则中新增了紧急仲裁员程序;[⑩]

(9)SCIA 于 2016 年在其仲裁规则中新增了紧急仲裁员程序。[⑪]

根据《华南规则》的规定,SCIAHK 在受理紧急申请后,应争取在收到紧急申请与预付款后 24 小时内指定紧急仲裁员。紧急仲裁员应自 SCIAHK 向其移交案件之日起 14 日内,就紧急申请作出决定、指令或裁决。此期限可根据当事

---

① See Nigel Blackaby, Constantine Partasides QC with Alan Redfern & Martin Hunter, *Redfern and Hunter on International Arbitration* (*6th Edition*), Oxford University Press, Section 4.17 “Emergency Arbitrators”, p. 235.

② See Chan Leng Sun & Weiyi Tan, *Making Arbitration Effective*: *Expedited Procedure*, Emergency Arbitrators and Emergency Relief, 6(2) Contemp. Asia Arb. J. 349, at 352 (2013).

③ 《国际争议解决程序(包括调解和仲裁规则)》(2006 年版)。

④ 《斯德哥尔摩商会仲裁院仲裁规则》(2010 年版)第 32 条以及附录。

⑤ 《新加坡国际仲裁中心仲裁规则》(2010 年版)第 26(2)条以及 Schedule 1。

⑥ 《国际商会仲裁规则》(2012 年版)第 29 条。

⑦ 《香港国际仲裁中心仲裁规则》(2013 年版)Schedule 4: emergency arbitrator procedures。

⑧ 《伦敦国际仲裁院仲裁规则》(2014 年版)第 9b 条。

⑨ 《中国国际经济贸易仲裁委员会仲裁规则》(2015 年版)附件三“中国国际经济贸易仲裁委员会紧急仲裁员程序”。

⑩ 《北京仲裁委员会仲裁规则》(2015 年版)第八章“国际商事仲裁的特别规定”第 63 条。

⑪ 《深圳国际仲裁院仲裁规则》(2016 年版)第四章“临时措施”第 24 条。

人的约定延长,也可在适当情况下由 SCIAHK 延长。这样紧凑的时间安排可以确保申请人的诉求得到及时有效的处理,也与大多数国际仲裁机构的规定保持了一致。①

(二)紧急仲裁员的裁断标准

《华南规则》第 26 条第 10 款规定:“一方当事人需要采取紧急临时措施,且无法等到仲裁庭组成的,可以按照《附件 1》规定的程序,申请紧急临时或保全性救济(‘紧急仲裁员程序’)。”

《华南规则》附件 1 第 5 条第 1 款规定,紧急仲裁员可以其认为适当的方式进行紧急救济程序,但应考虑到此程序内在的紧迫性,确保各方当事人均有合理的机会就紧急申请陈述意见。国际仲裁实践中的通行做法是,只要保证双方有合理的机会发表意见,紧急仲裁员有权决定是否进行开庭审理,或是在申请人、被申请人书面交换文件后进行书面审理。由此可见,《华南规则》对于紧急仲裁员程序审理方式的规定与国际仲裁中的通行做法相吻合。②

关于是否准予申请人临时救济措施的衡量标准,包括《华南规则》在内的各个机构仲裁规则都给予了紧急仲裁员较大的自由裁量权。通常,紧急仲裁员会从以下四个方面考虑,从而决定是否给予临时救济措施:

(1)时间紧迫性(urgency),即不能等待组成仲裁庭后再决定采取临时

---

① 例如,现行的《香港国际仲裁中心机构仲裁规则》(2018 年版)也规定了仲裁机构应在 24 小时内指定紧急仲裁员,紧急仲裁员应在收到案件材料的 14 日内作出决定。See also Article 4(1) of SCC Arbitration Rules (2017) Appendix II, “The Board shall seek to appoint an Emergency Arbitrator within 24 hours of receipt of the application.” Article 8(1) of SCC Arbitration Rules (2017) Appendix II, “Any emergency decision on interim measures shall be made no later than 5 days from the date the application was referred to the Emergency Arbitrator pursuant to Article 6 of this Appendix. The Board may extend this time limit upon a reasoned request from the Emergency Arbitrator, or if otherwise deemed necessary.” Article 2(1) of ICC Arbitration Rules (2021) Appendix V, “The President shall appoint an emergency arbitrator within as short a time as possible, normally within two days from the Secretariat's receipt of the Application.” Article 6(4) of ICC Arbitration Rules (2021) Appendix V, “The Order shall be made no later than 15 days from the date on which the file was transmitted to the emergency arbitrator pursuant to Article 2(3) of this Appendix. The President may extend the time limit pursuant to a reasoned request from the emergency arbitrator or on the President's own initiative if the President decides it is necessary to do so.”

② See *Report of the ICC Commission on Arbitration and ADR Task Force on Emergency Arbitrator Proceedings* (2019), “Consequently, EAs could in appropriate circumstances decide the case on documents only, with no hearing and no examination of witnesses, and limit the number, scope and length of submissions. The only limit to the EA's discretion is to ensure that each party has a reasonable opportunity to present its case.”

措施；[①]

(2)若不采取临时措施，将对申请人的权益造成不可弥补的损害(irreparable harm)；[②]

(3)比例原则(proportionality 或称 balance of convenience)，即采取临时措施不会给被申请人造成不合理的负担；[③]

(4)申请人提交了可以支持仲裁管辖权和申请人的实体(merits)仲裁请求的表面证据(*prima facie evidence*)。[④]

(三)紧急仲裁员程序的意义

上文提到的2015年伦敦玛丽女王大学的国际仲裁调查报告显示，93%的被调查者认为，机构仲裁规则纳入紧急仲裁员程序是一项积极的发展，38%的被调查者甚至认为紧急仲裁员程序必须成为机构仲裁规则的一部分。[⑤]

《华南规则》设置了紧急仲裁员程序，符合当前国际商事仲裁的发展趋势，为当事人在紧迫情况下申请临时救济措施以维护自身权利打下了良好的制度基础。

---

① See American Cyanamid Ltd. v. Ethicon Ltd., AC 396 (1975). See also *Yahoo!, Inc. v. Microsoft Corp.*, 983 F. Supp. 2d 310 (S. D. N. Y. 2013): The [Emergency] Arbitrator also concluded, inter alia, that "based on [his] evaluation of the testimony and affidavits submitted," it is "critical that the Ramp phase follow the Demand phase that has been successfully completed because advertiser orders and preferences change over time." Therefore, he found that the "urgency of the transition establishes the emergency required by the Emergency Rules."

② See Loana Knoll – Tudor, Chapter II: The Arbitrator and the Arbitration Procedure, *Emergency Arbitration: Evidence and Practice from Seven Arbitral Institutions Austrian Yearbook on International Arbitration*, (2019). See also *Yahoo!, Inc. v. Microsoft Corp.*, 983 F. Supp. 2d 310 (S. D. N. Y. 2013): [The Emergency Arbitrator] further concluded that the testimony and affidavits demonstrated that the Yahoo's breach of the Agreement "establishe[d] irreparable harm to Microsoft."

③ See *Report of the ICC Commission on Arbitration and ADR Task Force on Emergency Arbitrator Proceedings* (2019). See also Grant Hanessian & E. Alexandra Dosman, Songs of Innocence and Experience: Ten Years of Emergency Arbitration, Am. Rev. Int'l Arb. (2018).

④ See Moser & Bao, *Guide to the HKIAC Arbitration Rules* (2017). See also Christopher Boog & Bertrand Stoffel, *Preliminary Orders and the Emergency Arbitrator: Urgent Interim Relief by an Arbitral Decision Maker in Exceptional Circumstances*, Ten Years of Swiss Rules of International Arbitration – ASA Special Series No. 44 (2014).

⑤ See Queen Mary University of London, 2015 Improvements and Innovations in International Arbitration, https://arbitration.qmul.ac.uk/research/2015/，最后访问日期：2022年6月14日。

七、总结

《华南规则》体现了 SCIAHK 的灵活性管理与适应机构仲裁结合的价值取向：SCIAHK 提倡仲裁机构进行“轻管理”，充分尊重当事人的意思自治，增强仲裁的灵活性并提高效率。例如，《华南规则》第 10A 条允许当事人指定 SCIAHK 网站上公布的仲裁员名册之外的仲裁员，这有别于多数国内仲裁机构只从仲裁员名册里选择仲裁员[①]的做法。另外，上述提到的快速程序、请求和答辩的即决驳回，以及紧急仲裁员程序的制度设计，也是 SCIAHK 意在增强机构仲裁灵活性的体现。同时，由于自身机构仲裁的属性，《华南规则》也吸收了适应机构仲裁的规则和经验，如仲裁程序的起算时间、仲裁地的表述等。此外，《华南规则》在较前沿的问题上也有重要突破，如将选择性复裁程序引入仲裁规则。

综上所述，《华南规则》充分借鉴了国际上通行的做法，积极回应了当事人对仲裁公正和效率的要求，为各国当事人进行商事及投资仲裁提供充分和高效的规则指引。《华南规则》的发布和施行，将有助于进一步推动中国仲裁的国际化，扩大中国仲裁在国际上的影响力，标志着中国仲裁在国际化的道路上又迈出了一大步。

① 《中国国际经济贸易仲裁委员会仲裁规则》(2015 年版)第 26 条规定，当事人可从仲裁委员会制定的仲裁员名册中选定仲裁员，也可约定在名册之外选定仲裁员，但需经仲裁委员会主任确认。《北京仲裁委员会仲裁规则》(2019 年版)第 19 条规定：“本会制定有仲裁员名册，当事人从本会提供的仲裁员名册中选择仲裁员。”

国际仲裁对当事人意思自治原则的限制

高　杨[*]

摘　要:当事人意思自治原则是国际仲裁的基础性原则,在国际仲裁中通常被奉为圭臬。然而,即使是在高度自治和“去本地化”的国际仲裁中,当事人意思自治原则也并非绝对的,而是受限于一系列程序性和实体性条件,以平衡国际仲裁中涉及的多元利益。本文从国际仲裁对当事人意思自治原则的限制着手,论证了国际仲裁限制当事人意思自治原则的理论基础,即规范性证成和非规范性证成,系统性地梳理了国际仲裁程序的不同阶段对该原则不同程度上的限制和制约,并讨论了对我国仲裁立法和实务的相关启示,以期弥补我国仲裁理论界和实务界对该问题的相对不足。

关键词:意思自治原则　仲裁协议　仲裁员任命　可受理性

一、问题的提出

当事人意思自治原则是国际仲裁的基础性原则,通常被视为国际仲裁相较于法院诉讼而言最吸引人的优点之一。诚然,当事人选择将争议提交国际仲裁解决(而非归本国法院管辖),在很大程度上是因为其在国际仲裁中可以通过意思表示、针对自身需求而灵活约定程序性和实体性事项,通过意思自治实现个体化需求。但是,在单方面强调当事人意思自治原则重要性的同时,往往容易被忽视的是国际仲裁中存在各种对该原则的限制和制约。换言之,即使是将当

---

* 高杨,澳洲国立大学法学博士、研究员。

事人意思自治原则奉为圭臬的国际仲裁,当事人意思自治原则也并非绝对的,而是受限于程序和实体上的诸多限制和束缚。

目前,我国仲裁的理论界和实务界对当事人意思自治原则的研究,常常集中在对国际仲裁及外国法如何尊重和保障当事人意思自治原则,并对比我国相关法律中对当事人意思自治原则的限制和约束。但往往没有看到,即使在高度自治和"去本地化"的国际仲裁中,当事人意思自治原则也不是毫无约束的,而是受制于一系列程序性和实体性条件,以平衡国际仲裁中涉及的多元利益。本文着眼于国际仲裁对当事人意思自治原则的限制,论证了限制当事人意思自治原则的理论基础即限制意思自治的规范性证成和非规范性证成,系统性地梳理了在国际仲裁程序不同阶段对该原则的不同限制,并讨论了对我国仲裁立法和实务的相关启示,以期弥补我国仲裁理论界和实务界对该问题的相对空白。

本文的"国际仲裁",特指由我国内地以外的仲裁机构管理、适用国际仲裁机构的仲裁规则的仲裁程序,以及仲裁地约定在我国内地以外、适用《联合国国际贸易法委员会国际商事仲裁规则》(UNCITRAL Arbitration Rules)管理程序进行的临时仲裁(ad hoc arbitration)。

二、国际仲裁的基石:当事人意思自治原则

当事人意思自治原则在国际仲裁中通常被奉为圭臬。该原则不仅得到各国仲裁法律的尊重和认可,还被各大主要国际仲裁机构的仲裁规则、《承认及执行外国仲裁裁决公约》(以下简称《纽约公约》)、《联合国国际贸易法委员会国际商事仲裁示范法》(以下简称《示范法》)普遍视为国际仲裁中的基础性原则。①

首先,该原则体现为当事人对仲裁协议的自治。仲裁协议通常被视为当事人意思自治的典范:根据其意思表示,当事人可以约定将争议提交仲裁,以排除法院的管辖。

其次,该原则体现为当事人享有决定仲裁程序的相关程序和实体性事项的权利,包括当事人选择机构仲裁还是临时仲裁、任命仲裁员(决定仲裁员的人

---

① See Alan Redfern et al. , *Law and Practice of International Commercial Arbitration* 315, Sweet & Maxwell, 4th ed. ,2004.

数、背景、经验、资质、语言、人选等方面)、选择仲裁地和开庭地点、仲裁时间、开庭的程序性要求(选择书面审理还是开庭审理、线上还是线下开庭)、仲裁庭的权力、仲裁规则及仲裁语言等诸多方面。

最后,该原则体现在当事人选择争议适用的准据法的权利。当事人对准据法的选择既包括仲裁程序法(lex arbitri),也包括对争议适用的实体法(lex causae);既可以选择某个特定司法辖区的法律以管辖争议(如英国法、美国纽约州法律、香港法、我国合同法等),也可以选择适用相关的国际公约(如《联合国国际货物销售公约》)和其他法律渊源[如国际商会制定的《2010年国际贸易术语解释通则》、商人习惯法(lex mercatoria)等]。此外,英美法系下,还存在与"法律仲裁"不同的"衡平仲裁"(amiable composition 或 ex aequo et bono):基于当事人的同意,仲裁庭可以不严格依据法律规定或合同约定,而依据公平、正义、衡平原则对特定争议进行裁判。当事人往往基于维护双方的长期商事合作关系等考虑而选择"衡平仲裁",反映了其特殊的价值判断(如认为双方之间友好、合作关系比严格的合同约定或技术性的法律问题更重要等)。而无论是《1996年英国仲裁法案》还是《示范法》,均明确承认当事人选择"衡平仲裁"的决定应该被法院认可和承认。①

总之,通过赋予当事人对这些程序性和实体性方面的选择权,国际仲裁可以让当事人针对自身需求而灵活约定争议解决的诸多问题,当事人行使意思自治以更好地实现其在具体争议中的个体化需求。

但值得注意的是,即使是在非常尊重当事人意思自治的国际仲裁中,当事人意思自治原则的行使也不是绝对的,而是受限于自然正义、公共利益、第三人利益、准据法的强行性规定等规范性和非规范性因素。事实上,从起草仲裁协议到任命仲裁员、仲裁程序开庭审理、后裁决阶段,当事人意思自治原则均在不同程度上受到程序和实体上的诸多限制。

---

① See Arbitrations Act 1996, s. 46(1)(b) (Eng.); United Nations Commission on International Trade Law Model Law on International Commercial Arbitration, 1985 (With Amendments as Adopted in 2006), U.N. Doc. A/40/17, Annex 1, art. 28(3).

三、国际仲裁对当事人意思自治原则限制的证成

(一)规范性证成

1. 自然正义(natural justice)原则

国际仲裁中,当事人意思自治原则首先受限于自然正义原则(principle of natural justice)所提供的"兜底性"保护。虽然原则上当事人可以行使意思自治的权利指定仲裁员、选定仲裁程序、决定仲裁的程序性事项,但如果这些决定违反了自然正义原则,则不仅可能让决定本身自然无效,还可能构成拒绝承认和执行仲裁裁决或撤销仲裁裁决的法定事由。

首先,无论是《示范法》还是《纽约公约》,均注重对仲裁程序的程序正义(due process)的尊重和保障,以确保仲裁程序的正当性和合法性,保证当事人在仲裁程序中得到平等对待。例如,《示范法》第 18 条规定:"当事人应当受到平等对待,并应当被给予充分的机会陈述其案情。"[①]值得注意的是,国际仲裁中,适用该条款意味着虽然当事人可以自由地选择仲裁员,但如果存在证据证明其选定的仲裁员对某方当事人存在歧视或偏见(bias),则其任命仲裁员的选择将被视为无效。[②]此外,即使是裁决作出之后,仲裁员对一方当事人的歧视或偏见也可以构成申请仲裁地法院撤销仲裁裁决的法定理由之一。例如,在"孙杨案"中,2021 年瑞士联邦最高法院以国际体育仲裁法庭仲裁庭中一名仲裁员存在歧视和偏见为由,撤销了该仲裁庭作出的对孙杨禁赛的仲裁裁定。[③]

其次,如果当事人约定适用管理仲裁程序的规则对某一方当事人提供不公平的待遇致使其不能得到充分的机会以陈述其案情,则构成撤销或拒绝承认或执行该仲裁裁决的法定事由,这也是自然正义原则的体现。例如,《示范法》第 34 条第 2 款第 a 项第 iii 目规定,"未向申请的当事人发出指定仲裁员的适当通知或仲裁程序的适当通知,或因他故致使其不能陈述案情"的,仲裁地法院可以

---

① Model Law, art. 18.

② See Mia Louise Livingstone, *Party Autonomy in International Commercial Arbitration—Popular Fallacy or Proven Fact?*, 25(5) Journal of International Arbitration 529, 532 (2008); See, e. g., Gas & Fuel Corporation of Victoria v. Wood Hall, [1978] V. R. 385 (Sup. Ct. Vict.).

③ 参见《孙杨禁赛判决撤销原因公布,网友呼吁仲裁需公正!》,载中国新闻网,https://www.chinanews.com.cn/ty/2021/01-16/9388921.shtml。

撤销该仲裁裁决。①《纽约公约》也规定,这种情况可以构成申请承认和执行裁决地法院拒绝承认和执行裁决的法定理由。②因此,自然正义原则要求仲裁程序不得出现重大的程序性瑕疵、不得严重侵犯当事人的正当程序的权利,这不仅在一定程度上会限制当事人的意思自治,还会限制当事人选定的仲裁员的相关权力行使。

最后,自然正义原则决定了仲裁程序应当具有正当性(integrity)和合法性(legitimacy)。这意味着,当事人不得利用仲裁的合法形式追求非法目的。例如,如果当事人利用"虚假仲裁"的形式,由其任命的仲裁员依据其虚构的调解协议(settlement agreements)作出一个"合意裁决"(consent awards),以"合法"形式追求洗钱、贿赂、走私、资助腐败、恐怖主义行为等非法目的,则可能导致仲裁裁决被撤销或被拒绝承认和执行。

总之,自然正义原则提供的"兜底性"保护,保障了仲裁程序的正当性和合法性,决定了当事人必须在合法的范围内进行意思自治。

2. 保护弱势一方当事人

国际仲裁中当事人意思自治原则的存在的传统理论预设前提为当事人是符合现代经济学理论假设中的"理性人"(rational actor),其行为的逻辑在于通过意思自治行使自由意志,以追求个人福利的最大化(最大化原则)。③因此,意思自治原则所假定的前提条件是当事人是理性的主体,且具备相应的能力,可以作出最符合自身利益的选择。基于此,通过市场机制这一看不见的手的运作,这种制度设计认为当事人在互相协商中往往可以选择最符合其自身利益的争端解决机制,包括程序法、实体法和争议解决的各种安排等。④但是,现实中这种过于理想化的情况往往难以实现。

首先,不少当事人并不具有充分的"理性"(rationality)。诚然,商事交易中的当事人均追求自身利益的最大化,但因为信息不对称、缺乏专业的法律知识、

① See Model Law, art. 34(2)(a)(ii).

② See New York Convention, art. (v)(1)(b).

③ See Friedrich Rosenfeld, Limits to Party Autonomy to Protect Weaker Parties in International Arbitration, in Limits to Party Autonomy in International Commercial Arbitration 419 (Franco Ferrari ed.) (JURIS 2016).

④ Ibid.

经验不足等,不少当事人往往并不熟悉商事仲裁,也不擅长在跨境交易中选择最符合自身利益的争端解决安排。其次,当事人在跨境商事交易中可能并不具备充分的议价能力(bargaining power)。如果对方当事人是一家有充分市场份额的大型公司,可能会导致其交易对象被迫接受一些合同条款,包括仲裁条款,从而直接限制当事人意思自治的行使。因此,如果完全依赖放任自由的市场机制的调节作用,则可能出现"市场失灵"的结果,导致一方当事人凭借自身优势及市场地位强迫另一方当事人接受"霸王条款",从而造成双方权利义务的严重不对等。在极端情形中,还可能导致弱势的一方当事人寻求法律救济的基础性权利受到严重侵害。①

基于以上原因,各国法律体系中通常存在一些强行性法律规范(mandatory rules),如当事人的约定违反了这些规范,则其行为的法律效力应属于无效。值得注意的是,虽然这些强行性规范限制了当事人意思自治的权利,但其立法目的通常在于保护交易中的弱势方,防止其因为弱势地位而被强势的一方"剥削"或"压榨"。在此方面,典型的例子包括法律对雇佣合同和消费者合同的强行性规定。

例如,在 Akai Pty Ltd. v. People's Insurance Co. Ltd. 案中,澳洲联邦高等法院认为,当事人在消费者合同中通过格式条款选择适用英国法并在英国仲裁,该约定因违反《澳洲保险合同法案》(Australia Insurance Contracts Act)而无效,但不影响其他条款的效力。因为该法案规定消费者的合同应适用本法,即使当事人作出相反约定。类似条款还存在于一些国家的反垄断法案中。这些规定表明,一国法律体系中可能存在一些保护消费者、制衡大公司失衡的市场权利的强行性规定,如果仲裁协议对准据法和仲裁管辖的约定违反了这些规定,则可能会导致约定无效的法律后果。这种保护交易弱势方的立法目的,会导致仲裁当事人意思自治原则受到限制。

3. 保护公共利益

国际仲裁中,虽然原则上当事人可以基于其合意选择将任何争议提交仲

---

① See Friedrich Rosenfeld, Limits to Party Autonomy to Protect Weaker Parties in International Arbitration, in Limits to Party Autonomy in International Commercial Arbitration 419 (Franco Ferrari ed.) (JURIS 2016).

裁,但基于仲裁地或执行地法律的规定,当地法院可能对特定争议的可仲裁性(arbitrability)进行限制。通常而言,国内法可能规定刑事案件、婚姻家事纠纷、税务纠纷、知识产权纠纷、国家安全案件不得由当事人约定仲裁。此外,如果仲裁裁决违反了仲裁地或承认申请和执行地法院当地的法律中的"公共利益",则可能构成裁决被撤销或拒绝承认和执行的法定理由。在这两种情况中,仲裁地或执行地法律中的公共利益均被视为高于当事人意思自治的权利,故可能直接或间接地限制当事人对争议提交仲裁的意思自治。

例如,在 Mitsubishi Motors Corp v. Soler Chrysler – Plymouth 案中,争议的焦点在于当事人将《美国谢尔曼法案》项下的反垄断争议提交在日本仲裁的仲裁协议在美国联邦法律下是否有效的问题。该案中,虽然美国最高法院认定支持了该仲裁裁决的可仲裁性,但依然指出:下级美国法院在裁决的申请承认和执行阶段可以依据《纽约公约》第 5 条中"公共政策"的理由,审理仲裁裁决是否违反美国反垄断法的公共利益。[①]此外,在 Soleimany v. Soleimany 案中,英国上诉法院撤销了一个仲裁裁决,该裁决基于一个英国法项下的非法合同作出。法院认为,该合同对走私违禁品的约定,严重违反了当地的法律中的公共利益,故应当撤销该仲裁裁决。[②]

4. 保证司法主权与当事人法律救济的权利

国际仲裁程序通常被认为具有高度的独立性和自洽性(self – sufficiency),随之而来的问题是当事人能否通过约定,排除适用仲裁地的法律管理仲裁程序,以及能否以合意排除"当事人向法院寻求相关救济的权利"或对"仲裁裁决的司法追溯",包括申请撤销仲裁裁决、申请不予承认和执行仲裁裁决。[③]此问题的解决,主要取决于仲裁地或执行地法律的"强行性规定"(mandatory rules)是否允许、认可这种约定,目前各国对此规定并不一致。表面上,似乎可以通过当事人意思自治进一步排除地方保护主义的干预,让仲裁程序彻底地"去本地化"(delocalization)。但这个提议不仅不切实际,而且会产生各种难以解决的问题。

---

① See Mitsubishi Motors Corp v. Soler Chrysler – Plymouth, 2 July 1985, https://newyorkconvention1958.org/index.php? lvl = notice_display&id = 513.

② See Soleimany v. Soleimany, [1998] 3 W. L. R. 811 (C. A.).

③ See, e. g., Jan Paulsson, *Delocalisation of International Commercial Arbitration: Why and When It Matters*, 32 Int'l & Comp. L. Q. 53 (No. 1, 1983).

国际仲裁程序不是“空中楼阁”,不可避免地会与仲裁地或执行地法院发生联系,并在特定的情形中需要法院提供必要的司法协助,以保证当事人法律救济的实现。例如,仲裁庭虽然享有依据仲裁规则作出临时措施的权力,但其自身并不具有在仲裁程序之外“强制执行”这些临时措施的权力,故对这些临时措施的“执行”还需要依赖仲裁地或执行地法院的司法协助。同理,如果对方当事人拒绝主动履行裁决,仲裁裁决依然需要通过法院予以承认和执行。因此,虽然当事人享有高度意思自治的权利,但其不能也不宜以约定排除适用仲裁地法律对仲裁程序的管理,或排除其寻求相关法律救济的权利。[①]一是因为法律的适用涉及一国法律的司法主权,不能被作为私主体的当事人以合意排除适用,因为当事人无权也不宜以合意对仲裁地或执行地的司法主权作出处分。二是因为如此很可能导致国际仲裁程序难以在实际中有效地运作,例如,拒不履行仲裁庭作出的决定的一方当事人可以其不合作的“对抗”行为致使仲裁程序陷入“瘫痪”状态。对此,英国上诉法院在 *Coppee - Lavalin S. A. /N. V. v. Ken - Ren* 案中认为,虽然当事人理论上可以通过合意排除适用仲裁地的法律管理仲裁程序,但如此会让仲裁程序在实际中难以有效地运作,故不应支持。[②]三是因为即使承认该约定的效力,也容易导致仲裁程序中当事人在仲裁程序出现严重程序性问题(如未能保证一方当事人合理陈述案情的正当程序权利)或实体问题(如裁决严重违反当地公共利益)时合法权益难以得到保障。如此,这种约定即使可能在某些方面带来程序上的“快捷”“便利”(如实现“一裁终局”),整体而言依然弊大于利、得不偿失。

(二)非规范性证成

在国际仲裁中,当事人对程序性和实体性事项的选择往往是基于各种务实的考虑(pragmatic considerations)。其中,最重要的考虑因素之一即在于仲裁庭作出的仲裁裁决将来在某个外国司法辖区的可执行性,以及裁决是否存在被仲

---

① *Coppee - Lavalin S. A. /N. V. v. Ken - Ren*, [1994] 2 All E. R. 449 (H. L.)(认为当事人不能以协议排除其将向法院寻求救济的权利);*American Diagnostica v. Gradipore*, (1998) 44 N. S. W. L. R. 312 (Sup. Ct. N. S. W.)(认为当事人不能以协议排除仲裁地法律的适用);See Mia Louise Livingstone, *Party Autonomy in International Commercial Arbitration—Popular Fallacy or Proven Fact?*, 25(5) Journal of International Arbitration 529, 534 (2008).

② See *Naviera Amazonica v. Compania Internaciona*, [1988] 1 Lloyd's Rep. 116 (C. A.).

裁地法院撤销的可能性。值得注意的是,这些非法律本身的考虑因素可能在不同程度上构成对当事人意思自治原则的限制。例如,如果当事人选择在某大陆法系国家进行仲裁而仲裁协议约定对争议适用美国纽约州的法律,那么在处理赔偿金额时,如果仲裁庭选择适用纽约州的法律项下的惩罚性赔偿(putative damages)规则,而仲裁地的法律并不承认惩罚性赔偿的规则,则这个裁决在将来存在被仲裁地法院适用本国法律进行撤销的可能性。此外,如果执行地并未加入《纽约公约》,当地的法律中并不承认惩罚性赔偿的规则,则该裁决还有可能存在被执行地法院拒绝承认或执行的风险。

此外,虽然当事人理论上可以约定适用"商人习惯法"(lex mercatoria)作为实体法解决争议,但是并非所有的司法辖区均认可适用"商人习惯法"作出的裁决具有可执行性。虽然英国法下法院倾向于执行此类裁决,但不少其他《示范法》项下的司法辖区对其可执行性的态度并不明确。①因此,该裁决在部分司法辖区可能面临不能被当地法院承认和执行的风险。

在这些情况中,一些非法律性的因素(如仲裁裁决将来的可执行性和被撤销的可能和概率)会间接影响当事人行使意思自治原则,在不同程度上限制、制约当事人对争议实体法律等事项的选择。正因如此,澳大利亚新南威尔士州最高法院法官 Giles CJ 在 *American Diagnostica v. Gradipore* 案中指出:"在原则上,当事人意思自治并不意味着当事人享有完全的自由,并可以据此在彼此的法律关系中排除适用一个法律体系或其中的某些要素。"②

综上所述,本部分论证了国际仲裁限制当事人意思自治的理论基础,包括规范性因素和非规范性因素。值得注意的是,这些因素之间并不存在非此即彼的"排他"关系,即不同因素之间可能在特定的情形中存在重合、交叉的关系。例如,法院撤销虚假仲裁的"合法"形式掩盖洗钱、贿赂、腐败、走私等非法目的之仲裁裁决,该类裁决必然违反一个正常现代社会的基本公共政策,因此其之撤销不仅是自然正义原则的要求,也是实现公共利益的应有之义。再者,如果一方当事人利用优势地位强迫对方当事人接受"排除对仲裁裁决的司法追溯权

---

① See Mia Louise Livingstone, *Party Autonomy in International Commercial Arbitration—Popular Fallacy or Proven Fact?*, 25(5) Journal of International Arbitration 529, 534 (2008).

② Gerold Herrmann, *The UNCITRAL Model Law on International Commercial Arbitration*, *in* Essays on International Commercial Arbitration 93 (P. Sarcevic ed., 1989).

利”的格式仲裁条款,法院认定该条款无效不仅是为了尊重仲裁地的司法主权,也可能是出于保护当事人获得法律救济的权利、保护处于弱势一方的当事人的考虑,同时还可能因为该约定违反了仲裁地法律的强行性规定。总之,这些因素从不同的方面论证了限制当事人合意的合理性和必要性,反映了国际仲裁中涉及利益的多元性和复杂性。

正因为这些因素,一些学者认为,即使是高度鼓励当事人意思自治的《示范法》,亦不希望赋予当事人绝对的意思自治或毫无限制的选择自由。《示范法》的主要立法目的在于提供一个鼓励仲裁、具有自由化属性的法律框架,从而为满足不同案件当事人具体需求的各种仲裁协议提供便利。①

四、限制当事人意思自治原则的具体体现

(一)仲裁协议

在起草仲裁协议时,当事人享有极大的意思自治空间。基于其合意,当事人可以约定将争议提交仲裁以排除法院管辖、如何选择仲裁员、适用何种仲裁规则、选择机构仲裁还是临时仲裁、如何开展仲裁程序、选择仲裁的语言、争议适用的准据法、法律救济的形式(如金钱赔偿还是继续履行,是否适用惩罚性赔偿等)等涉及程序和实体的诸多方面。然而,值得注意的是,即使是集中反映当事人意思自治的仲裁协议,在国际仲裁中依然受限于一些或明示或默示的程序性和实体性要求。

第一,在形式要件上,无论是《纽约公约》还是《示范法》,均规定仲裁协议需为“书面协定”(an agreement in writing),即排除了口头协议和其他形式的协议。②值得注意的问题是如何认定协议是否属于“书面”形式。对此,《纽约公约》没有直接定义,应依据《维也纳条约解释公约》关于条约解释的相关规定对此进行解释,即取决于“书面”的正常字面含义,也可以参考缔约方国内法对书面的通常认定方法。此外,《纽约公约》第 2 条第 2 款规定:当事人之间签订或互换的信件、电报中所包含的仲裁协议或合同中的仲裁条款,亦构成“书面协

① See Gerold Herrmann, *The UNCITRAL Model Law on International Commercial Arbitration*, in Essays on International Commercial Arbitration 9 – 10 (P. Sarcevic ed., 1989).

② See New York Convention, art. 2(1); Model Law, art. 7.

定”。[①]

《示范法》第 7 条第 3 款对“书面协议”有更详细的规定:“仲裁协议的内容以任何形式记录下来的,即为书面形式,无论该仲裁协议或合同是以口头方式、行为方式还是其他方式订立的。”[②]第 7 条第 4 款还规定:“电子通信所含信息可以调取以备日后查用的,即满足了仲裁协议的书面形式要求;‘电子通信’是指当事人以数据电文方式发出的任何通信……包括但不限于电子数据交换、电子邮件、电报、电话或传真。”[③]此外,第 7 条第 5 款和第 6 款规定:“仲裁协议如载于当事人相互往来的索赔声明和抗辩声明中,且一方当事人声称有协议而另一方当事人不予否认的,即为书面协议。在合同中提及再有仲裁条款的任何文件的,只要此种提及可使该仲裁条款成为该合同一部分,即构成书面形式的仲裁协议。”[④]

在实体层面上,仲裁协议的法律效力必须得到相关法律的认可。在《纽约公约》和《示范法》项下,如果仲裁协议无效(如一方当事人不具有相应的权限或意思表示能力),则不仅对方当事人可以不受仲裁协议关于将争议提交仲裁的约束,而且依据该协议作出的仲裁裁决将来也可能被仲裁地法院撤销或被执行地法院拒绝承认和执行。[⑤]值得注意的是,对仲裁协议效力的准据法的认定,应当首先取决于当事人的约定,如果没有约定,则应当属于仲裁地法律或执行地法律的规定。[⑥]可见,无论是《纽约公约》还是《示范法》均以“书面协议”的形式要件和“协议有效”的实质要件限定了当事人意思自治的范围。

第二,如前所述,虽然当事人理论上可以在仲裁协议中以合意排除适用仲裁地法律管理仲裁程序,或者约定排除当事人向法院申请撤销仲裁裁决或申请拒绝承认和执行裁决的权利,但并非所有司法辖区的法院都会认可这些约定的法律效力,例如英国法、新西兰法均不承认其效力。这种对当事人意思自治的限制,主要是出于保障当事人法律救济权利、便利仲裁程序、维护司法主权的

---

① See New York Convention, art. 2(2).

② Model Law, art. 7(3).

③ Model Law, art. 7(4).

④ Model Law, art. 7(5) - (6).

⑤ See New York Convention, art. 2(3), art V(1)(a); Model Law, art. 8(1), 34(2)(a)(i), art. 36(2)(a)(i).

⑥ Ibid.

考虑。

此外,仲裁协议本质上属于一种合同约定,故亦受限于合同的“相对性”(privity of contract)。原则上,当事人不能约定通过仲裁涉及第三人的利益,除非第三人亦签署该仲裁协议。因此,如果当事人约定的仲裁协定约定将涉及第三人利益的纠纷提交仲裁,则可能导致该约定部分或全部无效。

第三,仲裁协议的自治受限于争议的“可仲裁性”和“公共政策”。“可仲裁性”和“公共政策”的具体适用,由仲裁地或执行地法院依据本国法进行具体判断。在“可仲裁性”的适用上,各国法律通常规定刑事案件、婚姻、家事、继承纠纷、税务纠纷、知识产权纠纷、国家安全案件不得由当事人约定仲裁。此外,部分国家法律还规定不得将侵权纠纷、反垄断争议、行政许可争议、主权债券违约(sovereign bonds default)纠纷、虚拟货币(如比特币等)纠纷提交仲裁解决。在“公共政策”的解读上,各国法律可能存在不同的理解。但通常而言,如果当事人利用“虚假仲裁”的形式,请求仲裁员以“合意裁决”的形式执行用以实现洗钱、贿赂、走私、资助腐败、恐怖主义行为等非法目的之仲裁裁决的,会导致仲裁裁决被撤销或被拒绝承认和执行。

(二)对仲裁员的任命

国际仲裁中,当事人选任仲裁员往往被视为一项至关重要的程序性权利,属于当事人意思自治的核心体现。这项权利的有效行使,不仅让当事人得以依据其意愿选择具有其认为适当的资质、背景、经验、专业特长、能力、语言的仲裁员对争议的程序和实体问题作出审理、裁决,还可以通过当事人直接参与仲裁庭的组庭程序,从而增强其对仲裁争端解决机制的认可和信任,增加国际仲裁程序的合法性基础,并增强当事人在裁决后主动履行仲裁决定的可能性。①

然而,在国际仲裁程序中,当事人选择仲裁员的权利并非绝对的,而是同样受限于不同的程序性和实体性条件。

1.“快速仲裁程序”规则对当事人任命仲裁员的限制

首先,一些主要国际仲裁机构的仲裁规则项下规定的“快速仲裁程序”(expedited arbitral procedure)或“简易仲裁程序”可能对当事人选择仲裁员的权利

① See George A. Bermann, Limits to Party Autonomy in the Composition of the Arbitral Panel, in Limits to Party Autonomy in International Commercial Arbitration chapter 3 (JURIS 2016).

行使设定限制。基于对国际仲裁普遍程序较为漫长、费用较为昂贵的批评，新加坡国际仲裁中心、香港国际仲裁中心、国际商会仲裁院等各大主要国际仲裁机构纷纷出台了各自的快速仲裁程序规则，通常规定该仲裁机构有权适当缩短选任仲裁员的组庭时间、仲裁庭享有在适当情形时仅依据提供的书面材料进行审理的自主裁量权、仲裁庭应当在组庭 6 个月内作出仲裁裁决的时间限制。[①]值得注意的是，如果适用这些快速仲裁规则，通常会对当事人选择仲裁员的权利行使构成不同程度的限制。

例如，《2016 年新加坡国际仲裁中心仲裁规则》(2016 SIAC Rules)第 5.2 条规定，快速仲裁规则项下应当由独任仲裁员审理，除非中心主席作出相反认定。[②]《2020 年国际商会仲裁庭仲裁规则》(2020 ICC Rules)也有类似规定，对此，国际商会仲裁庭解释为：适用快速仲裁程序时，国际商会仲裁庭通常仅会指定独任仲裁员审理争议，不论当事人的仲裁协议中是否存在相反规定。[③]对此，《2018 年香港国际仲裁中心机构仲裁规则》(2018 HKIAC Rules)存在不同规定。该规则第 42 条第 42.2 款第 b 项规定，简易程序中"如果仲裁协议约定了三位仲裁员，HKIAC 应建议当事人将案件提交独任仲裁员。若当事人不同意，案件应提交三位仲裁员"[④]。

可见，通过各大主要国际仲裁机构对仲裁规则的改革可以看出，快速仲裁程序通常对当事人自由选择仲裁员的权利行使进行了一定的限制，具体表现为默认规则倾向于选择独任仲裁员。这主要反映了仲裁机构对国际仲裁中传统选任仲裁员程序弊端的反思：国际仲裁中，当事人选任仲裁员的过程往往较为漫长，还经常因对方当事人基于利益冲突申请仲裁员回避 (challenge)而造成更多的程序拖延，往往可能需花费数周(甚至数月)的时间。而快速仲裁规则项下，如果仅由当事人约定或由仲裁机构指定独任仲裁员，则不仅更为便捷、快

① See Andreas Respondek et al., Limits to Party Autonomy in International Commercial Arbitration, Law Gazette (September 2019), https://lawgazette.com.sg/feature/limits-to-party-autonomy-in-international-commercial-arbitration/.

② See SIAC Rules, art. 5.2.

③ See Andreas Respondek et al., Limits to Party Autonomy in International Commercial Arbitration, Law Gazette (September 2019), https://lawgazette.com.sg/feature/limits-to-party-autonomy-in-international-commercial-arbitration/.

④ HKIAC Rules, art. 42.2(b).

捷,而且可能提高整个程序的效力,但对应的代价是当事人选任仲裁员的权利受到一定的限制和约束。

2. 利益冲突规则对当事人任命仲裁员的限制

无论是否适用快速仲裁规则,当事人选任仲裁员的权利均会受到关于避免仲裁员利益冲突(conflict of interest)的相关规则的约束。在此方面,由国际律师协会(international bar association)仲裁和替代性争端解决机制委员会制定的《国际律师协会关于国际仲裁的利益冲突的指南》(IBA Guidelines on Conflict of Interest in International Arbitration)(以下简称《利益冲突指南》),对国际仲裁中通常出现的可能影响仲裁员公正性和独立性的事项及仲裁员的披露义务提供了指引,适用于国际商事仲裁和国际投资仲裁。[①]虽然《利益冲突指南》并不具有严格意义上的法律拘束力(binding),但当事人可以约定适用其规定。事实上,基于其普遍适用的广泛影响力,《利益冲突指南》作为一项举足轻重的软法(soft law),构成了国际仲裁中认定仲裁员是否存在"利益冲突"、是否应当进行披露(disclosure)的重要依据。

根据《利益冲突指南》的规定,如果仲裁员现在或之前存在作为代理一方当事人或其相关联实体的相关行为(或其他相关行为),且该行为可能影响仲裁员对其公正、独立地履行本案仲裁员职责产生不当影响时,仲裁员应当拒绝担任仲裁员;已经接受仲裁员指定的,应当辞职。对另一方当事人选择仲裁员的决定,一方当事人可以基于利益冲突的理由提出申请仲裁员回避的请求。而认定是否会产生"不当影响"的标准,应当以一个了解具体案情的案外第三人是否会对仲裁员的独立性和公正性产生合理的怀疑(justifiable doubts)为准。[②]

《利益冲突指南》还为可能影响仲裁员独立性和公正性的具体事宜提供了详尽、细致的指引,并规定了仲裁员对可能发生利益冲突的事由应当履行披露义务。根据利益冲突的严重程度,《利益冲突指南》分列了"红色清单"、"橙色清单"和"绿色清单",对仲裁员是否需要披露、涉及利益冲突的具体情形进行了详尽(但非穷尽)而细致的规定。

① See IBA Guidelines on Conflict of Interest in International Arbitration, https://www.ibanet.org/MediaHandler?id=e2fe5e72-eb14-4bba-b10d-d33dafee8918.

② Ibid.

首先,《利益冲突指南》项下“不可弃权的红色清单”明确规定了仲裁员在任何情形下均不能担任该案仲裁员的情形。具体而言,包括以下情形:仲裁员不得同时担任当事人的代理人或雇员、不能是一方当事人公司的董事、监事或其他高级管理人员、不能对案件结果存在实质上的经济利益、不能对一方当事人具有显著的控制能力、仲裁员或其所在机构不能为一方当事人提供日常服务并从中获取实质性经济收入(significant financial income)。[①]

其次,《利益冲突指南》项下“可弃权的红色清单”规定了经过仲裁员披露、双方当事人同意之后仲裁员可以胜任的情形。具体而言,包括仲裁员就该争议已经向当事人或其关联机构提供过法律建议或服务、仲裁员与一方当事人的代理人同属于一家律师事务所、仲裁员所属的律师事务所与一方当事人具有实质性商业关系、仲裁员目前正在代理或向一方当事人或其关联机构提供法律咨询或服务、仲裁员之前已经接触过该争议、仲裁员直接或间接持有过当事人或其关联机构的股权、仲裁员的亲密家属对争议结果存在实质性的经济利益等情形。[②]

再次,《利益冲突指南》项下“橙色清单”规定了仲裁员需要主动向当事人披露的情形,在披露后,除非当事人即时反对,否则应视为当事人已经接受该仲裁员的指定。具体而言,主要包括仲裁员曾对该争议公开发表过观点、仲裁员在过去三年内就与本案争议无关事项担任过一方当事人或其关联机构的代理人、仲裁员在过去三年内就与本案争议无关事项担任过一方当事人或其关联机构的对方当事人的代理人、仲裁员与另一仲裁员属于同一家律所、仲裁员在过去三年内曾两次或更多次被一方当事人或其关联机构指定为仲裁员等情形。[③]

最后,《利益冲突指南》项下的“绿色清单”规定了一些仲裁员没有义务向当事人披露的情形,主要是指一些从客观的角度上不会影响仲裁员的独立性和公正性的因素。具体而言,包括仲裁员与一方当事人的代理人曾在另一起案件中共同担任仲裁员、仲裁员先前就案件中出现的问题公开发表过(并非针对本案事实作出的)一般性观点、仲裁员所在律师事务所或与其有合作或关联关系

---

① See IBA Guidelines on Conflict of Interest in International Arbitration, https://www.ibanet.org/MediaHandler? id = e2fe5e72 - eb14 - 4bba - b10d - d33dafee8918.

② Ibid.

③ Ibid.

(但并不分享收入)的其他律师事务所正在为本案无关的事项向一方当事人或其关联机构提供法律服务、仲裁员之间或仲裁员与一方当事人的代理人因同一律师协会或慈善机构或通过社交网络相识等其他情形。[①]

总之,通过对仲裁员可能存在的利益冲突进行规制,国际仲裁的主流实践不仅要求仲裁员对自身可能存在利益冲突的情形履行主动披露的义务,而且赋予当事人以重要的程序性权利,可以申请具有利益冲突的仲裁员回避。表面上,这是一项烦琐的工作,不仅会造成程序的拖延,还会限制当事人选任仲裁员的意思自治。但实质上,确认仲裁员不存在利益冲突不仅是保证仲裁员"公正性"和"独立性"的应有之义,也是维护仲裁程序正当性、合法性的重要保障,可以有效避免仲裁裁决程序瑕疵导致裁决将来被撤销或不予执行的风险。

(三)仲裁争议的可受理性

在国际仲裁中,在审理实体(merits)问题之前,仲裁庭往往需要审查争议的管辖权问题和争议的"可受理性"(admissibility)问题。不同于决定仲裁庭是否有权审理实体问题并作出裁决的管辖权问题,在"可受理性"问题上,仲裁庭享有自由裁量权(discretion),可以决定是否适宜继续审理争议的实体问题。此外,在对仲裁裁决的司法审查中,法院通常只审查仲裁庭的管辖权问题,而不会对仲裁庭关于"可受理性"问题的决定进行审查,除非涉及对正当程序原则的严重违反。[②]在国际仲裁程序的审理过程中,如果仲裁庭发现争议的主合同系当事人通过行贿、欺诈而取得,则可能以违反国际公共政策为由,认定争议不具有可受理性。

在此方面的典型案例是 World Duty Free v. Kenya 案。该案中,申请人就与肯尼亚政府签订的投资合同提交国际仲裁,约定适用英国法或肯尼亚法。仲裁庭通过申请人披露的文件,发现申请人曾经对肯尼亚政府前任总统支付一项秘密的巨额款项,认定争议合同系申请人通过贿赂政府高层人员取得,据此认定该争议不具有可受理性,驳回了仲裁请求。值得注意的是,仲裁庭在裁决中指

---

① See IBA Guidelines on Conflict of Interest in International Arbitration, https://www.ibanet.org/MediaHandler? id = e2fe5e72 - eb14 - 4bba - b10d - d33dafee8918.

② See Michael McErlaine & James Allsop, *Trends in Questions of Jurisdiction and Admissibility in International Arbitration*, Kluwer Arbitration Blog (November 2, 2021), http://arbitrationblog.kluwerarbitration.com/2021/11/02/trends - in - questions - of - jurisdiction - and - admissibility - in - international - arbitration/.

出,通过行贿而取得的商业合同不仅违反了准据法的相关规定,还违反了禁止腐败、贿赂的不法行为的国际公共政策,因为禁止这种不法行为的国际共识已经被相关国际公约、各国的法律和司法判决等众多法律渊源所广泛认可。①

值得注意的是,除了行贿、贿赂的腐败行为,仲裁庭还可能认定一方当事人严重的欺诈、虚假陈述行为违反国际公共政策,据此认为仲裁请求不具有可受理性。例如,在 Plama Consortum Ltd. v. Bulgaria 案中,申请人依据《能源宪章条约》(Energy Charter Treaty)提起条约项下的投资仲裁。仲裁庭以缺乏可受理性为由驳回了仲裁请求,依据是申请人在投资设立时存在严重的欺诈和虚假陈述行为,不仅违反了保加利亚当地的法律,还违反了国际法下的善意原则和国际公共政策。②

因此,在国际仲裁中,如果仲裁庭经过审理发现一方当事人存在行贿、贿赂的腐败行为或严重的欺诈、虚假陈述行为,无论对方当事人是否提出异议,均可能以案件缺乏可受理性为由驳回仲裁申请,以维护相关的国际公共政策。

(四)仲裁庭是否可以适用当事人诉状内容之外的法律进行裁判

传统意义上,受普通法系深远影响的国际商事仲裁中,仲裁庭的角色定位和大陆法系中法官的“纠问式”(inquisitory)角色有着显著不同。不同之处具体体现为国际仲裁中通常认为仲裁庭应当是一个“消极”的裁判者(a passive umpire),应仅就双方陈述的观点、提供的证据材料作出裁判,往往不会像大陆法系的法官一样更加“积极”地纠问双方以寻求“正确”的答案。值得注意的是,大陆法系国家的立法和司法实践通常认为法官不仅有“权力”而且有“职责”精准地“知晓”争议所应适用的法律,无论当事人是否在诉讼程序中提供相关观点,即存在“法官知法”(iura novit curia)的法律原则。而在国际仲裁中,对于仲裁庭是否“应当”适用当事人诉状内容之外的法律裁判争议的问题,理论和实务界一直存在争议。问题的关键在于“法官知法”的原则是否同样适用于国际仲裁的程序。

“法官知法”原则是否适用于国际仲裁程序这一理论问题对国际仲裁的实践具有直接的影响。如果“法官知法”原则适用于国际仲裁,则仲裁庭负有精准

① See World Duty Free v. Kenya, ICSID Case No. ARB/00/7 (October 4, 2006).

② See Plama Consortium Ltd. v. Republic of Bulg., ICSID Case No. ARB/03/24, Award (Aug. 27, 2008).

地“知晓”法律的义务,故应当主动超越双方当事人诉状的内容去更“积极”地研究、寻找所应适用的准据法,并可以在适当的情形中(如认为当事人聘请的法律专家未能充分阐述相应法律内容时,或一方当事人缺席仲裁时)直接聘请仲裁庭指定的法律专家,以提供相应的准据法的相关内容。

对此,传统观点认为,仲裁庭仅有“权力”但无“义务”主动、积极地掌握案件所应适用的法律,因为当事人负有阐述准据法的义务,故仲裁庭无义务超越当事人诉状观点去研究争议所应适用的准据法内容。①但近年来,这种传统观点日益受到冲击和挑战。例如,在 Enron v. Argentina 案中,国际投资争端解决中心(International Centre for Settlement of Investment Disputes,ICSID)上诉委员会认为,仲裁庭应当准确地适用相关的准据法,这一要求包含了仲裁庭应考虑当事人未在诉状中提到的相关法律内容的义务。②此外,知名仲裁员 Claus von Wobeser 认为,仲裁庭应当准确地认定和适用准据法,这是仲裁庭解决案件争端的法律义务应有之义。③此外,在越来越多的国际仲裁案件中,仲裁庭均认为“法官知法”原则同样地适用于国际仲裁,故即使双方当事人未能充分陈述涉案争议所应适用的准据法,仲裁庭也应当超越其诉状内容去积极、主动地研究、寻找准据法的相关内容。④

虽然就此问题依然存在争议,但在国际仲裁中认定仲裁庭存在“知法”之“义务”在审查管辖权阶段显得尤为重要。⑤表面上,让仲裁庭超越当事人诉状去“积极”地寻找准据法的相关内容似乎违反了当事人意思自治的原则。但实质上,仲裁庭确认其对争议享有管辖权往往需要其准确地适用准据法,因此仲裁庭妥善解决争议的管辖权问题正是对当事人意思自治原则的尊重和保障,如

---

① See CME Czech Republic BV v. Czech Republic(UNCITRAL),Final Award,14 March 2003,para. 411. Patrick Mitchell v. DRC(ICSID Case No. ARB/99/7),Decision on the Application for Annulment of the Award,1 November 2006,para. 57.

② See Enron Corporation v. Argentina (ICSID Case No. ARB/01/3),Decision on the Application for Annulment of the Argentine Republic,30 July 2010,paras. 385 – 395.

③ See Claus von Wobeser,*The Effective Use of Legal Sources: How Much is Too Much and What is the Role for Iura Novit Curia* in AJ van den Berg (ed.),Arbitration Advocacy in Changing Times(Kluwer 2011) 207.

④ See Iurii Bogdanov v. Moldova(SCC),Arbitral Award,22 September 2005,para. 2. 2. 1; Metal – Tech Ltd. v. Uzbekistan(ICSID Case No. ARB/10/3),Award,4 October 2013,para. 287; Albert Jan Oostergetel v. Slovakia(UNCITRAL),Final Award,23 April 2012,para. 141.

⑤ See Hepburn,Domestic Law in International Investment Arbitration (OUP,2016) 123.

此方能确保仲裁庭不会在当事人未达成将争议提交仲裁的合意(consent)时不会违背当事人的真实意思而推进仲裁程序的进行,防止缺乏法律依据的"滥诉"行为普遍出现。[①]此外,特别是在投资仲裁案件中,基于国际社会对投资仲裁程序普遍存在的周期漫长、费用昂贵等缺点的诟病,仲裁庭对管辖权要件的审查呈现日趋严格化的趋势。考虑到《解决国家与他国国民间投资争端公约》的缔约方也逐渐对欠缺法律依据的"滥诉"表现出强烈反对,《解决投资争端国际中心仲裁规则》(2006年修订版)对仲裁规则进行修改,开始明确赋予仲裁庭驳回"明显没有法律依据"(frivolous claims)的仲裁请求的权力。[②]这些近期发展,可以间接地支持仲裁庭在管辖权阶段承担更多的主动研究、积极寻找准据法相关内容的法律义务。

此外,国际法协会(International Law Association)在近期的一份报告中还指出,在一些具体的情形下,仲裁庭有"义务"对准据法的认定采取更主动、积极的态度。这些情形包括当事人提出的某些论点存在明显的错误(manifest wrong)、仲裁庭中明显存在一些精通涉案争议所适用的准据法的仲裁员、某些仲裁员显然是因为其对某些准据法的专长而被指定以及一方当事人缺席仲裁的情形。报告特别认为,在一方当事人缺席仲裁时,仲裁庭"应该"(而非"可以")依据准据法裁决,而不应仅依靠出庭的一方当事人的书状中提到的观点进行裁决。[③]这意味着,在缺席仲裁时,仲裁庭甚至可以就出庭方当事人的观点专门进行法律研究,并在必要时聘请仲裁庭指定的相关法律专家证人,以主动地反驳出庭方当事人提出的一些法律观点。而由此产生的额外费用,仲裁庭也可以裁定让缺席方按相应比例承担。[④]

值得注意的是,仲裁庭这种积极的(proactive)"知法"和"找法"的义务与传统观点下仲裁庭"消极裁判者"的角色定位存在较大不同。这表明在此问题上,国际仲裁的实践正由普通法系传统向大陆法系传统靠拢,可能给当事人意思自治原则带来一定的冲击与改变。

---

① See Hepburn, Domestic Law in International Investment Arbitration (OUP, 2016) 123.

② See M Potestà and M Sobat, "Frivolous Claims in International Adjudication: A Study of ICSID Rule 41(5) and of Procedures of Other Courts and Tribunals to Dismiss Claims Summarily" (2012) 3 JIDS 137.

③ See Hepburn, Domestic Law in International Investment Arbitration (OUP, 2016) 124.

④ See Hepburn, Domestic Law in International Investment Arbitration (OUP, 2016) 124.

(五)后裁决阶段

在仲裁裁决作出后,当事人的意思自治原则亦可能受到相当程度的限制和束缚。具体体现在两方面:一方面是仲裁地法院可能适用本国法律对严重违反程序正义或违反本国公共政策的仲裁裁决予以撤销;另一方面是在对方当事人拒绝履行裁决时,执行地法院也可能据此拒绝承认和执行该仲裁裁决。①对此,无论是《纽约公约》还是《示范法》的相关条文的规定,均体现了维护自然正义、保障当事人正当程序原则、保护弱势一方的当事人获得"兜底性"的法律救济、保护公共利益和公共秩序的规范性目的。值得注意的是,这里对"公共秩序"的保护,不仅体现在尊重仲裁地或执行地当地法律所保护的"本国公共秩序",也体现为尊重和保护各国普遍接受的"国际公共秩序"。例如,如果仲裁裁决所依据的合同以合法形式追求贩卖人口、种族灭绝、贩奴、买卖人口器官、走私、洗钱、行贿、资助恐怖主义和腐败行为等国际公认的严重违法犯罪行为,则通常会认为该裁决可能违反了国际法强行性规范(jus cogens rules)和相应的国际公共政策。②

五、结论及对我国仲裁的相关启示

当事人意思自治原则是国际仲裁的基础性原则,在国际仲裁中通常被奉为圭臬。然而,即使是在高度自治和"去本地化"的国际仲裁中,当事人意思自治原则也并非绝对的,而是受限于一系列程序性和实体性条件,以平衡国际仲裁中涉及的多元利益。本文从国际仲裁对当事人意思自治原则的限制着手,论证了国际仲裁限制当事人意思自治原则的理论基础即规范性证成和非规范性证成,系统性地梳理了国际仲裁程序的不同阶段对该原则不同程度上的限制和制约,以期弥补我国仲裁理论界和实务界对该问题的相对不足。

就我国仲裁相关法律而言,目前我国法律体系中对当事人意思自治原则的限制与国际仲裁对此的限制在根本原因和具体表现上存在相当程度的出入和差异。不同于国际仲裁,我国法律限制当事人意思自治的主要原因通常在于仲

① See New York Convention, art. V; Model Law, arts. 34, 36.

② See Karl – Heinz Boekstiegel, *Public Policy as a Limit to Arbitration and Its Enforcement*, Paper prepared for the 11th IBA International Arbitration Day, 1 February 2008.

裁市场不够对外开放、有关公权力机关对当事人和仲裁机构不够信任、对仲裁程序提供司法协助的公权力过于集中及防止对仲裁结果失去控制。①值得注意的是,此问题已经得到了很大程度的改善:由于司法部在 2021 年 7 月出台《仲裁法(修订)(征求意见稿)》,不少长期以来法律规定关于限制当事人意思自治的相关规定都已经得到极大的改善,包括仲裁协议、临时措施、仲裁员作出的临时仲裁、涉外仲裁协议效力等诸多方面,体现了立法部门支持鼓励仲裁、尊重并保护当事人意思自治的立法政策。但同时,依然应看到还存在一些问题。例如,《仲裁法》虽然规定了仲裁员的"回避"义务,但并未直接规定仲裁员对可能存在利益冲突的情形进行主动"披露"的法律义务;而仲裁员在仲裁实务中可能并不重视履行披露义务,因为相关信息不对称、不够透明,这往往会间接地制约当事人申请具有利益冲突的仲裁员回避之法定权利的行使。此外,无论是《仲裁法》还是最高人民法院的相关司法解释,对回避的法定事由规定得过于笼统,尚未细化仲裁员利益冲突和回避的具体类型,这可能导致实务中出现争议和困境。②

一方面,有必要进一步加大对我国仲裁法律体系的改革,进一步增强当事人意思自治的空间,促进我国仲裁法律体系和法律实践进一步与国际仲裁接轨。另一方面,我国法律仲裁服务可以借鉴国际仲裁的相关实践,为适当、合理地限制当事人意思自治原则提供"最佳国际实践"的范本参考和更清晰的指引。例如,就仲裁员利益冲突的披露和回避问题,可以参考《国际律师协会关于国际仲裁的利益冲突的指南》的相关内容,为利益冲突的披露和回避的具体事由提供更清晰、细致的指引,以明确判断标准。此外,基于我国仲裁机构逐渐推进的"走出去"战略部署、不断深化在境外提供国际化的仲裁法律服务的现实,我国法律仲裁服务可以借鉴国际仲裁的经验,既要注重对当事人意思自治原则的尊重和保护,同时也要认识到当事人意思自治的边界和限制,注重对国际仲裁中多元利益的平衡和保护。如此,方能顾全内外大局,实现我国仲裁法律服务的深化改革和创新发展。

---

① 参见顾维遐:《无涉外因素争议的域外仲裁问题》,载《中外法学》2018 年第 3 期。

② 参见牛磊、马瑞丰:《选定仲裁员如何避免利益冲突?》,载中伦资讯,http://www.zhonglun.com/Content/2020/04-08/1603282076.html。

论仲裁庭禁诉令之发布条件

徐　途*

摘　要：由于临时措施具有“临时性”，在仲裁庭禁诉令中，只有临时性质的禁诉令才构成临时措施。仲裁庭在发布禁诉令时，首先需要考虑是否符合发布的先决条件，包括有可能或已经违反仲裁协议以及有可能或已经出现平行程序。另外，临时性质的禁诉令还需要符合临时措施的发布前提。在例外情况下，仲裁庭可依据不加剧争议原则直接发布禁诉令。但是仲裁庭发布禁诉令的行为也受到不加剧争议原则的约束。仲裁庭可以从保障仲裁程序、保障仲裁裁决的效力两方面判断是否符合不加剧争议原则。

关键词：仲裁庭禁诉令　临时措施　平行程序　不加剧争议原则

在国际商事仲裁中，平行程序会带来许多不利影响，比如拖延仲裁、冲突裁判等。① 为解决这一问题，仲裁庭可以选择发布禁诉令，禁止一方当事人就涉案争议前往法院起诉或要求当事人中止已经存在的诉讼程序。《仲裁法（修订）（征求意见稿）》（以下简称《仲裁法意见稿》）赋予了仲裁庭发布临时措施的权力，规定仲裁庭可以依申请发布临时措施，包括保全措施和其他措施，且法院可以协助执行该种临时措施。② 这意味着，在未来，我国可能会承认仲裁庭有权力

---

* 徐途，中国政法大学国际法学院硕士研究生。

① 本文中提及的平行程序仅指在国际商事仲裁中，一方当事人提起仲裁，而另一方当事人就同一实体争议提起诉讼的情形。

② 参见《仲裁法（修订）（征求意见稿）》第四章第三节“临时措施”。

发布禁诉令。但仲裁庭发布禁诉令制度本身备受争议,从仲裁庭发布禁诉令的性质到仲裁庭发布禁诉令的效力,甚至仲裁庭是否有权发布禁诉令,学者们都莫衷一是。其中,仲裁庭在何种情况下可以发布禁诉令是仲裁庭发布禁诉令制度的中心问题。

为解决仲裁庭在何种情况下可以发布禁诉令这一问题,需要从两方面入手:一方面是仲裁庭发布禁诉令需要满足的先决条件,即在满足何种前提下,仲裁庭才会考虑发布禁诉令;另一方面是仲裁庭在发布禁诉令时需要考虑的因素,发布禁诉令往往涉及仲裁庭的自由裁量,但亦需要确定一套原则或是标准指导仲裁庭行使此种裁量权。

一、先决问题——仲裁庭发布的禁诉令与临时措施

如果认为仲裁庭发布禁诉令属于临时措施的一种,那么仲裁庭禁诉令的发布条件首先需要满足发布临时措施的条件。因此,如何定义仲裁庭发布禁诉令与临时措施的关系,是仲裁庭禁诉令发布条件的先决问题。

尽管学界主流观点认为仲裁庭发布的禁诉令属临时措施,①但是仍有学者对此提出了相反的意见,认为在某些情况下,仲裁庭发布的禁诉令不是临时措施。②

(一)临时措施的定义及性质

临时措施是指"为保护争议的一方或双方在仲裁过程中免受损害而发布的裁决或命令"③。仲裁庭临时措施的特点主要包括以下三点:第一,是在争议解决之前,即在仲裁裁决作出之前采取的,包括在仲裁程序开始之前或者在仲裁程序的进行之中采取的措施。第二,只是临时性的,即是暂时性和临时性的应

---

① See Gary B. Born, *International Commercial Arbitration* (*Third Edition*), *Kluwer Law International*, 2020, p. 2687 – 2688; also see Laurent Levy, *Anti – suit Injunctions Issued by Arbitrators*, in Emmanuel Gaillard ed., Anti – suit Injunctions in International Arbitration, Juris Publishing, 2005, p. 155; also see Olga Vishnevskaya, *Anti – suit Injunctions from Arbitral Tribunals in International Commercial Arbitration*: *A Necessary Evil*?, 2 Journal of International Arbitration 173(2015), p. 178.

② See Olivier Luc Mosimann, *Anti – suit Injunctions in International Commercial Arbitration*, *Eleven International Publishing*, 2010, p. 96 – 97; also see Rahim Moloo, *Arbitrators Granting Antisuit Orders*: *When Should They and on What Authority*?, 5 Journal of International Arbitration 675(2009), p. 679 – 683.

③ Gary B. Born, *supra* note 3, p. 2606.

急措施。第三,采取措施的要求通常是紧急的,如果不采取这些措施,存在可能给一方当事人造成伤害的威胁。①

《联合国国际贸易法委员会国际商事仲裁示范法》(以下简称《示范法》)第17条对仲裁庭发布的临时措施的定义作了如下规定:"临时措施是以裁决书为形式的或另一种形式的任何短期措施,仲裁庭在发出最后裁定争议的裁决书之前任何时候,以这种措施责令一方当事人实施以下任何行为:(a)在争议得以裁定之前维持现状或恢复原状;(b)采取行动防止目前或即将对仲裁程序发生的危害或损害,或不采取可能造成这种危害或损害的行动;(c)提供一种保全资产以执行后继裁决的手段;或(d)保全对解决争议可能具有相关性和重要性的证据。"从该条中可以看出,对临时措施的判断不拘泥于形式,仲裁庭可以以裁决的形式或者任何其他形式发布,但是这种措施必须是短期的。因此,"临时性"或者说"短期性",是构成临时措施的重要因素之一。

(二)仲裁庭发布禁诉令的"临时性"

《示范法》有意通过第17条赋予仲裁庭发布禁诉令的权力,②但这仅说明仲裁庭有权依据《示范法》第17条发布临时性质的禁诉令,并不能说明所有的仲裁庭禁诉令都构成临时措施。已有学者提出,应该将仲裁庭发布的禁诉令分为临时性质的禁诉令和永久性质的禁诉令。临时性质的禁诉令,当然可以视作临时措施,但是永久性质的禁诉令无法构成临时措施。③

仲裁庭发布禁诉令的性质与发布的形式无关,虽然仲裁庭一般通过发布程序性命令或是以部分裁决的形式发布禁诉令,但是,必须指出,禁诉令的发布形式不代表其性质,发布形式的"临时性"不能代表禁诉令实质上具有"临时性"。通常情况下,仲裁庭会要求当事人在仲裁程序的终结前中止法院的程序或者中止具体的诉讼程序,这是典型的临时性质的禁诉令。但依据意思自治原则,当事人选择仲裁,就排除了诉讼对相关争议的管辖,仲裁庭及法院应该尊重当事人的选择,并且法院对仲裁的司法审查理应保持克制态度。依据自裁管辖权原

---

① 参见赵秀文:《论国际商事仲裁中临时性保全措施的发布与实施(上)》,载《河南省政法管理干部学院学报》2002年第3期。

② See *Report of the United Nations Commission on International Trade Law on the work of its thirty-ninth session*, 19 June - 7 July 2006, para. 93 - 94.

③ See Olivier Luc Mosiman, *supra* note 4.

则,既然仲裁庭认为自己拥有管辖权,其就可以发布永久性质的禁诉令,禁止当事人就相同的争议另行诉讼,至于永久性质的禁诉令是否具有法律依据、是否侵害了当事人的诉权以及法院的司法管辖权,可以由执行地法院进行审查。

退一步说,实践中,确实存在仲裁庭通过最终裁决的方式发布永久性质禁诉令的案例,在 Telenor v. Storm 案中,仲裁庭在 2007 年 7 月 2 日作出的最终裁决书中裁定,禁止 Storm 公司以及所有一致行动人提起或者继续与该案争议有关的一切诉讼行为。[①] 无论是从发布的形式,还是仲裁庭的用语,都可以看出,仲裁庭意在永久地禁止一方当事人就该案争议进行另行诉讼,包括在仲裁程序结束后。因此,理论和实践都表明,仲裁庭可以发布永久性质的禁诉令。

(三)小结

将仲裁庭发布的禁诉令作为临时措施,无疑会减少仲裁庭禁诉令的适用争议。首先,与临时措施相关的法律会成为仲裁庭有权发布禁诉令的形式效力来源;其次,厘清仲裁庭禁诉令的发布条件问题,仲裁庭可以更好地把握在何种情况下可以发布禁诉令;最后,增加仲裁庭禁诉令的可执行性,比如《示范法》第 17 条规定了临时措施的承认和执行制度。[②]

但是,如上所述,仲裁庭可以发布永久性质的禁诉令,并且实践中也存在此类情况。永久性质的禁诉令并不符合临时措施的"临时性",必须加以区分。具有临时性质的仲裁庭禁诉令,可以被视为仲裁庭发布的临时措施,在临时措施制度项下适用。比如仲裁庭发布命令或裁决,要求一方当事人中止另诉程序,直至本仲裁最终裁决作出。而具有永久性质的仲裁庭禁诉令,不能被视为临时措施,但在这种情况下,关于仲裁庭发布禁诉令的权力来源、发布条件都存在较大的争议,不被执行地法院承认的风险也更高。

---

① See Telenor Mobile Communications AS v. Storm LLC, *Adhoc* Arbitration (Partial Award, 2 July 2007), holding that "Finally, the Tribunal orders that: a. Respondent Storm, and anyone acting in concert with it, is enjoined from the commencement or prosecution of any and all court actions concerning any disputes or controversies under, relating to, or in connection with, any obligations described in the Shareholders Agreement, including all of the existing litigations currently pending in the Ukraine and described herein."

② 参见《示范法》第四 A 章第四节"临时措施的承认和执行"。

二、仲裁庭禁诉令的发布条件之案例梳理

仲裁庭在发布禁诉令时,无可避免地会涉及自由裁量,但是此种自由裁量也需要符合一定的标准。为总结出实践中仲裁庭发布禁诉令的条件,本文依托 Jus Mundi 国际法与仲裁检索数据库,检索出八项涉及仲裁庭发布禁诉令的典型案件(见表 1)。虽然这八项案件中涉及的发布条件不完全相同,但仍有重合之处,比如存在平行程序、当事人违反仲裁协议等。

表 1 仲裁庭发布禁诉令的典型案件

序号	案件名称	仲裁庭是否发布禁诉令	仲裁庭发布禁诉令的条件
1	Four Seasons Hotels v. Consorcio Barr[1]	是	1. 仲裁协议是否有效 2. 是否存在平行程序
2	Telenor v. Storm[2]	是	1. 仲裁协议是否有效 2. 当事人是否违反仲裁协议
3	Ciments Francais v. Sibirskiy Cement and Istanbul Cimento[3]	否	适用发布临时措施的标准
4	Nexteer v. KDAC[4]	是	1. 当事人是否违反仲裁协议 2. 是否会干预仲裁程序或是加重争议
5	Cessna Finance v. Gulf Jet and others[5]	否	1. 保证仲裁程序的完整性 2. 保障裁决后续能被承认和执行
6	Ridge C. C. *v.* J. P. Morgan[6]	是	1. 以命令形式发布的禁诉令适用临时措施的标准 2. 以裁决形式发布的禁诉令,判断是否干预仲裁程序
7	Hotel TOC *v.* Trump International[7]	否	保障仲裁程序和仲裁庭的管辖权
8	Asia Cube *v.* Hans Chia[8]	是	适用发布临时措施的标准

〔1〕See Four Seasons Caracas C. A., Four Seasons Hotels and Resorts, B. *V.* and Four Seasons Hotel Limited *v.* Consorcio Barr S. A., AAA Case No. 50 – T – 180 – 00550 – 01 (Partial Award, 10 October 2002), p. 3 – 13.

〔2〕See Telenor Mobile Communications AS *v.* Storm LLC, Adhoc Arbitration, *supra* note 8, p. 17 – 33.

〔3〕See Ciments Francais *v.* Sibirskiy Cement and Istanbul Cimento, ICC Case No. 16240/GZ/MHM/GFG (Final Award, 3 December 2012), p. 3 – 13.

〔4〕See Nexteer Automotive Corporation *v.* Korea Delphi Automotive Systems Corporation, SIAC Case No. ARB105/13/SL [Procedural Order No. 3 (Decision on an Anti – Suit Injunction), 29 January 2014], para. 45 – 61.

〔5〕See Cessna Finance Corporation *v.* Gulf Jet LLC, Khalid Mohammad Saeed Al Mulla, Hussein Mohamed Salem Al Meeza, ICC Case No. 18769/VRO/AGF (Final Award, 17 Januanry 2014), para. 212 – 223.

〔6〕See Ridge C. C. At Reynosa Beneficiary LLC (U. S. A.) *v.* Banco J. P. Morgan, A. A. (Institución de Banca Multiple, J. P. Morgan Grupo Financiero, División Fiduciaria), as Trustee Under Administrative Business Trust Number F/0344 (Mexico), ICC Case No. 19134/CA/ASM (Procedural Order Relating to Interim Measures, 10 April 2013), para. 10 – 15; (Final Award, 14 August 2014), para. 145 – 151.

〔7〕See Hotel TOC, Inc. *v.* 1. Trump Panama Hotel Management LLC, 2. Trump International Hotels Management, LLC, ICC Case No. 23149/MK (Final Award, 20 March 2020), para. 25.

〔8〕See Asia Cube Energy Holdings, Ltd. *v.* Hans Chia and Inno Energy Tech Co., JAMS Case No. 1220066344 (Order Addressing Motion for Anti – Suit Injunction, 14 Feb 2021).

本文将在总结上述案例的基础上，结合相关法律和规则，对仲裁庭发布禁诉令的条件进行归纳和反思。下文详述。

三、仲裁庭发布禁诉令的先决条件

在满足一定的条件之后，仲裁庭才会考虑是否发布禁诉令，这种条件即是仲裁庭发布禁诉令的先决条件。与先决条件相关的标准往往较为清晰，尤其是临时性质的禁诉令，仲裁庭对此可以适用临时措施的发布前提。此外，无论是临时性的禁诉令还是永久性的禁诉令，仲裁庭在发布时都需要考虑两种特殊的先决条件。

（一）部分禁诉令适用仲裁庭发布临时措施的前提

仲裁庭在发布临时性质的禁诉令时，需要符合临时措施的发布要求，具体的发布要求取决于仲裁应适用的法律或仲裁规则。《示范法》第 17A 条第 1 款规定："一方当事人请求采取第 17(2)(a)、(b)和(c)条所规定的临时措施的，应当使仲裁庭确信：(a)不下令采取这种措施可能造成损害，这种损害无法通过判给损害赔偿金而充分补偿，而且远远大于准予采取这种措施而可能对其所针对的当事人造成的损害；以及(b)根据索赔请求所依据的案情，请求方当事人相当有可能胜诉。对这种可能性的判定不影响仲裁庭此后作出任何裁定的自由裁量权。"我国《仲裁法意见稿》第 44 条规定："一方当事人因其他当事人的行为或者其他原因，可能使裁决不能执行、难以执行或者给当事人造成其他损害的，可以申请财产保全和行为保全。"虽然各规则对于临时措施的发布条件的规定都不尽相同,但总结下来,最多会涉及 7 个方面的要求,分别是当事人的申请、表面证据证明管辖权成立、紧迫性、不涉及预先裁判、实质性损害、一方很有可能胜诉、相称性。

(二)仲裁庭发布禁诉令的特殊先决条件

无论是临时性质的禁诉令还是永久性质的禁诉令,由于禁诉令是一种性质特殊、争议性颇大的救济措施,仲裁庭在发布禁诉令时还会额外考虑以下两种因素:首先是当事人有可能或已经违反仲裁协议,其次是此种行为导致出现平行程序。

1. 有可能或已经违反仲裁协议

当事人应该依据诚实信用原则遵守自己达成的仲裁协议,仲裁庭有权采取措施规制当事人违反仲裁协议的行为。有学者认为,一方当事人违反仲裁协议的行为由以下几个因素构成:有意违反仲裁协议,两程序之间当事人相同,诉讼事项在仲裁范围之内,以及诉讼标的有重合。[①] 因此,认定当事人是否违反仲裁协议需要考虑主观和客观两个方面:主观上,当事人具有违反仲裁协议的意图;客观上,当事人已做出或可能做出引发平行程序的行为。另外,该条标准暗含一个前提,即仲裁庭初步认定涉案仲裁协议有效,尽管在实践中,仲裁庭往往在裁定仲裁庭拥有管辖权之后再发布禁诉令,但是理论上来说,如果存在特别紧急的情况需要仲裁庭立即发布禁诉令,只需存在"表面证据"证明仲裁协议有效即可。

2. 有可能或已经出现平行程序

如果当事人仅做出违反仲裁协议的另行诉讼行为,但是另诉法院由于种种原因未继续程序,此时,仲裁庭也无必要发布禁诉令。也就是说,只有存在另诉程序,仲裁庭才有必要发布禁诉令,因此,有可能出现或已经出现平行程序是仲裁庭发布禁诉令的特殊前提之一。

但是,对于如何认定平行程序,学界和实务界仍有争议。有学者认为,一般情形下,案件事实相同、诉讼理由相同、诉讼请求相同、法律关系相同的诉讼就判断为重复诉讼。[②] 也有学者认为,在我国,商事仲裁中的"一事"应理解为,同一当事人,基于同一法律(同一事实)而提出的同一请求。[③] 在 Asia Cube *v.*

---

① See Olivier Luc Mosimann, *supra* note 4, p. 112 – 113.

② 参见张卫平:《重复诉讼规制研究:兼论"一事不再理"》,载《中国法学》2015 年第 2 期。

③ 参见丁伟:《一事不再理:仲裁制度中的"阿喀琉斯之踵"》,载《东方法学》2011 年第 1 期。

Hans Chia 案中，仲裁庭在判断是否构成平行程序时考虑了当事人是否相同以及请求是否一致两项因素。[①]

虽然对于如何认定平行程序未有定论，但在仲裁实践中，认定平行程序的标准渐趋放松。在当事人方面，有案例表明如果两程序中涉及的是几乎相同的当事人，仲裁庭也支持发布禁诉令[②]；在争议方面，在 Asia Cube *v.* Hans Chia 案中，仲裁庭使用了美国法院的认定标准，即两程序中的请求并不要求完全相同，但至少是基于相同的争议。[③] 但本文认为，仲裁庭在认定是否构成平行程序方面应该持相对保守的态度，毕竟，仲裁庭发布禁诉令的正当性来源主要是存在有效的仲裁协议，因此应保证禁止的另诉程序涉及争议实质的内容处于仲裁协议项下、两程序之间的当事人实质性相同。

另外，有学者提出，仲裁庭发布禁诉令的前提还包括另诉程序不合理，也就是说对于违反仲裁协议向某国法院提起诉讼的一方当事人而言，其不存在正当理由，亦即不存在仲裁协议无效、失效、不可执行或另一方当事人弃权等情况，如果存在这些情况，则仲裁庭亦无权发布禁诉令制止当事人的诉讼行动。[④] 但本文认为，合理的另诉程序不能构成阻止仲裁庭发布禁诉令的理由，因为即使另诉程序合理，当事人也可能违反仲裁协议。比如在 Ridge C. C. *v.* J. P. Morgan 一案中，仲裁庭认为，即使当事人提起另诉程序合法，也存在拖延仲裁、破坏

---

① ICC Case No. 8307 (Interim Award, 14 May 2001), published extracts in Anti - Suit Injunctions in International Arbitration 308 - 315 (Emmanuel Gaillard ed., 2005), cited in Olivier Luc Mosimann, *supra* note 4, p. 114.

② See Olivier Luc Mosimann, *supra* note 4, p. 114.

③ See JAMS Case No. 1220066344 (Order Addressing Motion for Anti - Suit Injunction, 14 Feb 2021), *supra* note 18, holding that "As summarized by one court, '[c]ourts in this Circuit have found anti - injunctions appropriate even when the claims in the foreign and domestic actions were not precisely identical, but were at least based on the same underlying dispute'. Bailey Shipping Ltd., 2013 WL WL 5312540 at *9 (citing cases). The issues presented in the overseas suits and in this arbitration and related S. D. N. Y. proceeding crucially overlap even though ACE seeks only injunctive relief overseas while here it seeks both injunctive relief 'in aid of arbitration' (in the S. D. N. Y.) and damages (in the arbitration)."

④ 参见张建：《国际商事仲裁中禁诉令的适用问题研究——兼论我国仲裁禁诉令制度的立法构建》，载《国际法学刊》2021 年第 3 期。

仲裁程序的意图,因此其可以发布禁诉令。[①] 仲裁庭作出此认定的根据可以追溯到平行程序的产生原因。由于各国法律对仲裁协议适用法的规定不同,极有可能导致各受理机关对于仲裁协议应适用的准据法不同,从而导致对仲裁协议有效性出现判断上的差异,并最终导致平行程序的出现。[②] 因此,在仲裁庭和另诉法院对于仲裁协议效力认定不同的情况下,如果另诉法院认定仲裁协议无效,当事人提起的另诉程序也能具有合理性。但这种情况下,仲裁庭基于自裁管辖权有权发布禁诉令,另诉程序的合理性不构成阻碍发布禁诉令的理由。并且,在大多数情况下,仲裁庭在认为自身拥有管辖权的情况下,往往不会认为另诉程序的存在是合理的,因此仲裁庭是否应考虑该条件还值得商榷。

(三)不宜适用法院发布禁诉令的前提

在 Asia Cube *v.* Hans Chia 案中,[③]仲裁地是纽约,适用纽约州法律,于是仲裁庭运用纽约州法院发布禁诉令的法律来裁判该案是否符合发布禁诉令的条件。该案中,仲裁庭在判断平行程序[④]、临时措施的发布条件[⑤]方面均使用了法院关于禁诉令以及临时措施的判例法。本文认为此种裁决思路欠妥。

法院发布的禁诉令与仲裁庭发布的禁诉令存在本质上的不同,这些不同体现在以下两个方面:第一,权力的来源不同,法院发布的禁诉令具有司法主权的支撑,而仲裁庭发布禁诉令缺少该种权力来源,相反,仲裁庭发布禁诉令的权力

---

① See ICC Case No. 19134/CA/ASM (Procedural Order Relating to Interim Measures, 10 April 2013), *supra* note 16, holding that "However, the fact that the Respondents had a legitimate pretext to commence proceedings in Mexico DF against the DB Trust does not ipso facto mean there has been no breach of the arbitration agreement under the BRA in respect of the Mexican Lawsuit."

② 参见涂广建:《论国际民商事仲裁与诉讼的平行程序》,载《南大法学》2021 年第 4 期。

③ See JAMS Case No. 1220066344 (Order Addressing Motion for Anti – Suit Injunction, 14 Feb 2021), *supra* note 18.

④ See id, holding that "As summarized by one court, '[c]ourts in this Circuit have found anti – injunctions appropriate even when the claims in the foreign and domestic actions were not precisely identical, but were at least based on the same underlying dispute'. Bailey Shipping Ltd., 2013 WL WL 5312540 at *9 (citing cases). The issues presented in the overseas suits and in this arbitration and related S. D. N. Y. proceeding crucially overlap even though ACE *see*ks only injunctive relief overseas while here it *see*ks both injunctive relief 'in aid of arbitration' (in the S. D. N. Y.) and damages (in the arbitration)."

⑤ See id, holding that "The importance of this consideration in analyzing an anti – suit motion is emphasized in caselaw. E. g., Paramedics Electromedicina Comercial, Ltda, 369 F. 3d. at 653. Thus 'courts regularly exercise their discretion to issue anti – suit injunctions in aid of international arbitration agreements when they have previously or simultaneously compelled arbitration in the case.'"

来源于当事人的仲裁协议。但是,正是由于缺少司法主权的支撑,仲裁庭发布的禁诉令缺少司法权的对抗性。第二,执行力不同。法院发布的禁诉令可以通过法院的强制措施保障执行,但是仲裁庭发布的禁诉令仲裁庭本身是无法强制执行的,需要法院的协助执行。因此,仲裁庭发布的禁诉令无法类推适用法院发布禁诉令的前提。一般来说,仲裁庭发布禁诉令的条件理应比法院发布禁诉令的条件更宽松,因为如前所述,在仲裁庭发布禁诉令的场景中,往往不存在司法权与司法权的紧张对抗,因此一般无须考虑国际礼让原则等因素。

(四)小结

在发布禁诉令时,仲裁庭需要考虑两项先决条件:一是当事人是否违反仲裁协议,二是是否出现平行程序。对于当事人是否违反仲裁协议,仲裁庭需要考虑主观和客观两个方面;对于是否出现平行程序,仲裁庭仍应保持谨慎的态度严格认定。但是,合理的另诉程序不能阻碍仲裁庭发布禁诉令。而对于临时性质的禁诉令,还要适用仲裁庭发布临时措施的标准。另外,本文认为,仲裁庭不应该在考虑发布禁诉令的先决条件时适用法院发布禁诉令的考量标准。

四、仲裁庭发布禁诉令的自由裁量

在 Cessna Finance *v.* Gulf Jet and others 案中,仲裁庭在"发布禁诉令的条件"一节中提到,发布禁诉令需要考虑两方面的问题,首先是保证仲裁程序的完整性,其次是保障裁决能后续被承认和执行。[①] 有学者认为,即使不符合存在平行程序、损害等条件,如果出现另诉程序会加重争议、威胁仲裁程序的完整性和正常进行,仲裁庭也可以发布禁诉令。[②] 即使仲裁庭发布禁诉令存在先决条件,在特殊情况下,仲裁庭也可以突破上述发布条件的束缚。但是,仲裁庭必须谨慎适用此种例外。

(一)不加剧争议原则概述

在国际仲裁中,不加剧争议原则(the rule of non - aggravation of the dispute)是指一旦争议提交仲裁,各方就有义务避免采取可能加剧、加重或扩大此

---

① See ICC Case No. 18769/VRO/AGF (Final Award,17 Januanry 2014), *supra* note 15.

② See Gary B. Born, *supra* note 3, p. 2688.

类争议的任何作为或不作为。最初,这项原则起源于国际法,要求各国避免可能激起国际争端的行为,以维护国际和平、维护司法或仲裁程序的有效性,但是该项原则的内涵从诞生之时起就趋于模糊,很少有法庭或者当事人能明确该项原则的确切含义。[①] 后来,国际投资仲裁庭在裁判中逐渐适用此原则,但态度十分谨慎,国际投资仲裁庭往往运用“无法弥补的损害”的标准来判断是否会加剧争议。[②] 有学者认为,不加剧争议原则赋予了仲裁庭发布禁诉令的权力,因为将仲裁协议项下的争议提交给法院,会导致加剧争议的后果。[③] 因此,仲裁庭如果认为当事人的行为很有可能加剧争议,则可以突破某些条件的束缚而发布禁诉令。

从发展历史上看,不加剧争议原则虽然是规范当事人行为的一项原则,[④]但是,在国际商事仲裁的实践中,其效力同样也约束仲裁庭。有仲裁庭认为,发布禁诉令有可能会加重争议,根据不加剧争议原则,其不应发布禁诉令。[⑤] 本文认为,不加剧争议原则具有双向的约束力,一方面,当事人的行为如果违反该原则,仲裁庭有权对该行为采取措施;另一方面,仲裁庭在发布禁诉令时,需要考虑到此种发布是否会加剧争议。

但是,由于不加剧争议原则内涵的模糊性,仲裁庭适用该原则时往往难以下手,所以,在某些案件中,仲裁庭虽然提到了不加剧争议原则是发布禁诉令的考虑因素之一,但都未对该原则的内涵作出正面的解释。[⑥] 理论上来说,在仲裁

---

① See Steven R. Ratner, *The Aggravating Duty of Non – Aggravation*, 31(4) The European Journal of International Law1307 (2020), p. 1307.

② See Federico Campolieti, The Rule of Non – Aggravation of the Dispute in ICSID Arbitration Practice, ICSID Review – 1 Foreign Investment Law Journal 217(2015), p. 217 – 230.

③ See Emmanuel Gaillard, *Anti – suit Injunctions Issued by Arbitrators*, in Albert Jan van den Berg ed., International Arbitration 2006: Back to Basics?, Kluwer Law International, 2007, p. 239 – 240.

④ See Federico Campolieti, *supra* note 34, p. 217 – 218.

⑤ See ICC Case No. 18769/VRO/AGF (Final Award, 17 Januanry 2014), *supra* note 15, holding that "Second, the grant of an anti – suit injunction, when unnecessary to protect the integrity of the arbitral process, may exacerbate or aggravate the overall dispute and it may undermine the enforceability of this Final Award rather than enhance it."

⑥ See SIAC Case No. ARB105/13/SL (Procedural Order No. 3 (Decision on an Anti – Suit Injunction), 29 January 2014), *supra* note 14; also *see* ICC Case No. 18769/VRO/AGF (Final Award, 17 Januanry 2014), *supra* note 15, para. 217; also *see* ICC Case No. 19134/CA/ASM (Procedural Order Relating to Interim Measures, 10 April 2013), *supra* note 16.

案件中,所有平行程序的出现都可以被认为加剧争议,因此,仲裁庭盲目地适用不加剧争议原则可能会有滥用自由裁量权的嫌疑,不加剧争议原则在发布禁诉令的条件中只能作为一种辅助性的考虑因素,在例外的情况下才能适用。在国际商事仲裁中,仲裁庭可以参考国际投资仲裁中判断是否会加剧争议的标准,包括另诉的平行程序是否会干扰仲裁程序,或者是否会影响未来仲裁裁决的有效性。[①]

(二)不加剧争议原则的判断标准

1. 保障仲裁程序

仲裁庭需要保证仲裁裁决可被承认和执行,由此生发了仲裁庭有权利采取措施保障仲裁程序的原则,该种原则体现在众多仲裁规则中,比如《国际商会仲裁规则》(2021 年版)第 22 条第 2 款规定:"为确保有效管理案件,经洽商当事人后,仲裁庭应当采取其认为适当的程序措施,但该等措施不应违反当事人的任何约定。该等措施可以包括附件四中所描述的一项或多项案件管理方法。"在发布禁诉令时,仲裁庭理应考虑到保障仲裁程序的需要。

但是,必须指出,在某些情况下,存在平行程序并不一定会导致干预仲裁程序,比如在 Hotel TOC *v.* Trump International 案中,[②]仲裁庭认为另诉程序处于停滞状态,对于保障仲裁程序的影响不大,所以未发布禁诉令。因此,仲裁庭应结合个案情况认定平行程序是否会干预仲裁程序,以及此种干预的程度。

2. 保障仲裁裁决的效力

仲裁庭需要保证其作出的仲裁裁决是有效的,在仲裁庭发布禁诉令的语境下,该项判断标准包括两方面的内涵:一方面是针对当事人的行为,另一方面是针对仲裁庭的行为。

如果认为另诉程序会影响后续仲裁裁决的效力,仲裁庭就有权发布禁诉令。另外,仲裁庭在发布禁诉令时,需要考虑到对后续仲裁裁决的影响。现实的情况是,如果当事人成功地在某国法院提起了平行程序,则在仲裁裁决作出之后,该国法院也不太可能承认此裁决的效力。因此为了保障仲裁裁决可以被承认和执行,仲裁庭可以发布禁诉令,要求当事人中止另诉程序。但是,在 West

---

① See Federico Campolieti, *supra* note 34.

② ICC Case No. 23149/MK (Final Award, 20 March 2020), *supra* note 17.

Tankers 案中,欧盟法院认为法院发布的支持仲裁的禁诉令违反了《布鲁塞尔一号条例》。[①] 由此,有学者认为,包含禁诉令的仲裁裁决存在被拒绝承认和执行的风险,所以不推荐仲裁庭发布禁诉令。并且,为了保障仲裁裁决后续的效力,仲裁庭最好避免发布禁诉令。[②] 但是欧盟法院后续在 Gazprom 案中认为,仲裁庭发布的禁诉令不受布鲁塞尔条例的约束,因此不能被认定为违反了欧盟国家的公共政策。[③] 欧盟法院的立场更具合理性,毕竟,仲裁庭发布的禁诉令不同于法院发布的禁诉令,更加不存在司法权的紧张对抗。

结合以上观点,仲裁庭在发布禁诉令时,需要考虑仲裁裁决的后续效力问题,这一考虑因素包含两方面的内涵:一方面,仲裁庭需要考虑另诉程序的继续是否会影响仲裁裁决的承认和执行,因为存在管辖权争议,另诉程序一般会增加裁决不被承认和执行的风险,因此此种情况下,发布禁诉令会更有利于仲裁裁决的承认和执行。另一方面,仲裁庭需要根据裁决执行地法院对于仲裁庭发布禁诉令的态度决定是否发布禁诉令。仲裁庭需要预先判断裁决的主要执行地,如果裁决执行地法院对仲裁庭发布禁诉令持保守态度,那么仲裁庭可能需要考虑采取别的手段达到保护管辖权的效果;如果裁决执行地法院对仲裁庭发布禁诉令不多加限制,那么仲裁庭可以优先考虑发布禁诉令。

(三)小结

在例外情况下,仲裁庭可以突破先决条件而径行发布禁诉令,而衡量是否符合例外情况的标尺就是不加剧争议原则。在国际商事仲裁中,不加剧争议原则具有同时约束当事人和仲裁庭的双向效力,仲裁庭一方面可以采取措施防止争议加剧,另一方面也要对禁诉令的效果进行预判。不加剧争议原则的判断标准有二:一是保障仲裁程序,二是保障仲裁裁决的效力。

五、结论

仲裁庭发布的禁诉令包括临时性质的禁诉令以及永久性质的禁诉令,本文认为,只有临时性质的禁诉令才能构成临时措施,而永久性质的禁诉令不符合

---

① See Allianz SpA, Generali Assicurazioni Generali SpA *v.* West Tankers Inc., CJEU Case C – 185/07 (2009).

② See Olga Vishnevskaya, *supra* note 3, p. 193 – 202.

③ See Gazprom OAO *v.* Lietuvos Respublika, CJEU Case C – 536/13 (2015).

临时措施的“临时性”要件。

关于仲裁庭发布禁诉令的适用标准,本文认为,无论是临时性质的禁诉令还是永久性质的禁诉令,仲裁庭在发布禁诉令时都需要评估案件中的各种因素。禁诉令是一种非常特殊的救济手段,因此仲裁庭的此种自由裁量权并不完全自由。在总结相关实践之后,本文认为,仲裁庭需要在发布禁诉令时考虑两个先决条件:一是当事人是否违反仲裁协议,二是是否出现平行程序。此外,临时性质的禁诉令还需满足仲裁庭发布临时措施的标准。

在满足上述前提之后,仲裁庭可以考虑发布禁诉令,发布禁诉令的决定性考虑因素应是“不加剧争议原则”。在商事仲裁中,“不加剧争议原则”包含约束当事人和约束仲裁庭两方面的效力。首先,就算不满足上述前提,仲裁庭如果认为当事人的行为将会严重加剧争议,也可以发布禁诉令。其次,仲裁庭需要在发布禁诉令之前评估其发布的禁诉令是否会加剧争议。在具体内涵上,本文认为,“不加剧争议原则”包含两项评价标准:一是保障仲裁程序,二是保障仲裁裁决的效力。在保障仲裁程序的方面,仲裁庭应持谨慎态度评估另诉程序是否已经严重危害了仲裁程序;在保障仲裁裁决的效力方面,仲裁庭一方面要考虑另诉程序是否会导致无法作出有效的仲裁裁决的结果,另一方面要合理判断包含禁诉令的仲裁裁决能否被执行地法院承认和执行。

比较法视野下的自裁管辖理论消极效力研究

潘瑀瑭*

摘　要：目前不同国家对自裁管辖权的处理方式，特别在其“消极效力”方面，呈现多元化样态。鉴于我国仲裁法相较于国际通行做法之间的独特性，我国是否真正意义上确立了自裁管辖原则尚存在争议。争议的存在反映出我国立法中对自裁管辖学说概念尚不清晰，并与国际通行做法存在不一致。在这种情况下，厘清消极效力的概念并认识其他国家对于此的差异化实践，进而理解其做法背后的不同价值取向，是对中国目前的实践作出客观评价以及未来的改革方向提出前瞻建议的必要前提，也是本文的目标。

关键词：自裁管辖原则　管辖权/管辖权理论　消极效力　司法审查标准

仲裁作为一种当事人通过约定将对潜在争议默认的司法管辖权变更为仲裁庭管辖的争议解决机制，管辖权在法院和仲裁庭之间的分配方式一直是贯穿整个仲裁流程始末的根本性问题，也是分析仲裁案件的逻辑起点。实践中，若一方当事人提出抗辩认为此仲裁庭没有适格管辖权，具体的表现形式可能有在仲裁程序开始前向法院申请确认仲裁协议无效，直接将争议提交法院，在仲裁庭组成后向仲裁庭抗辩其不具有适格管辖权，在仲裁裁决作出后向法院申请撤销此裁决，或以没有管辖权为由拒绝承认与执行，等等。若此类抗辩被认同，即当仲裁庭的管辖权被否认时，那么仲裁庭则无权对实体争议作出裁决，仲裁庭

* 潘瑀瑭，康奈尔大学法学硕士。

作出的裁决(若有)也就同时失去了存在的合理性。① 因此管辖权在法院和仲裁庭之间的归属问题就成为仲裁争议的先决性问题。而在此之前,更为先决的问题在于,仲裁庭和法院谁有权利对管辖权争议作出决定。就此,为回应"谁有权利对管辖权归属作决定"的问题,对"管辖权的管辖权"作出判断,自裁管辖理论应运而生。

目前不同国家对自裁管辖权,特别在"消极效力"(下文详述)方面,处理方式呈现多元化样态,但广义上的自裁管辖原则,尤其在积极效力方面,已通过《承认及执行外国仲裁裁决公约》(以下简称《纽约公约》)和《联合国国际贸易法委员会国际商事仲裁示范法》(以下简称《贸易法委员会示范法》)得以确立。然而,由于我国仲裁法区别于国际通行做法,我国是否在真正意义上确立了自裁管辖原则尚存在争议。有学者指出,中国是唯一一个国内仲裁法从文义上明确与自裁管辖原则相悖的国家。更多学者则认为,中国的自裁管辖积极效力已经被承认,但消极效力仍尚未被确立。笔者认为,上述争议的存在本身就反映出我国立法中对自裁管辖学说概念尚不清晰,并与国际通行做法不一致。在这种情况下,厘清消极效力的概念并认识其他国家对于此的差异化实践,进而理解其做法背后的不同价值取向,是对中国目前的实践作出客观评价以及为未来的改革方向提出前瞻性建议的必要前提,也是本文的目标。

一、自裁管辖权的概念

自裁管辖权理论,又称管辖权/管辖权理论(Kompetenz – Kompetenz, Competence – Competence),已成为国际商事仲裁中被大多数国家普遍承认的理论。其核心概念指,仲裁庭一旦组成,即有权对其自身是否具有适格管辖权作出决定,无须等待法院的先决决定。

一般而言,仲裁庭在任何阶段是否具有适格的管辖权的问题将涉及三个具体问题:(1)当事各方之间是否已经存在仲裁协议;(2)当事各方之间现有的仲裁协议是否有效;(3)当事各方之间仲裁协议的范围是否足以涵盖他们之间争议的所有实质性问题。因此,仲裁庭是否具有适格的管辖权将取决于当事各方之间形成的仲裁协议的成立、有效性和范围。本文将把对消极影响理论的讨论

① See Gary B. Born, *International Commercial Arbitration*, 2nd edition, p. 1104.

局限于有关仲裁协议本身的成立、有效性和范围的问题,而不讨论与法庭的适当组成有关的问题。

(一)仲裁诉讼的三个阶段

为了提高讨论的便利性,本文将遵循一种较为普遍的分类方式,①以确定仲裁诉讼过程中可能出现仲裁管辖权问题的不同阶段,即第一阶段、第二阶段和第三阶段,以便下文中直接使用。值得注意的是,笔者发现尽管某些学术文章中也常出现三阶段的分类方式,但其含义与本文不尽相同。本分类方式中的三个阶段并不在每一个仲裁案件中都必然出现,也并不是单纯以时间先后顺序为标准进行划分的,几个阶段可能同时进行,第二阶段也可能在第一阶段之前发生。因此,为避免误读或混淆,在此处重新梳理一下本文三个阶段的划分标准。

"第一阶段"是指当事方在国家法院提起的诉讼,要求法院决定双方之间是否存在有约束力的仲裁协议,如果有,则法院将中止或驳回诉讼,并令当事双方提交仲裁。第一阶段的诉讼可能发生在假定的仲裁地(putative seat)或非仲裁地(non - seat)管辖区,或在多个管辖区同时进行。此外,也不一定存在第一阶段。有表面仲裁协议的当事人可能直接提交仲裁,尽管其中一方当事人(通常是被申请人)可以在仲裁庭上辩称仲裁庭没有适格的管辖权。但在一个具有强消极效力原则的法域,即倾向于将第一阶段产生的大多数管辖权问题交给仲裁员决定的法域,即使是更倾向于诉讼的当事人也可能被迫提起仲裁,再试图说服仲裁庭否认其自身管辖权。这也是某些国家和学者不支持强消极效力的原因之一。

"第二阶段"是指仲裁庭本身的程序。在这一阶段,遵循积极自裁管辖原则,仲裁庭将自行决定是否拥有适格管辖权。然而在大多数国家,仲裁庭肯定其自身管辖权的裁决并非最终裁决。在撤销或承认与执行裁决的程序中,法院都将重新进行司法审查。

"第三阶段"是指在法院对仲裁裁决进行撤销或承认与执行而进行的诉讼程序。该仲裁裁决可能是一项只涉及仲裁庭管辖权的初步裁决即确认或否认

① 此三阶段的分类方式也同时是 International Commercial Arbitration 教材中所用的分类方式。See Tibor Varady, John Barcelo III & Arthur T. Von Mehren, *International Commercial Arbitration*, West, 2003, p. 89.

管辖权,也可以是一项关于实体案情的最终裁决。

在仲裁诉讼程序的所有三个阶段都可能出现仲裁庭是否具有适格管辖权的问题。在第二阶段,正如上所述,积极自裁管辖原则几乎得到了普遍适用,即仲裁庭将自行决定其是否具有适格的管辖权,尽管不具有终局性。在第一阶段,法院对管辖权问题的审查力度将取决于该国法院适用的消极效力理论。一些法院将把多数管辖权争议提交给仲裁员进行首次判断,并保留在第三阶段的司法审查程序中重新独立对管辖权争议进行判断的权利。另一部分国家将在第一阶段决定自行对管辖权争议进行一裁终局的判断。

(二)积极与消极

自裁管辖权理论作为奠基性的理论,可以分为“积极效力”和“消极效力”两个层面。自裁管辖权的积极效力指向仲裁庭,指仲裁庭在第二阶段对其自身的管辖权有作出决定的积极权力。消极效力则指向法院,其核心含义是指在第一阶段“限缩”法院对于管辖权问题的介入和干涉。更强的消极效力指,法院在第一阶段更大程度地倾向于将管辖权争议交由仲裁庭进行优先判断,而不倾向于自己对仲裁协议的成立、生效和范围作出判断。[①] 但采纳强消极效力也并不意味着此仲裁庭的判断是终局性的,若当事人就此裁决向法院提起异议,法院在第三阶段仍有权对其做出司法审查以得出支持或否认的判断。因此,决定权分配在时间维度上的先后次序是自裁管辖权消极效力关注的重点。在美国,消极效力理论也影响到当法庭的裁决提交美国法院强制执行时美国法院对法庭先前管辖权裁决的尊重程度(deference),然而在大多数其他国家这一处理方式并不典型。

自裁管辖学说的积极和消极效力正如硬币的正反两面,虽内容侧重不同,但二者相辅相成且作用力同向。强大的消极效力理论让仲裁庭可以更充分地行使其积极的自裁管辖权。可以说,对于司法介入的限缩既是保障仲裁庭自裁管辖权利的良好前提也是必然结果。缺乏有效的消极自裁管辖机制,可能导致

---

① 就其消极效力而言,该原则认为赋予仲裁庭就其管辖权享有优先权,不受不适当的法院干扰是最合理的,即在法院优先受理了关于仲裁协议存在与否以及效力问题时以及在仲裁程序开始后,法院受理了关于仲裁协议存在与否以及效力问题的诉讼,允许仲裁庭继续仲裁程序时。在前一种情况下,优先规则要求法院经初步审查仲裁协议的存在与效力之后,令当事人提交仲裁解决争议;在后一种情况下,已经就其管辖权作出裁定的仲裁庭不必因未决诉讼程序的存在而中止仲裁程序。

实践中仲裁庭的积极自裁管辖权难以实现,又或者造成法院和仲裁庭管辖权重叠抑或分配不明的混乱局面。

自裁管辖理论和仲裁条款分离性理论(separability doctrine)[①]共同发挥作用,保障仲裁条款的有效执行和程序效率,以避免仲裁受到恶意异议而造成时间拖延和司法资源浪费。然而,并非所有当事人对于仲裁的异议都是出于恶意。任何真正支持仲裁并希望仲裁被更多当事人选择的法律体系,都需要维系一定程度的司法干预,以在缺乏有效的仲裁协议时保障当事人本应得的司法救济的同时,也避免当事人通过各种手段拖延或阻扰有效仲裁协议的执行。因此,由于不同国家对于上述价值的态度不同,实践中的做法呈现巨大的差异性。

尽管积极的自裁管辖权原则在绝大多数国家都或多或少得到了接受,但不同国家对于消极效力原则的处理态度非常多元化。这种多样性的存在也是处理仲裁合法性和效力相冲突的政策目标的体现。核心价值冲突在于:一方面,仲裁协议的效力需得到认可与尊重,以阻止已同意仲裁的当事人在争议发生后恶意妨碍仲裁程序的进行,从而避免由此造成的拖延以及高昂的司法成本;另一方面,在当事方并未通过仲裁协议自愿放弃将此争议提交法院寻求传统司法救济时,其诉诸法院的基本权利也应得到维护,以确保公平公正。与此同时,相比于在仲裁庭决定其管辖权后法院在事后司法审查中再重新决定管辖权这一情形,若法院在一开始就决定管辖权问题,然后再将当事方送交仲裁,将大大节省时间和费用,提高程序效率。[②] 因此后者的政策目标也被称为"公平/程序效率"目标。因此,一个国家对于消极效力原则的态度,根本上取决于其如何平衡"仲裁效力"和"公平/程序效率"这两个相互冲突的政策目标。[③]

(三)"管辖权"与"可受理性"

另一个值得注意的概念区分,即仲裁庭对于争议的"管辖权"(jurisdiction)

---

① 仲裁条款分离性理论是国际商事仲裁中另一个重要的原则。仲裁条款独立原则是指仲裁条款与其构成其中一个条款的主合同或者其附属的主合同是可分或者独立的,仲裁条款与主合同形成了两个分离或相互独立的合同。

② See F. Bachand, *Does Article* 8 *of the Model Law Call for Full or Prima Facie Review of the Arbitral Tribunal's Jurisdiction*?, 22 Arb. Int'l 463, 465 (2006).

③ See John J. Barcelo III, *Kompetenz – Kompetenz and It Negative Effect—A Comparative View*, (2017).

和“可受理性”(admissibility)之间的区别。特别是在大陆法系国家,法院和仲裁庭使用的“可受理性”的概念,指与提起争议的实效性以及提起诉请方式相关的问题。因此,“可受理性”涉及的问题,如申请人是否遵循了所有已获授权的仲裁前置程序步骤(如完成双方约定的和解谈判期,或遵守通知程序),或原告是否通过采取与试图提交仲裁不一致的步骤而误导了被告当事人,进而被视为放弃了其原本享有的仲裁权利。这些仲裁“可受理性”问题的核心是,申请人是否妥善进行了申请程序从而使其有权得到适当的裁决,而不是仲裁庭是否是适当的决策者。因此,“可受理性”问题在技术上不是“管辖权”问题,“管辖权”争议是关于仲裁庭或法院是不是适当的决策者的问题;相反,“可受理性”关心的是,提交的申请是否时机成熟,是否已超过时效,是否已经在其他流程上得到妥善处理。因此,“可受理性”问题并不受消极效力的制约。一旦确定或承认仲裁协议的存在、有效性和范围,此类问题就将由仲裁员作出裁决。

二、立法规定

仲裁管辖权的来源是当事人意思自治,也即有效的仲裁协议明确授权,管辖权争议同理。但在仲裁协议的成立和有效性受到质疑,最终可能被证明不存在或无效的情况下,自裁管辖学说的消极效力就丧失了以仲裁协议为依据的可能性。因为在这些情况下,自始没有任何协议可作为剥夺国家法院固有的司法管辖权的依据。因此,排除国家司法管辖权的来源应当是国内仲裁立法和国际公约,这些条文应作为判断国家法院缺乏或可能不会行使其固有的管辖权的依据。

《纽约公约》①和《贸易法委员会示范法》②作为国际层面实现仲裁原则统一的主要工具,应被视为讨论消极效力原则的逻辑起点。如果认为《纽约公约》清晰明确地对消极效力作出了规定,那么上述不同法域的多样化态度将不会存在,因为《纽约公约》对世界上大多数国家和所有重要的商业国家都具有约束

① U. N. Convention on the Recognition and Enforcement of Foreign Arbitral Awards, June 10, 1958, 330 U. N. T. S. 3, available at http://www. uncitral. org.

② U. N. Commission on International Trade Law [UNCITRAL] Model on International Commercial Arbitration of 1985, U. N. GAOR, 40th Sess., Annex I, U. N. Doc. A/40/17 (1985), available at http://www. uncitral. org.

力。截至本文撰写时,共有 106 个法域中的 75 个国家和地区以 1985 年《贸易法委员会示范法》为范本制定了其国家仲裁立法,这意味着许多法域采用了非常类似的国际仲裁法。如果《贸易法委员会示范法》包括一项明确的消极效力条款,或者存在对其较为统一的有说服力的解释,那么许多国家的做法将得到统一。然而事实上,《纽约公约》和《贸易法委员会示范法》的文本和立法历史都无法作出某种统一的解释。正如下所述,学者们观点各异。更合理的观点是,在如何处理这一消极效力的问题上,两部法规都没有采取"明确"的立场,可以由国家立法和司法自由裁量决定。

(一)《纽约公约》

《纽约公约》第 2 条第 3 款规定:"如果缔约方的法院受理一个案件,而就这案件所涉及的事项,当事人已经达成本条意义内的协议时,除非该法院查明该项协议是无效的、不再适用的或不可能实行的,应该依一方当事人的请求,令当事人把案件提交仲裁。"

1. 审查范围

显然,《纽约公约》第 2 条第 3 款规范的为第一阶段。该条文中"除非该法院查明"从字面理解,其含义为,当双方有清晰有效的仲裁条款时法院"应当"令当事人提交仲裁,这应当理解为关于自裁管辖学说的明文规定。根据通说,优先于并取代一审国家法院管辖权的仲裁管辖权取决于以下三方面:(1)当事方之间的仲裁协议存在,(2)现有协议有效,以及(3)争议属于双方同意仲裁的争议种类的范围。鉴于下文的讨论会涉及这三个要素中的哪一个有争议,因此有必要对其进行概念上的区分。"成立"是指在合同法下双方订立仲裁协议所需的要件已经满足。"有效性"涉及的是,一项客观存在的协议是否由于某些缺陷而无法强制执行,如欺诈、重大误解、违反公共政策等。这些避免执行理由中的大多数必须由反对协议有效的一方当事人主动提出。然而,"违反公共政策"一般可以由法院自行主张。"范围"是指争议中的特定问题是否属于本协议所要涵盖的问题的范围。

但值得注意的是,有学者 Gary Born 指出,虽然《纽约公约》条文字面涉及仲裁协议的成立、生效和范围这三个方面,但是这并不必然意味着《纽约公约》

“要求”法院在第一阶段对仲裁协议的效力进行审查。[①] Born 的理由是，一方面，《纽约公约》仅要求当法院在“查明该协议是有效的”时，把案件提交仲裁，并不是附加给法院一个必须判断仲裁协议是否生效的义务，因此若法院决定不审查仲裁协议的有效性而直接提交仲裁，也并不违反《纽约公约》。因此按照 Born 的观点，《纽约公约》的文义本身仅仅规定了法院查明仲裁协议确实有效后应提交仲裁，并没有明确要求法院应该进行审查，也没有对审查标准表示立场。

另一方面，Born 认为第 2 条第 3 款中仅规范了仲裁协议“无效的、不再适用的或不可能实行的”情况，也就是说应理解为仅与仲裁协议的成立和生效有关，没有明确提到“范围”的问题[尤其是将条文语言跟 V(I)C 相对比]。[②] 按此逻辑，涉及仲裁协议约定“范围”的争议应当由仲裁庭作出裁决。然而笔者认为，即使条文中的“无效的、不再适用的或不可能实行的”字面含义确实未涵盖“范围”，但条文前半段中“而就这案件所涉及的事项”的字句，也可以理解为暗含了所涉及争议落入仲裁协议所约定的争议范围内的意思。因此此处也存在争议，存在不同的解释空间。

2. 审查标准

对于此处“除非该法院查明”所指的法院的司法审查标准是“表面审查”(prima facie)还是对事实和法律进行“全面审查”(full review)，学界也争论已久。

对于此争议，学界尚未达成统一。《纽约公约》最早的评论员之一 Albert Jan van den Berg 于 1981 年撰文，[③]认为第 2 条第 3 款应理解为只要求在第一阶段作出“表面审查”，其是基于《纽约公约》支持仲裁裁决执行的立法精神，而不是基于第 2 条第 3 款的明确措辞或其立法历史。因此，他的结论也可以说是建立在较为薄弱的理由之上的。然而正如前所述，Born 反对 van den Berg 的观点，他认为第 2 条第 3 款不能理解为授权法院对所称仲裁协议的存在、有效性和范围进行“表面审查”，应将《纽约公约》理解为在第一阶段未就审查标准采

---

① See Gary B. Born, *International Commercial Arbitration*, 2nd edition, p. 1053 – 1055.

② Ibid.

③ Albert Jan van den Berg, The New York Arbitration Convention 155 (1981).

取立场,从而允许缔约方自行决定它们希望采纳的消极效力的强弱。这一观点是较为合理的,特别是如 Born 所说,如果考虑到许多缔约方国内法规定在第一阶段要求法院进行全面审查,①而 van den Berg 的观点认为《纽约公约》仅允许进行表面审查,那么这些国家都已违反了《纽约公约》。同理,Born 的观点和其他评论员的观点②也反对将《纽约公约》解读为要求在第一阶段全面审查管辖权,否则采取表面审查标准的国家也将被视为与公约要求相抵触。同样,我们可以举出对那些采取了初步检验的国家的同期解释,这些解释与任何此类解释相抵触。

但是 Born 认为,一方面,该条文中"除非该法院查明"从字面理解,其含义为,当双方有清晰有效的仲裁条款时法院"应当"令当事人提交仲裁,这应当理解为关于自裁管辖学说的明文规定。另一方面,第 2 条第 3 款中仅规范了仲裁协议"无效的、不再适用的或不可能实行的"情况,也就是说应理解为仅与仲裁协议的成立和生效有关,没有明确提到"范围"的问题[尤其是将条文语言跟 V(I)C 相对比]。按此逻辑,涉及仲裁协议约定"范围"的争议应当由仲裁庭作出裁决。

(二)《贸易法委员会示范法》

对于《贸易法委员会示范法》,情况就显得更加复杂。虽然在第 8 条中,《贸易法委员会示范法》采用了上文引述的《纽约公约》第 2 条第 3 款中相同措辞,但《贸易法委员会示范法》在第 16 条第 1 款中也对自裁管辖权作出了特别规定。《贸易法委员会示范法》第 16 条第 3 款规定,法院可以对仲裁庭裁定其自身具有良好管辖权的初步裁决进行早期且不可上诉的司法审查。此处的重点在于,立法者提供了一种与第一阶段的"表面审查"相协调的方式。如果(是假设)认为《贸易法委员会示范法》对第一阶段的司法审查采"表面标准",即更倾向于维护仲裁协议的"效力",那么对仲裁庭的初步管辖裁决进行早期司法审查会提供一定的对于"公平/程序效率"的平衡。

对于当事人没有真正达成将某一争议提交仲裁的合意,却面临被迫参与仲

---

① Born Treatise, Vol. 1, at 1052 – 1257. Germany, Switzerland, the U. S., and England are all jurisdictions in point. See the discussion in the text below dealing with each of these jurisdictions.

② See F. Bachand, *Does Article* 8 *of the Model Law Call for Full or Prima Facie Review of the Arbitral Tribunal's Jurisdiction*?, 22 Arb. Int'l 463, 471 (2006).

裁所造成的“缺乏公正”和“浪费成本”的情况，这种不正当和效率低下被两个因素抵消：(1)“表面审查”本身就会将某些仲裁请求在第一阶段否决；(2)对于进入第二阶段的案件来说，法院有权对仲裁庭肯定自身管辖权的初步裁决进行早期独立的司法审查。因此，被迫参与不当仲裁的当事人只会在有限的时间内承受仲裁成本。同时，一个有正当权利得到仲裁的仲裁请求人，在开始时将通过“表面审查”，诉讼程序在仲裁进行期间将暂时中止。法院的独立司法审查权仍然存在，但仅可能发生在仲裁庭在初步裁决中捍卫其自身管辖权之后。

尽管此论点很有吸引力，但《贸易法委员会示范法》的立法历史无疑可以被认为明确否认了“表面审查”的方式。支持在第一阶段进行全面审查的学者的论据通常来自早期的立法历史，即起草者明确拒绝了在《贸易法委员会示范法》第8条第1款中添加“明显”(manifestly)一词的提议。[①] 若在《贸易法委员会示范法》第8条第1款加入“明显”，即变更为“除非认定所称仲裁协议明显无效的、不再适用的或不可能实行的”，才代表“表面审查”标准。因此，从立法史推测，起草人不支持在第一阶段对管辖权进行“表面审查”。

然而，有学者认为，立法史的后半部分反映出起草人对“表面审查”态度的改变。[②] 他的论据是来自起草人放弃一项条款的理由中。该条款本应允许仲裁程序的被申请人在任何时候请求法院宣布仲裁庭无管辖权。起草人否决了这一规定，因为“不符合第16条(自裁管辖学说条款)所依据的原则，即管辖权问题是由仲裁庭优先并主要决定，受法院的事后审查约束”[③]。虽然没有明示，但从此逻辑可以推断出，起草人的观点与第一阶段的初步审查标准相符合。但起草人也并没有回到第8条第1款，添加他们先前拒绝使用的“明显”一词。因此，更好的结论似乎是，《贸易法委员会示范法》在第一阶段审查标准上没有定论。Barcelo认为应当将其理解为允许但不要求在第一阶段进行“表面审查”。

三、国际司法实践范例

鉴于《纽约公约》和《贸易法委员会示范法》对消极效力都没有定论，不同

---

① P. Binder, International Commercial Arbitration and Conciliation in Uncitral 91, para. 2 – 088 (2d ed. 2005).

② See F. Bachand, *Does Article 8 fo the Model Law Call for Full or Prima Facie Review of the Arbitral Tribunal's Jurisdiction?*, 22 Arb. Int'l 463, 465 (2006).

③ Born Treatise, Vol. I, at 1084.

的缔约方对待此原则的态度和司法实践各异。目前不同国家对待消极自裁管辖的态度和处理方式呈现较为多元的样态,这体现出不同政策的价值取向,对于具体方式的优劣仍有很大的讨论空间。但毋庸置疑的是,成熟并自洽的法律体系应当体现出司法审查介入强度在第一阶段和第三阶段的互补和平衡,并在其呈现结果上与其政策目标相一致。下文将介绍支持强消极理论的法国做法和支持弱消极理论的德国做法,以及比较有特色的美国做法,并重点关注其做法在第一阶段和第三阶段的平衡,对其利弊进行分析。

(一)强消极理论的法国做法

在所有采纳自裁管辖权原则消极效力的国家中,法国当属最激进的国家。法国法在诸多方面都被公认为非常有利于仲裁,包括其对消极影响理论的处理方式。2011 年《法国民事诉讼法典》第 1448 条规定了明确的管辖权冲突,其中规定:“当受仲裁协议约束的争议提交法院审理时,该法院应拒绝管辖权,但仲裁庭尚未受理争议,且仲裁协议明显无效或明显不适用的除外。法院不得自行主动拒绝管辖权。任何与本条相反的规定均应视为非书面规定。”此条文确定了法国在仲裁管辖权问题上采取了最纯粹的仲裁庭优先规则,同时明确否定了当事人意思自治对消极效力的任何修改作用。规则主要将情况分类为两类:在提交诉讼时争议尚未被仲裁庭受理(seized)和已经被仲裁庭受理。第一,若争议已经提交仲裁庭并被受理,那么法院不应做任何审查,应直接拒绝管辖,将争议交由仲裁庭解决。这表示,若一方当事人想要对所称仲裁协议的存在、有效性或范围质疑,必须在仲裁庭组成前提起诉讼,否则,管辖权问题将只能由仲裁员决定,司法审查只可能在第三阶段进行。此立法目的很明显是防止当事人阻挠仲裁的进行。第二,也是最重要的一点,即使仲裁庭尚未受理争议,法院仍然必须拒绝行使管辖权,除非在表面审查后就发觉仲裁协议的无效或范围不适用是“重大明显的”(manifestly)。换言之,任何证明存在有约束力的仲裁协议的初步证据足以让法院停止司法程序并将当事人提交仲裁,由仲裁庭对管辖权争议作出初次判断。

当然,允许第一阶段程序在法庭上继续并不会直接妨碍第二阶段仲裁程序的进行,两者可以同时进行。然而,Barcelo 指出,在这种情形下当事人将被迫主要关注法院诉讼,甚至可能中止仲裁。[1] 这是因为,一项由仲裁地出具的否认仲裁庭管辖权的法院判决将使仲裁裁决无效,从而导致《纽约公约》项下的执行无法实现,因此仲裁程序将失去意义。

法国的做法在很大程度上倾向于维护仲裁协议的效力,并支持仲裁。那么,对于与之相对的公平和程序效率的保护如何实现? 这主要体现在第三阶段法国的司法审查中。尽管法国在第一阶段支持仲裁,但第三阶段中的法国法院不会尊重或参照(defer)仲裁庭先前关于管辖权的决定,而是将完全独立自主决定管辖权问题。[2] 由于仲裁员审理案件的计费与个人利益有关,因此不能说在管辖权问题上完全没有偏见,这时第三阶段的完全自主的审理标准就很有意义。但与此同时,这似乎削弱了法国在第一阶段的态度。如果法国法院最终将在裁决执行阶段(第三阶段)独立自主决定管辖权问题,那么为什么不允许法院在第一阶段就作出决定,为当事人节省仲裁时间和费用,提高程序效率呢?

法国学者对此的解释是,仲裁庭在其管辖权受到质疑时,可以行使自裁管辖权,根据案情在初步裁决书或最终裁决书中决定管辖权问题。但是,如果仲裁庭在初步裁决中维持其管辖权,反对仲裁管辖权的一方可立即在仲裁地请求法院宣布裁决无效。[3] 这允许法院就管辖权较早进行独立自主的司法裁决,并且如果法院否认了仲裁庭管辖权,当事人将不必被迫承担全部仲裁费用。并且若法国是仲裁地,仲裁员也大概率将在法院程序开始后中止仲裁程序。这是因为,如上所述,如果仲裁地的法院撤销管辖权裁决,将不可避免地同时撤销任何之后的仲裁最终裁决。而根据《纽约公约》,在仲裁地被撤销的裁决通常无法在任何国家法院执行。[4] 因此,法国的做法形成了一种合理的折中办法,即仲裁庭将在初次决定其自身管辖权并阐明其理据。这种说理虽然对法院不具有约束力,但仍有说服力。法院有权利在仲裁程序的早期就管辖权作出重新裁决。

---

① See John J. Barcelo Ⅲ, *Kompetenz – Kompetenz and It Negative Effect—A Comparative View*, (2017).

② See Fouchard, Gaillard, Goldman, On International Commercial Arbitration 930, para 1608 (E. Gaillard & J. Savage eds., 1999).

③ See V. Pavic, "Appropriate Compromise: Article 16(3) of the Model Law and its Progeny", in Kröll, Mistelis, Perales and Rogers, eds., International Arbitration and Internationla Commercial Law: Synergy, Convergence and Evolution 387 – 410 (2011).

④ See N. Y. Convention Article V(1)(e).

(二)弱消极理论的德国做法

与法国相似,德国的民事诉讼法决定了德国对消极效力原则的处理方式,并且不允许当事人通过意思自治改变既定规则。[①] 然而,德国法在政策制定中反映出与法国截然不同的价值倾向,它更重视仲裁中的公平/程序效率。无论何时,只要当事人将可能受仲裁协议约束的"争议"起诉至德国法院,法院只会在另一方当事人提出根据约定应提交仲裁的抗辩,并且在全面审查后得出结论认为仲裁协议存在并可执行的情况下,才会拒绝管辖令当事人提交仲裁。否则,德国法院不会将关于管辖权的初次决定权交给仲裁庭。因此,仅仅为了请求仲裁庭拒绝管辖权而进行仲裁的情况并不会在德国发生。

此外,当事人还可以提交一份称为"申请"(application)的特别诉讼请求,只寻求法院判断争议是否必须提交仲裁。[②] 然而,这种"申请"必须在仲裁庭组成之前提交至法院,这一时间条件似乎是出于对效力目标的考量。如果仲裁庭已经成立,要求寻求管辖权裁决的一方当事人只能向仲裁庭提出,以避免出现更多的恶意拖延或不必要的费用。根据德国的规则,仲裁庭关于管辖权的裁决将作为初步裁决,一旦作出即可立即被德国法院进行独立的司法审查。

然而,此种时间条件并不适用于当事人向法院就实体争议的起诉。若允许当事人在仲裁庭组成后向法院提出所谓的诉讼,似乎会给当事人阻挠仲裁程序预留了空间。然而在实践中,若仲裁庭已经成立,德国法院倾向于中止其程序,以等待仲裁庭关于管辖权的初次仲裁裁决。《德国民事诉讼法》第 148 条规定:"如果对法律纠纷的判决结果将全部或部分取决于是否存在某种法律关系,且这种关系的构成取决于另一个未决的法律纠纷……法院可中止其审判程序,直到此未决的法律纠纷的被处理完毕……"据此,如果仲裁程序首先被提起,并已组成仲裁庭,德国法院很可能会中止其诉讼程序,并等待仲裁庭率先作出判断。

德国规则的另一个方面可以视为倾向于保护仲裁效力。即使当事人先向法院提出诉讼,德国法也允许仲裁程序开始并与法院程序同时进行。但是这对仲裁效力的保护作用十分有限。试图阻碍仲裁的当事人仍然可以在仲裁庭成

---

① See K. – H. Böckstiegel, S. Kröll, & P. Nacimiento, eds., Arbitration in Germany 118 & 216 (2d ed. 2015).

② German Code of Civil Procedure, section 1032(2).

立之前,通过起诉向对方施加诉讼成本。赞成仲裁的一方会被迫进入诉讼程序并对法院管辖权提出抗辩,因为德国法院可能不会主动令当事人提交仲裁。[①]此外,除非对仲裁管辖权特别有信心,否则仲裁申请人不太可能希望同时推进仲裁,因为仲裁成本可能被浪费。因此,德国做法被描述为法国的镜像。如果在仲裁庭成立之前提起诉讼,则在德国法院对管辖权问题进行全面审查时,仲裁程序大概率会暂停,除非法院管辖权"明显"(至少对仲裁申请人)不成立。

(三)赋予当事人意思自治特权的美国做法

美国的消极影响原则与法国和德国的规则在几个方面形成了对比。一方面,它不是以明确的立法规定为基础的,而是基于美国最高法院的判例。另一方面,美国做法最大的特色是允许当事人通过意思自治对自裁管辖权进行约定,正如上文所言,当事人通过自主约定在法国和德国都是不允许的。

美国也有关于仲裁的立法规定。在国际仲裁中,《美国联邦仲裁法》(Federal Arbitration Act,FAA)第二章将《纽约公约》引入为美国国内法。根据《纽约公约》第2款第3项的规定,如果法院收到受仲裁协议管辖的诉讼,法院应令当事人提交仲裁。然而正如前所述,《纽约公约》在第一阶段就仲裁管辖权应做全面审查(德国惯例)或表面证据审查(法国惯例)是模棱两可的,仲裁协议效力的审查标准将由各成员国自行决定。

某些观点认为,若推定仲裁地为美国,FAA第一章作为适用于美国国内的仲裁规则将可能被适用,在这种情况下,FAA第一章第4条的规定"如果一方因另一方未能、疏忽于或拒绝根据书面仲裁协议进行仲裁而不满,则该方可向任何美国地区法院提出申诉,除非该协议另有规定,否则该法院具有管辖权,法院应循简易程序对其进行审判",似乎表示法院在第一阶段应进行全面审查。然而,根据FAA,若某争议具有国际属性,那么即使仲裁地为美国,FAA第二章仍应适用,[②]并且在FAA第一章和第二章不一致的情况下,应以第二章为准。[③] 因此,关于在第一阶段的消极效力上,美国法中仍应以《纽约公约》第2条第3款中含糊不清的措辞为优先依据。

---

① See German Code of Civil Procedure, Section 1032(1).

② See FAA section 202.

③ See FAA section 208.

也有学者认为,在假设以美国为仲裁地的国际仲裁案件中,FAA 第一章和第二章同时适用,且由于第二章允许公约国在第一阶段选择其国内法选择的审查标准,因此 FAA 的两章之间并不存在冲突。因此,应按照第一章进行全面审查。然而,美国最高法院从未将其关于消极效力的判决建立在这一推理基础上。由于美国没有法律条文明确规定自裁管辖权的消极效力,因此给美国最高法院预留了解释的空间。

美国最高法院的两项判决对于理解美国处理消极效力的方法至关重要:First Options of Chicago v. Kaplan①(以下简称 First Options)和 Howsam v. Dean Witter Reynolds, Inc.②(以下简称 Howsam)。应该指出,美国最高法院对"可仲裁性"(arbitrability)的使用比许多其他法域"可仲裁性"一词的含义更广泛。在欧洲,"可仲裁性"一般特指公共政策是否禁止特定问题通过仲裁解决并将这些问题的管辖权保留给国家法院。而美国最高法院更广义地使用"可仲裁性"一词,即当事人已签订仲裁协议,协议有效,且争议中的特定问题(存在性、有效性和范围)包含在协议中时,争议才被认为是"可仲裁的"。

美国最高法院判例法的另一个重要特征是其在第一阶段和第三阶段之间的联系和平衡。法国和德国的做法中并不存在这种联系,无论第一阶段的审查标准如何,在第三阶段对仲裁庭管辖权的司法审查都是独立且重新开始的。然而在美国方法中,法院赋予当事人意思自治的优越性解释了第一阶段和第三阶段之间的联系,使这两个阶段可以彼此影响从而达到更佳的平衡。

First Options 是第三阶段的案例,美国最高法院在此案中需要回应的问题是,在被要求执行仲裁裁决时,美国法院对"可仲裁性"问题应适用何种审查标准。如果认为仲裁庭没有适格管辖权,那么仲裁裁决将被法院拒绝承认与执行。虽然 First Options 为一个美国国内的仲裁案件,但随后美国最高法院的 BG Group③ 裁决证明,此原则也同样适用于国际仲裁案件。

First Options 中法院主要将重点放在合同谈判期间双方当事人的真实意图上,并引入了一个很重要的推定。法院首先询问双方当事人是否曾就"应由谁

① See First Options of Chicago v. Kaplan, 514 U. S. 938 (1995).

② See Howsam v. Dean Witter Reynolds, Inc., 537 U. S. 79 (2002).

③ See BG Group v. Argentina, 572 U. S. 25; 134 S. Ct. 1198 (2014).

来决定所称的仲裁协议的存在、有效性或范围,是法院还是仲裁庭”,即“应由谁决定争议的可仲裁性”,作出过约定。事实上一般而言,双方当事人很少会想到这个“神秘”的问题。随后美国最高法院指示下级法院,推定在默认情况下当事人有意采用正常模式,即应由法院决定管辖权问题,有除非“明确无误”的证据可以证明当事人曾约定将关于可仲裁性(仲裁协议的存在、有效性和范围)的决定提交仲裁员决定,才能反驳上述推定。由于在 First Option 中,法院没有发现此类“明确无误”的证据,因此在第三阶段法院进行了独立审查。

First Options 清楚地表明,如果当事方明确约定了仲裁的可仲裁性,那么在裁决执行阶段,若仲裁庭按照当事人的约定对仲裁的可仲裁性作出裁决,那么法院将承认此仲裁庭对于管辖权的裁决。但在更多的国际商事仲裁案件中,在第三阶段中法院基本不会对仲裁庭关于实质案情的结论进行审查,法院通常决定相当彻底地遵从(deference)仲裁庭先前关于管辖权的裁决。然而,Barcelo 就认为法院在 First Options 的处理方式是存在很大问题的,他认为更合理的方式就是将关于可仲裁性的含义解释为仲裁员将有机会就管辖权作出优先决定,而不是最终的决定权。并且即使关注当事人意图,法院也应对当事人意图的“明确”提出更高的标准。

First Options 的判决只涉及第三阶段的问题,即在判断是否执行裁决时,法院应对仲裁员先前关于可仲裁性的裁决给予什么程度的遵从(若有)。尽管如此,本案也解释了消极效力理论在美国法院第一阶段扮演的角色。在第一阶段,消极效力取决于当事人的意图和法院适用的推定。除非有“明确无误”的证据表明当事人意图由仲裁员决定可仲裁性,法院在第一阶段将在充分审查的情况下决定可仲裁性。因此,若不存在第一阶段有关于此的法院判决,法院将在第三阶段独立作出判决。

在 First Options 几年后的 Howsam 案中,法院重述了 First Options 中的说理。Howsam 案提出的问题是,当争议不是关于仲裁庭的管辖权即仲裁协议的存在、有效性或范围的实体约定,而是申请人是否遵守了关于仲裁特定程序规则时,First Options 中的规则是否仍然适用。这一次,法院将争议的“实质性可仲裁性”(包括存在性、有效性和范围问题)与“程序可仲裁性”进行了区分。法院认为,“程序可仲裁性”问题,包括时间期限、通知要求、强制性事先调解义务、禁反言和弃权等,所适用的规则应当是不同的。在“程序可仲裁性”这类问题上,默认的推定为当事人意图将主要管辖权交给仲裁庭决定,而不是法院。当然此种假定可以被反驳,但只有在有“明确和令人信服的证据”表明当事人的意图是为法院保留管辖权的情况下。

“程序可仲裁性”理论有一个默认的前提,即若当事人已进入谈判仲裁协议的预期程序性细节,就意味着双方已经对“将争议提交仲裁解决”达成了共识。而这些程序性问题虽然不涉及实体问题,但与实体问题密切相关,因为违反约定的仲裁程序可能导致当事人丧失继续提请仲裁的权利。因此,“程序可仲裁性”问题似乎更自然地属于仲裁员的管辖范围。

由此可以看出,美国最高法院的“程序可仲裁性”概念与法国和德国等大陆法系国家将其归类为“可受理性”问题之间的重叠。例如,在法国和德国,人们在 Howsam 中发现的“程序可仲裁性”问题通常被视为“可受理性”问题。[①] 在这两个国家,可受理性问题是仲裁员的职责范围,与实体问题一样,不可由法院复审。然而,Howsam 的“程序可仲裁性”概念与大陆法系中的“可受理性”概念有一个重要区别。对于法国和德国来说,争议的可受理性问题的管辖权属于仲裁员,在第三阶段可受理性问题与实体争议一样是不可复审的,这并不被双方当事人在仲裁协议中约定的意图所影响。然而在美国,仲裁协议中明确的约定可以将“程序可仲裁性”问题保留给法院,让法院在第三阶段进行独立判断。

2019 年,美国最高法院在 Henry Schein, Inc. v. Archer & White Sales[②] 案中又一次肯定了对当事人意思自治的尊重,且明确了对“可仲裁性”的决定权也可由当事人约定。本案的争议焦点在于,当将争议提交仲裁“完全没有根据”(wholly groundless)时,法院是否仍需遵守当事人将可仲裁性问题交给仲裁庭决定的约定。最高法院认为,仲裁条款是当事人的合同,法院必须根据合同条款执行仲裁。[③] 签约的当事人可以同意让仲裁员不仅对某一争议的实体部分作出判断,也可以授权仲裁庭对“可仲裁性”这个“前提”问题进行判断。因此,当合同将可仲裁性问题授权给仲裁员时,即使法院认为可仲裁性主张完全没有根据,法院也不得推翻这种当事人对于管辖权的约定。

---

① See J. Barceló, Arbitrability Decisions Before, During, and After Arbitration in J. C. Betancourt, ed., Defining Issues in International Arbitration 74 para 7.29 (2016) and authorities cited id. in fn 16.

② See Henry Schein, Inc. v. Archer & White Sales, Inc., 586 U.S. 530, 139 S. Ct. 524 (2019).

③ See Rent – A – Center, West, Inc. v. Jackson, 561 U. S. 63, 67.

四、我国的立法和司法态度

目前,自裁管辖权在我国的法律中规定得较为模糊,甚至关于我国目前法律规则中是否明确确立了仲裁自裁管辖权,尚且没有统一的定论,关于消极效力理论是否被采纳则更少被提及。《仲裁法》第 20 条规定:"当事人对仲裁协议的效力有异议的,可以请求仲裁委员会作出决定或者请求人民法院作出裁定。一方请求仲裁委员会作出决定,另一方请求人民法院作出裁定的,由人民法院裁定。当事人对仲裁协议的效力有异议,应当在仲裁庭首次开庭前提出。"

《仲裁法》第 20 条给中国自裁管辖权的确立与否带来了极大的不确定性,主要体现在以下几个方面:首先,此条文将管辖权异议的决定权赋予仲裁委员会即仲裁机构和法院,而不是仲裁庭和仲裁员。这种极具中国特色的将管辖权赋予仲裁机构的做法与国际通行做法和自裁管辖的常规概念都存在差距,这也是引起争议的一个主要原因。由于仲裁机构在性质上并不真正负责审理实体争议,而只是事务管理机构,并且按照国际通说,仲裁机构虽可以按照仲裁机构规则来对案件的可受理性进行判断,但自裁管辖理论中所谓与法院相对的一直是仲裁庭和仲裁员。因此,此法规一直被广泛批判,同时也是很多学者认为中国尚未确立自裁管辖原则的重要原因。其次,此条文中仅规定了仲裁协议的"效力",而没有涉及"存在性和范围",也没有规定诸如"超过仲裁约定的时效"等程序可仲裁性事由。此种未明确狭义还是广义的用词在法律解释和适用方面留下了更多的不确定性和困难。最后,单纯对本条后半款进行理解,法院相较于仲裁机构有更优先的管辖异议决定权,这从广义上否定了自裁管辖原则的含义。然而,最高人民法院 2008 年修订的《关于适用〈中华人民共和国仲裁法〉若干问题的解释》(以下简称《仲裁法解释》)第 13 条规定,依照仲裁法第 20 条第 2 款[①]的规定,当事人在仲裁庭首次开庭前[②]没有对仲裁协议的效力提出异议,而后向人民法院申请确认仲裁协议无效的,人民法院不予受理。仲裁机构对仲裁协议的效力作出决定后,当事人向人民法院申请确认仲裁协议效力或者

---

① 《仲裁法》第 20 条第 2 款规定:"当事人对仲裁协议的效力有异议,应当在仲裁庭首次开庭前提出。"

② 值得注意的是,此条中"首次开庭"与更优先"受理"争议的概念仍存在不同,在时间维度上更为延后。

申请撤销仲裁机构的决定的,人民法院不予受理。从最高人民法院司法解释来看,这种在时间维度上"先到先得"的处理方式,尤其是在仲裁机构先于人民法院接受申请并作出决定的情况下,我国的做法与自裁管辖消极效力的做法并无二致。然而当仲裁机构先于法院受理即剥夺之后任何司法审查的可能性则颇为极端。

综上所述,在我国《仲裁法》和对应司法解释的规定都存在模糊和争议的情况下,最新的司法实践动态对于理解我国的自裁管辖原则意义重大。在2019年高晓力法官代表最高人民法院出席论坛,其讲话稿中指出:"而在我国尚未确立仲裁机构完全自裁管辖权时,确认仲裁协议效力案件理应对当事人是否存在提交仲裁的意思表示进行审查,即关涉当事人表意的事项均应纳入确认仲裁协议效力案件的审查范围,包括仲裁协议是否存在、是否成立、是否有效。"就此,笔者认为此篇讲话可以传递出最高人民法院国际商事法庭在最近的司法实践中的态度,并释放出三个信号:首先,最高人民法院认为,就我国目前的立法规定而言,自裁管辖原则尚未从立法层面得到明确的确立。其次,最高人民法院认为司法实践中应当从最广义的层面理解目前《仲裁法》第20条中对管辖异议规定中"效力"的含义,即涵盖了国际通行做法中的"成立、有效性和范围"三个方面。最后,最高人民法院在管辖权问题中着重强调了对"当事人意思表示"的关注,与上述美国法的做法有某种类似的逻辑。

最高人民法院第一国际商事法庭在2019年9月公布的裁判案例中,某案件的核心争议是涉案仲裁条款是否成立,在某种程度上也反映出最高人民法院目前关于自裁管辖学说的态度。① 本案中,一方当事人申请仲裁,而另一方当事人向法院起诉称仲裁协议不成立,此被公布的裁决是法院在此第一阶段诉讼作出的。可以看到,在法院受理之时,仲裁庭已先于法院受理,但应尚未作出裁决。在这种情况下法院对于仲裁条款是否成立的问题直接采取了全面审查,而不是表面证据审查。同时根据合同分离性理论,法院对主合同是否成立的实体争议未作判断,在裁决中仅判断了仲裁协议成立,随后令双方当事人提交仲裁解决。法院在此处援引了《仲裁法》第20条,以确认自己对于仲裁协议的效力

---

① 北京港中旅维景国际酒店管理有限公司、深圳维景京华酒店有限公司申请确认仲裁协议效力民事裁定书,(2019)最高法民特3号。

具有管辖权。笔者认为，最高人民法院在本案判断仲裁协议有效的说理过程中显示出倾向于支持仲裁的态度，然而，虽然结论上法院认为本案实体争议的管辖权应属于仲裁庭，但是此为对管辖权本身的判断。而关于"管辖权的管辖权"问题，显然法院在第一阶段进行了全面审查并直接作出了判断，并没有基于表面存在的仲裁协议令仲裁庭对此问题进行优先决定。因此，笔者认为，本案与《仲裁法》第20条的规定思路一致，显示了我国目前对仲裁自裁管辖原则的否认。

五、总结与建议

面对中国目前的对于自裁管辖权的立法和司法态度，《仲裁法》亟待进行修订以与国际通行做法更加接近。总体而言，笔者认为，一方面，中国目前在第一阶段给予仲裁庭自裁管辖的权力明显不足，法院仍然具有决定的优先权。这就给试图阻碍或拖延仲裁的当事人可乘之机，也大大降低了仲裁庭完整独立的管辖权。另一方面，司法解释又规定，若仲裁机构先于法院作出决定，那么法院将在第三阶段完全丧失对仲裁协议效力的司法审查权力，这一点与国际通行做法恰恰相反。在一个充分尊重仲裁并最大程度保障仲裁流程高效且顺利进行的法域，恰恰应当在第一阶段限制法院过早过多的司法介入，将对管辖权问题的首次决定权留给仲裁庭，但同时保留法院在第三阶段进行独立司法审查的权力。仲裁庭关于管辖权争议的判断应最好以初步裁决的形式下达，使法院可以更早介入，以免法院否认全部有关实体争议的判决时造成更多司法资源的浪费。同时，法院对于初步裁决的司法审查不必然导致仲裁程序的中止。若仲裁庭对于自身适格管辖权有较大程度的确信，则不必等待法院的裁决，应当有权继续进行对实体争议的审判流程，这样将更好地在仲裁效力和公平/程序效率原则之间实现平衡。

对境外仲裁机构入驻临港新片区相关问题的思考

王楚晴*

摘　要:2020 年 1 月 1 日开始,上海自由贸易试验区临港新片区开放境外仲裁机构进驻,是应对现阶段国际商事争议解决需求的现实需要,也是我国参与经济全球化的必然要求。虽已批准其入驻,但我国对境外仲裁机构在国内开展仲裁业务的相关规定仍未完善。主要存在入驻临港新片区的境外仲裁机构作出的判决在中国的执行问题、法院对其开展仲裁业务的支持问题以及如何处理境外仲裁机构与我国国内仲裁机构的关系这三个问题。对此我们应明确确立仲裁地标准,保障境外仲裁机构作出的仲裁裁决的承认和执行;通过国际商事法庭的"一站式"争议解决平台的形式来加强对境外机构开展仲裁业务的司法支持,提升我国作为仲裁地的魅力;通过境外机构的"引进来",吸收国际一流仲裁实务经验,加强合作交流,带动我国涉外仲裁机构"走出去"开拓海外仲裁市场。

关键词:机遇与挑战　仲裁地　司法支持　走出去

一、问题的提出

2020 年 1 月 1 日开始,上海自由贸易试验区临港新片区开放境外仲裁机构进驻,并允许其在临港新片区内开展仲裁业务。这是我国司法制度以及国内仲裁机构在处理国际商事上无法满足现阶段中国国际商事争议解决需求而带来

---

* 王楚晴,中国政法大学国际法学院师资博士后。

的现实需要,也是我国参与全球化经济导致的必然结果。这一政策的实施打破了境外仲裁机构和中国仲裁市场之间的多年寒冰,为境外仲裁机构开启中国市场大门的同时,也为中国仲裁市场通往国际仲裁市场搭建了阶梯。为中国仲裁事业、中国涉外商事争议解决的繁荣发展带来了无限生机。

在解决国际商事争议上,境外仲裁机构有望成为一项新的助力;随着境外仲裁机构在我国仲裁业务的开展,会让更多的外国当事人、外国仲裁员或者外国仲裁实务人员了解中国仲裁实务,提高中国作为仲裁地的魅力;境外仲裁机构的入驻也会促进境外仲裁实务与国内仲裁实务的交流,使我国仲裁实务与国际一流仲裁实务接轨;并且境外仲裁机构和我国仲裁机构交流合作,带动我国仲裁机构在国际商事仲裁领域的发展。

但是我国对境外仲裁机构在国内开展仲裁业务的相关规定未完善,因此,如何应对境外仲裁机构进入中国仲裁市场以后带来的问题引人担忧。主要存在下述三个问题:

第一,入驻临港新片区的境外仲裁机构作出的判决在中国的执行问题。从以往外国机构作出的判决在中国法院申请执行的案例来看,存在各地法院作出的裁定不一致的问题。同时,与以往不同,我国已经赋予了境外仲裁机构临港新片区办事处开展仲裁业务的权限。因此,中国法院应以何种方式来对临港新片区境外仲裁机构作出的仲裁裁决进行认定,并以何种方式在中国执行的问题还亟待解决。

第二,法院对入驻临港新片区的境外仲裁机构开展仲裁业务的支持问题。众所周知,仲裁机构虽是独立解决商事争议的机构,但其仅仅是私人机构,因此在开展仲裁业务时,仲裁的顺利进行离不开法院的支持。由于临港新片区配套司法保障建设还未完善,应如何对临港新片区境外仲裁机构开展仲裁业务进行支持的问题还需做好应对。

第三,如何处理境外仲裁机构与我国国内仲裁机构的关系的问题。境外仲裁机构的入驻给我国仲裁机构的发展带来机遇与挑战,我国仲裁机构应如何把握机遇、迎接挑战这一问题引人深思。

基于上述问题意识,本文的基本内容包括如下四个部分:第二部分结合中国国情分析境外仲裁机构入驻临港新片区的必要性以及对我国仲裁领域的影响;第三部分是结合中国实务界、专家界以及外国经验来解决境外仲裁机构作出的商事裁决在中国执行的问题;第四部分是思考如何来确保境外机构的仲裁业务顺利开展;第五部分是分析解决如何依靠境外机构的“引进来”带动我国仲裁机构的“走出去”。

二、境外仲裁机构的进驻——机遇? 挑战?

其实,对于外国的当事人来说通过对方当事人的国家司法诉讼来解决他们之间的争议会存在一定的担忧:“大多数在国际上开展业务的公司都不愿由其客户所在地的法院来处理争议。他们害怕腐败或地方保护主义的法官;他们不熟悉当地的法律(因此对其持怀疑态度);他们试图避免不一致的结果;他们更喜欢私下解决争议,而不是公开审判;他们可能不熟悉当地的语言和习俗;他们希望达成统一的协议,而不是修改合同,来符合许多司法管辖区不明确的要求。”①

同时,中国涉外民事诉讼制度在处理涉外民商事关系方面存在滞后性。②中国民事诉讼制度中关于涉外民事诉讼程序部分的特别规定自 2012 年到现在,并没有实质上的改变。③ 但是现今中国社会的经济结构,对外开放程度,以及国际商事的参与都不可同日而语。随着对外开放程度的提高,我国逐渐成为世界上的贸易大国,也就意味着越来越多的中国当事人和中国涉外商事争议解决工作者将参与到国际商事争议解决中来。④ 自然地现今对于涉外商事争议解决的需求也就与以往不同。

因此,中国一直重视坚持多元化纠纷解决机制的发展,灵活运用仲裁的优

---

① F. Peter Phillips, *The Challenges of International Commercial Dispute Resolution*, CPRhttps://www.businessconflictmanagement.com/pdf/BCMpress_01.pdf. “[M]ost companies doingbusiness internationally are reluctant to enter their customer’s courts. They fear corrupt or protective judges; they are unfamiliar with (and therefore skeptical of) local law; they seek to avoid inconsistent outcomes; they prefer private conflict resolution to public trial; they may be unfamiliar with local language and custom; they wish to pursue uniform agreements rather than modifying their contracts to comply with the sometimes obscure requirements of scores of jurisdictions”.

② 参见何其生:《大国司法理念与中国国际民事诉讼制度的发展》,载《中国社会科学》2017 年第 5 期。

③ 同上注。

④ 参见李庆明:《境外仲裁机构在中国内地仲裁的法律问题研究》,载《环球法律评论》2016 年第 3 期。

势来弥补中国司法制度在解决涉外商事纠纷上的不足。

在改革开放初期，中国司法系统还未成熟，仲裁成为外国投资者和中国企业之间解决争议的重要手段。[①] 这成为奠定仲裁在中国国际商事争议解决领域的优势地位的关键因素，也是仲裁作为国际商事争议解决手段在中国得以快速发展的决定性因素。1995 年仲裁法实施以来，27 年间中国仲裁机关受理的案件数量逐年递增，年均增长率超 30%。[②] 从 1995 年平均 1000 多件案件到 2018 年 54 万案件，可以说我国仲裁事业的发展有了长足的进步。[③]

随着仲裁制度在中国的发展，中国仲裁机构的数量也在不断增加。现阶段，已经有 250 多家仲裁机构。但是在数量众多的仲裁机构当中，有能力受理涉外商事仲裁案件的仲裁机构屈指可数，比如说中国国际经济贸易仲裁委员会、北京仲裁中心、上海国际仲裁中心、深圳国际仲裁中心等少数仲裁机构。这几个少数能够胜任涉外商事仲裁案件的仲裁机构所在的区域可以反映出，各地经济贸易繁荣程度带来的中国仲裁发展不均衡的现实问题。[④] 此外，中国国际经济贸易仲裁委员会秘书长王承杰先生认为，在中国国际商事仲裁领域，“我国仲裁事业还存在着全社会对仲裁意识比较淡薄、仲裁制度尚需完善、国际仲裁专家人才不足、国际仲裁话语权亟待提高等现象，这些问题在一定程度上束缚了我国仲裁的发展”[⑤]。

由于我国仲裁在处理国际商事争议方面存在上述问题，我国通过仲裁来解决日益增多的国际商事争议的策略受到了限制。因此，可以说引入境外仲裁机构成为了必然趋势，也是解决我国国际商事争议的客观需求。

但是一直以来，境外仲裁机构在中国进行仲裁业务是不被允许的。而随着上海自由贸易试验区的扩张并于2019 年 8 月 6 日设立临港新片区以来，上海人民法院受理的临港新片区的案件也一直在增加。从 2019 年 9 月 1 日到 12 月

---

① See Jerome A. Cohen, *Settling International Business Disputes with China: Then and Now*, Cornell International Law Journal, Fall, 2014, p. 558.

② 参见《仲裁已成为解决民商事纠纷主渠道之一》，载《法治日报》2019 年 3 月 26 日。

③ 同上注。

④ 参见何晶晶、惠宁宁：《全力打造贸仲委国际一流争端解决机构助力我国国际仲裁中心建设——专访中国国际经济贸易仲裁委员会副主任兼秘书长王承杰》，载《人民法治》2018 年第 5 期。

⑤ 同上注。

25日的统计数据来看,仅仅设立了四个多月的临港新片区就有了2487件案件。[①] 这体现了临港新片区内国际商事争议解决机制的构建的必要性与紧迫性。

2019年12月13日,最高人民法院发布了《关于人民法院为中国(上海)自由贸易试验区临港新片区建设提供司法服务和保障的意见》(以下简称《自贸区意见》),明确了对未来临港新片区的司法建设的总体方针,其中也包括了构建临港新片区国际商事争议机制的总体方针。

《自贸区意见》在国际商事争议解决机制的司法建设方面,特别强调应坚持改革创新(第2条),加强新片区国际商事审判组织建设(第4条),完善诉讼、仲裁与调解一站式纠纷解决机制(第7条)等。但是从效力上来讲,《自贸区意见》仅仅是对于如何推进构建临港新片区的国际商事争议解决机制的指导性意见,还需要通过相关法律规定来具体落实《自贸区意见》中的指示精神,而这个意见为具体落实提供了一个总体的工作方向。

《自贸区意见》中强调为营造新片区国际一流法治化营商环境,在2020年开始引入经登记备案的境外仲裁机构在新片区就国际商事、海事、投资等领域发生的民商事纠纷开展仲裁业务(第6条),并完善新片区内多元化纠纷解决机制,确定打造上海成为亚太仲裁中心的工作方向与目标。

上海市司法局出台的《境外仲裁机构在中国(上海)自由贸易区试验区临港新片区设立业务机构管理办法》[②](以下简称《自贸区管理办法》),虽早于《自贸区意见》,却也体现了意见中提到的建设临港新片区的精神。

根据《自贸区管理办法》,2020年1月1日开始,外国和我国香港、澳门特别行政区、台湾地区合法成立的不以营利为目的的仲裁机构,以及我国加入的国际组织设立的开展仲裁业务的机构(第3条),可就国际商事、海事、投资等领域发生的民商事争议开展以下仲裁业务:案件受理、庭审、听证、裁决;案件管理和服务;业务咨询、指引、培训、研讨(第14条)。

在临港新片区开展业务的境外仲裁机构还需要向上海市司法局进行设立

---

① 参见《上海高院发布服务保障临港新片区建设实施意见》,载中国新闻网,http://www.chinanews.com.cn/cj/2019/12-30/9047090.shtml。

② 参见《境外仲裁机构在中国(上海)自由贸易试验区临港新片区设立业务机构管理办法》,沪司规〔2019〕5号,2019年10月21日发布。

申请。提出申请的境外机构需在境外合法成立并存续5年以上；在境外实质性开展仲裁业务，有较高国际知名度；业务机构负责人没有因故意犯罪受过刑事处罚（《自贸区管理办法》第6条）。

早在2015年国务院批准《进一步深化中国（上海）自由贸易试验区改革开放方案》之后，HKIAC、ICC、SIAC就相继在上海自由贸易试验区设立了办事处。该方案指出："进一步对接国际商事争议解决规则，优化自贸试验区仲裁规则，支持国际知名商事争议解决机构入驻，提高商事纠纷仲裁国际化程度。探索建立全国性的自贸试验区仲裁法律服务联盟和亚太仲裁机构交流合作机制，加快打造面向全球的亚太仲裁中心。"[①]其明确表明了上海市自由贸易试验区支持境外知名仲裁机构的入驻，但是没有许可境外仲裁机构在自由贸易试验区内开展仲裁业务。而据北京天同律师事务所合伙人顾嘉律师所述，入驻的三家境外知名机构虽未立即开展业务，但也开始进行进驻中国仲裁市场的筹备工作。

"笔者和上述三家国际仲裁机构的驻华首席代表有过多次深入交流，得知他们在中国《仲裁法》没有明确赋予境外仲裁机构在华管理仲裁案件之前，都采取了较为保守和稳妥的动作，即仅在中国内地推广境外仲裁机构的仲裁规则，加强与境内企业、律师事务所和其他仲裁机构的联系，而不会公开地管理在华仲裁案件。"[②]

对于是否应该向境外仲裁机构开放市场的问题，可能会有人存在一定的担忧，但是如前所述，引入境外仲裁机构是现阶段解决国际商事争议的现实需要，也是必然结果。尽管在中国国际商事仲裁市场领域与中国国内仲裁机构有产生竞争的可能性，也面临境外仲裁机构的业务开展对法院的司法审查工作和仲裁相关法律制度带来新的挑战，但是总体上会为我国仲裁事业的发展带来巨大的机遇。

相比于挑战来说，境外仲裁机构在中国开展仲裁业务带来更多的应该是机遇。境外仲裁机构在我国开展仲裁业务可以让更多的外国当事人、外国律师以及外国仲裁实务界了解到我国作为仲裁地的魅力，从而带动更多的国际商事争

① 《进一步深化中国（上海）自由贸易试验区改革开放方案》。

② 顾嘉：《境外仲裁机构在华管理仲裁案件的"蝴蝶效应"》，载微信公众号"天同诉讼圈"2019年8月23日，http://www.tiantonglaw.com/Content/2020/06-28/1608085120.html。

议解决来到中国,扩大我国国际仲裁市场。境外仲裁机构在中国开展仲裁业务也会使我国国内仲裁机构在国际商事争议解决领域的知名度变高,在国际上的公信力随之增加,使我国国内仲裁机构走出中国去往境外开办分支办事处变为可能,同时也使我国仲裁法、仲裁机构吸收国际上的一流的创新制度与经验成为可能。[①]

面对巨大的机遇,我们应该完善相关法律制度,以及便利仲裁机构开展工作的配套措施,才能够把握住机遇,借此之际发展我国仲裁事业。同时,也借此之际,发展壮大我国国内仲裁机构,使其更多地参与到国际商事仲裁实务中去,与国际接轨。

三、确立仲裁地标准

随着政策的开放,HKIAC、ICC、SIAC 等早期就意识到中国仲裁市场的世界有名的仲裁机构也有望入驻上海临港新片区,在新片区开展仲裁业务。这就带来了一个实务问题,即在临港新片区登记备案的境外仲裁机构作出的仲裁裁决应该以何种形式在我国承认和执行的问题,是应该认定上述的仲裁裁决为外国仲裁裁决,按照《纽约公约》的相关规定进行承认和执行仲裁裁决的司法审查,还是应该认定上述的仲裁裁决为中国仲裁裁决,由于包含涉外因素,因而适用中国涉外仲裁裁决的特别规定进行司法审查?这就涉及应该如何认定临港新片区内境外仲裁机构作出的仲裁裁决的国籍。

仲裁裁决国籍的认定标准,通常有仲裁地标准和仲裁程序法标准两种。[②]采用仲裁地认定标准的话,在中国以外的国家作出的仲裁裁决在中国申请承认和执行时应被认定为外国仲裁裁决。采用仲裁程序法认定标准的话,无论仲裁地是哪里,适用外国程序法作出的仲裁裁决在中国申请承认和执行时应被认定为外国仲裁裁决。

从中国的实务上来看,中国法院在审查是否承认和执行境外仲裁机构作出

---

① 参见牛磊、刘震:《静待花开——境外仲裁机构中国之路的机遇与挑战》,载微信公众号“中伦视界”2019 年 11 月 14 日,https://mp. weixin. qq. com/s? _biz = MjM5ODI5MzI0NA = = &mid = 26513110258idx = 1&sn = 1ba89be3f3e72084584d62e005bb8ed。

② 参见高晓力:《司法应依仲裁地而非仲裁机构所在地确定仲裁裁决籍属》,载《人民司法(案例)》2017 年第 20 期。

的仲裁裁决时到底是按照仲裁地标准还是按照仲裁程序法标准，目前还不明确。根据大多数学者的意见以及最高人民法院的近期裁定来看，更偏向于采用仲裁地标准来确定仲裁裁决的国籍。①

在中国法院对仲裁裁决国籍进行判断的实务当中，以仲裁地为判断基准进行司法审查的案件较多。2015 年到 2017 年对仲裁裁决进行司法审查的 81 件案件当中，有 50 件采用了仲裁地标准。② 并且在 2015 年的一起向北京第四中级人民法院申请执行 ICC 在中国香港作出的仲裁裁决的案件当中，北京第四中级人民法院也采用了仲裁地标准。在该司法审查当中，北京第四中级人民法院采用仲裁地标准，认定 ICC 在中国香港作出的仲裁裁决应属于中国香港的仲裁裁决，按照内地与中国香港之间执行仲裁裁决的规定进行执行。③

因此，按照多数的意见，临港新片区的境外仲裁机构作出的仲裁裁决的国籍的判断应采用仲裁地标准。而仲裁地并非一个具体的地理地点，有些情况下仲裁庭的开庭地、仲裁机构所在地，或者合意地可能存在与仲裁地不一致的现象。④ 因此，我们不能单纯地认为临港新片区境外仲裁机构作出的仲裁裁决的仲裁地都是中国，都应看作中国国内的涉外仲裁裁决来进行承认和执行。

那么，接下来需要考虑的问题就是如何确定仲裁地。按照国际实务经验、仲裁机构的相关规定，以及国内仲裁实务，当事人自治原则都是普遍接受的，即当事人可以自由约定仲裁地。如果双方当事人约定其他国家作为仲裁地，尽管仲裁庭的开庭地点、审理地点或者仲裁机构的办公地点是在中国的领域内，仲裁裁决也应视为由仲裁地作出而认定其为外国仲裁裁决，通过《纽约公约》在中国承认和执行。如果双方当事人约定中国作为仲裁地，由于临港新片区境外仲裁机构作出的仲裁裁决具有涉外因素，应认定为中国涉外仲裁裁决来进行承认

---

① 参见李庆明：《境外仲裁机构在中国内地仲裁的法律问题研究》，载《环球法律评论》2016 年第 3 期；宋连斌、王珺：《国际商会在中国内地仲裁：准入、裁决国籍及执行——由宁波中院的一份裁定谈起》，载《西北大学学报（哲学社会科学版）》2011 年第 3 期；高晓力：《中国法院承认和执行外国仲裁裁决的积极实践》，载《法律适用》2018 年第 5 期。

② 参见刘敬东、王路路：《“一带一路”倡议下我国对外国仲裁裁决承认与执行的实证研究》，载《法律适用》2018 年第 5 期。

③ 参见季境、温志军：《国际商事仲裁裁判国籍籍属的认定》，载《人民司法》2019 年第 14 期。

④ Gary B. Born, *International Commercial Arbitration*, 2nd edition (Kluwer Law International 2014), p. 2051.

和执行。

那么,如果双方当事人没有约定仲裁地,一般来说是由仲裁庭或者仲裁机构来决定。① 以 SIAC 和 ICC 的仲裁规则为例进行说明。

《SIAC 仲裁规则》(第 6 版)第 21 条规定,当事人可以约定仲裁地。当事人没有约定的,仲裁地由仲裁庭在考虑全部案情后予以确定。仲裁庭有权按照仲裁庭认为便捷、适当的任何方式,在仲裁庭认为便利、适合的任何地点开庭和举行会议。②

《ICC 仲裁规则》(2012 年版)第 18 条规定,(1)仲裁地由仲裁院确定,但当事人另有约定者除外。(2)经与各当事人协商,仲裁庭可在其认为适当的任何地点开庭和举行会议,但当事人另有约定者除外。(3)仲裁庭可以在其认为适当的任何地点进行合议。③

一般来说,临港新片区的境外仲裁机构受理的案件大多是在中国产生的与中国联系紧密的国际民商事案件,因此,在中国开庭,接受中国法院的支持,很大可能会被认为是便利且适合的。

另外,对于仲裁地的确定,我们也可以参考在迪拜国际金融中心(Dubai International Financial Centre, DIFC)内部设立办事处的伦敦国际仲裁法院(The London Court of International Arbitration, LCIA)的经验。④

LCIA 是总部设在伦敦的解决国际商事纠纷的组织。⑤ 2008 年 LCIA 和 DIFC 合作,在 DIFC 内部成立了 DIFC - LCIA 仲裁中心。⑥ 其实境外机构进驻上海临港新片区的政策与总部位于伦敦的 LCIA 进驻 DIFC 的举措很相似。因此,DIFC - LCIA 仲裁中心的仲裁规则对于仲裁地的确定的条款也可以说是为即将入驻临港新片区的境外仲裁机构提供了样本。DIFC - LCIA 仲裁中心仲裁规则(2016 年版)第 16 条第 2 款规定:"当事人若无约定,除非仲裁庭根据情况

---

① Gary B. Born, *International Commercial Arbitration*, 2nd edition (Kluwer Law International 2014), p. 2053.

② 《新加坡国际仲裁中心仲裁规则》(第 6 版)第 21 条。

③ 《ICC 仲裁规则》(2012 年版)。

④ 参见石静霞、董暖:《我国国际商事法庭的若干核心问题》,载《西安交通大学学报(社会科学版)》2019 年第 3 期。

⑤ 参见 LCIA 官网介绍的部分。

⑥ 参见 DIFC - LCIA Arbitration Centre 官网 Overview 部分。

并在给予当事各方合理的机会向仲裁庭提出书面意见后作出认为其他仲裁地更合适的命令以外，仲裁地应该是迪拜国际金融中心，迪拜。”①

因此，根据上述的国内实务以及国际实务上的经验来看，在各方当事人没有约定仲裁地的情况下，中国被指定为仲裁地的可能性很大。如果中国（香港特别行政区、澳门特别行政区及台湾地区除外）作为仲裁地，那么临港新片区境外仲裁机构作出的仲裁裁决应视为中国涉外仲裁裁决，按照中国《民事诉讼法》第 281 条以及第 282 条的规定进行承认和执行司法审查。

四、加强司法支持

如上所述，在临港新片区的境外仲裁机构受理的仲裁案件中，中国作为仲裁地的可能性极大，因此我国在引入境外仲裁机构的同时，应充分明确仲裁地的意义，意识到我国作为仲裁地的责任与使命。确定仲裁地的意义，就在于若各方当事人对适用法律约定不明，那么仲裁地的法律就会成为认定仲裁协议效力的准据法、仲裁规则以外的程序的准据法以及仲裁中争议的实体法，并且仲裁地法院对仲裁程序中的保全措施以及撤销仲裁裁决司法审查提供支持。② 实践中，当事人除了考虑交通、基础设施等方面以外，也会考虑法律环境来确定仲裁地。③ 但是我国司法实践对于境外仲裁机构在内地仲裁的认定存在不一致的问题，导致境外的法院和当事人对我国仲裁界的实务以及我国法院的仲裁司法审查水准的判断有所偏差。④ 司法审查认定不一致问题带来的对我国法律环境的负面评价会影响外国当事人对我国作为仲裁地能力的判断。在中国香港高等法院⑤和新加坡高等法院⑥的判决中都显示了，我国司法实践中的不确定性带来的潜在风险会阻碍外国当事人或者境外仲裁机构选定我国作为仲裁地。

---

① DIFC－LCIA Arbitration Rules 2016，Art. 16（2）.

② 参见高晓力：《司法应依仲裁地而非仲裁机构所在地确定仲裁裁决籍属》，载《人民司法（案例）》2017 年第 20 期。

③ 参见宋连斌、王珺：《国际商会在中国内地仲裁：准入、裁决国籍及执行——由宁波中院的一份裁定谈起》，载《西北大学学报（哲学社会科学版）》2011 年第 3 期。

④ 参见李庆明：《境外仲裁机构在中国内地仲裁的法律问题研究》，载《环球法律评论》2016 年第 3 期。

⑤ See Z v. A［2015］HKEC 289.

⑥ See BNA v. BNB［2019］SGHC 142.

因此，应该统一我国对于境外仲裁机构以中国作为仲裁地的仲裁协议和仲裁裁决的认定标准，并完善我国人民法院对境外机构在中国开展仲裁业务的司法支持机制，创建良好的营商环境。① 不然会影响我国国际商事仲裁公信力的建立和仲裁事业国际化的发展，也不利于越来越多“走出去”的中国企业寻求司法救济。

根据最高人民法院公布的指导意见来看，为了做好临港新片区的司法建设工作，有必要创建国际商事审判组织。而在上海高级人民法院根据指导意见颁布的具体方案中，也提到了构建国际商事专门审判组织。但是，具体是什么样的国际商事审判组织还不明确。基于2018年在西安市和深圳市分别设立了专门的国际商事法庭这一背景来考虑，在上海临港新片区设立国际商事法庭作为国际商事专门审判组织是具有现实可能性的。

我国新设立的国际商事法庭开创了调解、仲裁、诉讼“一站式”国际商事纠纷解决机制，对于通过仲裁来解决国际商事争议、仲裁过程中涉及的保全措施以及仲裁裁决的承认和执行的司法审查都大力支持。该“一站式”纠纷解决机制体现了诉讼与仲裁并非敌对关系，通过互帮互助优劣互补而达到共赢的目的这一思想。②

目前为止，由于最高人民法院指定的仲裁机构只有五家，且国际商事法庭（China International Commercial Court，CICC）对所支持的仲裁案件的标的额也有所限制，因此，能够得到CICC支持的仲裁案件还很局限。但《最高人民法院关于设立国际商事法庭若干问题的规定》第11条规定：“最高人民法院组建国际商事专家委员会，并选定符合条件的国际商事调解机构、国际商事仲裁机构与国际商事法庭共同构建调解、仲裁、诉讼有机衔接的纠纷解决平台，形成‘一站式’国际商事纠纷解决机制。”从该条中我们可以得知，最高人民法院选取的符合规定的国际商事仲裁机构，将不仅仅是国内仲裁机构。这就意味着国际商事仲裁机构也有机会被纳入“一站式”国际商事纠纷解决机制当中。因此，为了得到更好的支持，无论是在临港新片区设立新的国际商事专门法庭，还是通过

① 参见沈红雨：《贺荣在2015年“中国仲裁高峰论坛”上强调继续完善仲裁司法审查制度促进仲裁公信力提升》，载《人民法院报》2015年9月26日，第1版。

② 参见汪祖兴、郑夏：《自治与干预——国际商事仲裁当事人合意问题研究》，法律出版社2016年版，第36页。

已有的国际商事法庭来支持境外仲裁机构的运作,都有必要把入驻临港新片区的境外机构纳入“一站式”纠纷解决机制的仲裁机构的名单当中。

考虑到临港新片区内对允许入驻的境外仲裁机构的资格作出了限制,因而把有资格入驻临港新片区的境外知名的国际商事仲裁机构纳入国际商事法庭的“一站式”纠纷解决机制中去也并无不妥。此种做法可以为境外仲裁机构提供最优质的司法支持,向外国当事人、境外机构以及外国仲裁界实务人士展示我国仲裁友好型的形象以及我国法院对国际商事仲裁的司法审查的能力,提高我国仲裁事业的公信力。

当然,在加强对境外机构的司法支持使其仲裁程序高效运作的同时,也必须坚持维护境外机构的独立性。仲裁机构,说到底是解决私人间争议的组织,应该独立于政府体制之外,不受司法体制的制约和控制。这种独立于司法的特点也正是仲裁的魅力之一。而我国的“一站式”纠纷解决机制所提供的司法服务,从表述上来看,并不是法院对仲裁机构的司法监督(judicial supervision)或者司法干预(judicial intervention),而是司法支持。因此,可以看出,CICC 所采取的“一站式”纠纷解决机制不是要对仲裁机构内部的仲裁程序的运营进行监督干预。仅对被纳入“一站式”纠纷解决争议的仲裁机构在需要司法支持的时候,为其提供必要的司法支持。也就是说,境外仲裁机构即使被纳入“一站式”纠纷解决机制,也无须担心会丧失仲裁机构的独立性。

五、境外机构的“引进来”v. 我国仲裁机构的“走出去”

随着仲裁机构的“引进来”,不可否认,在分配中国仲裁市场中国际商事争议解决份额时,国内仲裁机构可能会受到来自境外知名仲裁机构的竞争压力。如果国际商事争议的当事人是外国当事人,对比国内仲裁机构可能会更加信任境外的比较熟悉的仲裁机构。但是,我国的仲裁市场很大,我国的涉外商事仲裁机构的竞争力也并不弱,因此足以面对境外仲裁机构入驻带来的压力。并且,从长远利益来看,境外仲裁机构的入驻为我国仲裁机构发展国际商事仲裁业务带来了新的机会。如前所述,尽管我国仲裁机构取得了长足的发展,但是在国际商事争议解决方面还存在问题。因此,我国仲裁机构更应在境外仲裁机构带来的良性竞争中谋求发展。

一直以来,我国仲裁机构都尤其重视与境外仲裁机构的交流,如与境外仲裁机构通过签订合作备忘录的形式,一起举办仲裁研讨会,或者仲裁员培训会等交流活动来让我国国内仲裁机构吸收国际商事仲裁实务的经验。[①] 现在,随着境外仲裁机构的进驻,我国仲裁机构与国际一流仲裁机构的距离缩短了,交流也就变得更为方便。并且此次对于入驻临港新片区的境外机构的资格作出了严格的限制,只有在国际上有很高知名度的境外仲裁机构才会被许可。而在境外具有高度知名度的境外仲裁机构被"引进来"的同时,也为我们带来了国际商事仲裁领域有丰富经验的仲裁员和律师等人才资源,国际一流的仲裁实务经验,以及完备的国际商事仲裁规则。

因此,我国仲裁机构应该把握住机遇,不断吸纳优秀的国际商事仲裁领域的人才,不断完善现阶段的国际商事仲裁规则,不断提升中国仲裁机构的公信力和影响力,为争议当事人提供更高品质的法律服务。[②] 同时也应该通过圆桌会议、研讨会等会议的形式来增加交流,有助于我国仲裁机构掌握现阶段国际商事争议领域的热点问题、把握国际商事仲裁领域新动态、及时了解外国国际商事仲裁环境。

在充实我国仲裁机构在中国境内的发展以外,随着我国更多企业的"走出去",我国的仲裁机构也应该"走出去",为在境外谋求法律服务的我国企业争议解决提供支持。中国国际经济贸易仲裁委员会早在2018年就开始了我国仲裁机构"走出去"的第一步。除了国内的各个分会以外,中国国际经济贸易仲裁委员会于2018年7月1日在加拿大设立了北美仲裁中心,紧接着在2018年9月28日设立了欧洲仲裁中心。这也为我国其他的涉外仲裁机构起到了示范作用,也是今后我国涉外仲裁机构的发展方向。

因此,应当把握境外仲裁机构仲裁业务的开展带来的崭新机遇,提高我国作为仲裁地的魅力,扩大我国国际商事仲裁市场。并且,使我国国内仲裁机构的国际商事仲裁实务与国际上的一流仲裁实务保持一致。在发展中国国内仲裁机构,保障"一带一路"相关商事争议解决的同时,[③]也期待通过境外仲裁机

① 以北京仲裁委员会为例,其于2019年与新加坡国际仲裁中心的签订了合作备忘录来增进交流合作。

② 参见沈红雨:《贺荣在2015年"中国仲裁高峰论坛"上强调继续完善仲裁司法审查制度促进仲裁公信力提升》,载《人民法院报》2015年9月26日,第1版。

③ 参见漆彤:《"一带一路"国际经贸法律问题研究》,高等教育出版社2018年版,第81页。

构的“引进来”来促进双方的交流合作，带动我国更多的仲裁机构“走出去”。[①]

六、结语

境外仲裁机构入驻中国仲裁市场，是应对现阶段国际商事争议解决需求的现实需要，也是我国参与经济全球化的必然要求。其为我国解决国际商事争议带来助力，也为我国涉外仲裁事业发展带来新的可能性的同时，如何应对境外仲裁机构入驻带来的法律问题也是当前面临的重要挑战。

首先，对于临港新片区内境外仲裁机构所作出的仲裁裁决的承认和执行，按照近些年的司法审查实践以及专家学者的意见来看，应明确确立采用仲裁地的标准。如若采用仲裁地的判断基准，那么在仲裁地为中国（除香港特别行政区、澳门特别行政区及台湾地区）的情况下，仲裁裁决视为中国作出的仲裁裁决，按照中国涉外仲裁裁决来承认和执行仲裁裁决（仲裁地为香港特别行政区、澳门特别行政区及台湾地区的情况下按照内地与该地区之间的安排进行对仲裁裁决承认和执行）；仲裁地为中国境外的情况下，仲裁裁决视为在中国境外作出的仲裁裁决，按照《纽约公约》在中国承认和执行。对于仲裁地的确定问题，若当事人之间有约定的应从其约定，无约定的应由仲裁庭决定。从目前仲裁机构的仲裁规则中指定便利适合的地点为仲裁地的规定以及 LCIA 在 DIFC 的设立的 DIFC - LCIA 的仲裁规则中指定迪拜为仲裁地来看，中国极有可能被仲裁庭指定为仲裁地。那么临港新片区内境外仲裁机构所作出的仲裁裁决极有可能按照中国涉外仲裁裁决承认执行的相关规定或者内地和香港特别行政区、澳门特别行政区及台湾地区之间仲裁裁决承认和执行的相关安排来进行司法审查。

其次，为确保境外仲裁机构的仲裁业务顺利开展，还应加强司法的支持。目前在我国司法实践中存在的司法审查认定不一致的问题所带来的不确定性不利于我国作为仲裁地的作用的发挥，也就会影响境外仲裁机构在中国开展仲裁业务的确定性。因此，可以考虑把临港新片区境外仲裁机构加入调解、仲裁以及诉讼“一站式”纠纷解决机制的仲裁机构的名单当中，通过国际商事法庭来为境外仲裁机构开展仲裁业务中的仲裁裁决效力认定、仲裁保全措施申请、仲

① 参见季境、温志军：《国际商事仲裁裁判国籍籍属的认定》，载《人民司法》2019 年第 14 期。

裁裁决承认和执行以及仲裁裁决的撤销等方面提供更优质高效的司法审查。此外,也可以在临港新片区成立 CICC 来为仲裁机构提供更好的司法支持。并且,在加强司法支持的同时还应当保持仲裁机构的独立性。

最后,通过境外仲裁机构入驻带来的良性竞争带动中国涉外仲裁机构的发展,带动我国更多的仲裁机构"走出去"。在临港新片区允许开展仲裁业务的境外仲裁机构的资格上有较高的要求,因此高评价的机构可以带来优秀的仲裁员人才、先进的仲裁程序制度和互助互利的合作机会。把握境外机构的"引进来"政策带来的机遇,引领我国更多涉外机构"走出去",为走出去的中国企业提供更便利的仲裁服务。

境外仲裁机构开放中国仲裁市场,带来的不仅仅是挑战,更多的是发展机遇。我们应明确确立仲裁地标准,保障境外仲裁机构作出的仲裁裁决的承认和执行;通过 CICC 的"一站式"争议解决平台的形式来加强对境外机构开展仲裁业务的司法支持,提升我国作为仲裁地的魅力;通过境外机构的"引进来",吸收国际一流仲裁实务经验,加强合作交流,带动我国涉外仲裁机构"走出去"开拓海外仲裁市场。我们应以此来应对挑战,迎接机遇。

国际商事仲裁中快速程序的困境与消解

——兼评 UNCITRAL 快速仲裁规则

陈凡凯*

摘　要:国际商事仲裁中的快速程序以恢复仲裁效率性特征为目标,实践中成效显著,同时也面临困境,即程序简化与正当程序的冲突以及仲裁机构管理权扩张与当事人意思自治的冲突,其本质是仲裁效率价值和公正价值的冲突。为了消解这一困境,一方面应当坚持程序公正,保障当事人基本程序性权利,另一方面应当尊重当事人意思自治,从对当事人真实意思的解释、仲裁机构内部监督和司法外部监督维度提供解决问题的方案。最后,UNCITRAL 快速仲裁规则作为快速程序规则的最新发展,在对高效的实现、对当事人程序性权利的保障和对当事人意思自治的尊重方面有重要的促进作用。

关键词:快速程序　正当程序　仲裁机构管理权　意思自治　UNCITRAL 快速仲裁规则

一、快速程序的产生及其价值

商事仲裁作为一种争议解决方式,自产生之初就被冠以“快速、便捷和廉价”的特征,商事仲裁的效率是商人创造和选择这一途径以替代诉讼的原因之

* 陈凡凯,中国政法大学国际法学院硕士研究生。

一。[①] 然而,近年来,仲裁的效率优势被频频质疑。根据玛丽女王大学 2015 年的调查报告[②]和 2018 年的调查报告[③],在被问到"国际仲裁三个最糟糕的特征是什么"这一问题的时候,仲裁费用高昂被认为是国际仲裁中最糟糕的特征,"在仲裁过程中缺乏有效的制裁"的特征位于第二,缺乏速度同样备受诟病,同时当事人还对他们对仲裁员和仲裁机构办事效率的了解程度不满。2021 年的调查报告虽然没有对这一问题展开调查,但是这一报告援引 2018 年调查报告的内容,指出时间和成本一直被认为是仲裁用户最关心的问题,提高效率则被认为是仲裁未来发展的主要驱动因素。[④] 因此,仲裁效率在实践中的减损已经成为了制约仲裁发展的一个重要因素。

仲裁的"诉讼化"趋势是制约仲裁程序效率的原因之一。所谓仲裁的"诉讼化",是指仲裁在程序运作上像诉讼程序那样复杂和正式。[⑤] 尽管有学者认为仲裁的"诉讼化"并不一定是一件坏事,因为它兼顾了国际商事仲裁的质量,[⑥]然而这种"诉讼化"意味着仲裁沦为诉讼的附庸,在程序上越来越繁杂,受到的司法干预和审查也越来越多,[⑦]显然已经减损了仲裁的效率性,与仲裁产生伊始当

---

① See Andrew I. Okekeifere, *Commercial Arbitration as the Most Effective Dispute Resolution Method: Still a Fact or Now a Myth?*, 15 Journal of International Arbitration 81 (1998).

② 在 2015 年的调查中,仲裁费用被调查者认为是国际仲裁中最糟糕的特征(68% 的被调查者选择该项),46% 的人选择了"在仲裁过程中缺乏有效的制裁",36% 的人选择了"缺乏速度",39% 的人选择了"不够了解仲裁员的办事效率",12% 的人选择了"不够了解仲裁机构的办事效率"。See Mary Queen University of Londen, 2015 *Improvements and Innovations in International Arbitration*, p. 7, at http://www.arbitration.qmul.ac.uk/media/arbitration/docs/2015_International_Arbitration_Survey.pdf (Last visited on December 20, 2021).

③ 在 2018 年的调查中,67% 的人选择了"仲裁费用",45% 的人选择了"在仲裁过程中缺乏有效的制裁",34% 的人选择了"缺乏速度",30% 的人选择了"不够了解仲裁员的办事效率",11% 的人选择了"不够了解仲裁机构的办事效率"。See Mary Queen University of London, 2018 *International Arbitration Survey: The Evolution of International Arbitration*, p. 8, at http://www.arbitration.qmul.ac.uk/media/arbitration/docs/2018 – International – Arbitration – Survey – – – The – Evolution – of – International – Arbitration – (2).PDF (Last visited on December 20, 2021).

④ See Mary Queen University of London, 2021 *International Arbitration Survey: Adapting Arbitration to a Changing World*, p. 13, at http://www.arbitration.qmul.ac.uk/media/arbitration/docs/LON0320037 – QMUL – International – Arbitration – Survey – 2021_19_WEB.pdf (Last visited on December 20, 2021).

⑤ 参见丛雪莲、罗楚湘:《仲裁诉讼化若干问题探讨》,载《法学评论》2007 年第 6 期。

⑥ See Leon Trakman & Hugh Montgomery, *The Judicialization of International Commercial Arbitration: Pitfall or Virtue*, 30 LJIL 432 – 434 (2017).

⑦ 参见邓杰:《商事仲裁改革国际潮流下的加速仲裁程序》,载《上海师范大学学报(哲学社会科学版)》2018 年第 6 期。

事人希望更有效率解决纠纷的初衷不符。除此之外,更有观点称,现今的国际商事仲裁是病态而荒谬的,非专家仲裁员的出现使得仲裁过程需要寻求外界帮助,律师的参与使得诉讼式的思维方式引入仲裁而加剧仲裁"诉讼化",当事人对程序的滥用使仲裁逐渐"平庸化",既快速又便宜的仲裁程序离我们渐行渐远。①

因此,寻求新的程序规则以重拾仲裁制度的效率性成为必要,快速仲裁程序应运而生。从某种程度上来说,快速仲裁程序是一种对效率的复归或者重拾,其高效和快速的中心目标也是仲裁制度本身所追求的价值。②

二、快速程序的两大困境

快速程序以快速高效为目标,重拾仲裁的效率价值。然而,在追求这种效率价值的同时,快速程序的困境也由于实践的深入而不断浮出水面:一是程序简化与当事人程序性权利的冲突,二是仲裁机构管理权扩张与当事人意思自治的冲突。

困境一:程序简化与当事人程序性权利的冲突

一方面,程序简化可能导致对正当程序的违反。正当程序要求当事人被倾听和被告知,要求当事人获得通知并对案件发表主张,③而快速仲裁程序中一些程序性事项的简化给可能导致当事人这一基本程序性权利受到减损,主要体现在开庭方式、证据和听证程序上。

根据各个仲裁机构的快速仲裁规则,一些程序上的简化成为仲裁机构之间的共识。首先,在征求当事人意见之后,仲裁庭可以决定案件仅仅根据当事人提交的书面材料进行审理,而可不进行开庭审理,也可不进行听证程序或者询问证人或专家。④ 其次,仲裁庭可以限制当事人书面提交的证据材料和证人证

① See Michael Mustill, *Comments on Fast - Track Arbitration*, 10 Journal of International Arbitration, 122 - 125 (1993).

② See Irene Welser and Christian Klausegger, *Fast Track Arbitration: Just Fast or Something Different?*, 2009 Austrian Arbitration Yearbook 2009, 272 - 274 (2009).

③ 参见中国国际仲裁30人:《1958年〈承认与执行外国仲裁裁决公约〉(〈纽约公约〉)理论与适用》,法律出版社2020年版,第113页。

④ For example, 2021 ICC Arbitration Rules Appendix VI Art. 3.5, 2016 SIAC Rules Act. 5.2(c) and 2018 HKIAC Administered Arbitration Rules Act. 42.2(e).

言的数量、长度、范围。①

虽然这些规则的前提都要求仲裁庭与当事人进行协商，但是在实践过程中，这些程序的简化给当事人造成的麻烦是显而易见的。已经有学者对此产生了担忧，认为根据仲裁规则，仲裁庭可以对当事人提交证据的数量和时间进行限制，因此必须要确保当事人之间的平等性和遵守正当程序的重要性，因为可能出现这种情况：申请人在启动仲裁程序之前有充足的时间准备案件，但由于快速程序严格的时间限制，被申请人的准备将是不充分的，这对被告而言不公平，因此保障各方当事人尤其是被申请人充分陈述案情的权利尤为重要。② 如果当事人陈述案情的权利在快速仲裁程序中未得到保障，将可能招致国家法院对最终仲裁裁决的撤销或者不予承认与执行，所以应当对当事人这一程序性权利报以最大的谨慎和关注。③

另一方面，对裁决说理的简化可能导致裁决难以得到承认与执行。要求仲裁员在裁决中进行说理是当事人的一项程序性权利，但是在仲裁机构制定的仲裁规则中，当事人可以通过一致意见要求仲裁庭简化说理甚至不说理。④ 从仲裁庭与当事人沟通和协商这一做法来看，这一规定本身没有什么问题，但是在最终的承认与执行程序中，缺乏裁决理由的仲裁裁决可能会因为违反公共政策而不被承认与执行。已经有学者注意到了这一点，例如德国、西班牙、奥地利等国法院都有先例认为在裁决中说理是该国的一项基本原则，从而认定缺乏说理的裁决违反当地的公共政策，最终根据《承认及执行外国仲裁裁决公约》（以下简称《纽约公约》）第 5 条第 2 款乙项拒绝承认与执行这样的裁决。⑤ 故当事人应当注意到这一点，在追求效率的同时应当考察执行地的公共政策以规避这种风险。

---

① For example, 2021 ICC Arbitration Rules Appendix VI Art. 3. 4.

② See Javier Tarjuelo, *Fast Track Procedures: A New Trend in Institutional Arbitration*, 11 Disp. Resol. Int'l 114 (2017).

③ See Irene Welser and Christian Klausegger, *Fast Track Arbitration: Just Fast or Something Different?*, 2009 Austrian Arbitration Yearbook 2009, 270 – 271 (2009).

④ For example, 2016 SIAC Rules Act. 5. 2(e) and 2018 HKIAC Administered Arbitration Rules Act. 42. 2(g).

⑤ See Javier Tarjuelo, *Fast Track Procedures: A New Trend in Institutional Arbitration*, 11 Disp. Resol. Int'l 115 – 116 (2017).

困境二:仲裁机构管理权扩张与当事人意思自治的冲突

在国际仲裁实践中,仲裁机构管理权呈现扩张的趋势,这既是人类社会从无序到有序发展过程的体现,也是对仲裁效率的一种现实需求,是对仲裁程序灵活性特征下当事人基于意思自治所引发的负面效应的回应和规制。① 然而,当事人意思自治是仲裁程序的基石,应当贯穿仲裁程序的始终,仲裁机构管理权的扩张必然导致两者之间发生冲突,使两者在某些情况下处于一种紧张关系,所以如何解释当事人的仲裁条款以及仲裁机构的仲裁规则就显得尤为重要。

仲裁机构管理权扩张与当事人意思自治的冲突主要体现在是否强制适用独任仲裁员上。针对仲裁规则的适用方式,各个仲裁机构之间存在不同的实践,其中如国际商会仲裁院(The ICC International Court of Arbitration)采取的是限额自动适用模式(opt out),即如果争议金额不超过规定的限额,除非当事人合意排除适用快速程序,否则自动适用该程序。② 类似地,新加坡国际仲裁中心(Singapore International Arbitration Centre,SIAC)快速程序的适用本质上和限额自动适用模式一致,只是增加了一方当事人提出申请以启动程序的行为要求。③ 因此,如果当事人选择了如国际商会仲裁院或 SIAC 这样的仲裁规则,那么案件极易落入限额自动适用快速程序的范畴,其关于独任仲裁员的规定也将得到适用。此时,如果仲裁规则并未进一步规定当事人有相反约定的后果,那么如何解释当事人的真实意思和仲裁规则的意图将成为一个难题。在实践中,也确实发生了这种冲突,并且关于当事人意思的解释问题还存在分歧。

对于当事人意思的一种解释体现在"来宝案"中,该案认为当事人的三人仲裁庭的约定排除了独任仲裁员的规定。在该案中,上海市第一中级人民法院认为当事人已经在仲裁条款中约定了三人仲裁庭也未排除对快速程序的适用,因此推测当事人的真实意思是适用快速程序的同时组成三人仲裁庭,SIAC 适用独任仲裁员的决定违反了当事人之间的约定,从而根据《纽约公约》第 5 条第 1

① 参见刘晓红、冯硕:《论国际商事仲裁中机构管理权与意思自治的冲突与协调——以快速仲裁程序中强制条款的适用为视角》,载《上海政法学院学报(法治论丛)》2018 年第 5 期。

② See 2021 ICC Arbitration Rules Art. 30. 2.

③ See 2016 SIAC Rules Act. 5. 1.

款丁项拒绝承认与执行该裁决。①

另一种解释体现在“AQZ v. ARA”中,该案认为当事人选择了《新加坡国际仲裁中心仲裁规则》(以下简称 SIAC 规则),就意味着他们通过意思自治授予仲裁机构院长指派独任仲裁员的裁量权,当事人关于三人仲裁庭的约定并不意味着对快速程序中适用独任仲裁员的排除,反而是对独任仲裁员的默示适用。② 对此,Gary Born 教授表示赞同,③他认为:根据双方所选择的 SIAC 规则的第 5.2 条,新加坡法院正确地认可了仲裁机构的院长有决定仲裁程序的自由裁量权,其中就包括了组庭方式的裁量权。因此,只要自由裁量权行使明智,在院长充分考虑所有相关因素的情况下,如果当事人不能举出其他严重的程序瑕疵或违反自然正义的情况,仅仅是任命与当事人约定数量不同的仲裁员并不能充分构成挑战这一快速仲裁裁决的事由。

上述两个案件存在两个共同特点:(1)仲裁规则不明确;(2)都是当事人一方面选择如国际商会仲裁院或 SIAC 这些仲裁机构的仲裁规则,另一方面约定三人仲裁庭。由于上述案件分别涉及 2013 年的 SIAC 规则和 2010 年的 SIAC 规则,这两个规则均未对当事人有相反约定的情况提供处理方案,所以就存在对当事人关于三人仲裁庭的约定是否排除独任仲裁员问题的解释空间。仲裁机构院长指定独任仲裁员的行为代表仲裁机构对于仲裁过程的内部监督,是仲裁机构管理权的体现,而当事人对于三人仲裁庭的约定是意思自治的体现,二者之间的矛盾和冲突在上述的案件中早已昭然。

三、问题的本质:仲裁价值的冲突

美国著名仲裁员 Jennifer Kirby 曾针对仲裁程序发表过著名的“铁三角”(Iron Triangle)理论(见图 1):一个仲裁程序在实施过程中将会出现多重矛盾,若想追求质量和效率,那么价格将会提升;若想追求质量和价格,那么效率将得

---

① 参见来宝资源国际私人有限公司与上海信泰国际贸易有限公司申请承认和执行外国仲裁裁决案,上海市第一中级人民法院(2016)沪 01 协外认 1 号民事裁定书。

② See AQZ v. ARA. [2015] SGHC 49.

③ Gary Born and Jonathan Lim, *AQZ v. ARA: Singapore High Court Upholds Award Made under SIAC Expedited Procedure*, at http://arbitrationblog.kluwerarbitration.com/2015/03/09/aqz-v-ara-singapore-high-court-upholds-award-made-under-siac-expedited-procedure/ (Last visited on December 26, 2021).

不到保障;若想追求价格和效率,那么质量就会变差。① 所以,在她看来同时兼顾质量、效率和价格几乎是不可能的事情。②

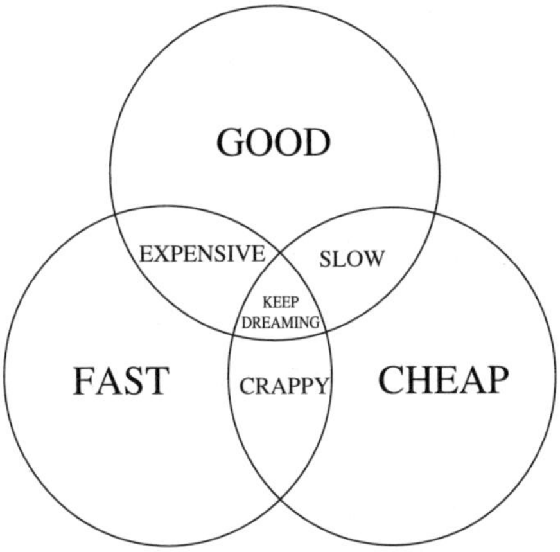

图 1 "铁三角"理论

快速仲裁中,在价格固定甚至希望价格降低的时候,效率和质量就容易产生冲突,即上述快速程序困境的本质其实是仲裁效率和代表质量的公正价值之间的冲突。如果要追求仲裁的效率,那么就要求对程序进行简化,就可能会损害到当事人的程序性权利;同样地,对仲裁效率的强调就将促使仲裁机构管理权的扩大和对独任仲裁员的指定,当事人事先对于三人仲裁庭的约定就将可能被进一步解释。

就效率价值而言,快速程序使得仲裁重拾"高效"。程序的简化以及采取独任仲裁员的方式大大提升了程序的效率。③ 事实证明,快速程序在实践过程中成效显著。在联合国国际贸易法委员会(United Nations Commission on International Trade Law,UNCITRAL)对快速程序机制的一项调查中,各个仲裁机构对

---

① See Jennifer Kirby, *Efficiency in International Arbitration: Whose Duty Is It?*, 32 Journal of International Arbitration, 689 – 690 (2015).

② 她认为同时兼顾三者的仲裁程序(图 1 中三者交叉的地方)是独角兽生活的天堂(that paradise is where the unicorn lives),仍然处于梦中(keep dreaming)。意旨同时兼顾三者是不可能实现的。Ibid., p. 690 – 691.

③ 从仲裁程序的高效性考虑,独任仲裁员更可取:(1)开庭时间更容易确定;(2)更快捷解决纠纷,当事人难以在组庭程序上滥用程序构成拖延;(3)更具有保密性;(4)程序灵活,审限较短,可以更为迅速地审结案件。参见马占军:《我国仲裁庭组成方式的修改与完善》,载《法学》2009 年第 1 期。

快速程序的现实效果表示满意。[①] 例如,中国国际经济贸易仲裁委员会(China International Economic and Trade Arbitration Commission, CIETAC)表示在其受理的案件中,采用简易程序的案件仅需 105 天作出裁决,普通程序则需要 195 天。[②] 又如,在香港国际仲裁中心(Hong Kong International Arbitration Centre, HKIAC)适用快速程序的案件中,案件提交至作出最终裁决的中位数值为 5.8 个月,平均值为 5.4 个月,而普通程序的中位数值和平均值为14.3个月和 16.2 个月;在费用上,HKIAC 快速仲裁的费用中位数和平均数分别为 19,065 美元和 35,056 美元,而普通程序的费用中位数和平均数分别为 62,537 美元和 117,045 美元。[③] 由此可见,在实践中快速程序确实发挥了其促进仲裁效率、便利、低费的作用和价值。

就公正价值而言,在快速程序中仲裁当事人仍然对正当程序的保障和其意思自治的实现保持关注。一方面,当事人关注快速程序对正当程序原则的保障。在仲裁程序中,特意加快程序进程可能引发当事人权利弱化、正常程序公正性受到质疑等诸多副作用。[④] 尤其是在仲裁庭采取书面审理,限制证据的数量、长度、范围的时候,当事人陈述案件的权利将受到减损。因此,在裁决作出后被申请人可能会根据正当程序提出拒绝承认与执行的主张(或撤裁),这是《纽约公约》第 5 条第 1 款乙项所允许的。另一方面,当事人关注其意思自治是否实现。在前述当事人选择三人仲裁庭的案件中,仲裁机构规则要求快速程序适用独任仲裁员但并未对当事人的相反约定规定处理方式,所以当事人的意思和仲裁机构规则均需要进一步解释,此时当事人意思自治可能受到机构仲裁管理权的制约。这种制约是基于仲裁效率的考虑而产生的,最终采取的程序与当事人的约定不一致,因此当事人可能会基于程序违法进行抗辩。另外,仅仅由

---

① See UNCITRAL, *Responses to the UNCITRAL Questionnaire on Expedited Arbitration* (Jan. 2020), p. 16 – 23, at https://uncitral.un.org/sites/uncitral.un.org/files/media-documents/uncitral/en/responses_to_questionnaire_30_january_2020.pdf (Last visited on December 26, 2021).

② Ibid., p. 17.

③ Ibid., p. 19 – 20.

④ 参见唐塞潇:《国际商事仲裁早期处置机制的价值平衡和制度构建》,载《武大国际法评论》2019年第2期。

一名仲裁员处理纠纷在某些情况下可能会导致当事人的失望。[①]

因此，为了消解快速程序的困境，如何平衡程序的效率和公正价值则值得深思。对此，不同学者提出了不同看法。有学者认为，仲裁制度理性构建的初衷是公平和效率的兼顾，不能两全其美时，公正应优先于效率，即"公正说"。[②]另有学者认为国际商事仲裁与市场交易行为挂钩，应当基于当事人的意思自治，以效益为最高价值准则，即"效率说"。[③] 亦有学者认为应当具体问题具体分析，仲裁条款和仲裁规则发生冲突时，不能简单指出任何一方具有当然的优先性。[④] 还有一种观点称，公正和效率并不矛盾，追求效率也是当事人追求公正的目标和组成部分。[⑤] 然而，就快速程序本身而言，一方面，其以效率为逻辑起点，效率应当是其底色；另一方面，快速程序是仲裁制度的一部分，应当遵循当事人的意思自治，故考察当事人的真实意思尤为必要，如果当事人的意思本身就包含了对效率的追求，那么效率应当是追求的目标，如果当事人本身想通过一种公正的方式解决纠纷或者说当事人对快速程序保持担忧，那么应当放弃对于快速程序一些具体安排的过于偏执。

四、快速程序困境之消解

（一）坚持程序公正：保障当事人基本程序性权利

上述第一种困境主要是基于仲裁程序的简化减损正当程序和当事人基本程序性权利展开的，因此，如何坚持程序公正，保障当事人程序性权益则成为消解这一困境的重心。

正当程序要求快速程序中当事人听证、举证、开庭的要求得到保障，这些程

---

① See Michael W. Bühler & Pierre Heitzmann, *The* 2017 *ICC Expedited Rules*: *From Softball to Hardball*?, 34 Journal of International Arbitration, 147 (2017).

② 参见孙志煜、郑钧洋：《公正与效率：国际商事仲裁调解中立人制度的价值博弈及中国因应》，载《时代法学》2020 年第 6 期；刘晓红、冯硕：《论国际商事仲裁中机构管理权与意思自治的冲突与协调——以快速仲裁程序中强制条款的适用为视角》，载《上海政法学院学报（法治论丛）》2018 年第 5 期。

③ 参见宋连斌：《刍议国际商事仲裁的价值取向》，载《中国国际私法与比较法年刊》2000 年第 0 期；汪祖兴：《效率本位与本位回归——论我国仲裁法的效率之维》，载《中国法学》2005 年第 4 期。

④ 参见杜焕芳、李贤森：《国际商事仲裁当事人程序自治边界冲突与平衡》，载《法学评论》2020 年第 2 期。

⑤ 参见朱若菡：《快速仲裁中强势独任仲裁员条款之检视》，载《上海对外经贸大学学报》2019 年第 5 期。

序涉及当事人到庭(present the case)发表意见的权利。[①] 值得肯定的是,在各个仲裁程序中,对这些程序的简化均要求与当事人进行沟通和协商。[②] 然而,如前所述,实践中当事人的程序性权利仍可能在实际上受到损害,基于程序上的不公平,当事人可能会提出正当程序抗辩。故虽然当事方可以自由就程序规则达成协议及放弃任何程序权利,但任何时间的限制或对当事方提交案件可能性的其他限制都不应与基本的正当程序要求相违背。[③] 因此,内部监督变得十分重要,只有从内部监督进行规制,才可能从程序启动伊始到程序结束保证当事人基本程序性权利的实现,而减少司法上对于正当程序违反的认定,从而保证仲裁裁决得到执行。

首先,仲裁庭应当注意考虑简化程序对当事人的影响,既要兼顾程序简化的灵活性,又要符合正当程序的内在要求。第一,应当保证当事人程序性权利的实现。如在作出限制当事人举证的决定之后,如果当事人要求举证并且其认为该证据十分必要,应当予以准许。并且,仲裁规则中的一般正当程序规则也应当被适用于简易程序之中。[④] 第二,应当保证程序的效率。如若当事人在同意限制举证之后,还想提出更多的证据,仲裁庭可以要求当事人提供该证据与待证事实具有关联性的初步证明。第三,裁决本身应该明确和精确,以尽量减少挑战或不可执行的风险。[⑤] 如前所述,简化裁决说理可能导致执行地法院对公共政策违反的认定,所以仲裁庭要以保障仲裁裁决可执行性为目标。例如,在 UNCITRAL 组织的一项对快速仲裁的调查中,HKIAC 表示,即便其仲裁规则

---

① See Peter J. Pettibone, *Due Process Considerations in Expedited Arbitrations*, 10 Indian J. ARB. L, 181(2021).

② For example, 2021 ICC Arbitration Rules Appendix VI Art. 3.4 and 3.5, 2016 SIAC Rules Act. 5.2(c) and 2018 HKIAC Administered Arbitration Rules Act. 42.2(e).

③ 参见张卫彬:《快车道仲裁规则的比较及借鉴》,载《政法论丛》2010 年第 6 期。

④ 例如 CIETAC 表示,其规则中的一般正当程序规则应当被适用于简易程序之中,如其规则的第 31、32、35、49、51 条。See UNCITRAL, *Responses to the UNCITRAL Questionnaire on Expedited Arbitration* (*Jan.* 2020), p. 68, at https://uncitral.un.org/sites/uncitral.un.org/files/media - documents/uncitral/en/responses_to_questionnaire_30_january_2020.pdf (Last visited on December 26, 2021).

⑤ See Irene Welser and Christian Klausegger, *Fast Track Arbitration: Just Fast or Something Different?*, 2009 Austrian Arbitration Yearbook 2009, 278 (2009).

规定了可以简化裁决的说理,但实践中还没有选择这样做。[①]

其次,仲裁机构的内部监督亦应当发挥重要作用。纵观世界范围内仲裁机构的实践,仲裁庭之外的机构内部监督被认为是保证正当程序的主要办法之一。例如,SIAC 仲裁规则规定仲裁机构可缩短程序中的任何时限,[②]在决定是否应缩短 SIAC 仲裁规则下的时限时,仲裁机构应考虑正当程序和公平性等因素,在快速仲裁中作出的裁决,在发布前也会由仲裁机构仔细审查。[③] HKIAC 虽然不正式审查裁决,但其案件负责人协助仲裁庭确保裁决符合 HKIAC 仲裁规则下的形式要求,同时 HKIAC 案件办理人员也会监督仲裁程序,如果他们怀疑仲裁庭违反正当程序,可能会在内部对仲裁庭提出问题。此外,HKIAC 还提供法庭秘书服务,这为仲裁过程提供了一层额外的制度监督。[④] 另外,比利时仲裁和调解中心(Belgian Centre for Arbitration and Mediation, CEPANI)和大韩商事仲裁院(The Korean Commercial Arbitration Board, KCAB)同样强调机构内部的秘书处对于正当程序的监督作用。[⑤]

因此,在快速程序中,为了符合正当程序的要求,保障当事人的基本程序权利,应当依靠仲裁庭和仲裁机构进行内部监督。

(二)尊重意思自治:当事人真实意思解释、仲裁机构内部监督、司法外部监督维度

当事人的意思自治是仲裁的基石,也是仲裁庭获得管辖权的基础,所以尊重当事人的真实意思是消解上述第二种困境的关键,应当从解释当事人真实意思、仲裁机构内部监督、司法外部监督三重维度消解困境。

1. 合理解释当事人真实意思

首先,自主性是仲裁制度的根本属性。仲裁充分尊重当事人的意思自治,

---

① See UNCITRAL, *Responses to the UNCITRAL Questionnaire on Expedited Arbitration* (Jan. 2020), p. 64, at https://uncitral.un.org/sites/uncitral.un.org/files/media-documents/uncitral/en/responses_to_questionnaire_30_january_2020.pdf (Last visited on December 26, 2021).

② See 2016 SIAC Rules Act. 5.2(a).

③ See UNCITRAL, *Responses to the UNCITRAL Questionnaire on Expedited Arbitration* (Jan. 2020), p. 69, at https://uncitral.un.org/sites/uncitral.un.org/files/media-documents/uncitral/en/responses_to_questionnaire_30_january_2020.pdf (Last visited on December 26, 2021).

④ Ibid., p. 70.

⑤ Ibid., p. 71.

当事人在仲裁庭的组成、仲裁机构的选择、仲裁法律适用的约定、仲裁员的指定、仲裁事项范围的确定等方面具有自主权。所以,在仲裁规则范围之内当事人可以灵活约定程序。例如,当事人可以在机构仲裁中约定临时仲裁规则进行程序。以 UNCITRAL 仲裁规则为例,HKIAC 出台了《UNCITRAL 下仲裁管理程序》以满足当事人选择这一临时仲裁规则开展程序的需要。① 而我国内地司法实践中也通过司法先例明确了当事人这一做法的合法性。② 甚至有观点认为,仲裁程序应当是反剧场化的,在尊重双方当事人合意的前提下,仲裁程序的开展不拘泥于任何程序规则,仅需符合自然法意义上的正当程序。③

其次,平衡两种意思自治,考察当事人的真实意思。第一,应当明确的是,当事人对三人仲裁庭的选择和仲裁机构的管理权均基于当事人的意思自治而产生,没有孰先孰后之分。当事人对仲裁规则的选择实际上是将程序置于仲裁机构和仲裁庭的之下,仲裁庭的组成是当事人对仲裁机构院长的授权,是一种默示的意思自治,当事人在仲裁条款中对于三人仲裁庭的约定则是一种明示的意思自治。无论是默示意思自治还是明示意思自治均是当事人意思的体现,不应当说谁当然优先,而应当看谁更真实。所以,一些学者谈到的明示意思自治应当优先于默示意思自治的推测难称合理。④ 第二,应当寻求一种能很好平衡这两种意思自治的解释方法。以“AQZ v. ARA”和“来宝案”为例,⑤由于 2010 年和 2013 年的 SIAC 规则并没有对当事人存在相反约定的情形作规定,⑥所以,

---

① See HKIAC, Procedures for the Administration of Arbitration under the UNCITRAL Arbitration Rules.

② 参见《最高人民法院关于浙江逸盛石化有限公司申请确认仲裁条款效力一案请示的复函》,〔2013〕民四他字第 60 号。

③ 参见傅攀峰:《商事仲裁:一种“去剧场化”的司法方式》,载《重庆理工大学学报(社会科学)》2020 年第 10 期。

④ 参见桑远棵:《国际商事仲裁快速程序:问题与完善》,载《国际商务(对外经济贸易大学学报)》2019 年第 5 期。

⑤ 参见来宝资源国际私人有限公司与上海信泰国际贸易有限公司申请承认和执行外国仲裁裁决案,上海市第一中级人民法院(2016)沪 01 协外认 1 号民事裁定书。See AQZ v. ARA[2015] SGHC 49.

⑥ SIAC 之后在其 2016 年版的规则中增加了即便当事人存在相反的约定,也应当按照 SIAC 确立的具体程序规则行事的规定,这意味着当事人具有注意这种限制的义务,有利于对于当事人真实意思的解释。See 2016 SIAC Rules Act. 5. 3: By agreeing to arbitration under these Rules, the parties agree that, where arbitral proceedings are conducted in accordance with the Expedited Procedure under this Rule 5, the rules and procedures set forth in Rule 5. 2 shall apply even in cases where the arbitration agreement contains contrary terms.

对当事人真实意思的解释尚存空间，新加坡法院认为当事人对三人仲裁庭的约定仅适用于普通程序而非快速程序，上海市第一中级人民法院认为当事人约定快速仲裁不排除可以同时适用三人仲裁庭。但是，从理性商业人的角度来看，当事人既然选择了 SIAC 规则，自然能意识到未来适用快速程序的可能，毕竟 SIAC 规则的快速程序有明显的“opt out”特征。而无论是独任仲裁员还是三人仲裁庭，仲裁员秉持着自然正义作出的裁决最终却没有被执行，这似乎不太符合“支持执行”(pro－enforcement)的态度。故从“支持执行”和“理性商业人”的角度来看，诸如 Gary Born 教授提出的解释路径似乎合理而且能被接受，他认为对当事人意思最好的解释是，当事人同时约定了两种机制：一是在小额案件中适用快速仲裁程序，指定独任仲裁员；二是在其他案件中，按照三人仲裁庭组庭，这样兼顾了效率与公正。①

2. 仲裁机构内部监督维度

首先，仲裁机构的规则应当进一步细化和明确。由“AQZ v. ARA”和“来宝案”可知，对当事人真实意思的解释是一大难题，仲裁机构规则规定的不明确则是产生这一难题的主要原因，这在前文已着笔墨。所以，进一步细化和明确仲裁机构的规则尤为必要。例如，在经历裁决未被承认与执行之后，SIAC 在其 2016 年版的仲裁规则中增加了即便当事人存在相反的约定，也应当按照 SIAC 确立的具体程序规则行事的规定，②随着规则的进一步明确，理性商事主体的意思自治表现得更为明显，因此，我国法院是否还应当像“来宝案”那样裁判则值得进一步考虑。可以肯定的是，规则的明确带来当事人意思的明确，使当事人意思的推定更容易，即便当事人在仲裁条款中约定了三人仲裁庭，仲裁裁决被认定为程序违法的可能性将大大降低。

其次，应当注重与当事人的协商，根据当事人的意思自治作出决定是仲裁制度和仲裁机构提升其竞争力的需要。仲裁机构作为一个服务机构，本质是要向案件当事人提供优质的法律服务。③ 随着《选择法院协议公约》和《海牙判决

---

① See Gary B. Born, *International Arbitration and Forum Selection Agreements*, 6*th ed.*, Wolters Kluwer, 2021, p. 1800－1802.

② See 2016 SIAC Rules Act. 5. 3.

③ 参见杜焕芳、李贤森：《国际商事仲裁当事人程序自治边界冲突与平衡》，载《法学评论》2020 年第 2 期。

公约》的出台,一旦判决流通性增强,将可能影响当事人对争议解决方式的选择,因为他们可能会冲击国际仲裁可执行性的优势。[①] 另外,国际商事法庭的建立从某种程度上来说是对国际商事仲裁缺陷的一种回应,其介于仲裁和内国法院之间的制度安排,在内国法院的框架中做了制度性调整,兼顾了一些仲裁的意思自治因素和诉讼制度的审级原则,所以可能会吸引一部分当事人选择诉讼。[②] 因此,有必要从服务当事人的角度来构建仲裁规则以及解释当事人之间的约定,这是仲裁制度和仲裁机构提升竞争力的需要,故应当注重与当事人的协商,从效率和公正角度为商事主体的利益考虑。

3. 司法外部监督维度

司法外部监督应当坚持“支持执行”的态度,既要尊重商事主体的选择,也要尊重仲裁地和仲裁机构对其法律和规则的解释。

首先,司法外部监督应当尊重商事主体的选择,这是自序理论的要求。自序理论要求司法监督应当尊重当事人的自由行为。自我决定是自由的核心,个人通过其自我决定而感受并且实现自由,这种自我决定权被自由主义哲学认为是意思自治的基本思想。[③] 处于社会中的个人可以依据自己的生活规划,自由选择和行为,否定这种自由,就是否定个人自治,否定人们自我决定的基本权利。[④] 所以,在自序理论和个人自治的驱使下,每个人都是自己利益最可靠的代表和守护人,应该承担自主决定和选择下的责任和后果,即行为自由与责任相匹配。而在此时,法院可能基于某种考量(很多情况下是基于对当事人权益保护的考量),有时会构成对当事人权益的过度保护,这是司法上的“家长主义”的结果。

在“来宝案”中,上海市第一中级人民法院认为当事人的意思可能是既要选

---

① See Lucas Clover Alcolea, *The* 2005 *Hague Choice of Court and the* 2019 *Hague Judgments Conventions versus the New York Convention*: *Rivals*, *Alternatives or Something Else*?, 6 MCGILL J. Disp. Resol. 197 (2019 – 2020). See also Rouzana Kasem, *The Future of Choice Court and Arbitration Agreements under the New York Convention*, *the Hague Choice of Court Convention*, *and the Draft Hague Judgments Convention*, 10 Aberdeen Student L. Rev. 112 (2020).

② 参见苏伟康:《竞争或协作——论国际商事法庭与国际仲裁的关系定位》,载《仲裁研究》2021 年第 1 期。

③ 参见车浩:《自我决定权与刑法家长主义》,载《中国法学》2012 年第 1 期。

④ 参见杨海、胡亚球:《诉讼中家长主义的若干问题研究》,载《当代法学》2012 年第 3 期。

择快速程序，又要适用三人仲裁庭，这种论断也许本身有其合理性，[①]但是当事人的意思自治却是有边界的，在机构仲裁的情况下，当事人可以选择仲裁规则，但是这种选择应当是该机构仲裁所允许的，[②]所以某种程度上来说，当事人选择了仲裁规则，就选择了接受仲裁机构的管理。这是自序理论在发生作用，当事人应当为其选择行为负责。

其次，司法外部监督也要尊重仲裁地和仲裁机构对其法律和规则的解释。一方面，尊重仲裁地对其法律的解释是执行地国法院对裁决地国法院的一种“礼让”，如果执行地国忽视仲裁地国法院对其自身法律的解释，将可能导致对《纽约公约》义务的违反，特别是对于作出了“互惠保留”的国家而言，对仲裁地国法院解释的忽视将可能使得其仲裁裁决在对方国家的执行举步维艰。也难怪有学者对“来宝案”的裁判持批判态度。[③] 另一方面，司法外部监督要尊重机构自治。仲裁机构作为民间机构，有自主权。仲裁机构的自主权是意思自治原则在仲裁制度中的表现之一，其独立自主，可以自行制定或修改自己的仲裁规则，同时也在组庭方面能行使自主权而不受干涉，当事人不行使权利或者行使权利之后不能达到组庭目的的，仲裁机构有权决定仲裁庭的组成。[④] 如果仲裁机构的决定不是明显违反正当程序、法律程序、当事人约定、公共政策等，应当秉持支持执行的态度。[⑤] 而在“来宝案”中，在当事人没有明确排除独任仲裁员且仲裁规则对快速程序规定不明确的情况下，SIAC 的决定有其合理性，并不越界。

五、UNCITRAL 快速仲裁规则之效果评估

《联合国国际贸易法委员会仲裁规则》（以下简称 UNCITRAL 规则）作为全

---

① 参见杜焕芳、李贤森：《国际商事仲裁当事人程序自治边界冲突与平衡》，载《法学评论》2020 年第 2 期。

② 参见宋连斌：《国际商事仲裁管辖权研究》，法律出版社 2000 年版，第 141 页。

③ Gary Born 教授认为中国法院对于“来宝案”的裁决考虑不当，违反了中国在《纽约公约》下的义务。See Gary B. Born, *International Arbitration and Forum Selection Agreements*, 6th *ed.*, Wolters Kluwer, 2021, p. 1800 – 1802.

④ 参见董连和：《论我国仲裁制度中的意思自治原则》，载《清华大学学报（哲学社会科学版）》2006 年第 3 期。

⑤ 参见宋连斌：《国际商事仲裁管辖权研究》，法律出版社 2000 年版，第 224 ~ 225 页。

世界最受欢迎的临时仲裁规则,其变化和发展势必影响当事人对仲裁规则的选择和世界范围内的仲裁立法。[①]《联合国国际贸易法委员会快速仲裁规则》(以下简称 UNCITRAL 快速仲裁规则)的出台填补了 UNCITRAL 规则的空白。作为快速程序规则的最新发展,有必要评析该规则在高效的实现、对当事人程序性权利的保障、对当事人意思自治的尊重方面的效果。评析这一规则的意义主要在于这一规则将对快速程序领域的国际仲裁立法和仲裁规则的发展趋向产生重要的指导作用。

(一)对高效的实现

从 UNCITRAL 快速仲裁规则的规定可看出,该规则以"高效"为目的,并从多方面得到体现。

具体而言,体现在如下八个方面:第一,该规则要求无论是当事人还是仲裁庭,都应当在整个过程中保持高效和迅速。[②] 第二,被申请人应当在收到仲裁通知之后的 15 天内对仲裁通知进行答复,并且在仲裁庭组成之后的 15 天内对仲裁请求进行答辩。[③] 第三,除非当事人另有约定,否则默认独任仲裁员审理,有利于提高仲裁程序的效率,降低当事人的费用。[④] 第四,如若当事人未就独任仲裁员的产生达成一致意见,将由仲裁员指定机构进行制定,[⑤]这很好地防止了程序的拖延。第五,仲裁庭可以基于对效率的考量,决定对程序中的任何期限进行缩短或延长。[⑥] 第六,仲裁庭在征求当事人的意见之后,可以不进行开庭审理。[⑦] 第七,仲裁庭在证据的提交、范围等方面有较大的自主权,因此可以更高效地推进程序进行。[⑧] 第八,该规则规定审理期限一般不能超过 6 个月,最长不

① 根据 2021 年玛丽女王大学的国际仲裁调查报告,有 76% 的被调查者认为在过去五年中 UNCITRAL 规则作为一项临时仲裁规则被选择和适用得最多。See Mary Queen University of Londen, 2021 *International Arbitration Survey*: *Adapting Arbitration to a Changing World*, p. 9, at http://www.arbitration.qmul.ac.uk/media/arbitration/docs/LON0320037 – QMUL – International – Arbitration – Survey – 2021_19_WEB.pdf (Last visited on December 20, 2021).

② See 2021 UNCITRAL Expedited Arbitration Rules, Act. 3.1 and 3.2.

③ Ibid., Act. 5.

④ Ibid., Act. 7.

⑤ Ibid., Act. 8.

⑥ Ibid., Act. 10.

⑦ Ibid., Act. 11.

⑧ Ibid., Act. 15.

能超过9个月,保证当事人纠纷的迅速解决,防止仲裁程序拖延。[①]

（二）对当事人程序性权利的保障

由前述可知,快速程序中由于程序的简化,可能会导致当事人程序性权利的减损和对正当程序的违反。而UNCITRAL快速仲裁规则很好地保障了当事人的程序性权利,主要体现在两个方面:

首先,对当事人程序性权利的积极保护。具体体现在:(1)仲裁庭可以在邀请当事各方发表意见并考虑案件的情况后,利用其认为适当的任何技术手段进行诉讼,包括与当事各方沟通、远程进行协商和听证。[②] (2)该规则强调仲裁通知和对仲裁请求的告知,[③]这有利于对当事人出庭发表意见权利进行保护,是正当程序的要求。(3)要求组庭之后的15天内仲裁庭应当立即通过案件管理会议或者其他的方式,对于仲裁的进行方式与当事各方进行协商。[④] (4)在征求当事人的意见之后,仲裁庭可以决定是否要求当事人做进一步的书面陈述,[⑤]这有利于在保证效率的同时,兼顾当事人举证的权利,从某种意义上来说,是对公正的维护。

其次,对当事人程序性权利的消极保护。前文已述,简化裁决事由可能会导致裁决因为违反公共政策而被拒绝承认与执行。而在UNCITRAL快速仲裁规则中,并没有出现简化裁决理由的规定,这从消极层面规避了裁决中不附裁决理由或者简化裁决理由带来的裁决承认与执行危机,是对当事人程序性权利的消极保护。

（三）对当事人意思自治的尊重

UNCITRAL快速仲裁规则本身不存在机构管理权扩张的问题,因为其依附于作为临时仲裁规则的UNCITRAL仲裁规则。并且,该规则在适用方式上和仲裁庭的组成上很大程度尊重了当事人的意思自治。

一方面,UNCITRAL快速仲裁规则采取协议适用模式(opt in),即需要当事

---

① See 2021 UNCITRAL Expedited Arbitration Rules, Act. 16.

② Ibid., Act. 3. 3.

③ Ibid., Act. 4.

④ Ibid., Act. 9.

⑤ Ibid., Act. 14.

人合意选择才能适用,[①]这有利于规避前文所述的“opt out”模式带来的对当事人真实意思表示认定困难的问题。

另一方面,该规则第 7 条规定,除当事人另有约定外,应由 1 名仲裁员审理案件。[②] 其实是尊重当事人选择程序的自由,使得组成仲裁庭的规定兼顾灵活性与确定性。

六、结论

由于国际仲裁的效率性受到仲裁“诉讼化”等因素的减损,快速仲裁程序以恢复仲裁“快速、便捷和廉价”为目的应运而生。但是,随着实践深入,快速仲裁面临程序简化与正当程序的冲突以及仲裁机构管理权扩张与当事人意思自治的冲突问题。而问题的本质其实是仲裁效率和公正的价值冲突。为了消解这种困境,一方面应当坚持程序公正,保障当事人基本程序性权利,另一方面应当坚持当事人意思自治这一仲裁的基石,从对当事人真实意思的解释、仲裁机构内部监督和司法外部监督多维度提供解决问题的方案。最后,UNCITRAL 快速仲裁规则作为快速程序规则的最新发展,在对高效的实现、对当事人程序性权利的保障和对当事人意思自治的尊重方面有重要的促进作用。

① See 2021 UNCITRAL Expedited Arbitration Rules, Act. 1.

② Ibid. , Act. 7.

已撤销国际商事仲裁裁决的域外效力及中国立法优化研究

蔡晓雯*

摘　要：在《纽约公约》的推动下，国际商事仲裁因得到承认和执行的范围扩大了而被广泛运用，但跨境执行仲裁裁决仍需要面临仲裁地法院和执行地法院的双重审查。尽管《纽约公约》在很大程度上统一了国际商事仲裁的司法审查标准，但由于各国国内法规定千差万别和法院司法实践各不相同，已撤销的国际商事仲裁裁决的域外效力问题，目前在国际上仍然未形成一致看法。本文拟以新近备受关注的UNI－TOP案为切入点，首先，对已撤销的国际商事仲裁裁决的域外效力的含义做简要概述；其次，分析被撤销的国际商事仲裁裁决的域外效力来源的两大依据，即《纽约公约》文本本身的模糊空白和各国对被撤销的国际商事仲裁裁决效力认定所持的理论立场不同；再次，归纳主要国家在该问题上的司法实践形成的基本轨迹；最后，探讨我国对已撤销的国际商事仲裁裁决的域外效力的立场、执行可能性并提出改革优化路径。

关键词：已撤销国际商事仲裁裁决　域外效力　承认与执行　纽约公约　自由裁量权

* 蔡晓雯，复旦大学硕士研究生。

一、问题的提出

作为一种在很大程度上兼具效率与公平的争端解决机制,国际商事仲裁伴随着经济全球化在世界范围内被广泛采用。一份仲裁裁决作出后,将受到仲裁地国家的司法监督,裁决作出地或仲裁准据法国当地法院通常通过仲裁协议效力的判定、仲裁裁决的撤销以及仲裁裁决的不予执行三种方式来对仲裁行使司法审查权;如果仲裁裁决的执行地在他国,则还要受执行地国法院的审查来决定是否予以承认和执行。通常情况下,仲裁裁决被撤销即因丧失效力而不存在被外国承认和执行的可能性,但在近二十几年来的国际仲裁实践中,出现了不少承认已撤销国际商事仲裁裁决域外效力的案例。

尽管 1958 年《承认及执行外国仲裁裁决公约》(以下简称《纽约公约》)规定统一司法审查标准并推动了国际商事仲裁裁决在缔约方范围内的承认与执行,被撤销的国际商事仲裁裁决能否得到另一缔约方的承认与执行,无论在理论还是实践层面,长久以来在仲裁界都存在不小争议。其核心的问题在于如何回答:缔约方法院是否承认已被其他缔约方法院撤销的国际商事仲裁裁决具有域外效力?缔约方法院在《纽约公约》第 5 条第 1 款 e 项[①]下是否享有对被撤销的国际商事仲裁裁决予以承认和执行的自由裁量权?[②] 目前,针对该问题的回答可大致分为肯定派和否定派。肯定派认为,已撤销国际商事仲裁裁决具有域外效力,依据《纽约公约》第 5 条第 1 款 e 项和第 7 条"更优惠权利条款"以及《纽约公约》的立法本意就是为了扩大仲裁裁决被承认与执行的范围,执行地国法院对被他国法院撤销的仲裁裁决的承认执行拥有自由裁量权。相反,否定者指出,《纽约公约》第 5 条第 1 款 e 项下不存在缔约方法院的自由裁量空间,一项仲裁裁决被撤销后即不复存在,不可能再获得承认与执行,所有已撤销国际商事仲裁裁决不存在域外效力。

2020 年 4 月 27 日,北京第四中级人民法院(以下简称北京四中院)撤销了

---

① 《纽约公约》第 5 条第 1 款 e 项规定,裁决只有在受裁决援用的一方向请求承认与执行地的主管机关提出证据,证明有下列情形之一时,才可以根据该方的请求拒绝承认与执行:……(e) 裁决对各方尚无约束力,或被裁决地所在国或裁决所依据法律的国家主管机关撤销或停止执行。

② 参见傅攀峰:《未竟的争鸣:被撤销的国际商事仲裁裁决的承认与执行》,载《现代法学》2017 年第 1 期。

(2017)中国贸仲京裁字第 0836 号裁决,2020 年 6 月 29 日,裁决申请人UNI - TOP Asia Investment Limited(以下简称 UNI - TOP 公司)向美国哥伦比亚特区法院申请承认和执行该被撤销的裁决。该案再度引发学界和实务界对于上述议题的强烈讨论,特别是 UNI - TOP 公司所选择的法院是于 1996 年作出 Chromalloy 案①执行决定的哥伦比亚特区法院,且两案在事实方面具有一定的相似性,所以有预测指出该案很可能将"复活"Chromalloy 案,成为美国法院再一次承认与执行被外国法院撤销的仲裁裁决的标志性案件,也是我国贸仲裁决被法院撤销后被申请域外承认执行的第一案。

本文拟以 UNI - TOP 公司向美国法院申请承认和执行被我国法院撤销的仲裁裁决一案(以下简称 UNI - TOP 案)为引入,从概念梳理、效力依据、各国的司法实践角度,分析被撤销的国际商事仲裁裁决的域外效力问题,最终落脚到我国对该问题的立场与执行可能性问题,希望能对相关立法和实践的完善提出有参考价值的建议。

二、UNI - TOP 案:对已撤销仲裁裁决效力的思考

(一)案情概要

UNI - TOP 公司,一家在中国香港登记注册的公司,与中国石化集团国际石油勘探开发有限公司(以下简称国勘公司)于 2005 年 3 月 4 日签订《代理协议》,约定国勘公司委托 UNI - TOP 公司作为其排他的代理人协助国勘公司根据相关法律或规定直接或通过国勘公司的关联公司获得哈萨克斯坦的 PetroKazakhstan(以下简称 PK 公司)股份,并协助国勘公司获得相关政府批准(以下简称完成交易),完成交易后 UNI - TOP 公司可获取约定的代理费用。双方约定,由此产生的争端由贸易仲裁委员会的三名仲裁员根据其相关规则在北京予以仲裁。本协议适用中国法。后中石油集团收购了 PK 公司 67% 股份并与中石化集团商讨 PK 公司股权转让事宜。

2012 年 8 月 30 日,UNI - TOP 公司向贸易仲裁委员会申请仲裁,请求国勘公司支付逾期的代理酬金及相应的利息、预期利益损失以及律师费和仲裁费用。2013 年 12 月 30 日,仲裁庭作出了对国勘公司有利的仲裁裁决(以下简称

① See Chromalloy Aero services v. Arab Republic of Egypt. ,939 F. Supp. 907(D. D. C. 1996).

裁决一),认为由于国勘公司并没有实际取得PK公司的股权或与此相关的其他权益或补偿,《代理协议》规定的酬金支付条件未成就,因而驳回了UNI-TOP公司的全部仲裁请求。

2015年12月30日,UNI-TOP公司再次向贸易仲裁委员会提起仲裁,基于其所谓"新的事实",即发现国勘公司怠于履行向中石油集团追索PK公司股权和其他权益补偿的《代理协议》义务,阻碍对UNI-TOP公司给付义务的成就,其向仲裁庭作出了大致相似的请求(除款项具体金额数目改变)。仲裁庭于2017年6月30日作出了支持UNI-TOP公司大部分请求的(2017)中国贸仲京裁字第0836号裁决(以下简称裁决二),认为国勘公司怠于追索的行为不正当地阻止代理酬金支付条件的成就,根据《合同法》(已失效)第45条第2款应认为条件成就。

北京四中院依国勘公司撤销申请对裁决二进行审查后认定,裁决二违背了《仲裁法》第9条规定的"一裁终局"制度,对属于"同一纠纷"的两案进行两次裁决,且最高人民法院复函中也答复:由于国勘公司未取得PK公司股权这一客观状态的延续并未使任何一方的权利义务产生新的变化,故UNI-TOP公司所称的国勘公司怠于追索相关权益的情况并不属于"新的事实"。[①] 综上所述,2020年4月27日,北京四中院依《仲裁法》第9、70条和《民事诉讼法》第281条第1款第4项之规定撤销了裁决二。

(二)争议焦点

UNI-TOP公司代理人在向美国法院提交的申请承认与执行裁决二的备忘录[②]中对北京四中院撤销裁决二的做法大肆抨击,认为国勘公司向法院提起撤销仲裁裁决的诉讼的行为违背双方当事人在《代理协议》第10.3.2条仲裁条款中作出的"仲裁结果是终局的且不得提起诉讼"的约定,[③]而北京四中院无视仲裁裁决的既判力,对裁决的实体部分进行审查,"明显不适当地"作出了"有利于中国政府的一个机关、单位或机构的新结果"。[④] 其申请承认与执行被撤销的

① 参见北京市第四中级人民法院民事裁定书,(2017)京04民特39号。

② Memorandum of Law in Support of Petition to Confirm an International Arbitral Award.

③ Agency Agreement:"10.3.2... The result of the arbitration shall be the final resolution of the dispute, and there shall be no litigation."

④ 参见北京市第四中级人民法院民事裁定书,(2017)京04民特39号。

裁决二的主要逻辑可以概括为以下几点:首先,承认美国法院拥有《纽约公约》第5条第1款e项下对被撤销的仲裁裁决予以承认和执行的自由裁量权。其次,北京四中院作出的撤销裁决二的决定是基于国勘公司违背双方仲裁后不得诉讼约定的前提,且不适当地对裁决的实体问题进行审查,所以该撤销决定不构成美国法院依据《纽约公约》第5条第1款e项拒绝承认与执行的合法基础。最后,如果据此拒绝承认和执行该仲裁裁决将违背美国支持仲裁终局性和约束性的公共政策。此外,哥伦比亚法院在Chromalloy案形成的先例是良法(good law),且本案的事实与Chromalloy案相似,所以应得出一致的结果。

综上所述,可概括本案的争议焦点为:(1)缔约方是否拥有《纽约公约》第5条第1款e项下对被撤销的仲裁裁决予以承认和执行的自由裁量权;(2)当事人对仲裁裁决不得提起诉讼的约定是否可以排除法院对仲裁裁决的撤销审查;(3)法院对仲裁裁决的审查是否能涉及实体部分;(4)基于"一裁终局"原则对仲裁裁决撤销是否属于当地标准。

(三)对已撤销仲裁裁决效力的思考

很显然,UNI－TOP公司并不认同北京四中院基于我国法院对仲裁裁决的司法审查权撤销裁决二的效力,这是私主体对国家司法机关行使司法监督权这一行为的质疑,这本质上是一方仲裁当事人意思自治与一国法院的裁决撤销权之间的冲突。然而,要探讨已撤销仲裁裁决的域外效力,必须先回答一个根本性的先决问题:被仲裁地法院撤销的国际商事仲裁裁决本身是否从根本上、当然地丧失效力?而要回答该问题,有必要厘清国际商事仲裁裁决被撤销的基本含义到底意味着什么,或者说裁决撤销之后的效力范围或边界在何处?

从美国该区法院接受立案后进行司法审查可见,一项被撤销的仲裁裁决的效力并不是当然丧失,执行地国法院还需考虑该仲裁裁决是否被"有效"撤销。查询案件进展,该案双方当事人主要就管辖和送达的程序问题提交动议,而法院目前也尚未作出进一步的裁判。根据美国以往的判例,裁决二存在被承认和执行的可能性,下文评析司法实践部分将结合前述争议对此焦点进一步展开。

三、已撤销国际商事仲裁裁决的域外效力概述

(一)国际商事仲裁裁决被撤销的含义

国际商事仲裁裁决,是指不同国家的当事人通过书面协议合意将双方之间

的跨国商事争议交由第三方进行评判所作出的对双方具有约束力的终局性结果。国际商事仲裁裁决的跨国性质，是探讨其被撤销后域外效力的基本前提，因为一个纯国内性质的仲裁裁决一般不具有到域外执行的可能性，所以下文讨论的仲裁裁决均指代国际商事仲裁这一类别的仲裁裁决，本文在此不展开关于仲裁裁决“国际性”的认定问题。

比较普遍的观点认为，国际商事仲裁裁决被撤销是指法院在具有本国国籍的仲裁裁决存在法律所规定的特定情形时，根据当事人请求撤销仲裁裁决，使之归于无效。我国学术界通说认为，国际商事仲裁裁决被撤销是指当存在民事诉讼法和仲裁法所规定的撤销情形时，人民法院根据当事人申请，决定组成合议庭，撤销在我国境内作出的仲裁裁决，使之归于无效的制度。① 国际商事仲裁裁决撤销制度的设立，一方面给予法院对仲裁适度监督权，有利于约束仲裁员裁决过大的自由裁量权，保证仲裁的中立性和公正性，是法院代表国家行使司法主权的重要体现；另一方面赋予当事人对仲裁裁决效力存在异议时的救济权，从而保护正当利益不当受损的当事人的权益，因而该制度是维护国际商事仲裁正常运转以及国际商事秩序稳定的重要保障。

（二）已撤销国际商事仲裁域外效力的含义

谈论到域外效力，通常对象是一国法律，由于法律具有严格的国家主权烙印和属地性，一国法律仅在其领土主权管辖范围内对法律关系产生约束力，而国内法要发生域外效力，也即约束主权管辖范围外的法律关系，须以另一国的承认为前提，否则他国基于国家主权平等原则没有遵守其他国家法律的义务。一国法院撤销国际商事仲裁裁决是依据其本国国内法作出的决定，具体而言，已撤销的国际商事仲裁裁决如果能够得到执行地国法院的承认和执行，那么说明其具有域外效力；反之，则意味着不具有域外效力。②

对上文提及的已撤销国际商事仲裁裁决是否当然丧失效力问题，传统绝对属地主义观点持肯定态度，认为被撤销的仲裁裁决完全丧失效力，且该效力具有普遍性，这种普遍效力要求其他国家不能承认与执行该裁决。按照此种观点，撤销仲裁裁决具有普遍效力则不需要以国家领土范围作为区分边界，从而

---

① 参见赵秀文：《国际商事仲裁法》，中国人民大学出版社2004年版，第35页。

② 参见栾海萍：《已撤销国际商事仲裁裁决的域外效力研究》，辽宁大学2011年硕士学位论文。

也无域内和域外效力之分,似乎否定了本文的论题,但笔者认为,从执行地国对已撤销仲裁裁决是否能被本国承认和执行的态度角度而言,可以区分为已撤销国际商事仲裁裁决的消极域外效力和积极域外效力。认为已撤销仲裁裁决具有普遍效力,某种程度上也是已撤销仲裁裁决的域外效力的一种表现形式,由于执行地国在该过程中扮演消极尊重仲裁地国司法监督权的角色,属于其消极域外效力。而本文所欲探讨的,是已撤销仲裁裁决的积极域外效力,也即执行地国积极地以其本国的法律作为监督仲裁裁决的最终依据,自由裁量是否执行被撤销的仲裁裁决,故在此明确,下文出现的"域外效力"均指积极域外效力。

那么,已撤销国际商事仲裁裁决拥有的域外效力源于何处?换言之,该域外效力得以存在的原因或依据为何?为更深入地理解该问题的缘起、其内在逻辑以及在各国的发展趋势,接下来将阐述已撤销国际商事仲裁裁决具有域外效力的依据。

四、已撤销国际商事仲裁裁决的域外效力依据

之所以会产生关于被撤销的国际商事仲裁裁决是否具有域外效力,或者执行地国法院是否具有对此予以承认和执行的自由裁量权的问题,主要原因有以下两个:第一,《纽约公约》文本本身的模糊与空白,不仅在于其第5条第1款的表述模糊,且文本仅规定了仲裁裁决的承认与执行的审查标准而未对仲裁裁决撤销制度进行规定;第二,各国对被撤销的国际商事仲裁的效力认定遵循不同的理论基础,导致对撤销国际商事仲裁裁决有无域外效力认定不一。同时,这两个原因也是已撤销国际商事仲裁裁决域外效力产生的来源和依据。

(一)《纽约公约》文本本身的模糊与空白

1.对《纽约公约》第5条第1款的"may"的理解

由于公约的法文版使用了"seront"这一意为"必须"的表达,与中文、英文、俄文和西班牙文一致的措辞相反,这两种截然相反的表述引发了对缔约方依据《纽约公约》第5条第1款e项以裁决被撤销为由拒绝承认与执行的权力性质到底是强制性还是裁量性的争议。如果综合考察公约的立法背景,运用文义解释、体系解释及目的解释的方法分析公约文本,可以得出第5条第1款e项具有明确的授权性质,即执行地国法院具有承认和执行被撤销的仲裁裁决的自由裁量权。

首先,起草《纽约公约》的最初就是为了要废除原本《日内瓦公约》和《日内瓦议定书》形成的阻碍仲裁裁决承认与执行的"双重许可机制"(double exequatur mechanism),而第 5 条第 1 款的"may"正好扩大了裁决得到承认与执行的可能性,与公约确保一项国际商事裁决在全球范围内获得有效落实的宗旨相吻合。

其次,仅从文义上进行解释,必须同时考虑除法文版本外的其他四个版本的用词,如果仅凭法文版就把具有授权性质的"may"解释成强制性的"shall"或"must",将歪曲公约本身的内涵。①

最后,将第 5 条第 1 款与第 7 条②的"更优惠权利条款"(more favorable right provision)结合起来考察,两者都服务于使外国仲裁裁决尽可能得到执行的目的。根据体系解释原理,为了使公约条文之间形成逻辑自洽、不自相矛盾的一体,第 5 条第 1 款应解释成授权性条款,否则第 7 条便无存在的意义。

综上所述,尽管有观点认为赋予执行地法院承认和执行被撤销的仲裁裁决可能导致与《纽约公约》追求的裁决的稳定性和一致性相背离,但从上述法律解释方法来看,明确了缔约方享有《纽约公约》第 5 条第 1 款 e 项下的自由裁量权,肯定了已撤销仲裁裁决存在具有域外效力的可能性与前提。

2.《纽约公约》缺乏对仲裁裁决撤销制度的统一规定

《纽约公约》为废除双重许可机制而弱化了仲裁地的对仲裁裁决效力认定的绝对地位,但仍在第 5 条第 1 款 e 项中将仲裁地国法院对仲裁裁决行使撤销权作为执行地国法院拒绝承认和执行仲裁裁决的情况之一,并且由于公约没有对仲裁裁决的撤销制度进行具体规定,将之留待仲裁地国法院根据其国内法自行裁断,而各缔约方对撤销事由的不同规定直接导致了被撤销的仲裁裁决在不同缔约方获得承认与执行。

笔者认为,《纽约公约》对撤销制度的"建设性空白"一定程度上是为了平

---

① 参见肖永平、廖卓炜:《已撤销仲裁裁决在美国的承认与执行》,载《经贸法律评论》2019 年第 2 期。

② 参见《纽约公约》第 7 条第 1 款规定:"本公约的规定不影响缔约方间所订立的关于承认与执行仲裁裁决的多边或双边协定的效力,也不剥夺任何利害关系人可援引裁决地所在国的法律或条约所允许的方式和范围内援用仲裁裁决的任何权利。"

衡为尽量扩大仲裁裁决被承认和执行范围的公约宗旨与缔约方之间对仲裁裁决的司法审查权的矛盾,平衡的效果暂且不论,缺乏国际统一认可的规定,各国国内法对仲裁裁决的撤销依据和撤销程序的多样化导致仲裁裁决效力及被他国认可程度的不确定是必然发生的,为已撤销国际商事仲裁裁决的域外效力创造了生存空间。

（二）各国对被撤销的国际商事仲裁的效力认定遵循不同的理论基础

对被裁决作出地撤销的仲裁裁决是否应该予以承认与执行的问题,除了《纽约公约》文本本身的模糊与空白外,还由于国际社会对被撤销的国际商事仲裁裁决的效力认定问题还未形成统一认识,各国都奉行不同的理论基础,主要存在三种观点,分别为“绝对属地主义理论”(absolute territorial theory)、“非当地化理论”(delocalization theory)和“相对属地主义理论”(comparative territorial theory)。[①]

1. 绝对属地主义理论

正如《纽约公约》重要起草者桑德斯(Sanders)认为的,“由于被仲裁地法院撤销的仲裁裁决已经不存在,且执行一项已经不存在的仲裁裁决乃为不可能之事,或者甚至会与执行地的公共政策相抵触,因此执行地法院将会拒绝执行”[②]。以研究《纽约公约》著称的范登伯格(van den Berg)也表示,撤销一项仲裁裁决具有普遍效力(erga omnes effect),被撤销的仲裁裁决丧失了在《纽约公约》缔约方获得承认与执行的资格,因此裁决的撤销制度能提供法律的确定性(legal certainty)。[③] 在该观点看来,《纽约公约》第 5 条第 1 款的“可以”(may)应被解释为“应当”,就此否定了执行地法院对于被撤销的仲裁裁决的自由裁量权存在的空间,也否定了被撤销仲裁裁决具有积极域外效力。

绝大多数国家的立法与司法实践都明确遵循该理论,执行地法院根据国际礼让原则对仲裁地的司法监督结果予以尊重或服从,一定程度上有利于仲裁裁决的法律确定性和《纽约公约》框架下仲裁裁决效力的一致性。我国最高人民

① 参见桑远棵:《超越属地主义:已撤销仲裁裁决的承认与执行》,载《武大国际法评论》2020 年第 4 期。

② P. Sanders, *New York Convention on the Recognition and Enforcement of Foreign Arbitral Awards*, Netherlands International Law Review ,1959, p. 41 – 53.

③ See A. J. Van den Berg, *Enforcement of Arbitral Awards Annulled in Russia*, Journal of International Arbitration, 2010, p. 182.

法院于2003年《关于人民法院处理涉外仲裁及外国仲裁案件的若干规定(征求意见稿)》中第36条坚持了拒绝承认和执行被撤销的外国仲裁裁决的基本立场,此外1998年《德国民事诉讼法》第1060条和第1061条、2010年《意大利民事诉讼法典》第840条第5款以及1986年《荷兰民事诉讼法典》第1076条第1款中都明确遵循绝对属地主义理论,否定已撤销国际商事仲裁裁决具有域外效力。

2. 非当地化理论

非当地化理论不承认仲裁地法院作出的撤销仲裁裁决的裁决具有普遍效力,认为执行地法院对是否承认与执行被撤销的仲裁裁决具有自由裁量权。在该观点的支持者看来,仲裁地并不是仲裁与一国法律秩序的唯一联系点,执行地法院需要判断仲裁地与仲裁是否存在紧密而非偶然的联系,对于与仲裁地不存在紧密联系的仲裁裁决应当由执行地法院来监督。[①] 国际著名仲裁员 Paulsson 将裁决撤销依据区分为"当地标准"和"国际标准",国际标准为《纽约公约》第5条第1款前4项与《联合国国际贸易法委员会国际商事仲裁示范法》(以下简称《示范法》)第36条第1款a项列出的情况,而除国际标准外都属于当地标准。[②] 他们认为,这种安排与《纽约公约》扩大仲裁裁决被承认执行的范围的立法宗旨具有内在一致性,从而避免那些因仲裁地特有的、不符合国际标准的当地标准的撤销依据或不公正的撤销程序导致仲裁裁决被撤销的当事人的合法权益无法得到保护的情况发生。

总的来说,非当地化理论要求摆脱仲裁地对仲裁裁决的司法监督控制,赋予执行地国法院最终的审查权,以及尊重当事人高度的意思自治权,符合国际贸易的发展需要而获得了一众国家的支持。1982年《瑞士联邦国际私法(草案)》曾包含了一条由当事人双方意定放弃对仲裁裁决提起撤销之诉的"弃权条款",旨在避免瑞士受理与其不存在任何实际关联的裁决撤销申请。1985年《比利时仲裁法》也增加了强制性规定:禁止提起与比利时当事人无关的在比利时作出的仲裁裁决的撤销申请,尽管该规定在1998年再次修订《比利时仲裁

---

① See E. Gaillard, *The Enforcement of Awards Set Aside in the Country of Origin*, ICSID Review, 1999, p. 19.

② See J. Paulsson, *Enforcing Arbitral Awards Notwithstanding Local Standard Annulments*, Asia Pacific Law Review, 1998.

法》时又被废除,原因在于许多当事人因忌惮自身权利无法在比利时得到救济而纷纷排除将比利时作为仲裁地的选项,这背离了比利时欲成为国际知名仲裁地的追求。《法国民事诉讼法典》第1522条、《瑞典仲裁法》第21条也都明确赋予当事人排除仲裁裁决撤销程序的权利。

前述国家的立法展现的非当地化的趋势是为了避免仲裁地对仲裁裁决的绝对控制,将裁决撤销制度相对化,这很大程度上为确认已撤销国际商事仲裁裁决的域外效力大开方便之门。但由于当今国际商事仲裁尚且无法普遍接受非当地化理论激进、过于自由的观点,很少有国家愿意完全放弃对本国境内的国际商事仲裁裁决的监督,因而其适用范围有限。

3. 相对属地主义理论

在对前述两种理论取舍之间逐渐形成了相对属地主义理论,也即在一般情形下执行地法院应秉承礼让原则遵从仲裁地法院的撤销判决,只有在例外情形下才能执行已撤销的仲裁裁决。① 执行地法院在有充分的说理或确信的事实支撑其认为仲裁地存在撤销依据不符合被国际社会广泛认可的标准、撤销程序违反国际公共政策或损害一般公平正义的基本理念的"例外情况"下,可发挥自由裁量权承认与执行已撤销仲裁裁决。采用该理论最典型的国家就是美国,尽管在早期坚持的是绝对属地主义理论,但经过近几十年来的案件积累,其逐渐形成了自身的一套标准。

4. 对上述理论的评价及对我国的建议

绝对属地主义理论虽然可以维持形式上的一致性,但由于仲裁地法院的撤销依据和撤销程序未必合法正当,容易造成实质上的不公平现象,其僵化的适用越来越难以获得国际社会的普遍认可。非当地化理论通过执行地法院对仲裁地撤销裁决的矫正来避免产生对当事人不公的结果,但这种做法破坏了仲裁裁决效力的稳定性和当事人对争议解决的合理期待,不符合国际礼让原则和《纽约公约》追求仲裁裁决在国际层面的确定性的目的。至于相对属地主义理论则较好地平衡了绝对属地主义理论的僵化与非当地化理论的过度自由化,对执行地法院自由裁量权加诸一定限制,能够防止被随意滥用,还能保证在一定

① 参见桑远棵:《超越属地主义:已撤销仲裁裁决的承认与执行》,载《武大国际法评论》2020年第4期。

程度上维护《纽约公约》所要求的确定性与可预见性。

虽说因各国对撤销国际商事仲裁裁决的效力认定的理论各不相同,使得已撤销仲裁裁决被承认和执行的情形获得存在空间,但在现实性上,相对属地主义理论能为已撤销国际商事仲裁裁决的域外效力存在的合理性提供较优的理论基础。

我国目前所遵循的是绝对属地主义理论,认可和接受仲裁地法院撤销的仲裁裁决并不予承认和执行,不承认已撤销裁决的域外效力。但就前述理论的对比可见,我国应当考虑向相对属地主义理论转变,作为执行地国时不应过于绝对放弃对被撤销的仲裁裁决进行司法审查的自由裁量权,在追求仲裁裁决法律效果的确定性与一致性和国际礼让的一般原则下,考虑个案的实质性影响因素特别是仲裁地法院基于明显不合理理由撤销仲裁裁决的例外情况,对被撤销的仲裁裁决予以承认和执行,实现支持仲裁与司法监督的动态平衡。

五、已撤销国际商事仲裁裁决在各国的域外效力司法实践

以上对作为确认撤销仲裁裁决效力依据的不同理论的辨析,有利于更好地理解采取不同理论立场的国家在具体司法实践中的做法,尽管各国相关案例的具体情况各不相同,但通过比较分析可以归纳出共有的特征供我国借鉴,以优化我国对已撤销仲裁裁决的司法审查制度的构建路径。从各国法院的实践来看,法国是典型的非当地化理论支持国,美国法院则逐渐形成坚持相对属地主义理论的传统,以及其他国家法院也有相关案例可作参考。

(一)法国:一贯承认撤销仲裁裁决域外效力——以适用有利于撤销仲裁裁决执行的本国法为原则

1. Pabalk v. Norsolor[①](1984 年,以下简称 Pabalk 案)

法国公司 Norsolor 和土耳其公司 Pabalk 因代理协议发生争议提交奥地利维也纳的仲裁庭进行仲裁,仲裁庭作出有利于 Pabalk 的裁决。Norsolor 不服裁决提起上诉,维也纳上诉法院认为仲裁庭适用的实体法不当,属于越权仲裁,撤销了部分裁决。Pabalk 根据该已撤销仲裁裁决在法国法院提出执行申请并获

① See Award of 26 October 1984 in ICC Case No. 3131. IXY. B. Com. Arb. [1984], p. 109 - 110; French Supreme Court, decision of 09 September 1984, Rev. Arb., 1985, p. 341.

得执行裁定,巴黎上诉法院依 Norsolor 申请和《纽约公约》第 5 条第 1 款 e 项撤回了法国法院的执行裁定。但最终法国最高法院基于 Pabalk 的申请恢复对该裁决的执行裁定,其理由在于:根据《纽约公约》第 7 条“更优惠权利条款”,法国有优先适用本国法促使仲裁裁决得到执行的权利。

2. Hilmarton v. OTV①(1994 年,以下简称 Hilmarton 案)

英国公司 Hilmarton 和法国公司 OTV 因咨询服务合同的费用产生纠纷,在日内瓦提出了仲裁,仲裁庭以合同无效为由驳回 Hilmarton 的申请。Hilmarton 不服上诉,日内瓦上诉法院以“仲裁裁决是武断的”为由撤销了仲裁庭作出的仲裁裁决,并且随后得到了瑞士最高法院的进一步认可。OTV 仍然向法国提出执行被撤销仲裁裁决的请求。巴黎一审法院作出执行裁定,得到巴黎上诉法院和法国最高法院的维持判决。法国最高法院认为,OTV 可以援引法国法律,《法国民事诉讼法典》第 1502 条没有规定《纽约公约》第 5 条第 1 款 e 项下的已撤销仲裁裁决是拒绝承认与执行仲裁裁决的理由,最终根据《纽约公约》第 7 条“更优惠权利条款”执行了该项已被撤销的国际商事仲裁裁决。

3. Putrabali v. Rena Holding②(2007 年,以下简称 Putrabali 案)

印尼公司 Putrabali 就法国公司 Rena Holding 拒绝支付在海难中丧失的货物的款项,向位于伦敦的国际综合生产协会(International General Produce Association,IGPA)提起仲裁。2001 年仲裁庭作出支持 Rena Holding 的裁决(以下简称裁决三)。伦敦高等法院根据 Putrabali 申请部分撤销裁决三,认为 Rena Holding 拒绝支付货款的行为构成违约,该争议又重新回到仲裁庭。2003 年仲裁庭作出支持 Putrabali 的裁决,要求 Rena Holding 支付货款(以下简称裁决四)。

Rena Holding 向巴黎大审法院请求执行已被伦敦高院撤销的裁决三,2003 年巴黎大审法院作出准予执行裁决三的决定。巴黎上诉法院驳回 Putrabali 的上诉申请,认为一项仲裁裁决在外国被撤销的事实并不阻碍相关当事人请求法国法院将其执行,而且执行裁决三不会违背国际公共政策。该裁定获得法国最

① See Soc. HilmartonLtd. v. Soc. OTV, French Supreme Court, decision of 23 March 1994, XIXY. B. Com. Arb. (1994), p. 665; Courd' Appel, Paris, 18January2007, Yea rbook XXXII(2007), p. 297 - 298.

② See PT Putrabali Adyamuliav. Rena Holding, in XXXIIY. B. Com. Arb. (2007), p. 299.

高法院的认可，其认为一项国际仲裁裁决不囿于任何国家法律秩序之下，所以其有效性及是否蕴含国际争议必须由裁决执行地国的准据规则来确定。所以 Rena Holding 可向法国寻求执行裁决三，并且可以援用法国关于国际仲裁的法律规则，因为法国并未将裁决已被仲裁地法院撤销列为一项拒绝承认与执行的理由。同时，Putrabali 向巴黎大审法院申请执行裁决四获得肯定。2005 年巴黎上诉法院推翻巴黎大审法院的决定并获得法国最高法院的认可，理由在于：裁决四与裁决三处理的是相同当事人之间的相同争议，而裁决三已获准执行，产生了既判力，因此，裁决四不能在法国获得执行。

4. 归纳小结

通过上述三个典型案件可见，法国法院的实践遵循一贯的轨迹——以《纽约公约》第 7 条"更优惠权利条款"为"铠甲"武装其以更有利于仲裁裁决执行的法国国内法来判断仲裁裁决被撤销的合理性的观点，因为法国国内法拒绝承认和执行仲裁裁决的规定中不包含裁决已撤销这项理由。而且，尽管《纽约公约》法文译本将第 5 条第 1 款的"may"译为"必须"，但法国法院的实践与之恰恰相反，法国积极行使该条下的自由裁量权，承认已撤销国际商事仲裁裁决的域外效力，认为国际商事仲裁具有非当地化性质，不附属于任何一个国家的法律体系，因而仲裁地的撤销判决不具有普遍效力。

需要说明的是，Putrabali 案中法国最高法院也认为本案属于针对"同一纠纷"作出两份相反结果裁决的情况，案情上与 UNI - TOP 案存在一定相似之处，法国法院和中国法院在说理时都采用了既判力或"一裁终局"原则论证其裁判结果，尽管该原则并非 Paulsson 所谓的撤销仲裁裁决"国际标准"，但作为撤销仲裁裁决标准或不予执行理由在国际上也具有一定支持度，[①]如 2012 年《示范法判例汇编》所示："'仲裁庭无权对终局裁决进行修改或推翻'，'重新仲裁'可被认为属于《UNCITRAL 示范法》第 34 条第 2 款（a）项（iii）涵盖的情形。"因而将之归为"当地标准"有失偏颇。然而两者也有一定的差异：Putrabali 案是当两份裁决（裁决三、裁决四）进入执行阶段后，法国最高法院肯定了裁决三的既判力阻却裁决四得以执行的可能性；而 UNI - TOP 案是在两份裁决（裁决一、裁决二）效力审查阶段，法院就判定后裁决的产生违背"一裁终局"而应被撤销，但这

① See UNCITRAL 2012 Digest of Case Law on International Commercial Arbitration, p. 153, para. 91.

并不妨碍北京四中院采用“一裁终局”原则作为撤裁依据存在合理性。

（二）美国：自成一套判断规律——仅在限缩的例外情况承认撤销仲裁裁决域外效力

1. 承认和执行的案例

（1）Chromalloy v. Arab Republic of Egypt[①]（1996 年，以下简称 Chromalloy 案）

美国公司 Chromalloy 与埃及政府国防部于 1988 年订立军事采购合同纠纷，1991 年埃及政府因 Chromalloy 没有履约而单方面终止合同。1992 年 Chromalloy 根据仲裁条款提出仲裁，1994 年开罗仲裁庭认为埃及政府违约，应当对 Chromalloy 予以补偿。同年 Chromalloy 向美国哥伦比亚法院提出执行申请，埃及政府紧随向埃及上诉法院提起撤销仲裁裁决请求，向美国法院提出中止执行申请。埃及上诉法院以“仲裁员适用法律错误”为由撤销仲裁裁决，美国哥伦比亚法院没有认可该项撤销裁定，依然准予执行仲裁裁决，其理由是：首先依据《纽约公约》第 5 条执行地法院拥有自由裁量权；其次，根据《纽约公约》第 7 条，法院可以优先适用国内法以更好地执行仲裁裁决，并且埃及上诉法院的撤销理由不在《美国联邦仲裁法》（Federal Arbitration Act，FAA）第 10 条规定的撤销事由范围内；最后，当事人在仲裁条款中约定，一旦裁决作出，任何一方当事人不得对仲裁裁决提起诉讼，法院认为应尊重当事人的合意，而埃及法院违反了美国的基本公共政策，故应承认和执行该被撤销的仲裁裁决。

（2）Corporación Mexicana de Mantenimiento Integral（COMMISA）v. Pemex – Exploracióny Producción[②]（2013 年，以下简称 Pemex 案）

美国公司 COMMISA 针对其与墨西哥所有的石油天然气公司 Pemex 的天然气平台建设争议提起仲裁并获得了对其有利的裁决。后来，墨西哥法院根据仲裁程序开始之后的墨西哥法律，认为仲裁庭在解除合同这一仲裁事项上超越了其权力，因为行政事项具有不可仲裁性，所以撤销了该仲裁裁决。美国南区地方法院审查了仲裁裁决被撤销的理由后，认为墨西哥法院适用双方订立仲裁

---

① See Chromalloy Aeroservices v. Arab Republic of Egypt. ,939 F. Supp. 907（D. D. C. 1996）.

② See Corp. Mexicana de Mantenimiento Integral v. Pemex – Exploraciony Prod. ,962 F. Supp. 2d 642（S. D. N. Y. 2013）.

协议之后生效的法律违背了法不溯及既往的基本法理,与美国社会基本的公平正义观念相违背,且根据 Chromalloy 案形成的良法,美国法院认为该被撤销的国际商事仲裁满足拒绝承认和执行的例外情况,应予承认和执行。

2. 拒绝承认和执行的案例

(1)Baker Marine (Nig.) Ltd. v. Chevron (Nig.) Ltd.[①](1999 年,以下简称 Baker 案)

一起船舶服务合同争议的三方当事人均是尼日利亚籍公司:Baker 公司、Chevron 公司和 Danos 公司。Baker 认为 Chevron 和 Danos 违反合同,根据仲裁条款在尼日利亚的拉各斯提起仲裁,两起仲裁裁决都支持 Baker 的主张。Baker 向尼日利亚联邦高等法院申请执行两项裁决,但该院以"缺乏足够证据支持"和"超越权限仲裁"为由撤销了两项裁决。Baker 向美国法院提出执行申请,但美国法院以尼日利亚法院撤销了两项裁决为由拒绝承认与执行,理由在于:本案当事人非美国国籍,案件与美国无关联;当事人没有约定不得对仲裁裁决提出上诉;尼日利亚的撤销判决程序正当,美国没有足够理由行使自由裁量权;拒绝执行不违背美国的公共政策。

(2)Martin Spier v. Calzaturificio Technica.[②](1999 年,以下简称 Martin 案)

美国工程师 Martin 和意大利制造商 Calzaturificio 因制造靴子的服务合同产生纠纷提交仲裁,仲裁庭作出了对 Martin 有利的仲裁裁决,但意大利法院以"仲裁员超越权限"为由撤销了该仲裁裁决,并得到威尼斯上诉法院和意大利最高法院的认可。美国纽约南区法院认为,意大利法院作出的撤销判决本身是公正的;当事人没有明确作出放弃其他救济权利的意思表示,因此拒绝承认和执行该仲裁裁决。

(3)Termorio & Leas Co. Group S. A. E. S. P. v. Electranta S. P.[③](2007 年,以下简称 Termorio 案)

在美国 Leas Co. Group 的全资子公司 Termorio 与哥伦比亚国有电力公司 Electranta 的仲裁案件中,仲裁庭作出对 Termorio 有利的仲裁裁决,但被哥伦比

① See Baker Marine, Ltd. v. Chevron, Ltd., 191 F. 3d 194(2d Cir. 1999).

② See Spier v. Calzaturificio Technica, S. p. A., 71 F. Supp. 2d 279(S. D. N. Y. 1999).

③ See Termorio S. A. E. S. P. v. Electranta S. P., 376 U. S. App. D. C. 242, 487 F. 3d 928(2007).

亚行政法院以“仲裁庭适用国际商会(International Chamber of Commerce,ICC)的仲裁规则违反了哥伦比亚法律”为由撤销。美国哥伦比亚巡回上诉法院认为哥伦比亚作为《纽约公约》项下的具有“首要管辖权”的国家,其作出的撤销判决是合法的,美国作为“次要管辖国”不能轻易否决该判决;该案事实与 Chromalloy 案有“明显区别”,没有违反美国基本公平正义观念,不属于拒绝承认和执行的例外情况,最终拒绝执行该被撤销的裁决。

(4)Thai – Lao Lignite Co. ,Ltd. v. Government of the Lao People's Democratic Republic[①](2014 年,以下简称 Thai – Lao 案)

马来西亚上诉法院撤销了 Thai – Lao Lignite 两家泰国公司与老挝政府之间关于采矿和经营权项目开发协议的仲裁裁决,理由是仲裁员判断两份合同的管辖权及承认和裁定非协议方的索赔有误,该判决获得马来西亚高等法院认可。美国纽约地区法院认为马来西亚上诉法院和高等法院的判决都是公平、程序正当的,不存在适用《纽约公约》第 5 条第 1 款项下的自由裁量权,不属于违反公平正义原则的例外情形,且当事人也不能提供充分证据证明另外情形存在。因此,美国法院不予承认和执行该仲裁裁决。

(5)Getma International v. Republic of Guinea[②](2017 年,以下简称 Getma 案)

法国公司 Getma 与几内亚共和国就特许协议产生的争端提交仲裁,仲裁庭作出对 Getma 有利的裁决,但被非洲司法和仲裁共同法院(Common Court of Justice and Arbitration,CCJA)撤销,理由是违反了仲裁员费用的强制性规定。Getma 希望美国法院能执行这个被撤销的仲裁裁决。美国哥伦比亚上诉巡回法院维持了哥伦比亚地区法院的一审判决,不予承认和执行该裁决,理由在于:Getma 未能充分证明撤销判决达到了违反最基本的道德和正义理念的例外情形,考虑国际礼让原则,美国需要尊重 CCJA 的首要管辖权,即使美国具有支持仲裁的联邦政策,也不能承认和执行该被撤销仲裁裁决。

---

① See Thai – Lao Lignite(Thail.)Co. ,Ltd. v. Gov' t of the Lao People's Democratic Republic,997 F. Supp. 2d 214(S. D. N. Y. 2014).

② See Getma Int'l v. Republic of Guinea,862 F. 3d 45(2017).

3. 归纳小结

不难看出美国法院在对被撤销的国际商事仲裁裁决的承认与执行方面态度相对谨慎,且存在前后不一的判例,虽并非像法国法院有相对连贯一致的态度,但也形成了一套有迹可循的、具有本国特色的、较为完善的标准——在承认本国法院具有承认和执行被撤销国际商事仲裁的自由裁量权这个基本前提下,依据国际礼让原则拒绝承认和执行被撤销裁决为一般原则,仅当申请执行人能够充分证明严格的"例外情形"存在时才能承认和执行被撤裁决,比如是否明显违反公平正义原则、违反美国公共政策等,根据个案情形加以考虑诸多因素如美国国内法规定、案件当事人与美国的联系、当事人在仲裁协议中合意排除诉讼、区分首要管辖权和次要管辖权等。

由上述美国法院案例可发现,Chromalloy 案中形成的"尊重当事人的意思自治"先例被后续案件的法官反复援引,足以看出在美国司法界意思自治对认定已撤销仲裁裁决域外效力的重要性。UNI - TOP 公司认为其所涉案件与 Chromalloy 案具有实质上的相似性,最关键的一点就是指出双方当事人明确合意"不得起诉",进而认为国勘公司提起撤销之诉以及北京四中院审理并作出撤销仲裁裁决决定的行为显然违反了合同约定,①美国法院很可能揪住这点而认为北京四中院作出的撤销仲裁裁决决定侵害当事人依仲裁协议约定的合理期待利益。但是当事人意思自治是否能避免裁决作出地国对仲裁的司法监督,目前仍存在极大争论,基本认识是强制性规定不能由当事人意定排除。

值得注意的是,UNI - TOP 公司还认为如果法院拒绝承认和执行该被撤销的裁决就违背了美国支持仲裁终局性和约束力的公共政策,Chromalloy 案中提及的"公共政策"在后案说理中也出现过,虽然没有明确说明违反公共政策的内涵,但从法院说理可归纳出其大致包括是否无视当事人意思自治、存在 FAA 中"明显漠视"(manifest disregard)法律的情形、适用实体法审查案件撤销裁决等不公正、带有偏见的做法,有观点认为公共政策实际上构成了美国法院判断撤销裁决效力问题的标准。② 关于 UNI - TOP 公司就北京四中院审查仲裁裁决时

① Memorandum of Law in Support of Petition to Confirm an International Arbitral Award.

② 参见[西]帕德罗·马丁内兹 - 弗拉加:《国际商事仲裁:美国学说发展与证据开示》,蒋小红、谢新胜等译,中国社会科学出版社 2009 年版,第 169 ~ 170 页。

涉及实体部分的质疑，可能会被美国法院认定为违背美国公共秩序，但笔者认为此处应与 Chromalloy 案进行区分：UNI－TOP 案存在两项仲裁裁决，而 Chromalloy 案仅涉及单独一项裁决；北京四中院的审查目的是回应 UNI－TOP 公司在提起第二项仲裁时的请求理由，以此来认定裁决二是否抵触了裁决一产生的既判力、是否存在如 UNI－TOP 公司所称的"新的事实"，如果不审查比对裁决一和裁决二双方实体权利和义务内容有无变化则无法作出合理、合法判断；而且如果要考虑仲裁的终局性和约束力，那么提起第二次仲裁的 UNI－TOP 公司才是不遵守一裁终局、引起一切后续纠纷的始作俑者，国勘公司不得已向法院申请撤销仲裁裁决是其维护自身权利的一种救济方式。基于此，笔者认为美国法院如果因审查涉及实体内容和"违背"仲裁终局性而认定国勘公司和北京四中院的撤销仲裁裁决决定违背美国公共秩序不能让人信服。

（三）其他国家：基于主观或客观的撤销仲裁裁决效力认定思路

其他国家如荷兰、德国、奥地利也曾有少数执行已撤销仲裁裁决的实践。

1. Yukos Capital SARL v. OAO Rosneft[①]（2009 年，以下简称 Yukos 案）

卢森堡的 Yucos 集团下的金融公司 Yukos Capital 在 2005 年 12 月向莫斯科商会国际商事仲裁院（International Court of Commercial Arbitration of the Moscow Chamber of Commerce）提起仲裁请求 Rosneft 归还其四项贷款及利息。仲裁庭支持 Yukos Capital 的大多数请求，Rosneft 向俄罗斯法院请求撤销裁决，莫斯科商事法院作出撤销裁决决定，得到上诉法院支持。荷兰阿姆斯特丹地方法院依据《纽约公约》第 5 条第 1 款 e 项拒绝 Yukos Capital 的执行申请。[②] 阿姆斯特丹上诉法院推翻地方法院决定，认为《纽约公约》并没有对荷兰法院应否拒绝承认被俄罗斯法院撤销了的仲裁裁决提供答案，这个问题应由荷兰国际私法来回答。由于俄罗斯法官所作出的撤销仲裁裁决的判决很可能被认定为"缺乏公正和独立性且存在偏见"（a dispensing of justice that must be qualified as partial and dependent）的产物，因此，在考虑 Yukos Capital 所提起的执行涉案裁决之申请时，俄罗斯法院撤销仲裁裁决的情形须被忽略。Rosneft 上诉，荷兰最高

① See Yukos Capital SARL v. OAO Rosneft, Gerecht－shof Amsterdam (Amsterdam Court of Appeal) LJN: BI 2451, 200.005.269 (28 April 2009) s3.5; (2009) 34 YB Com Arb 703.

② See Albert Jan Van DenBerg, *Should the Setting Aside of the Arbitral Award be Abolished*? ICSID Review, 2014, p. 17－18.

法院认为 Rosneft 向其提出的上诉申请不具备可受理性。[①] 荷兰法院被批判存在随意滥用例外情形进行自由裁量的嫌疑——因其上诉法院只是根据与案件无关的新闻和报告,并在没有确凿证据的情形下,主观地径直认定俄罗斯法院在涉及俄罗斯国家利益的案件中缺乏公正性和独立性而漠视俄罗斯的撤销判决。

2. Do Zdravilisce Radenska v. Kajo – Erzeugnisse Essenzen GmbH(1993 年,以下简称 Kajo 案)

奥地利法院依据奥地利和南斯拉夫签订的《相互承认与执行仲裁裁决》的双边协定和双方加入的《欧洲国际商事仲裁公约》(以下简称《欧洲公约》)第 9 条第 1 款规定的不予执行的外国仲裁裁决理由,执行了斯洛文尼亚最高法院以违反国内公共政策为由被撤销的仲裁裁决。[②] 同样是 Kajo 案,申请人在获得奥地利法院执行许可后也向德国法院申请执行,德国法院也根据《欧洲公约》第 9 条第 1 款作出了执行判决。由此可见,不似荷兰法院基于主观判断,德国和奥地利承认已撤销裁决域外效力的依据是两国签订的双边协定或同为缔约方的区域性公约客观的法律依据,显然更具说服力和可预见性。

从前述国家法院对已撤销仲裁裁决域外效力认定的司法实践案例可以归纳出:不同国家承认和执行被撤裁决的依据各不相同;即使是在同一国家对该问题的认定也没有完全可复刻照搬的模板或公式,不论是积极承认与执行的“法国模式”,还是例外承认且尊重当事人意思自治的“美国套路”,或者荷兰主观认定不公平以及德国、奥地利的客观公约依据,都需要根据个案案情加以具体分析,不加区分地一概拒绝或者同意承认和执行被撤销的仲裁裁决都是非理性之举。

六、已撤销国际商事仲裁裁决在我国的域外效力和优化进路

在各国奉行的不同仲裁体制中,关于已撤销仲裁裁决的域外效力问题,应

---

① 在荷兰申请执行《纽约公约》项下的仲裁裁决程序:如果申请人的执行申请被初审法院拒绝,其有权将初审法院的裁定诉至上诉法院;如果上诉法院同样作出拒绝执行的裁定,其还可以继续诉至最高法院。但是,如果初审法院或上诉法院作出了准许执行外国仲裁裁决之裁定,那么,若不考虑特殊情况,另一方无权再上诉,申请人可在获取执行准许后即刻推进执行裁决。

② Do Zdravilisce Radenska v. Kajo – Erzeugnisse Essenzen GmbH, decision of 23 February 1998, in-XXIVa Y. B. Com. Arb(1999),925;Rev. Arb. (1999),p. 385.

寻求仲裁地与执行地法院司法监督权以及当事人意思自治扩张与法院职权监督强制之间的平衡,可以预见到未来承认和执行被撤销的国际商事仲裁裁决将成为一种国际趋势。对此,我国应先完善自身的仲裁制度,充分借鉴国际主流经验并结合本国目前仲裁发展水平形成具有中国特色的仲裁体制。趁着我国仲裁法修订的契机,基于前述关于被撤销国际商事仲裁裁决的域外效力认定问题的思考和比较法研究,对我国仲裁裁决撤销制度的改革优化路径提出建议。

(一)检视我国对撤销仲裁裁决域外效力认定的现有立场

最高人民法院发布的《关于执行我国加入的〈承认及执行外国仲裁裁决公约〉的通知》(以下简称《外国仲裁通知》),其将《纽约公约》第 5 条第 1 款 e 项视为强制性条款,未赋予我国法院自由裁量权。[①] 但最高人民法院与我国香港特别行政区、澳门特别行政区及台湾地区的区际安排或规定[②]中的相关规定与内地并不一致——对被撤销的香港和澳门仲裁裁决,内地法院在一定情形下可以承认和执行;对被撤销的台湾地区仲裁裁决无法在大陆得到认可和执行。除此之外,最高人民法院在我国目前唯一一例涉及《纽约公约》第 5 条的邦基农贸新加坡私人有限公司申请承认和执行英国仲裁裁决案[③]中对 e 项采取回避性态度,让人难以琢磨其真正的观点。

(二)在我国承认撤销仲裁裁决域外效力并予以执行的可能性

1. 我国目前致力于构建国际商事仲裁中心

改革开放以来,我国企业与他国企业通过国际仲裁解决纠纷的实践也越来越多。从国务院 2015 年推进上海自由贸易试验区改革后吸引众多国际知名仲裁机构在上海设立代表处,到 2019 年允许先前设立代表机构就特定领域的国际民商事争议开展实质业务,再到沿海地区自由贸易试验区“遍地开花”,我国不断向外界释放我国仲裁友好的积极讯号,为我国承认已撤销仲裁裁决域外效力拓展了创新空间。

---

① 《外国仲裁通知》规定,如果被执行人提供证据证明裁决具有公约第 5 条第 1 款中规定的情形,我国法院“应当”拒绝执行该仲裁裁决。

② 《最高人民法院关于认可和执行台湾地区仲裁裁决的规定》第 14 条;《最高人民法院关于内地与香港特别行政区相互执行仲裁裁决的安排》第 7 条第 1 款第 5 项;《最高人民法院关于内地与澳门特别行政区相互认可和执行仲裁裁决的安排》第 7 条第 1 款第 5 项。

③ 《最高人民法院关于邦基农贸新加坡私人有限公司申请承认和执行英国仲裁裁决一案的请示的复函》,民四他字〔2006〕第 41 号。

2. 仲裁法修订为契机

2021 年 7 月 30 日司法部公布《仲裁法(修订)(征求意见稿)》(以下简称《仲裁法意见稿》),无论从体例还是内容上都为中国仲裁制度进一步改革和发展指明方向,当然部分条文也存在有待完善的地方。①《仲裁法意见稿》贯彻"统筹推进国内法治和涉外法治"思想,积极借鉴仲裁领域国际法律规则,引入仲裁地概念、在涉外部分引入临时仲裁、赋予仲裁庭临时措施决定权等,都展现我国力行改革的决心与魄力,也为承认已撤销仲裁裁决域外效力或减少我国法院撤裁判决被外国法院作出否定评价的情况出现提供了创新动力。

3. 除《纽约公约》第 7 条外,其他国际公约或双边协定的规定

1965 年《关于解决国家和他国国民之间投资争端公约》(以下简称《华盛顿公约》)第 54 条第 3 款规定,裁决的执行应受被请求在其领土执行的国家关于执行判决的现行法律支配,赋予了执行地国依据其本国法律审查已撤销裁决的域外效力问题。此外,还可以依据中国与他国签订的双边司法协助协定中的承认和执行条款的具体规定处理该问题。

(三)改革与优化路径

通过审视我国长久以来对已撤销国际商事仲裁裁决域外效力持有的消极态度,分析我国承认并执行被撤裁决存在的可能性空间,为寻找我国自身的改革与优化路径,笔者提出以下几点构想:

1. 明确基调:承认我国法院对被撤销国际商事仲裁裁决域外效力认定有限缩的自由裁量权

我国应通过最高人民法院的司法解释或更高层级的法律明确,基于国际礼让原则在一般情况下尊重外国法院撤销仲裁裁决的决定,但我国保留作为执行地法院拥有《纽约公约》第 5 条第 1 款 e 项下对被撤销的外国仲裁裁决予以承认和执行的自由裁量权,为我国的仲裁裁决司法监督在执行问题上留有一定的空间,不仅有利于保障我国当事人的权利,也在国际上释放了我国仲裁友好的积极信号。为了防止该自由裁量权被滥用,我国可借鉴美国法院的审慎做法,采用如违反基本的公平公正原则等"例外情况"的规定为该权力套上一定枷锁,

① 参见刘晓红、冯硕:《对〈仲裁法〉修订的"三点"思考——以〈仲裁法(修订)(征求意见稿)〉为参照》,载《上海政法学院学报(法治论丛)》2021 年第 5 期。

并且建立一套基于个案的审查机制，根据具体情况分析外国法院的撤销依据和撤销程序是否符合国际通行的标准而非仅为其本国的特殊规定，防止对当事人造成不公的现象。此外，我国 1998 年《最高人民法院关于人民法院撤销涉外仲裁裁决有关事项的通知》(已被修改)确立了撤销涉外仲裁裁决的层报制度，应继续遵守，将最终决定权交由最高人民法院。

2. 同步配套：回归国内仲裁裁决与涉外仲裁裁决撤销审查标准的分轨制

基于我国目前国内仲裁与涉外仲裁的二元体制，我国现行《仲裁法》第 70 条及《民事诉讼法》第 281 条一同规定了我国涉外仲裁裁决的撤销以及不予执行的事由，审查的都属于程序性事项，对国内仲裁裁决才审查实体内容，采用与二元体制相配套的分轨制。但《仲裁法意见稿》第 77 条对撤销国内裁决和涉外裁决审查标准采"并轨制"，将原仅适用于国内裁决的"伪造证据""仲裁员腐败"等实体审查标准延伸至涉外仲裁裁决，极易导致适用上的不适配，而且这种做法是与国际通行标准相悖的。如果《仲裁法意见稿》第 77 条最终通过，当我国法院依照《仲裁法》对在我国作出的涉外仲裁裁决审查后予以撤销，执行地法院在审查时未必会认可我国的撤销依据，如果该国法院非坚持绝对属地主义理论，可能会发挥其自由裁量权对我国撤销的仲裁裁决予以承认和执行。这样一来当事人对仲裁裁决救济的合理期待落空，我国与该国的互惠关系可能会受影响，还将影响当事人对我国仲裁审查水平的信任度。因而，笔者认为应当保留我国对国内仲裁裁决和涉外仲裁裁决审查标准的分轨制，对涉外仲裁裁决采取仅审查程序的"程序监督论"模式，借鉴其他国家仲裁法的做法，允许当事人以明确书面方式合意约定是否排除撤销权、选择是否允许司法审查延及实体事项等事项，以最大化地保证当事人的意思自治，可以缓解僵化的审查标准，寻求公平与效率之间的平衡。与此同时，我国《民事诉讼法》等一系列相关的法律文件也必须形成一致的审查模式，避免国内法规之间发生冲突。

3. 国际接轨：撤销依据与撤销程序的基于本土考量的合理选择

作为仲裁地国时，为了让被我国法院撤销的仲裁裁决在域外得以被尊重，我国应完善涉外仲裁裁决撤销制度。在撤销依据上应采用国际标准，可参照《示范法》第 34 条第 2 款所规定的撤销事由及两种提出方式：一是当事人提供证据证明；二是法院依职权主动认定，通过当事人和法院的协同作用平衡双方当事人的利益。[①] 由于《示范法》是对《纽约公约》继承基础上的优化,体现了国际仲裁的核心价值,通过借鉴该种机制,有利于我国打造国际仲裁中心,提升国际影响力。在撤销程序上,我国也必须秉承善意和正义规范和行使司法监督权,不得为了本国利益而恶意违反正当程序撤销裁决,否则我国法院撤销仲裁裁决的合法性和合理性都将受到执行地法院的质疑。

而作为执行地国时,我国应充分利用《纽约公约》第 7 条"更优惠权利条款",如果外国法院的撤销依据不符合国际标准,不能给予当事人更多的权利保障,而我国法律相对更有利于仲裁裁决目的的实现,且承认和执行该被撤销的裁决不违背我国的社会公共利益,我国可援引《纽约公约》第 7 条予以承认和执行。

① 参见苟应鹏:《我国临时仲裁裁决撤销制度的建构》,载《北京仲裁》2020 年第 3 期。

外国仲裁裁决在中国的承认与执行

——2019~2022年司法实践

林一飞　蔡璐璐*

摘　要:国际仲裁相比其他争议解决方式更受各国商事主体欢迎,一个重要的原因是《纽约公约》可以有效确保仲裁裁决在国际范围内的承认与执行。自1987年中国正式加入《纽约公约》以来,我国法院在适用《纽约公约》审查外国仲裁裁决方面积累了丰富的经验。通过定期追踪司法审查案例,我们或许可一窥我国法院在践行《纽约公约》过程中存在的问题、争论以及新的转变。本文梳理了2019~2022年法院审理的44个承认与执行外国仲裁裁决案例,通过评述案例涉及的主要抗辩事由,包括仲裁协议、正当程序、裁决范围、可仲裁性、公共政策等,以呈现近年来我国法院理解和适用《纽约公约》的司法实践新发展,并希望未来能日臻完善。

关键词:《纽约公约》　外国仲裁裁决的承认与执行　仲裁协议　仲裁裁决

在国际商事争议解决领域,仲裁相比于其他争议解决方式受到更多商事主体的青睐,除了仲裁具有的专业性、保密性、灵活性等特点之外,最为关键的吸引力在于裁决的可执行性。《纽约公约》成员国数量不断增加,从最初的24个

---

* 林一飞,法学博士、法学研究员,一裁律师事务所顾问;蔡璐璐,一裁律师事务所顾问。

发展至今已达171个,几乎覆盖世界范围主要的国际经济贸易主体所在国及地区,裁决可被承认与执行的范围之广是外国法院判决无法媲美的。尽管公约仅对仲裁协议和仲裁裁决的承认与执行作出相对框架性的规定,不可否认,公约在确保裁决获各缔约方司法机关承认与执行、推动国际商事仲裁理念一致化、平衡商事主体私权利与缔约方司法监督权等方面始终发挥着至关重要的作用;同时,客观上《纽约公约》也对各缔约方国内仲裁立法及司法实践相应地产生重要影响。

中国1987年正式加入《纽约公约》后,法院在适用公约审查当事人申请承认与执行外国和境外仲裁裁决方面积累了丰富的司法实践。本文通过概述2019～2022年的立法规定以及外国裁决在我国法院申请承认和执行的案例情况,按可能涉及的《纽约公约》项下的抗辩事由以及当事人所提主要抗辩,包括仲裁协议抗辩、正当程序抗辩、裁决范围抗辩、可仲裁性抗辩、公共政策抗辩等,选取相关案例进行简要介绍及评述,[①]供业界了解近此阶段我国法院适用《纽约公约》审查外国仲裁裁决的裁判立场和解释标准。

一、概述

中国承认与执行外国仲裁裁决的主要国内法依据包括《中华人民共和国民事诉讼法》(以下简称《民事诉讼法》)以及最高人民法院发布的各项司法解释。根据规定,法院主要依照我国缔结或参加的国际条约或基于互惠原则承认与执行外国仲裁裁决。1987年《纽约公约》正式对我国生效后,《纽约公约》成为我国法院承认与执行外国仲裁裁决最主要的法律依据。为解决法院适用《纽约公约》之初产生的各种问题,1991年《民事诉讼法》从立法层面上明确法院承认与执行外国仲裁裁决的司法审查标准应与《纽约公约》精神保持一致。此后,最高人民法院通过发布系列司法解释,明确涉及外国仲裁裁决的承认与执行案件《纽约公约》优先于国内法的位阶而应优先适用,建立拒绝承认与执行外国仲裁裁决案件的层层上报至最高人民法院的报核制度。此外,最高人民法院通过公

---

① 有关此前的中国法院适用《纽约公约》的实践及评析,参见林一飞:《外国仲裁裁决的承认与执行:中国二十年的司法实践》,载《国际经济法学刊》2009年第1期;林一飞:《外国仲裁裁决在中国的承认与执行:1987年—2009年的司法实践》,载韩健主编:《商事仲裁评论》(第1辑),对外经济贸易大学出版社2008年版;林一飞、叶珊珊:《〈纽约公约〉下外国仲裁裁决的承认与执行:2008～2018年的中国实践》,载刘晓春、潘剑锋主编:《中国国际仲裁评论》(总第二卷),法律出版社2020年版,第101～156页。

布一系列答复典型个案审查意见等具有司法解释性质的文件，逐步规范各级法院关于外国仲裁裁决的审查标准和裁判尺度。

2019～2022年，在统一裁判尺度、规范适用标准、明确支持仲裁的司法态度方面，我国法院一如既往地做了大量工作。2021年1月8日，《最高人民法院关于人民法院为海南自由贸易港建设提供司法服务和保障的意见》第30条"推进国际司法协助和交流合作"中规定，"恪守国际公约义务，依照《纽约公约》承认和执行外国仲裁裁决，严格适用公共政策，便利裁决跨境执行。"2021年3月22日，《最高人民法院关于人民法院为北京市国家服务业扩大开放综合示范区、中国（北京）自由贸易试验区建设提供司法服务和保障的意见》第19条"加强国际商事纠纷解决机制建设"中规定，"依法支持和保障中外当事人在仲裁前和仲裁中的财产保全、证据保全、行为保全的申请和执行。支持在自由贸易试验区内注册的企业之间约定在特定地点、按照特定仲裁规则、由特定人员对相关争议进行仲裁。恪守国际公约义务，依照《纽约公约》承认和执行外国仲裁裁决。"2022年1月24日，《全国法院涉外商事海事审判工作座谈会会议纪要》第105～109条中专门对申请承认和执行外国仲裁裁决案件的审查作出规定。① 2022年10月28日，《最

① 《全国法院涉外商事海事审判工作座谈会会议纪要》第105条规定："【《纽约公约》第四条的理解】申请人向人民法院申请承认和执行外国仲裁裁决，应当根据《纽约公约》第四条的规定提交相应的材料，提交的材料不符合《纽约公约》第四条规定的，人民法院应当认定其申请不符合受理条件，裁定不予受理。已经受理的，裁定驳回申请。"

第106条规定："【《纽约公约》第五条的理解】人民法院适用《纽约公约》审理申请承认和执行外国仲裁裁决案件时，应当根据《纽约公约》第五条的规定，对被申请人主张的不予承认和执行仲裁裁决事由进行审查。对被申请人未主张的事由或者其主张事由超出《纽约公约》第五条第一款规定的法定事由范围的，人民法院不予审查。人民法院应当根据《纽约公约》第五条第二款的规定，依职权审查仲裁裁决是否存在裁决事项依我国法律不可仲裁，以及承认和执行仲裁裁决是否违反我国公共政策。"

第107条规定："【未履行协商前置程序不违反约定程序】人民法院适用《纽约公约》审理申请承认和执行外国仲裁裁决案件时，当事人在仲裁协议中约定'先协商解决，协商不成再提请仲裁'的，一方当事人未经协商即申请仲裁，另一方当事人以对方违反协商前置程序的行为构成《纽约公约》第五条第一款丁项规定的仲裁程序与各方之间的协议不符为由主张不予承认和执行仲裁裁决的，人民法院不予支持。"

第108条规定："【违反公共政策的情形】人民法院根据《纽约公约》审理承认和执行外国仲裁裁决案件时，如人民法院生效裁定已经认定当事人之间的仲裁协议不成立、无效、失效或者不可执行，承认和执行该裁决将与人民法院生效裁定相冲突的，应当认定构成《纽约公约》第五条第二款乙项规定的违反我国公共政策的情形。"

第109条规定："【承认和执行程序中的仲裁保全】当事人向人民法院申请承认和执行外国仲裁裁决，人民法院受理申请后，当事人申请财产保全的，人民法院可以参照民事诉讼法及相关司法解释的规定执行。申请人应当提供担保，不提供担保的，裁定驳回申请。"

高人民法院关于人民法院涉外审判工作情况的报告》中肯定某地方法院首次将境外仲裁机构在我国内地作出的裁决认定为我国涉外仲裁裁决的做法,某种程度上间接规范了《纽约公约》的适用标准。鉴于本文主要立足于司法实务,上述规定在此暂不详述。

通过公开途径检索 2019 ~ 2022 年申请承认与执行外国仲裁裁决案例裁判文书,本文主要以法院审结的 44 个涉外国仲裁裁决案例(不包含申请人撤回申请、当事人和解等法院未实质阐明关于承认与执行案涉裁决裁判观点的案例)为样本进行研究。为直观了解情况,表 1 对案例相关情形作出简单说明。

表 1　2019 ~ 2022 年申请承认与执行外国仲裁裁决的案例

序号	裁决年份	申请人	被申请人	裁决地	执行法院	仲裁机构	案号/编号	判决结果
1	2018	香港泉水有限公司 Water Solutions (Hong Kong) Limited	宏柏家电(深圳)有限公司	美国	深圳中院	美国仲裁协会	(2016)粤03民初366号	承认与执行部分裁决事项
2	2018	特郎索网络有限公司(Telenco Networks SAS)	内蒙古北特通信有限责任公司	瑞士	内蒙古自治区呼和浩特市中级人民法院	瑞士国际商会仲裁机构	(2019)内01民初268号	承认[1]
3	2019	肯考迪亚农产品贸易有限公司(Concordia Agritrading Pte Ltd.)	山东晨曦集团有限公司	英国	山东省日照市中级人民法院	国际油、油籽和油脂协会(FOSFA)仲裁庭	(2018)鲁11协外认5号	承认[2]
4	2019	沃泰思航运有限公司(Vertex Shipping Co.,Ltd.)	华风国际海运有限公司	英国	上海海事法院	临时仲裁	(2019)沪72协外认2号	承认与执行
5	2019	别尔基私人股份有限公司	青岛金润琪橡胶机械有限公司	乌克兰	青岛市中级人民法院	乌克兰工商会国际商事仲裁院	(2019)鲁02协外认4号	承认与执行

续表

序号	裁决年份	申请人	被申请人	裁决地	执行法院	仲裁机构	案号/编号	判决结果
6	2019	信息管理服务全球有限公司(IHS Global Limited)	新疆美克化工股份有限公司	新加坡	上海市第一中级人民法院	新加坡国际仲裁中心	(2018)沪01协外认23号	承认与执行
7	2019	昌盛贸易公司(Chang Sheng Trading Co. Inc)	河南江河机械有限责任公司	瑞典	河南省郑州市中级人民法院	斯德哥尔摩商会仲裁院	(2017)豫01协外认11号	承认与执行
8	2019	株式会社现代家庭购物(TION)	家有购物集团股份有限公司	新加坡	北京市高级人民法院	新加坡国际仲裁中心	(2019)京民辖终98号	承认与执行
9	2019	利奇食品株式会社(Rich Food 株式会社)	元某	韩国	天津市第一中级人民法院	大韩商事仲裁院	(2018)津01协外认1号	承认与执行
10	2019	华联力宝医疗有限公司(Oue Lippo Health Care Limited)	林某	新加坡	上海市第一中级人民法院	新加坡国际仲裁中心	(2019)沪01协外认5号之一	承认与执行
11	2019	世安株式会社(SEAN INC.)	天津市天锻压力机有限公司	新加坡	天津市第一中级人民法院	国际商会仲裁院	(2018)津01协外认13号	承认与执行
12	2019	ACME清洁技术解决方案私人有限公司	中电电气(上海)太阳能科技有限公司	新加坡	上海市第一中级人民法院	新加坡国际仲裁中心	(2019)沪01协外认12号	承认与执行
13	2019	斯万斯克蜂蜜加工公司(Svensk Honungsforadling AB)	南京常力蜂业有限公司	瑞典	江苏省南京市中级人民法院	临时仲裁	(2018)苏01协外认8号	承认与执行

续表

序号	裁决年份	申请人	被申请人	裁决地	执行法院	仲裁机构	案号/编号	判决结果
14	2019	鲁彼昂姆公司(Lubiam Moda Per L'uomo S. P. A.)	宁波杉杉时尚服装品牌管理有限公司	法国	浙江省宁波市中级人民法院	国际商会国际仲裁院	(2019)浙02协外认5号	承认与执行
15	2019	特莱顿国际集装箱有限公司(Triton Container International Limited)	洋浦经济开发区建设投资开发有限公司、海南泛洋航运有限公司	美国	海口海事法院	美国国际争议解决中心	(2015)琼海法他字第1号	部分承认与执行
16	2019	大宝产业株式会社	山东浩瀚能源有限公司	日本	山东省日照市中级人民法院	日本商事仲裁协会	(2018)鲁11协外认3号	承认与执行
17	2019	南太平洋风险投资有限公司(South Pacific Venture SFZE)	盘锦辽河油田凯特石油设备有限公司	新加坡	辽宁省大连市中级人民法院	新加坡国际商会国际仲裁院	(2019)辽02协外认8号	承认与执行
18	2019	Fairdeal物资供应有限公司(Fairdeal Supplies Ltd.)	山西煤炭进出口集团有限公司	法国	山西省太原市中级人民法院	国际商会国际仲裁院	(2018)晋01民初921号	驳回申请
19	2019	贸达商品有限公司	北京和美汉艺进出口有限责任公司	英国	北京市第四中级人民法院	英国咖啡协会	(2018)京04协外认8号、(2018)京04协外认7号	承认与执行

续表

序号	裁决年份	申请人	被申请人	裁决地	执行法院	仲裁机构	案号/编号	判决结果
20	2019	VM有限公司（Valentine Maritime Ltd.）	江苏中汇进出口有限公司南京天舜船舶有限公司	英国	湖北省武汉海事法院	临时仲裁	（2018）鄂72协外认1号之一	承认
21	2020	科兹集团分销有限公司	广东省东莞畜产进出口有限公司	俄罗斯	广东省东莞市中级人民法院	俄罗斯联邦工商会国际商事仲裁法院	（2019）粤19协外认1号	承认与执行
22	2020	满升航运有限公司（Amarante Shipping Pte Ltd.）	卓联海运有限公司（Intermarine Shipping Co.，Ltd.）	英国	天津海事法院	临时仲裁	（2019）津72协外认1号之一	承认与执行
					天津高级人民法院		（2019）津民辖终121号	管辖权异议
23	2020	皇家食品进口公司（Royal Food Import Corp.）	烟台洛克西进出口有限公司	美国	山东省烟台市中级人民法院	美国食品工业协会	（2017）鲁06民初382号	驳回申请
24	2020	安富尔自由贸易区公司（Emphor FZCO）	广东粤新海洋工程装备股份有限公司	新加坡	广州海事法院	新加坡海事仲裁院	（2020）粤72协外认1号	承认与执行
25	2020	翱兰国际有限公司（Olam International Limited）	青岛中商恒通国际贸易有限公司	英国	山东省青岛市中级人民法院	国际棉花协会	（2020）鲁02协外认5号	承认与执行

续表

序号	裁决年份	申请人	被申请人	裁决地	执行法院	仲裁机构	案号/编号	判决结果
26	2020	奥克塔福系统有限公司	华浚塑料建材有限公司	加拿大	浙江省湖州市中级人民法院	加拿大不列颠哥伦比亚省国际商事仲裁中心	(2019)浙05协外认1号	承认与执行
27	2020	UNID国际商社(UNID Global Corporation)	宁波保税区长荣国际贸易有限公司	韩国	浙江省宁波市中级人民法院	大韩商事仲裁院	(2019)浙02协外认4号	承认与执行
28	2020	布兰特伍德工业有限公司(Brentwood Industries, Inc.)	广东阀安龙机械成套设备工程有限公司	法国	广东省广州市中级人民法院	国际商会国际仲裁院	(2015)穗中法民四初字第62号	终结审查
29	2020	上海佳船机械设备进出口有限公司	美克斯海洋工程设备股份有限公司	英国	浙江省嘉兴市中级人民法院	伦敦海事仲裁员协会	(2019)浙04协外认2号	承认与执行
30	2020	招商银行股份有限公司厦门分行	新加坡星展银行有限公司(DBS BANK Ltd.)	新加坡	厦门海事法院	新加坡国际仲裁中心	(2019)闽72民特1042号	承认与执行
31	2020	嘉能可有限公司	昆山立益纺织有限公司	英国	江苏省苏州市中级人民法院	国际棉花协会	(2019)苏05协外认2号	承认与执行
32	2020	IM全球有限责任公司(IM Global, LLC)	天津北方电影集团有限公司	美国	天津市第一中级人民法院	美国独立电影电视联盟国际仲裁院	(2018)津01协外认2号	拒绝承认与执行

续表

序号	裁决年份	申请人	被申请人	裁决地	执行法院	仲裁机构	案号/编号	判决结果
33	2020	FSOJ 国际有限责任公司（FSOJ International LLC）	天津北方电影集团有限公司	美国	天津市第一中级人民法院	美国独立电影电视联盟国际仲裁院	（2018）津01协外认3号	拒绝承认与执行
34	2021	商行荣耀国际航运有限公司	东盛航运有限公司	英国	上海市高级人民法院	伦敦海事仲裁委员会	（2020）沪民辖终110号（2020）沪72协外认1号	承认与执行
35	2021	世界商品智能交易中心私人有限公司（Commodities Intelligence Centre Pte. Ltd.）	天津航物国际贸易有限公司	新加坡	天津市第三中级人民法院	新加坡国际仲裁中心	（2021）津03协外认2号之一	承认与执行
36	2021	Ecomagro Industrial Corp. Ltd. Switzerland	青岛锦华东国际贸易有限公司	英国	山东省青岛市中级人民法院	国际棉花协会	（2021）鲁02协外认3号	承认与执行
37	2021	爱迪玛有限公司	张家港万晟新材料有限公司	乌克兰	江苏省苏州市中级人民法院	乌克兰工商会国际商事仲裁庭	（2019）苏05协外认7号	承认与执行
38	2021	斯芙拉玛特有限公司	张家港万晟新材料有限公司	乌克兰	江苏省苏州市中级人民法院	乌克兰工商会国际商事仲裁庭	（2019）苏05协外认6号	承认与执行
39	2021	NHE 航运有限公司（NHE Shipping INC）	江苏四海荣进出口有限公司	英国	南京海事法院	伦敦仲裁协会	（2020）苏72协外认1号	承认与执行

续表

序号	裁决年份	申请人	被申请人	裁决地	执行法院	仲裁机构	案号/编号	判决结果
40	2021	路易达孚瑞士公司（Louis Dreyfus Company Suisse SA）	青岛保税区棉花交易市场有限公司	英国	山东省青岛市中级人民法院	国际棉花协会	（2021）鲁02协外认5号	承认与执行
41	2021	安塞尔多能源有限公司（Ansaldo Energia S. P. A.）	哈尔滨空调股份有限公司	意大利	北京市第四中级人民法院	米兰仲裁院	（2020）京04协外认29号、（2021）京04执异13号、（2021）京04执37号	承认与执行/驳回异议申请
42	2021	瑞欧太阳能公司（Rioglass SolarS. A）	华夏聚光（内蒙古）光伏电力有限公司	新加坡	内蒙古自治区呼和浩特市中级人民法院	新加坡国际仲裁中心	（2020）内01民特100号	承认与执行
43	2021	KSP Co. ,Ltd.	抚顺中兴重工有限公司	韩国	辽宁省抚顺市中级人民法院	大韩民国大韩商事仲裁院	（2020）辽04民再7号	承认与执行
		KSP Co. ,Ltd.	抚顺中兴重工有限公司	韩国	辽宁省抚顺市中级人民法院	大韩民国大韩商事仲裁院	（2020）辽04民监1号民事裁定	
		KSP Co. ,Ltd.	抚顺中兴重工有限公司	韩国	辽宁省抚顺市中级人民法院	大韩民国大韩商事仲裁院	（2019）辽04协外认13号	

续表

序号	裁决年份	申请人	被申请人	裁决地	执行法院	仲裁机构	案号/编号	判决结果
43	2021	KSP Co. ,Ltd.	抚顺中兴重工有限公司	韩国	辽宁省抚顺市中级人民法院	大韩民国大韩商事仲裁院	(2020)辽01协外认10号	
44	2020	上海诺基亚贝尔股份有限公司	乌兹特拉斯加斯股份有限公司	新加坡	上海市第一中级人民法院	国际商会国际仲裁院	(2018)沪01协外认4号	承认与执行

资料来源:中国裁判文书网、一裁仲裁数据库等。

〔1〕本案当事人仅提出承认的裁决申请,法院基于申请作出裁定。

〔2〕同上注。

根据《纽约公约》第5条的规定,被申请承认与执行裁决的当事人(以下简称被申请人)仅可以下述事由抗辩裁决的承认与执行:(1)仲裁协议无效;(2)未给予适当通知导致当事人未能申辩;(3)超裁;(4)仲裁庭组成或仲裁程序不当;(5)裁决不具有约束力或已被撤销/停止执行;(6)裁决事项不具有可仲裁性;(7)违反公共政策。中国的司法实践中,被申请人援引《纽约公约》第4条进行抗辩,法院通常会要求当事人补正,如当事人确无法提交,法院则裁定不予受理或驳回申请。除此之外的抗辩事由,一般会被法院驳回。

本文研究的上述44个案例中,从被申请人的抗辩事由来看,被申请人向法院提出抗辩主要系援引《纽约公约》第5条规定,少部分被申请人援引《纽约公约》第4条递交材料形式要件之规定提出抗辩,另有个别被申请人以申请超出法定期限、隐瞒证据、裁决不公等为由抗辩。从法院裁定结果来看,裁定承认与执行的案例35个、裁定承认的案例2个、裁定部分承认与执行的案例2个、裁定拒绝承认与执行的案例2个、裁定驳回申请的案例2个,裁定终结审查的案例1个。下文将基于法院适用《纽约公约》的具体司法案例,结合可能涉及的法律依据及裁判观点,对部分案件进行简要分析。

二、仲裁协议效力

仲裁协议是仲裁庭管辖权的来源,也是仲裁程序启动的前提和基础。《纽约公约》第5条将仲裁协议瑕疵作为第1项法院可拒绝承认与执行外国仲裁裁决的情形。根据《纽约公约》第5条第1款甲项规定,依据当事人选择的法律或仲裁地法律,被申请人提供证据证明仲裁协议无效或仲裁协议当事人存在无行为能力的情形,法院则可拒绝承认与执行。司法实践中,如被申请人能够提供证据证明当事人之间无仲裁协议,法院也将援引《纽约公约》第1款第1项拒绝承认和执行仲裁裁决。

本文研究的44个外国裁决的承认与执行案例中,有13个案例的被申请人抗辩不存在仲裁协议;5个案例的被申请人抗辩仲裁协议无效;另有6个案例的当事人对仲裁协议适用的准据法存在争议。以上案例中,仅有2个案例被法院以仲裁协议存在瑕疵拒绝承认与执行。

(一)关于仲裁协议准据法

基于仲裁协议的"独立性"推定,仲裁协议的成立、效力和解释的准据法,与当事人签订的基础合同所适用的法律,以及仲裁程序适用的法律可能均不同。国际商事仲裁纠纷涉及的法律适用问题,通常包括实体争议适用的实体法、仲裁程序适用的程序法以及仲裁协议的适用法律。司法实践中,常常存在案涉合同中未明确仲裁协议法律适用的情形。在缺乏当事人明确选择时,法院审查仲裁协议效力之前,首先要确定仲裁协议的准据法。

在我国,法院确定仲裁协议准据法的法律渊源主要为《纽约公约》《涉外民事关系法律适用法》及其司法解释、《最高人民法院关于审理仲裁司法审查案件若干问题的规定》等。在当事人无明确约定仲裁协议准据法的情况下,适用何种系属标准判断准据法,《纽约公约》与我国立法规定稍存差异。按《纽约公约》规定,[①]无约定则适用裁决地法,裁决地与仲裁地实质指向同一概念;而按我国法律相关规定,"仲裁机构所在地"曾是法院认定仲裁裁决国籍以及确定仲裁协议准据法的主要标准;近年司法实践中才逐渐呈现与《纽约公约》规定一致的系属,即采取"仲裁地"标准。

采取"仲裁机构所在地"标准还是采取"仲裁地"标准,除了可能直接影响法院认定仲裁协议效力的结果,还影响法院受理执行裁决申请适用的法律依

① 《纽约公约》第5条第1款规定,仲裁协议准据法依照当事人约定,如无约定,适用裁决地所在国法律。

据。布兰特伍德工业有限公司(Brentwood Industries,Inc.)与广东阀安龙机械成套设备工程有限公司申请承认与执行仲裁裁决案[①]中,法院未支持申请人关于仲裁机构决定仲裁裁决国籍的主张,而是将外国仲裁机构在中国内地作出的仲裁裁决认定为中国涉外仲裁裁决,继而认为案涉裁决的司法审查应适用我国《民事诉讼法》而非《纽约公约》。该案中,合同约定将争议提交国际商会仲裁委员会根据国际惯例在项目所在地进行仲裁。申请人认为,仲裁机构决定仲裁裁决的国籍,无论按国际商会仲裁院总部所在地法国巴黎,还是按裁决作出的分支机构所在地中国香港,均应分别依据《纽约公约》或《关于内地与香港特别行政区相互执行仲裁裁决的安排》(以下简称《相互执行安排》)的规定认可并执行。法院则认为,案涉仲裁裁决系外国仲裁机构在中国内地作出的仲裁裁决,可视为中国涉外仲裁裁决,而非外国仲裁裁决。申请人依据《纽约公约》或《相互执行安排》规定申请承认与执行案涉裁决,法律依据明显错误。申请人应参照《民事诉讼法》第288条规定向具有管辖权的法院申请执行,经多次释明后申请人拒不撤回,故法院裁定终结审查。

采用"仲裁地"标准确定仲裁协议效力准据法,意味着法院将面临更多适用外国法对仲裁协议进行审查的情况。不同法域下关于仲裁协议效力的规定存在差别,大陆法系和普通法系的法律渊源、法律适用逻辑亦不相同,这对法院解释、适用外国法的裁判能力则提出更高要求。

在利奇食品株式会社(Rich Food 株式会社)与元某申请承认与执行仲裁裁决案[②]中,当事人之间关于未明确约定具体的仲裁机构是否导致仲裁条款无效产生争议,法院通过援引、解释韩国仲裁法相关规定,认可了案涉仲裁条款的效力。该案中,案涉合同约定,"双方发生与本合同有关的纠纷、分歧、异议或违约事项时,可通过友好协商进行解决。如协商未果,可根据大韩民国法律通过贸易仲裁委员会进行仲裁……"法院查明,《韩国仲裁法》第3条第2项规定,"仲裁合意"是指,无论是否为合同上的争议,关于一定的法律关系,当事人之间已经发生或者将要发生的争议的全部或者部分,当事人之间希望通过仲裁解决的合意。《韩国仲裁法》第17条第1项规定,仲裁庭可以关于自身的权限以及与

① (2015)穗中法民四初字第62号。
② (2018)津01协外认1号。

之相关的仲裁协议的存在与否或者有效性提出的异议作出决定。据此,法院认为,首先,韩国仲裁法并未规定仲裁机构约定不明确会导致仲裁合意或仲裁条款无效的后果;其次,大韩商事仲裁院依据韩国法律对于案涉仲裁协议的效力已经作出决定,并详细论述了决定理由。元某以仲裁机构不明确为由主张仲裁条款无效不符合《纽约公约》第 5 条第 1 款甲项规定的情形,并且也未举证证明该决定存在违反韩国法的证据,故法院认定案涉合同仲裁条款有效。

在信息管理服务全球有限公司(IHS Global Limited)与新疆美克化工股份有限公司申请承认和执行外国仲裁裁决案[①]中,仲裁协议准据法为新加坡法律,法院通过援引新加坡上诉法院作出的一则判例[②],指出新加坡上诉法院在该案中确定的基本原则对该案认定仲裁协议效力具有约束力。该案中,被申请人抗辩,合同中包含两种不同的争议解决条款,即案涉合同第 6.7 条仲裁条款和第 6.11 条诉讼条款,两者存在冲突,仲裁条款应属无效。法院首先归纳出上述判例确立的基本原则,即当事人明确表示有意通过仲裁解决任何争议,即使协议中的某些方面可能含糊不清、不一致、完整或缺少某些细节,只要仲裁可以在不损害任何一方权利的情况下进行,并且生效,即可实施这种仲裁意愿,这种意愿不会导致仲裁不属于任何一方的考虑和期待。据此,法院认定双方当事人之间将争议提交仲裁的意愿是明确的,仲裁条款有效。

(二)无仲裁协议的抗辩

仲裁协议是否成立是认定仲裁协议效力的前提。实践中,被申请人常常提出仲裁当事人之间不存在仲裁协议,以此挑战裁决的可执行性。本文研究的 44 个案例中,近 30% 的案例被申请人以双方之间无仲裁协议为由提出抗辩。

被申请人抗辩提出的具体事实依据主要包括不认可合同的真实性、当事人主体不适格、尚未达成书面仲裁协议、合同约定期限已过等。其中仅有 1 个案例被法院以被申请人并非仲裁协议当事方、申请不符合受理条件为由裁定驳回申请:皇家食品进口公司(Royal Food Import Corp.)与烟台洛克西进出口有限公司申请承认和执行外国仲裁裁决案[③]中,被申请人抗辩,合同签署主体与被申

---

① (2018)沪 01 协外认 23 号。

② Insigma Technology Co., Ltd. v. Alston Technology Ltd. [2009]3SLR(R).

③ (2017)鲁 06 民初 382 号。

请人非同一商事主体，二者公章、注册经营地等工商登记信息均不一致，被申请人并非仲裁裁决当事人。被申请人还提出，其从未参与案涉合同的签订及履行，仲裁条款对其不具有约束力。法院认为，申请人虽提供的仲裁裁决和含有仲裁条款的合同，但未提交充分证据证明该仲裁裁决及合同的当事人“Adu International Group Corp. Ltd.”即为被申请人洛克西进出口有限公司，即未能提供与洛克西进出口有限公司之间的仲裁裁决及仲裁协议，其申请不符合受理条件，驳回申请人的申请。

除上述案例以外，下文所列被申请人提出的其他关于无仲裁协议具体抗辩事由，均未得到法院支持。

抗辩合同是虚假合同，申请对合同签章进行鉴定。别尔基私人股份有限公司与青岛金润琪橡胶机械有限公司申请承认和执行外国仲裁裁决案①中，被申请人抗辩，其与申请人之间从未签订过仲裁裁决所裁定的两份合同，两份合同是虚假的。法院指出，仲裁纠纷涉及的两份合同中载明的合同价款、合同标的物与申请人提交的《委托付款函》及本院查询的收款底单电子传文中载明的货物名称、收付款数额均一致，可以对应。被申请人认可收到款项，但无证据推翻申请人提交的两份合同。被申请人申请对合同公章及签字申请鉴定，考虑到国际货物买卖合同签订通常采用电子传输方式而非当面签订的特殊性，法院认为被申请人申请理由不足，不予支持。

抗辩合同系伪造拼凑，签字虽属实，但未曾签署包含仲裁条款的合同。华联力宝医疗有限公司(Oue Lippo Health Care Limited)与林某申请承认与执行仲裁裁决案②中，被申请人称案涉《购股协议》末签字页上的“D”系其本人所签，但《购股协议》系变造，该签字页是从其他协议中拿过来的，且协议每页签署的“D”缩写签名均不是林某本人所签。法院查明，《购股协议》由协议文本及5个附件构成，在最末签字页上签名的各方当事人与协议记载的主体一致，除签字页外，其他页面下方均有各方当事人的缩写签名，包括代表林某的“D”签名，整个协议文本及附件的内容连续、完整，且申请人出示了《购股协议》原件，故据此确认《购股协议》的真实性，其中约定的仲裁条款亦合法有效。林某称该签字页

① (2019)鲁02协外认4号。
② (2019)沪01协外认5号之一。

系其他协议的签字页,但未能出示其所称的该其他协议,而每页“D”签名是否林某本人所签,亦不足以否定签字页上林某签名的真实性。

抗辩合同签字非公司法定代表人且无公司印章,签字人也无授权文件。信息管理服务全球有限公司(IHS Global Limited)与新疆美克化工股份有限公司申请承认和执行外国仲裁裁决案①中,被申请人提出,案涉合同无申请人法定代表人签字及公司印章,也无公司授权文件,双方之间未订立合法有效的仲裁协议。法院认为,信息管理公司向本院提供了经公证认证的关于公司注册信息材料、授权委托书以及法定代表人身份证明,可以证明信息管理公司是合法存续的公司。合同中代表信息管理公司签字一方系该公司的授权代表 JP,虽然并未加盖信息管理公司公章,但是该合同中记载的主体即为信息管理公司,信息管理公司对授权代表 JP 签署合同的行为予以认可并依据此合同提起仲裁,在仲裁过程中美克公司对信息管理公司的合同主体资格也从未提出过异议。合同中记载的信息管理公司的地址与公证认证的公司注册信息记载的地址不尽相同,但公司名称是相同的,表明案涉合同是信息管理公司真实意思的表示。

抗辩双方之间尚未达成书面仲裁协议。Fairdeal 物资供应有限公司(Fairdeal Supplies Ltd.)与山西煤炭进出口集团有限公司申请承认和执行外国仲裁裁决案②中,被申请人抗辩从未签署过涉案仲裁协议,也从未向申请人发出含仲裁条款的传真或者收到申请人的传真;双方之间的购销合同仍处于要约磋商阶段,并未形成有约束力的书面仲裁协议。

抗辩合同期限已过,仲裁协议已失效。科兹集团分销有限公司与广东省东莞畜产进出口有限公司申请承认和执行外国仲裁裁决案③中,被申请人称合同期限至 2012 年 11 月 18 日,但申请人申请仲裁的事实依据为 2015 年的款项,该事实发生时双方已无合同关系,亦无仲裁条款。法院认为,被申请人未提交任何证据表明依据俄罗斯联邦法律案涉仲裁协议在双方发生连续交易的情况下已失效。

---

① (2018)沪 01 协外认 23 号。

② (2018)晋 01 民初 921 号、(2018)京 04 协外认 7 号。

③ (2019)粤 19 协外认 1 号。

（三）仲裁协议无效的抗辩

根据《纽约公约》第 5 条第 1 款甲项后半段规定“该项协定依当事人作为协定准据之法律系属无效，或未指明以何法律为准时，依裁决地所在国法律系属无效者”，当事人签订的仲裁协议如果存在某些“缺陷”而应被认定为无效时，根据该条规定，法院可拒绝承认与执行裁决。至于何种“缺陷”将导致仲裁协议无效，《纽约公约》仅于第 2 条作出“书面形式”的要求，将最终认定仲裁协议是否有效的权利赋予各缔约方法律。然而，不同法域下关于仲裁协议效力的规定不尽相同，需要法院根据准据法规定作出具体认定。

从我国法院的司法实践来看，被申请人抗辩仲裁协议无效的常见情形有：缺乏明确提交仲裁的意思表示，未约定仲裁机构或约定不明确、不符合书面形式的形式要件、超出法定可仲裁范围、非当事人真实意思表示、无涉外因素约定境外仲裁等。

抗辩合同同时约定仲裁和诉讼，缺乏明确提交仲裁的意思表示。在香港泉水有限公司 Water Solutions（Hong Kong）Limited 与宏柏家电（深圳）有限公司申请承认和执行外国仲裁裁决案[①]中，法院维持在审查仲裁协议效力案[②]裁定中的意见，即仲裁协议有效。首先，法院确认，仲裁协议是否有效应适用美国《联邦仲裁法》、加利福尼亚州民事诉讼法、美国联邦法院和州法院的判例进行判定。接着，法院在查明《美国联邦法》第 2 条、加利福尼亚州《民事诉讼法》第 1281 条成文法具体规定之后，通过查明美国最高法院适用《联邦仲裁法》判例对有争议的仲裁协议进行解释时所确立的原则，法院指出“美国最高法院在判例中确立了支持仲裁的原则包括三个方面：其一，一个自由的联邦政策应当有利于仲裁协议；其二，一个明确的联邦政策应当有利于仲裁争议解决方式；其三，任何与可仲裁范围相关的疑问的解决应当有利于仲裁。”继而，法院查明美国联邦法院和州法院对既约定诉讼又约定仲裁的情况下如何认定仲裁协议效力的判例，通过对比判例与该案，认定两案当事人约定内容存在实质区别，不能适用判例而否定该案仲裁协议效力。法院认为，判例中，诉讼送达条款明确清晰，相比仲裁条款更加具体。本案中，当事人对仲裁和诉讼两种争议解决方式

① （2016）粤 03 民初 366 号。
② （2015）深中法涉外仲字第 91 号。

的选择,处于同等地位,选择诉讼方式并不占优;判例中,双方当事人缔约意图不同,法院认为保险单可以作如下解释:如果是产生于保险单或与保险单有关的争议,可以进行仲裁;如果是出现被告违约,不支付到期款项,则应要求被告将争议交付法院。而本案中当事人对争议只进行了概括约定,并未明确哪一种争议申请仲裁,哪一种争议提出诉讼;判例中,原告根据诉讼送达条款选择向法院起诉。而本案中,申请人选择向美国仲裁协会申请仲裁。据此法院认为应当认定仲裁协议有效。

抗辩未明确约定仲裁机构,仲裁协议无效。在肯考迪亚农产品贸易有限公司(Concordia Agritrading Pte Ltd.)与山东晨曦集团有限公司申请承认与执行仲裁裁决案①中,案涉合同约定"按照FOSFA(国际油籽和油脂协会)规则在伦敦仲裁解决",如上所述,在被申请人提出"没有明确约定仲裁机构的视为没有约定,申请人所依据的仲裁条款因此不具任何效力"后,法院根据英国法和FOSFA规则相关规定,驳回被申请人的主张。在株式会社现代家庭购物(TION)与家有购物集团股份有限公司申请承认与执行仲裁裁决案②中,案涉合同约定"双方发生与本合同有关的纠纷、分歧、异议或违约事项时,可通过友好协商进行解决。如协商未果,可根据大韩民国法律通过贸易仲裁委员会进行仲裁。"法院援引韩国仲裁法规定,认为韩国仲裁法并未规定如果仲裁机构约定不明确会导致仲裁合意或仲裁条款无效的后果,据此认定仲裁条款有效。

此外,需要特别指出的是,在适用中国法审查仲裁协议效力时,约定不具有涉外因素的合同纠纷提交仲裁,仲裁条款无效。至于是否具有涉外因素的判断标准,由法院在个案中具体把握,其认定结果将直接决定仲裁条款的效力。嘉能可有限公司与昆山立益纺织有限公司申请承认与执行仲裁裁决案③中,法院基于三个理由认定案涉合同具有涉外因素并据此承认仲裁协议的效力。其一,申请人嘉能可有限公司系在我国自由贸易试验区注册的外商投资企业,其与被申请人约定将商事争议提交国际棉花协会仲裁。其二,在仲裁过程中,被申请

① (2018)鲁11协外认5号。
② (2019)京民辖终98号。
③ (2019)苏05协外认2号。

人在仲裁过程中未对仲裁协议提出异议，现被申请人又以争议不具有涉外因素为由主张仲裁协议无效，不符合《最高人民法院关于为自由贸易试验区建设提供司法保障的意见》第9条第2款规定[①]。其三，案涉合同标的物为美国进口原棉，原棉进口的目的即是由申请人销售给包括被申请人在内的国内买方，原棉一直堆放在保税区仓库。

（四）仲裁协议当事人无行为能力的抗辩

《纽约公约》第5条第1款甲项提及"某种无行为能力情形者"，可理解为签署仲裁协议的一方当事人缺乏合法有效的契约能力。本文研究的44个案例中，有2个系列案被申请人抗辩合同签署方无权代表公司，获法院支持并裁定拒绝承认与执行外国仲裁裁决。

IM全球有限责任公司（IM Global，LLC）与天津北方电影集团有限公司申请承认与执行外国仲裁裁决案[②]中，被申请人援引《纽约公约》第5条第1款甲项，提出其从未与IM公司达成任何仲裁协议或合意，理由是依据《法国民法典》规定，签字人"孙某"与被申请人不存在合法有效的委托代理关系，孙某无代表被申请人签订契约的行为能力。申请人则认为，孙某是否有权代表被申请人时案件实体问题，应由仲裁庭审理，不属《纽约公约》项下法院有权审查的问题。法院指出，《纽约公约》第5条第1款甲项"无行为能力"应理解为"缺乏契约能力"，包括行为人无权代表或代理公司签订协议。孙某是否有权代表被申请人签订案涉合同，根据《涉外民事关系法律适用法》第14条规定，应当适用中国法进行判断。依据《中华人民共和国民法典》（以下简称《民法典》）规定，孙某不能代表被申请人；关于孙某能否代理被申请人，根据《涉外民事关系法律适用法》第16条规定，应当适用代理关系发生地法国法律进行认定。依据法国民法典规定，由于孙某本人及被申请人也称孙某既非被申请人高管，亦非普通员工，IM公司既未能提供证明孙某与被申请人存在委托代理关系的相关证据，也未

---

① 一方或者双方均为在自由贸易试验区注册的外商投资企业，约定将商事争议提交域外仲裁，发生纠纷后，当事人将争议提交域外仲裁，相关裁决作出后，其又以仲裁协议无效为由主张拒绝承认、认可或执行的，人民法院不予支持；另一方当事人在仲裁程序中未对仲裁协议效力提出异议，相关裁决作出后，又以相关争议不具有涉外因素为由主张仲裁协议无效，并以此主张决绝承认、认可或执行的，人民法院不予支持。

② （2018）津01协外认2号。

能充分证明其在签约过程中对孙某的身份构成法律规定的“合理信赖”,故法院最终认定,孙某无权代表或代理被申请人签订案涉仲裁协议,当事人之间不存在有效仲裁协议。

另有被申请人抗辩公司已破产经核准注销,不具有法人主体资格,未获法院支持。昌盛贸易公司(Chang Sheng Trading Co. Inc)与河南江河机械有限责任公司申请承认和执行外国仲裁裁决案[①]中,被申请人抗辩,案涉被申请人河南江河机械有限责任公司成立于2004年2月18日,申请人所述的河南江河工业有限责任公司于2006年10月因资不抵债经平顶山市中级人民法院破产程序终结了法人主体资格。河南江河机械有限责任公司与河南江河工业有限责任公司不存在法律上的继承关系,被申请人不应属案涉仲裁裁决的仲裁范围。法院经查明认定,河南江河工业有限责任公司系原河南江河机械厂改制而来,改制后全部承担原机械厂的债权债务。由于本案被申请人系从改制公司分立而来,注册资本由改制公司实收资本划出,两者注册登记的法定代表人及经营场所一致;被申请人曾出具说明,称对分立前的债务在分离后的改制后公司无力偿还的情况下,由被申请人代为偿还。尽管改制后公司已核准注销,本案涉仲裁纠纷为原机械厂与申请人之间的合营合同纠纷,故被申请人作为原机械厂改制后的公司,其主体资格适格。

此外,有被申请人抗辩公司已破产清算,亦未获法院支持。特莱顿国际集装箱有限公司(Triton Container International Limited)与洋浦经济开发区建设投资开发有限公司、海南泛洋航运有限公司申请承认与执行外国仲裁裁决案[②]中,被申请人称当地法院已经受理泛洋公司破产清算的申请,根据《中华人民共和国企业破产法》第20条规定,被申请人泛洋公司在案涉裁决作出时处于无民事行为能力情形。法院阐明,纽约公约规定“无行为能力”是指当事人不具有缔约行为能力,案件被申请人泛洋公司在订立案涉仲裁时具有缔约行为能力,被申请人关于裁决期间不具有民事行为能力的主张不能支持。

三、正当程序的抗辩

正当程序的抗辩,是当事人挑战仲裁裁决效力及执行力常见的理由之一。

① (2017)豫01协外认11号。

② (2015)琼海法他字第1号。

依据《纽约公约》第5条第1款乙项、丁项规定，违反正当程序原则的情形主要分为两大类：一是送达程序问题导致一方当事人丧失申辩陈述权利、丧失指派仲裁员的权利；二是仲裁程序违反协议约定或法律规定。

（一）送达程序问题的抗辩

作为裁决执行对象的当事人，未得到进行仲裁程序的适当通知，未能进行充分陈述，对于仲裁裁决而言，后果往往是致命性的。尽管当事人在承认与执行外国仲裁裁决的案件中经常将之作为抗辩事由，但从大量司法实践案例可以看出，法院在审查送达程序时始终持谨慎态度，绝大多数情况下，当事人仅以未收到相关通知为由提出抗辩，无明显证据表明仲裁庭或仲裁机构送达程序存在重大瑕疵，很难抗辩成功。本文研究的案例中近50%的案件当事人抗辩送达程序存在问题，仅有1个案例关于送达的抗辩得到法院认可。

Fairdeal物资供应有限公司（Fairdeal Supplies Ltd.）与山西煤炭进出口集团有限公司申请承认和执行外国仲裁裁决案①中，法院支持了被申请人关于送达程序的抗辩，裁定驳回申请人关于承认和执行裁决的申请。法院认为，申请人提供了ICC出具的关于被申请人已收到裁决书的证明，该证明未经相关公证、认证程序，依据《最高人民法院关于民事诉讼证据的若干规定》第11条之规定，不予采信。法院查明，裁决书载明被申请人及其代理人通讯地址为"中国山西省太原市新建路39号乡海大厦707号房间"，在仲裁过程中，被申请人和仲裁机构之间也一直在使用上述通讯地址。然而，ICC邮寄的裁决书地址为"山西太原南内环街168号盛伟大厦F室"，同日，ICC邮寄另一份提示双方"案件已经结案，双方提交的任何文件将被销毁"的文件邮寄地址为"中国山西省太原市新建路39号乡海大厦707号房间"。因此，法院无法确认案涉裁决已实际送达被申请人，也无法认定案涉裁决在境外已经发生法律效力。

关于送达方式、视为送达、适当送达，各仲裁机构仲裁规则对此均有明确界定，该类规定是法院审查送达是否适当的重要依据。通常情况下，向当事人注册地址、合同载明地址、申请人提供的送达地址进行送达可以视为是适当有效的，至于被申请人是否实际收到仲裁文件，并非判断仲裁送达程序是否合法的依据。法院审查送达程序是否适当，本质上是判断当事人是否因送达程序确有

① （2018）晋01民初921号。

问题而丧失了如指派仲裁员、举证、申辩陈述等可能影响裁决公正性的重要权利。司法实践中,即便送达程序事实上存在轻微的瑕疵,也并不一定足以导致否定仲裁裁决的效力及可执行性。例如,在爱迪玛有限公司与张家港万晟新材料有限公司申请承认与执行外国仲裁裁决案①中,法院认为,乌克兰工商会国际商事仲裁庭通过DHL公司以信函方式向万晟公司送达仲裁程序通知等仲裁材料过程中,虽在第一次送达时,邮寄地址栏中存在轻微瑕疵,但载明的地址信息能够明确指向万晟公司且函件被签收,故该送达符合乌克兰仲裁程序通知的法律规定,程序合法有效。

另外,需要指出的是,有时送达程序的审查可能涉及对实体法律关系的查明,存在送达程序与是否存在仲裁协议问题的竞合。在上述法院裁定拒绝承认与执行的IM全球有限责任公司(IM Global,LLC)与天津北方电影集团有限公司仲裁案②中,法院认为,审查当事人关于送达的异议,需先厘清被送达人是否为仲裁案件的适格主体,则须就被送达人与案件当事人之间的法律关系进行判断。法院基于被申请人未与IM公司签订仲裁协议、涉案仲裁协议并非被申请人所签署的认定,认为协议上所列联系方式并不能当然视为被申请人的联系方式,而应当根据送达的实际情况判断被申请人是否"接获关于指派仲裁员或仲裁程序之适当通知"。关于仲裁文件的送达情况,仲裁裁决和仲裁庭秘书的事后表述存在冲突,此种情况下,被申请人提供了较为充足的证据予以反驳,因此,可以确认被申请人并未接获此种方式的送达。关于传真方式送达,根据证据显示,仲裁庭秘书向被申请人发送传真两页,但传真的两页文件未包括《仲裁通知书》和《仲裁规则》,该传真送达不能确认为"接获关于指派仲裁员或仲裁程序之适当通知"。

(二)仲裁程序违反协议约定或法律规定的抗辩

根据《纽约公约》第5条第1款丁项规定,仲裁机构/仲裁庭组成或仲裁程序与当事人协议或适用法律规定不符,法院可拒绝承认与执行该仲裁裁决。本文将研究案例分为两类分别进行陈述,一类是抗辩仲裁庭组成违反规定,另一类是抗辩其他仲裁程序不符合规定。

① (2019)苏05协外认7号。

② (2018)津01协外认2号。

针对仲裁庭组成方式是当事人可能提出的一种抗辩。仲裁实务中,除非适用法律有相反的强制性规定,否则当事人可依其意思自治对仲裁庭组成作出约定。如果裁决由未按当事人协议约定组成的仲裁庭作出,该裁决也属于可被异议的情形,但这并不意味着不符合协议约定将一定导致法院判定仲裁庭组成不当。本文研究的案例中,被申请人就仲裁员人数与协议约定、法律规定不符提出的抗辩,均未得到法院支持。

抗辩仲裁规则与适用法律关于仲裁员人数的规定不一致。株式会社现代家庭购物(TION)与家有购物集团股份有限公司申请承认与执行外国仲裁裁决案①,被申请人提出,根据《韩国仲裁法》规定,如果没有约定,仲裁员的人数应为 3 人;仲裁规则规定,标的额在两亿韩元以下适用独任仲裁。据此,本案不应由独任仲裁员审理。法院认为,韩国仲裁法与大韩商事仲裁院国际仲裁规则在仲裁庭的人数规定上略有不同,但韩国仲裁法并未禁止独任仲裁庭的存在,因此该法关于仲裁庭人数的规定不应认定为强制性规定。实践中,每个仲裁机构都有各自仲裁规则规定相应的仲裁程序,大韩商事仲裁院国际仲裁规则第 3 条第 1 项第 2 款规定,当事人通过书面合意同意根据仲裁院的裁决来解决争议,而相关仲裁又属于国际仲裁时,适用该国际仲裁规则。在上海佳船机械设备进出口有限公司与美克斯海洋工程设备股份有限公司申请承认与执行外国仲裁裁决案②中,被申请人也提出类似抗辩。法院指出,涉案仲裁协议约定仲裁庭由 3 名仲裁员组成,但是并未对一方当事人未能按期指定仲裁员时,如何组成仲裁庭的事项进行约定。按合同约定,此情况下应当适用 LMAA2017 年仲裁规则和英国《1996 年仲裁法》。而根据 LMAA2017 年仲裁规则及英国《1996 年仲裁法》规定,本案中,申请人按仲裁协议约定通知被申请人,要求其按期指定己方仲裁员未果后,又根据英国《1996 年仲裁法》的规定,再次通知被申请人要求其按期指定己方仲裁员,并告知逾期未指定仲裁员的后果,但是被申请人仍未予以理会。此种情况下,申请人单方指定的仲裁员可以作为独任仲裁员组成仲裁庭,仲裁庭组成符合双方仲裁协议、LMAA2017 年仲裁规则以及英国《1996 年仲裁法》规定。

---

① (2019)京民辖终 98 号。

② (2019)浙 04 协外认 2 号。

抗辩适用临时仲裁规则与协议约定的快速仲裁不符。斯万斯克蜂蜜加工公司（Svensk Honungsforadling AB）与南京常力蜂业有限公司申请承认和执行外国仲裁裁决案[①]中，被申请人提出，仲裁程序适用临时仲裁规则，与双方合同约定的仲裁条款不符，临时仲裁不等同于快速仲裁。法院认为，在临时仲裁庭审中，被申请人法定代表人赵某并未就仲裁管辖权提出任何异议，应当认定被申请人对临时仲裁庭的管辖并不持异议。双方对在瑞典通过快速仲裁解决争端不存异议，仅对快速仲裁是否可以通过临时仲裁产生争议。法院认为，快速仲裁相对于普通仲裁而言，更加高效、便捷、经济，其核心在于简化了仲裁程序、缩短了仲裁时间、降低了仲裁费用等，从而使当事人的争议以较为高效和经济的方式得到解决。而临时仲裁庭相对于常设的仲裁机构而言，也具有高效、便捷、经济的特点。具体到本案，因双方已经明示同意争议通过快速仲裁的方式解决，且案涉争议标的数额不大，该快速仲裁并未排除通过临时仲裁的方式解决。此前，申请人向瑞典斯德哥尔摩商会仲裁院申请仲裁，该仲裁院以其无管辖权为由驳回了申请人的申请。被申请人在该仲裁中称："很显然，双方当事人就在瑞典进行快速/加快的仲裁程序达成一致，但不适用 SCC 仲裁规则。""仲裁条款可以指临时仲裁或瑞典西部规则或瑞典南部规则下的快速仲裁规则。"由此可以反映出，被申请人当时对以临时仲裁处理的方式并不持异议，且在本案中又不能明确、具体指出由哪一家仲裁机构处理，适用何种仲裁规则，在此情形下，案涉仲裁由临时仲裁庭作出裁决，符合双方当事人的合意。

四、裁决范围的抗辩

《纽约公约》第 5 条第 1 款丙项将超裁列为可拒绝承认与执行仲裁裁决的情形之一。仲裁庭的管辖权来自于当事人授权，这就要求仲裁庭在推进仲裁程序和作出决定的过程中，必须将自己的权限严格把控在界限之内，不可越权。超裁通常可分为两类情形，一类是超越仲裁协议约定范围，另一类是裁决事项超出仲裁请求。

（一）关于超越仲裁协议约定范围

裁决项涉及的当事人非仲裁协议签署方，是实务中常见的超裁情形之一。

---

① （2018）苏 01 协外认 8 号。

特莱顿国际集装箱有限公司(Triton Container International Limited)与洋浦经济开发区建设投资开发有限公司、海南泛洋航运有限公司申请承认与执行外国仲裁裁决案[①]中,法院基于部分当事人未实际签订包含仲裁条款的合同的事实,拒绝承认与执行针对部分当事人的裁决事项。该案涉及多方当事人基于一系列交易签署的多份合同,法院通过对合同进行文义、体系解释,结合多份合同的签字盖章情况,认定包含仲裁条款合同与其他合同系各自独立,部分当事人并非案涉包含仲裁条款的合同的缔约方,继而认定案涉仲裁条协议对该部分当事人不具有约束力,认为仲裁庭仅可基于当事人签署的包含仲裁条款的合同涉及的纠纷行使管辖权。涉案仲裁裁决被申请人洋浦经济开发区建设投资开发有限公司就 HPO42 号协议之外的其他五份协议向申请人承担责任,超出了仲裁协议约定的范围,且超裁部分与有权裁决部分不可分,故根据《纽约公约》第 5 条第 1 款丙项的规定对于案涉仲裁裁决涉及被申请人洋浦经济开发区建设投资开发有限公司部分的裁决,应当不予承认和执行。不过,需要说明的是,当事人之间的系列交易涉及多份合同的,仅有部分合同不包含仲裁条款,也不一定意味着该部分合同不受仲裁管辖,需要结合交易整体情况、协议签署过程、协议的具体条文等事实因素综合判断。

纠纷事项不在于仲裁协议约束范围内,也是关于超裁一种可能的抗辩。在前述香港泉水有限公司 Water Solutions (Hong Kong) Limited 与宏柏家电(深圳)有限公司申请承认和执行外国仲裁裁决案[②]中,被申请人抗辩包含仲裁协议的合同期限已到,仲裁协议失效。法院认为,基于协议到期后双方未签订新的协议且未变更争议解决方式、双方继续按原有方式交易的行为等事实,应视为对案涉协议的继续履行,仍受仲裁协议约束,因此,当事人之间在书面合同约定的期限届满后发生的订单纠纷并未超过仲裁协议的范围。同样地,被申请人在奥克塔福系统有限公司与华浚塑料建材有限公司申请承认与执行外国仲裁裁决案[③]中抗辩案涉标的物与合同约定标的物不同,该标的物项下的纠纷不属仲裁协议约束范围。被申请人提出,案涉协议系就异型材(模板)产品采购达成的

① (2015)琼海法他字第 1 号。
② (2016)粤 03 民初 366 号。
③ (2019)浙 05 协外认 1 号。

约定,而双方另行交易的快线面板产品纠纷不受该协议的约束。法院认为,双方签署的质量保证确认函中载明,双方就申请人遭受的质量保证问题、损失及损失赔偿等事项达成协议,损失赔偿部分载明按照案涉协议规定由被申请人承担更换所有缺陷或瑕疵货物等赔偿责任,而后附瑕疵货物明细中系包含案涉快线面板产品。故可认定双方在实际交易过程中对快线面板产品适用了供应协议约定;并且在仲裁过程中,被申请人曾就快线面板产品提出反请求;此外,根据不列颠哥伦比亚省国际商事仲裁中心仲裁规则规定,仲裁庭可以就仲裁事项超出仲裁庭权限的抗辩以初步的问题或在仲裁裁决中就争议实质作出裁定。而仲裁庭曾对此问题作出专门分析认定。故法院判定,仲裁庭就快线面板产品作出仲裁裁决并未超出仲裁协议的约定,不存在《纽约公约》第 1 款丙项之情形。

(二)关于裁决事项超越仲裁请求

仲裁庭超越权限的第二类情形,是指裁决事项属于仲裁协议范围,但当事人并未将之作为诉求向仲裁庭提出,这种情况下,仲裁庭对此部分进行裁决,也超出了仲裁庭权限。一般地,裁决项是否超越当事人请求事项,形式上较容易识别判断。但涉及某些如欠付费用的利息、律师费等特定费用时,适用不同准据法法院具有的自由裁量权不同,认定结果也会有所不同。在安富尔自由贸易区公司(Emphor FZCO)与广东粤新海洋工程装备股份有限公司申请承认与执行外国仲裁裁决案①中,被申请人抗辩,申请人仅提出要求被申请人支付视察费用,仲裁庭关于视察费用利息的裁决超出申请人请求范围,属超裁。法院认为,虽然申请人未对中山船厂视察费用的利息提出仲裁请求,但其仲裁反请求中包括了中山船厂视察费用,根据新加坡海事仲裁院仲裁规则第三版第 37.2 条规定,仲裁庭可以对于裁决的任何金额按其认为公正的利率裁定单利或复利,本案仲裁裁决 8.1 条对此也作出了说明。因此,在申请人已向仲裁庭请求视察费用的情况下,法院认定仲裁庭关于视察费用利息的裁决不属于仲裁范围以外的事项。

---

① (2020)粤 72 协外认 1 号。

五、裁决效力的抗辩

根据《纽约公约》第5条第1款戊项规定，裁决尚未生效、或经管辖机关裁定撤销或停止执行的，缔约方法院有权拒绝承认与执行该仲裁裁决。该项规定一方面是为保护仲裁中败诉方权益，另一方面也维护了各缔约方的司法主权。但需指出，法院在作出拒绝承认与执行或延缓程序的决定之前，须明确申请撤销仲裁裁决的一方并未违反诚实信用原则，即利用撤裁程序拖延执行。为此，《纽约公约》第6条作出规定，法院受理败诉方援引上述规定提出的拒绝或延缓执行的申请，须令其提供相应担保。我国的司法实践中，法院通常还要求败诉方承担举证证明义务。

前述香港泉水有限公司 Water Solutions (Hong Kong) Limited 与宏柏家电（深圳）有限公司申请承认和执行外国仲裁裁决案①中，法院认为，美国加利福尼亚州洛杉矶郡高等法院已经作出确认涉案仲裁裁决的判决书，被申请人对此提出的上诉和不予执行的申请尚未得到有效支持，且被申请人未对其中止本案审理的申请提供担保，亦未提供充分证据证明涉案仲裁裁决将会被美国法院撤销或不予执行，故法院不支持被申请人的该项抗辩。

沃泰思航运有限公司（Vertex Shipping Co., Ltd.）与华风国际海运有限公司申请承认与执行外国仲裁裁决案②中，被申请人称，其已就案涉裁决向英国法院提起诉讼，该仲裁裁决是否生效需要进一步核实。法院认为，根据《纽约公约》规定，裁决不具约束力或在裁决作出地国被撤销或停止执行，可裁定拒绝承认与执行，但须由负有裁决履行义务的被申请人举证证明，而被申请人并未提交符合法律形式要件的证据，以证明涉案仲裁裁决已被英国法院撤销。

六、可仲裁性及公共政策的抗辩

意思自治原则是商事仲裁的基石，但当事人的意思自治并非不受限制。由于商事仲裁是一种可以产生公共后果的私人程序，《纽约公约》在起草制定之时，除考虑保护当事人仲裁自治权，同时也考虑尊重各缔约方的司法监督权。

---

① (2016)粤03民初366号。

② (2019)沪72协外认2号。

基于此,《纽约公约》第 5 条第 2 款规定,缔约方法院可主动审查裁决争议是否具有可仲裁性、承认与执行裁决是否违反本国公共政策。

(一)可仲裁性的抗辩

当事人可以约定是否将争议提交仲裁,也可以约定提交仲裁的争议范围,但并非所有约定争议都可通过仲裁解决。《纽约公约》第 2 条将不可仲裁性作为缔约方承认仲裁协议推定义务的一项例外,同时第 5 条第 2 款第 1 项规定,争议事项不具有可仲裁性,该裁决无须被承认。

可仲裁性问题往往与国家社会公共利益存有直接联系,各国法律对于某类事项能否提交仲裁解决有不同的规定,有可能存在某类争议在 A 国可仲裁而在 B 国不可仲裁的情况。早年,以案涉争议不具有可仲裁性为由否定裁决的可执行性的情形并不少见;近年,以可仲裁性成功抗辩的案例已显著减少。本文研究的案例中,没有法院通过主动审查可仲裁性而否定裁决的情况;有个别当事人将之作为抗辩事由之一提出,例如昌盛贸易公司(Chang Sheng Trading Co. Inc)与河南江河机械有限责任公司申请承认和执行外国仲裁裁决案[①],但并未获法院认可。

事实上,随着国际商事仲裁制度的发展,各国仲裁立法和司法实践中"支持仲裁"的立场愈加明确,逐步扩大可仲裁的争议范围似乎已成主流趋势。如此,被申请人以此项规定抗辩或法院主动援引此项规定否定外国仲裁裁决的案例或将逐步减少。

(二)公共政策的抗辩

公共政策作为缔约方法院审查外国仲裁裁决的最后一道安全阀,是国际商事仲裁中极易被提出但也最难以得到支持的一种抗辩。根据《纽约公约》第 5 条第 2 款的规定,即便被申请人未提出抗辩,缔约方法院亦有权主动审查执行裁决是否会违反本国的公共政策。然而,何为公共政策,这并不易于界定。通常地,公共政策主要指涉及一国的重大社会利益、国家政策或一般的道德观念及风序良俗等。《纽约公约》对此未明确阐明,各个国家或地区立法及司法实践对于公共政策的理解也存在诸多差异。基于顺应国际商事仲裁发展趋势、支持仲裁的立场,我国法院对公共政策采取十分审慎严格的解释标准,仅在极少数

① (2017)豫 01 协外认 11 号。

情形下才会以此理由拒绝承认与执行外国仲裁裁决。本文研究的案例中,被申请人关于违反公共政策的抗辩均未得到法院支持,法院在相关案例中对违反公共政策的情形作出详细阐述。

例如,在奥克塔福系统有限公司与华浚塑料建材有限公司申请承认与执行外国仲裁裁决案①中,被申请人主张,裁决将已在我国获得专利的产品认定为违反保密义务,推翻了我国法律关于商业秘密定义的基本原则,违反我国公共政策。法院认为,《纽约公约》第5条第2款乙项规定的违反公共政策情形,应当理解为承认和执行外国仲裁裁决将严重违反我国法律基本原则、侵犯我国国家主权、危害社会公共安全、违反善良风俗以及危及我国根本社会公共利益的情形。法院查明,案涉协议适用不列颠哥伦比亚省法律,裁决载明双方当事人均确认以普通法中的规定作为违反保密义务的验证标准,即信息必须具有必要的保密特性,提供信息的情形必须引起保密义务,被申请人在未经授权的情况下使用该信息。法院指出,仲裁裁决作出是否违反保密义务的认定,所影响的只是奥克塔福公司与华浚公司的经济利益,不违反我国的基本法律制度、损害我国根本社会公共利益;且各个国家授予的专利权彼此独立,被申请人并未举证证明其在加拿大亦就该产品申请并获得专利授权从而得到加拿大国家的保护。故认定被申请人关于承认与执行案涉裁决将违反公共政策的抗辩不能成立。

此外,在嘉能可有限公司与昆山立益纺织有限公司承认与执行仲裁裁决案、昌盛贸易公司(Chang Sheng Trading Co. Inc)与河南江河机械有限责任公司申请承认和执行外国仲裁裁决案②、株式会社现代家庭购物(TION)与家有购物集团股份有限公司申请承认和执行外国仲裁裁决案③中,被申请人以程序方面或实体方面的事由主张案涉裁决违反我国公共政策,均未获法院支持。

七、其他

从《纽约公约》第五条的条文表述来看,《纽约公约》关于缔约方法院拒绝承认和执行仲裁裁决的事由采取穷尽性的方式,换言之,只有裁决确实存在第

---

① (2019)浙05协外认1号。

② (2017)豫01协外认11号。

③ (2019)京民辖终98号。

五条所列七项中的一项或多项情形时,法院才可决绝承认和执行,除非缔约方在加入纽约公约时作出保留声明。不过,仲裁实践中,常常有当事人提出《纽约公约》第五条规定之外的抗辩。

本文研究的案例中,有7个案例被申请人主张申请人递交的承认与执行外国仲裁裁决的申请材料不符合我国法律或《纽约公约》规定的形式,据此挑战承认与执行外国仲裁裁决案件审理程序的正当性。其中,Fairdeal物资供应有限公司(Fairdeal Supplies Ltd.)与山西煤炭进出口集团有限公司申请承认和执行外国仲裁裁决案①,法院以申请人提交的材料未经相关公证、认证程序,不符合《最高人民法院关于民事诉讼证据的若干规定》第11条规定而不予采信。

另外,《纽约公约》并未明确规定当事人申请承认和执行时应当遵照的申请程序,具体程序规则由各缔约方法律进行规定。司法实践中,承认与执行外国仲裁裁决的申请不符合我国《民事诉讼法》规定,可能成为法院裁定不予受理或被申请人提出抗辩的事由之一。

我国《民事诉讼法》第288条规定,国外仲裁机构的裁决,需要我国人民法院承认和执行的,应当由当事人直接向被执行人住所地或者其财产所在地的中级人民法院申请。在昌盛贸易公司(Chang Sheng Trading Co. Inc)与河南江河机械有限责任公司申请承认和执行外国仲裁裁决案②中,江苏省某法院认为,案件被执行人住所地在河南省,且被执行人在本地已无财产,法院对该申请无管辖权,故裁定不予受理。

《民事诉讼法》第246条规定,申请执行的期间为二年。申请执行时效的中止、中断,适用法律有关诉讼时效中止、中断的规定。前款规定的期间,从法律文书规定履行期间的最后一日起计算;法律文书规定分期履行的,从规定的每次履行期间的最后一日起计算;法律文书未规定履行期间的,从法律文书生效之日起计算。例如,在Fairdeal物资供应有限公司(Fairdeal Supplies Ltd.)与山西煤炭进出口集团有限公司申请承认和执行外国仲裁裁决案③中,被执行人抗辩,申请人未在我国法律规定期限内申请承认和执行本案,申请人申请承认及

---

① (2018)晋01民初921号。

② (2017)豫01协外认11号。

③ (2018)晋01民初921号。

执行仲裁裁决时，该申请承认及执行的时效已经届满，不应得到支持。

此外，本文研究的案例中，有个别被申请人还曾提出其他较为“另类”的抗辩事由，例如，证据系伪造[①]、隐瞒事实导致裁决不公[②]、合同履行受中美贸易战争影响[③]、执行汇率计算不当[④]等“另类”抗辩，均未得到法院支持。

八、结语

“支持仲裁”“支持裁决执行”，是目前国际上绝大多数国家的主流做法。《纽约公约》采取穷尽式地列举性的方式，仅规定 7 种情形下法院才可拒绝与承认外国仲裁裁决。通常认为，一方当事人已向管辖法院证明裁决存在，且满足管辖权要件，那么，《纽约公约》缔约方应当承认与执行该裁决。从 2019 年至 2022 年的司法审查案例来看，我国法院近年在适用《纽约公约》规定审查外国仲裁裁决过程中，虽仍有不足，如法院裁定类型的统一性问题，但整体上呈现比以往更加明确的支持仲裁、倾向于仲裁的司法立场，例如在转变确定仲裁协议准据法及裁决国籍的系属标准、灵活解释和判定送达程序及仲裁程序是否适当、审慎审查可仲裁性问题及公共政策等方面。

然而，仲裁某种程度上作为一种私权利的产物，仍需司法的适度监督和审查，才能最大程度地保障平等当事人的权益。仲裁制度如何在鼓励仲裁和司法监督之间找到更适合当下的平衡，需在每个案例中积累司法实践经验。同样，每个个案的尺度和质量亦离不开仲裁制度本身的不断完善与发展。

① (2019)沪 01 协外认 5 号之一。
② (2019)浙 04 协外认 2 号。
③ (2021)鲁 02 协外认 3 号。
④ (2020)内 01 民特 100 号。